Discursive Research in Practice

CU00706910

Over the past few decades new ways of conceiving the relation between people, practices and institutions have been developed, enabling an understanding of human conduct in complex situations that is distinctive from traditional psychological and sociological conceptions. This distinctiveness is derived from a sophisticated analytic approach to social action which combines conversation analysis with the fresh treatment of epistemology, mind, cognition and personality developed in discursive psychology. This volume is the first to showcase and promote this new method of discursive research in practice. Featuring contributions from a range of international academics, both pioneers in the field and exciting new researchers, this book illustrates an approach to social science issues that cuts across the traditional disciplinary divisions to provide a rich participant-based understanding of action.

Alexa Hepburn is a Senior Lecturer in the Department of Social Sciences at Loughborough University.

Sally Wiggins is a Lecturer in the Department of Psychology at the University of Strathclyde.

Discursive Research in Practice

New Approaches to Psychology and Interaction

Edited by

Alexa Hepburn and Sally Wiggins

CAMBRIDGE
UNIVERSITY PRESS

CAMBRIDGE UNIVERSITY PRESS
Cambridge, New York, Melbourne, Madrid, Cape Town, Singapore, São Paulo

Cambridge University Press
The Edinburgh Building, Cambridge CB2 8RU, UK

Published in the United States of America by Cambridge University Press,
New York

www.cambridge.org
Information on this title: www.cambridge.org/9780521614092

First published 2007

Printed in the United Kingdom at the University Press, Cambridge

A catalogue record for this publication is available from the British Library

Library of Congress Cataloging-in-Publication Data

Discursive research in practice: new approaches to psychology and inter-
action/edited by Alexa Hepburn and Sally Wiggins.
p. cm.
Includes bibliographical references and index.

ISBN: 978-0-521-84929-6 (hardback)
ISBN: 978-0-521-61409-2 (pbk)

1. Discursive psychology.   I. Hepburn, Alexa.   II. Wiggins, Sally, 1975–
III. Title.
BF201.3.D572 2007
150.19′8–dc22
2006038546

ISBN: 978-0-521-84929-6 (hardback)
ISBN: 978-0-521-61409-2 (paperback)

Contents

Figures

Contributors

SIMON ALLISTONE is a Lecturer in Social Policy and Social Work at the University of York

CHARLES ANTAKI is Professor of Language and Social Psychology in the Department of Social Sciences at Loughborough University

KARIN ARONSSON is a Professor in the Department of Child Studies at Linköpping University, Sweden

MARTHA AUGOUSTINOS is a Professor in the Department of Psychology at the University of Adelaide

REBECCA BARNES is a Research Fellow in the Peninsula Medical School at the University of Plymouth

RICHARD BUTTNY is Professor of Communication and Rhetorical Studies at Syracuse University, New York

JAKOB CROMDAL is Associate Professor in the Department of Child Studies at Linköpping University, Sweden

PAUL DENVIR is a Graduate Student in the Department of Communication at the University at Albany, SUNY

DEREK EDWARDS is Professor of Psychology in the Department of Social Sciences at Loughborough University

ALESSANDRA FASULO is Professor in Psychology at the University of Rome 'la Sapienza', Italy

FRANCESCA FIORE is a Research Assistant in Psychology at the University of Rome 'la Sapienza', Italy

KATHRYN FOGARTY is a Research Assistant in the Department of Psychology at the University of Adelaide

VIRGINIA TEAS GILL is an Associate Professor in the Department of Sociology and Anthropology, Illinois State University

ALEXA HEPBURN is Senior Lecturer in Social Psychology in the Department of Social Sciences, Loughborough University

SANDRA KELLOGG RATH is a Graduate Student in the Department of Communication and Rhetorical Studies at Syracuse University, New York

CURTIS D. LEBARON is an Associate Professor in the Marriott School of Management at Brigham Young University, Provo, Utah

AMANDA LECOUTEUR is Senior Lecturer in Psychology at the University of Adelaide

IVAN LEUDAR is Reader in Psychology at the University of Manchester

CLARE MACMARTIN is an Assistant Professor in the Department of Family Relations and Applied Nutrition at the University of Guelph, Ontario, Canada

PIRJO NIKANDER is Assistant Professor in the Department of Sociology and Social Psychology at the University of Tampere, Finland

CERI PARSONS is Senior Lecturer in Psychology at Staffordshire University

ANITA POMERANTZ is Director of Graduate Studies and Associate Professor in the Department of Communication at the University at Albany, SUNY

JONATHAN POTTER is Professor of Discourse Analysis at Loughborough University

CLAUDIA PUCHTA is a Professor at the University of Applied Science, Lueneburg, Germany

SUSAN A. SPEER is Lecturer in the Department of Sociology at Brunel University, London

MICHAEL THOLANDER is Research Fellow in the Department of Child Studies at Linköpping University, Sweden

SALLY WIGGINS is Lecturer in Psychology in the Centre for Applied Social Psychology at the University of Strathclyde

ROBIN WOOFFITT is Reader in Sociology in the Department of Sociology at the University of York

Acknowledgements

Thanks are due to various people and organisations for practical, intellectual and psychological support. First and foremost, we would like to thank our contributors both for their sustained efforts in producing their excellent chapters to various deadlines, and for their speedy responses to our comments and suggestions. The Discourse and Rhetoric Group at Loughborough University provides a stimulating intellectual context, in particular, Derek Edwards and Elizabeth Stokoe are inspirational friends and colleagues. We would also like to thank Jonathan Potter for his helpful comments on our own chapters. Finally, thanks to Sarah Caro and Cambridge University Press for commissioning the book.

1   Discursive research: themes and debates

Alexa Hepburn and Sally Wiggins

There has been a quiet revolution in the social sciences. Over the past few decades new ways of working and new ways of conceiving the relation between people, practices and institutions have been developed. These have started to make possible an understanding of human conduct in complex situations that is distinct from the traditional conceptions offered by disciplines such as psychology and sociology. This distinctiveness is derived from the sophisticated analytic approach to social action that has been developed by conversation analysis combined with the fresh treatment of mind, cognition and personality developed in discursive psychology. Both of these approaches work with the displayed perspectives of participants in interaction, perspectives embodied in people's constructions and orientations. In addition, this research has exploited the new recording technology and representational forms that enable it to engage more immediately with human practices; that is, to study 'the world as it happens' (Boden, 1990) instead of working through the mediation of interviews, questionnaires or ethnographic field notes. This work offers a sophisticated and theoretically nuanced empiricism that focuses on discourse as the central medium for action, psychology and understanding.

This book brings together researchers who have been doing discourse research in this new tradition. It features well-known contributors, some of them pioneers in their field, as well as exciting new researchers who are still early in their careers. Most come from the fields of discursive psychology and conversation analysis. It provides a range of analyses, which illustrate and exemplify new ways in which institutional and everyday settings can be researched and understood, as well as showing how key psychological topics can be reworked. All of the contributors work with direct records of interaction from various institutional and everyday settings. These are highly varied, and include: family conversations with young children; mundane telephone calls; therapeutic and medical sessions; psychological experiments; market research focus groups; sex offender therapy; political speeches and emails; relationship

1

counselling; psychiatric assessment for gender reassignment; school group evaluation and school counselling sessions; therapy for autistic children; and a child protection helpline. Taken together, the chapters illustrate an approach to social science issues that cuts across the traditional disciplinary divisions to provide a rich participant-based understanding of action.

In this opening chapter we will set this work in context, outlining developments in ethnomethodology, conversation analysis and discursive psychology, and distinguishing those developments from traditions of discourse work that make different assumptions.

Talking organisations

Conversation analysis

Conversation analysis (occasionally CA) originated in the 1960s in the lectures of Harvey Sacks (now published as Sacks, 1992). It was refined and rethought with his colleagues Emanuel Schegloff and Gail Jefferson. Conversation analysis offers an approach to analysis that combines a focus on the systemic nature of conversation and the way it is heard and understood by its participants. CA highlights three key elements of conversation:

1. Talk is a medium of action. Central to conversation analysis is the notion that any utterance can be examined for the action that it performs. This focus on action (and on the way actions are parts of broader practices) is in contrast to traditional linguistic approaches where talk is treated in terms of sentences or similar structures.
2. Actions done in talk are both context-dependent and context-renewing. That is, any action is oriented to the immediately prior turns of talk, and the action done in the current turn of talk provides a context for what comes next. Hence CA has a particular focus on sequences of action, which are often organised around paired actions such as invitations and acceptances, questions and answers, or assessments and second assessments.
3. In producing a next action, a speaker displays their understanding of the prior action. For example, if an invitation is issued by a speaker, the recipient not only accepts (or declines) the invitation, but *in doing one of these acts* (or relevant alternatives) shows that they have understood what has been issued *as* an invitation. This, in turn, provides further opportunities for the issuing speaker to acknowledge or initiate repair of a problem. This turn by turn display

of understanding is crucial, both for participants, as it allows them to coordinate their actions, and for analysts, as it allows them to ground their claims in participants' own understandings.

In the thirty years since the publication of the foundational turn-taking paper (Sacks, Schegloff and Jefferson, 1974) conversation analysis has resulted in a cumulative set of studies that map out some of the systemic features of the organisation of interaction – the very 'structures of social action' (Atkinson and Heritage, 1984) that provide the building blocks for social life. The power of these structures is that they are not brittle templates that must be followed; rather, they are normative. If an invitation is not followed by an acceptance or refusal (or some other normatively relevant action) this may occasion possible inferences (the recipient has not heard, is rude, is embarrassed or some other contextually relevant possibility).

Sacks worked on a range of materials from settings such as suicide-prevention lines and therapy groups. His focus was on the basic conversational phenomena – he was less concerned with how these conversations were refined in, or did the work of, institutions. The first major work that explicitly and systematically applied conversation analysis to institutional materials was Atkinson and Drew's (1979) study of courtroom interaction. This considered the way the practices that make up the work of the courts are achieved, for example, how the constraints of cross-examination questions necessitate more than one turn to generate an accusation, and how witnesses produce different kinds of defences in the sequential positions before and after the blaming is completed.

Although a series of studies on various topic areas was produced in the intervening time it was not for another decade until conversation analytic work on institutional interaction came to major prominence in four collections (Duranti and Goodwin, 1992; Watson and Seiler, 1992; and particularly Boden and Zimmerman, 1991, and Drew and Heritage, 1992a). Taken together, and despite some differences, this work revolutionises the way what it is to be an institution can be understood. In particular, it offers an alternative to the more common 'container' view of institutions, which treats them as broad societal boxes within which interpersonal actions take place in a way that is somewhat determined by features of the institutional box. At the same time it offers a radically different treatment of the role of broad social categories such as race, class and gender that sociologists have often taken to be central to the asymmetries of social institutions. Such categories are often a major focus of Critical Discourse Analysis (discussed below).

Constructing context: relevance and procedural consequentiality

The four collections on institutional interaction offered different arguments against the 'container' view of institutions. To better comprehend the radical direction of these four collections, we can focus on the arguments presented by Schegloff (1992). Schegloff presents two key challenges that illustrate the subtlety and complexity of addressing institutions in this way, one focused on the issue of *relevance* and one on the issue of *procedural consequentiality*. The argument about relevance starts with the observation that there is a wide range of alternative categorizations available for persons and settings. Put at its simplest, even though the analyst may have some judgements about what categorizations are appropriate or correct the key interactional issue is what categorizations are *treated* as relevant by the participants. Thus, whether a person is female, or Scottish, or a teacher is not a sufficient warrant for the analysts to invoke that person's membership of these categories (or any of the many other categories that the person could potentially occupy) to explain their utterances. The key issue is not *abstract* descriptive adequacy, but *practical relevance* to the interactional business at hand.

Schegloff suggests that there are two broad approaches to the problem of relevance. One can be described as positivist and requires that the success of a particular categorisation be assessed by statistical or historical methods, perhaps supplemented by interpretation on the basis of the appropriate theory. This approach works independently of participants' use of and/or orientation to the terms. The other approach is central to the conceptualisation of institutions and categories in conversation analysis. In this approach the social science categorisations are grounded in the conduct of the participants and in particular in the categorisations and orientations that they are themselves using. As Schegloff (1992) puts it, it is not just that social scientists find people 'to be characterizable as "president/assistant," "chicano/black," as "professor/student," etc. but that for them, at that moment, those are terms relevant for producing and interpreting conduct in the interaction' (p. 109).

The point, then, for Schegloff is not that these categories do not matter – they do. The problem is showing *analytically* that some features of the structure or some categories are what the participants *themselves* are orienting to. This will involve showing '*how the parties are embodying for one another the relevancies of the interaction and are thereby producing the social structure*' (p. 110, italics in original).

The problem of procedural consequentiality comes into play when some category or social structure has been shown to be relevant. The point is that even *if* some category or structure is oriented to as relevant, that does not mean that it is procedurally consequential for the unfolding interaction. Thus if a classroom context, say, is relevant for the parties to an interaction, that does not mean that it has specific *consequences* for the content or *trajectory* or character of the interaction. What needs to be established is the mechanism by which the context (as understood) is consequential for the ongoing interaction.

For example, if it is thought that some style of question asking is central to classroom teaching, the analytic challenge is to show how this style is produced institutionally rather than being a questioning style that is common elsewhere and which has simply been drawn in the classroom setting. What this challenge encourages is careful comparative work. It is easy to assume that some interactional practices in an institutional setting are a product of that setting when a broader study might show that these practices are more generic.

Talk at work

Although Schegloff's discussion of social organisation can seem more negative than positive it paves the way for a broader conversation analytic approach to institutions. Drew and Heritage (1992b) highlighted three features of institutions that would provide a framework for understanding the contribution of conversation analysis.

1. Goal orientation. In institutional settings at least some of the participants are oriented to basic goals or tasks. These can be clear cut and relatively consensual (such as in calls to emergency services) or ill defined and fluid (such as health visits to new mothers). There are often differences between the orientations of lay and institutional participants (the patient and doctor, for example).
2. Interactional constraints. Different institutional settings generate formal and informal constraints on conduct. Note that these can be inhibiting or promoting. In doctor–patient settings some talk is discouraged and some is encouraged.
3. Inferential frameworks. In institutional settings the 'inferential' properties of actions may be different. For example, withholding an expression of sympathy might be treated as disaffiliative in a mundane setting such as a phone call between friends but not treated as such in a television news interview (e.g. Clayman and Heritage, 2002); in contrast, inconsequent-seeming remarks in a chat between friends might be treated as critical or threatening in some institutional contexts (e.g. Heritage and Sefi, 1992).

Overall, they noted that interaction in institutional settings often involves both a restriction of what happens elsewhere and also a refinement. Certain kinds of activities and certain sorts of responses drop out, but basic institutional activities such as courtroom cross-examination, medical consultation or news interviewing involve a refinement of more basic mundane practices (cf. Drew, 1992; Peräkylä, 1995; Clayman and Heritage, 2002).

In the time since the publication of the Drew and Heritage (1992a) volume there has been a large amount of work on interaction in institutional settings. This has increasingly refined the alternative to the container view of institutions, highlighting a range of different levels at which the operation of institutionality can be revealed. Many of the themes in this work will be picked up in the chapters collected here.

Talking cognition

Discursive psychology

At around the same time that conversation analysts were offering this reworking of the nature of social institutions discursive psychology (sometimes DP) offered what can now be seen as a parallel reworking of the nature of psychology and, in particular, the status of cognition. Just as CA moved researchers away from the idea that institutions are separate entities that have some kind of determinist effect on interaction, so DP moved researchers away from the idea that cognition is a separate mental space that has a determinate effect on action (Potter, 1998). It criticised the assumptions of the kind of cognitivism which assumes that the explanation of human conduct is dependent on the understanding of prior and underlying cognitive processes and entities. In these traditions of work action is treated in a more *constitutive* than *dependent* relationship to either the institution or the cognition. Indeed, both perspectives provide a critical stance in relation to the reified and solidified versions of institutions and cognitions.

Edwards and Potter's (1992) volume *Discursive psychology* set out the foundations of the discursive psychological programme of work by way of a series of studies that reworked classic studies in cognitive psychology. For example, they examined the way Ulrich Neisser had used the testimony of John Dean to the Senate Committee investigating the Watergate break (ultimately crucial in the impeachment of President Nixon) as a basis for developing a theory of memory. They argued that by treating Dean's testimony as a product of cognitive processes (different kinds of memory) Neisser was failing to appreciate the *practical* role of different versions of what had happened as Dean dealt with cross-examination. They show how he *imposes* a cognitivist construction on Dean's testimony by treating it as determined by his memory and failing to attend to conversational and institutional pragmatics. In discursive psychology cognition is not the thing that explains interaction; rather, in a discursive psychological analysis we can see how versions of mind (memories, traits and attitudes) come to be produced for the purposes of action.

Core principles of discursive psychology

Discursive psychology works with three fundamental principles in its approach to discourse (Potter and Edwards, 2001).

1. Action orientation. As in CA, discourse is treated as primary means through which actions are done and interaction is coordinated. Actions are seen as typically embedded in broader practices. DP does not assume that there will be a one-to-one relationship between discrete acts and discrete verbs. Rather, DP has had a particular focus on the way actions are done indirectly through different kinds of descriptions.
2. Situation. DP treats discourse as situated in three complementary senses. First, it is organised *sequentially* in the way emphasised by conversation analysis, such that the primary environment for any utterance is the immediately prior utterance, and the new utterance sets up (although does not determine) what comes next. Second, discourse is situated *institutionally*, such that institutional identities (therapist and patient, perhaps) and tasks (managing problems, offering advice) will be relevant to what takes place. Third, discourse is situated *rhetorically*, such that any description can be inspected for how it counters relevant alternative descriptions (often, but by no means always, from the immediately prior talk).
3. Construction. DP treats discourse as both constructed and constructive. Discourse is constructed from a variety of different resources (words, categories, rhetorical commonplaces, interpretative repertoires). Discourse is constructive of different versions of the world, including versions of actions, events, histories, social structures and organisations, psychological characteristics and phenomenological experiences. DP studies both the actions done with these constructions (how a person uses a version of the traffic on the motorway to account for missing a meeting) and the way these constructions are built to be stable, objective and independent of the speaker.

There is a considerable overlap of these DP principles and the basic assumptions of conversation analysis. This is not surprising as discursive psychology was itself heavily influenced by work in conversation analysis. Moreover, some of the key alternative sources for the development of DP (Gilbert and Mulkay, 1984; Potter and Wetherell, 1987) were *themselves* somewhat influenced by CA. And all of this work was somewhat influenced by ethnomethodology which played a powerful role in the inception of conversation analysis.

One of the achievements of discursive psychology has been to move away from the individualist and cognitivist assumptions of recent psychology. For discursive psychologists, what people say is not taken to represent the contents of their mind (what they are really thinking) or reality (what really happened); rather things such as mind and reality are seen as first and foremost resources for participants in dialogue – which also makes them a useful resource for the analyst. DP has therefore focused on broadly 'psychological' topics such as cognition and emotions (Edwards, 1997, 1999; Locke and Edwards, 2003; Potter and Hepburn, 2003), attitudes and evaluations (Potter, 1996, 1998a; Puchta and Potter, 2002; Wiggins and Potter, 2003), racism and prejudice (Buttny, 1999; Edwards, 2005; LeCouteur, Rapley and Augoustinos, 2001), and memories and motives (e.g. Edwards and Potter, 1992). In doing so, it has offered an alternative to traditional psychological approaches to these topics, and also to how we theorise 'psychology'. Psychological concepts are treated in DP not as something we have or we are, but as resources for action. Psychology becomes more interactionally focused, dynamic and culturally specific as a result.

Themes in discursive psychology

Work in discursive psychology has developed around a number of different themes. These are cross-cutting, but it is useful to highlight some of their differences. Edwards (2004) picks out three themes.

1. Respecification and critique. Respecification involves the reworking of topics from cognitive psychology and social cognition from a discourse perspective. For example, the core social cognitive notion of script has been reworked in DP by considering the way descriptions of actions and events can produce them as standard and orderly (Edwards, 1994). Note that respecification is not intended in DP to just provide a different version of the same objects – rather it changes the whole perspective from a cognitive one to a constructed and action-oriented one. In many cases the coherence of the cognitive object will simply dissolve.

2. The psychological thesaurus. One of the key aims of DP is to explore the working of common sense, including the use of categories that would conventionally be treated as psychological. This includes the range of words for emotional and mental states such as remember, think, upset, angry and so on as well as the huge range of available idiomatic and metaphorical constructions – bear in mind, boiling, ragged and so on. Several of the studies collected in this volume address terms from the psychological thesaurus.

3. Management of psychological business. A major topic in DP since its inception has been the often implicit management of psychological themes. How are matters such as agency, doubt, prejudice and emotional investment displayed, built up or undermined through descriptions of actions, events or circumstances?

In addition to these three basic DP themes, some of the contributors to the current collection will pick up a newly emerging topic which is the discursive psychology of institutions (Edwards and Potter, 2001; Potter, 2005). Social psychology has traditionally had little interest in the specifics of social institutions, being focused instead on the operation of generic trans-historical social processes (Gergen, 1982). In contrast, DP has started to ask the question of how particular institutions and organisations – therapy sessions, classroom teaching, police interrogation – are done through the use of specific 'psychological' business. DP studies with this focus may ask how particular psychological notions and orientations are drawn on to do the work of the institution.

This emerging theme in DP builds on the ground-breaking work done by conversation analysts and adds a particular focus on the organisation and refinement of practices or issues that have more traditionally been understood as psychological. Issues of knowledge, stance, understanding, blame, guilt and responsibility are threaded through everyday situations and are at the core of many institutions. DP focuses on the way these issues are practically managed in interaction.

Differences between conversation analysis
and discursive psychology

As we have already indicated discursive psychology has drawn heavily on the theoretical ideas and analytic approach of conversation analysis. Sacks' (1992) early work not only laid the foundations for conversation analysis it also developed a sophisticated interactional approach to the relationship between utterances and psychological states which is, to some extent, a forerunner of modern discursive psychology. However, it is worth briefly considering three areas of potential tension between DP and CA.

First, DP developed a systematic approach to the relation between the way descriptions are assembled and the actions they are involved in. This drew as much on developments in the sociology of science and broader constructionist ideas as specifically CA work (see Potter, 1996, for an overview). For example, Edwards (1995, 1997) studied the way constructions of anger in relationship counselling can play a role in assigning problems to one of the partners, nominating them as the person who needs the therapy. Constructions of this kind are mutually inferential – people construct versions of their memories, feelings and cognitive states as part of establishing the nature of events or settings; and they construct versions of events or settings as part of establishing the nature of feelings or cognitive states. In addition, as we have noted DP draws on the rhetorical tradition of Billig (1996). This shows how descriptions are put together to counter actual or potential alternatives. DP is distinctive from other constructionist traditions (and closer to CA) in its focus on the business of constructing versions in talk and texts, and its emphasis on the way constructions are parts of situated practices. Conversation analysts have been less focused on constructionist themes of this kind (although they are not necessarily inconsistent with CA work).

A second area of potential contrast involves the way cognition is conceptualised. DP is a systematically non-cognitivist approach. It puts aside questions of the existence of cognitive entities and processes (technical or everyday) in favour of a focus on how cognitive entities are constructed in and for interactional practices. It can study 'upset' in a therapy session, for example, without trying to answer the question of whether the word 'upset' has an inner referent, and without trying to assess whether a 'display' of upset is 'authentic' or 'invented'. Nor is such a study required to decide on the reality of distinctions between, say, surface and depth psychology prior to analysis. These things can be treated as topics for study in their own right. For the most part CA has also been an enterprise that avoids cognitivist assumptions. However, at times CA researchers have had a more ambivalent approach to cognition. Sometimes this has involved an attempt to connect interactional phenomena to putative mental objects or at least to suggest the coherence of such a programme (Drew, 2005; Kitzinger, 2006; Schegloff, 2006). For an overview of these issues see the different papers in te Molder and Potter (2005) and the debate between Coulter (1999) and Potter and Edwards (2003b).

A third major area of contrast relates to the conversation analytic focus on turn-taking and sequence organisation. DP has tended to focus on participants' formulations and categories, and has picked up on issues of turn organisation and sequential placement in a less thoroughgoing way. Developing a more rigorous conversation analytic approach will allow further insights into the organisation and sequential placement of particular phenomena that are generated through a corpus of materials, and their relationship to constructions of mind and world. This will facilitate the further development of both discursive psychology and conversation analysis.

Discursive psychology and discourse analysis

Discursive psychology emerged out of a particular strand of discourse analytic work. It will help situate the contributions to this volume if we discuss this work and its relationship to DP as well its relationship to CA and the rather different tradition of Critical Discourse Analysis (CDA). This is a major challenge to understanding the disciplinary geography in this somewhat contested terrain – the best we can do is highlight some of the main features of interest and point the reader to some paths that might lead to higher ground.

Discursive psychology was developed from a particular strand of discourse work that was laid out in Potter and Wetherell (1987). They set out the fundamentals of a style of work that offered a new way of conceptualising the topic of social psychology and an alternative method of analysis to the hegemony of experiments and surveys. It drew on both conversation analytic and post-structural thinking, as well as ideas from the sociology of scientific knowledge. All of this potential confusion was disciplined by taking as its major focus discourse – talk and texts – and in particular the way discourse is embedded in and contributes to social practices. It laid down many of the features later refined in discursive psychology. Two areas of difference are worth considering because they have been consequential in subsequent work.

First, Potter and Wetherell (1987) had a major interest in identifying the organised resources that underlie and sustain interaction. Of course, linguists have highlighted the role of individual lexical items. Sacks (1992) in his early work highlighted the role of membership categories, and this has been a tradition recently revived by ethnomethodologists (e.g. Hester and Eglin, 1997). Billig (1996) emphasised the importance of rhetorical commonplaces as resources for action. Building on the work of Gilbert and Mulkay (1984), Potter and Wetherell developed the notion of interpretative repertoires. These are clusters of terms organised around a central metaphor, often used with grammatical regularity. They can be flexibly drawn on to perform particular actions (see Edley, 2001).

For example, in their major study of racist discourse in New Zealand Wetherell and Potter (1992) focused on 'culture' in a way different from previous anthropology and social psychology. They did not treat culture as a feature of the lifestyle, rituals and world view of Maoris; nor did they treat it as a mental stereotype organising the information processing of the Päkehä (White, European New Zealanders). Instead, they identified two interpretative repertoires through which culture was flexibly and locally constructed to perform different activities. On the one hand, the Culture-as-Heritage repertoire was used to build culture as an antiquated inheritance that should be treasured but requires protection from the rigours of the 'modern world'. On the other, the Culture-as-Therapy repertoire constructed culture as a psychological requirement that would stop Maori becoming rootless and mentally unstable. Wetherell and Potter (1992) note that these repertoires show a sensitivity to difference organised around social relations rather than genetics, and are thus free of many of the connotations of racism. Yet they can be powerfully used (in newspapers, parliamentary debates and everyday talk) to attack Maori political movements and undercut the legitimacy of Maori claims.

The repertoire notion offered a picture of complex, historically developed organisations of ideas that could be identified through research, and yet were flexible enough that they could be drawn on and reworked in the vagaries of practice. In this way, they have some advantages over some neo-Foucauldian notions of discourse (Parker, 2002) that are more brittle and tectonic. Nevertheless, as Wooffitt (2005b) has suggested, the notion fails to accommodate the sheer complexity of human conduct. Moreover, there are major issues in how interpretative repertoires can be reliably and accountably identified in a specific corpus of materials. There are very real debates here, illustrated in the influential exchange between Schegloff (1997) and Wetherell (1998).

The second area of difference between Potter and Wetherell's (1987) conception of discourse analysis and the later discursive psychology concerns the place of open-ended interviews in the generation of analytic materials. Potter and Wetherell draw on some work using naturalistic materials, but much of their discussion and the majority of the very large body of studies using interpretative repertoires have used open-ended interviews (e.g., Lawes, 1999; Liefooghe, 2003; Lumme-Sandt et al., 2000). Discursive psychology is distinct from the earlier tradition of discourse analysis in almost completely abandoning open-ended interviews as a research method. In contrast, from its very beginnings conversation analysis has been conducted on the basis of a critique of sociological and anthropological methods which has led to an exclusive focus on naturalistic materials. We will have more to say on this topic below.

Conversation analysis, discursive psychology and Critical Discourse Analysis

Critical Discourse Analysis is a much broader collection of approaches than either conversation analysis or discursive psychology (although there is some variation of assumptions within both). In their authoritative overview, for example, Fairclough and Wodak (1997) include French Discourse Analysis, Critical Linguistics, Social Semiotics, Socio-cognitive studies and the Duisburg School amongst others. One thing that collects these approaches together is a focus on social critique. Often this involves an interest in the ideologies and discourses that are treated as underpinning different forms of talk and text and sustaining relations of inequality. However, social critique in some form is not unique to these approaches. Work in both conversation analysis and discursive psychology has been involved with critical and political issues, such as the oppression of minority groups (see, e.g., Kitzinger, 2005; Sneijder and te Molder, 2005). Indeed, Phillips and Jørgensen (2002) suggest that discursive psychology satisfies many of the broader defining characteristics of Critical Discourse Analysis (CDA) while eschewing the title. And there is a judgement to be had about whether political and critical analysis is something to be earned by results or something that should be celebrated and asserted in the very name of a programme of work (see Hammersley, 1997).

However, our aim here is not to provide an assessment of CDA but to indicate some general areas of difference from the style of work included in the current volume. Even with the heterogeneity of CDA three areas can be highlighted: the role of linguistics, the theorising of context and the understanding of discourse and discourse practices. We will take them in turn.

CDA draws upon fields as diverse as Foucauldian discourse theory and cognitive psychology; nevertheless, most strands start with some form of linguistic analysis, often Halliday's functional grammar. Although the work collected here is concerned with discourse, it is cautious about *linguistic* analysis and the associated linguistic categories for the analysis of that discourse. Instead, the focus is on social practices, and how the categories that are used in understanding those practices are analytically connected to the participants' orientations and displayed understandings.

Linguistic analysis, even functional linguistics in the Halliday tradition, has not started with practices and how words and sequences are involved in those practices. Instead it has worked with textual and lexical organisations and processes (nominalisation, subject deletion).

With respect to theorising context this is an area where there have been some heated debates between conversation analysts and others. Schegloff's influential (1997) paper on text and context is often seen as directed at some CDA work. He highlights the challenge that issues of relevance and procedural consequentiality pose for work that opts to start with a historical or sociological account of context, and hopes to explain discourse practices by reference to that account. CA and DP work is particularly focused on the way context is a live issue for participants, and an issue that is locally and fluidly managed through various means (including formulations of relevant contextual particulars). Note that Schegloff is not suggesting that such work cannot be done, nor that it is uninteresting or unimportant; he is, however, highlighting the complexity of the analytic tasks that are involved.

There is a difference of emphasis between CDA and the work collected here on the issue of discourse practices. Broadly, CDA tends to adopt functional analyses that attempt to connect textual structures to social structures; DP and CA are concerned with activities done through talk and texts, and the way these may be coordinated in particular practices, and in turn, the way they constitute broader institutional organisations. This difference is reflected in differences in the way discourse is conceptualised. In CDA discourse is typically treated as a thing, something that can be counted. Thus in a doctor–patient interaction there can be a move between 'the discourse of medicine' and 'the discourse of counselling' (e.g., Fairclough, 1995) and much of the explanatory purchase of CDA comes from the structured nature of these organisations, both within each one and between them. In contrast, CA and DP work is more likely to see such textual organisations as a by-product of the way activities are done within settings. These are difficult issues, and we are not attempting to resolve them here. The key point to note is that the papers in the current collection focus on practices within settings and are not attempting to explain those practices in terms of broader discourse structures in the manner of CDA.

Naturalistic materials and empirical methods

Up to now we have laid out some of the features shared by the different contributions to this volume as well as considering some of the ways they are distinct from alternative perspectives such as Critical Discourse

Analysis. At the start we noted that one of the features of this work is that it has exploited new recording technologies and forms of representational practice that allow it to engage with human practices in all their detail. Looked at another way, it has moved away from the kinds of standard data-generation procedures that are common elsewhere in the social sciences, including in discourse work in sociology, anthropology and social psychology. In particular it has avoided the use of both interviews and the ethnographic observation-and-field-note approaches common in qualitative research. One key reason for this focus on naturalistic materials is that work in discourse and conversation analysis sees what Goffman (1983) called the interaction order as a foundational way of accessing how people live their lives. Interviews and other researcher-generated techniques such as questionnaires disrupt this order in complex and hard-to-identify ways. Ethnographic observation is very hard to conduct at a level of granularity that captures its operation. We will make some brief comments on the operation of interviews and basic issues that arise in conceptualising and collecting naturalistic materials.

Open-ended interviews

The style of discourse analysis laid out in Potter and Wetherell (1987) and exemplified in work by Billig (1992) and others used some form of open-ended interview as its principal data-generation technique. More recently, the style of critical discourse work that has addressed issues of subjectivity and neo-liberalism using a psychodynamic meta-theory has also been based almost exclusively on open-ended interviews (e.g. Hollway and Jefferson, 2000).

Potter and Hepburn (2005a) summarise some of the problems with the use of open-ended interviews. They note that they are often used in ways that wipe out many of their interactional features (by focusing on extracts from participants' 'answers' and using forms of transcript which wipe out many of the elements of talk that conversation analysts have shown to be live for participants). Even when more care is paid to these features interviews present challenging difficulties. It is very hard to disentangle the social science agendas that are imported with the question construction, terminology and the whole set-up of the interview. Both interviewer and interviewee move between complex and sometimes indistinct footing positions. For example, participants are often recruited as members of social categories (a schoolteacher, say), but they may position their talk in various complex ways with respect to that category membership. Widdicombe and Wooffitt (1995) highlight a range of difficulties of this kind. There are also complex and hard-to-analyse issues with respect to the stake or interest (Potter, 1996) that each party may show in what they are saying.

More generally, open-ended interviews are used with the assumption that they will access some competence or resources that underlie practices in other settings, or can access cognitive notions such as beliefs or events and actions that happened elsewhere. Conversation analysts and discursive psychologists have preferred to work from actual records of conduct rather than work via interviews. Given that researchers have demonstrated the possibility of working with records, and given the sorts of difficulties with interviews that have been highlighted, the onus is more with interview researchers to show the value of continuing to base their work on these instruments.

Naturalistic data

There are a further set of issues about natural and contrived data (Speer, 2002) and in particular whether researchers are offering a new positivism that underplays the active role of the researcher in the data-collection and analytic process. It is useful to make some distinctions here. First, we have referred to naturalistic rather than natural data to highlight cautions about its status. Researchers are often involved in the generation of such data (recruiting participants, training them to use recording equipment, working through ethics procedures). However, this is a different order of involvement than the open-ended interview, say, where the data is fashioned by direct interaction with the researcher. Second, although we can consider interview interaction to be fashioned by the researcher it is, nonetheless, possible to naturalise it. That is, it can be studied as research interview interaction, considering, for example, how it differs or does not from news interview interaction or from focus group interaction and so on. This tradition of work includes Lee and Roth (2004), Rapley (2001), Widdicombe and Wooffitt (1995) and several of the contributions to van den Berg et al. (2003). This is, in turn, part of the broader tradition of work on interaction in research settings (overviewed in the chapter by Potter and Puchta below).

Research using naturalistic records faces issues that are traditionally collected together with the notion of 'reactivity' (the participants' activities being 'influenced' by the recording process). Without trivialising this issue there are a number of responses. First, a period of acclimatisation can be used to let participants become familiar with the recording process. Moreover, they are often quite unconcerned with issues that are of research interest, but much more focused on issues that are not relevant (cursing, say, or the disclosing of intimate information). Second, recording technology is a pervasive and often unremarkable feature of people's lives in the West – people use video cameras and memo recorders for all kinds of things, and are often told that their talk is to be recorded for training purposes when they phone a big organisation. Third, recording is often done in situations where there are important and omnipresent practical goals – in courtrooms, police interrogations, NSPCC calls, psychotherapy and so on. The research process is unlikely to make much difference here – all parties will be focused on other issues.

This book records a tradition of work where a new kind of empiricism is being developed. This uses sophisticated theories of interaction derived from ethnomethodology and conversation analysis, combined with a discursive stance that avoids the cognitivism of more traditional work. This apparatus is able to work with high quality digital records of people acting and interacting in everyday and institutional settings, which can be stored, replayed, cut and pasted, anonymised, coded and searched. These records can be combined with Jeffersonian transcription, which captures talk as it is hearably relevant to the participants. This is the basis for a science of what people do that goes beyond a range of contemporary social science traditions and distinctions. In some sense, it is the start of a new way of doing social research. For the rest of this chapter we will overview the content of the book and highlight the ways in which it exemplifies this research agenda.

Talking psychology   Part I of this book sets out one of the major focuses of discursive psychology, with all five chapters advocating an action-orientated approach to what have traditionally been characterised as inner states. A major focus for discursive psychologists has been the role of dispositional formulations, which present actions as a product of features of individuals (their personality, views or moral shortcomings). Derek Edwards has been particularly active in highlighting the interactional usefulness that arises from being able to disclaim or refer to one's own or another's inner states and subjective biases. He has also shown the ways that these can be contrasted with what he terms 'script formulations', which present actions as normal, standard or expected (e.g. Edwards, 1994, 1997). Script formulations are a basic tool used by people when constructing and stabilising particular versions of social order. It is possible to see Edwards' chapter (Chapter 2) in this collection as both an extension and a refinement of his earlier work.

Using data from a variety of sources, Edwards builds an increasingly sophisticated project focused on managing dispositions, in particular on the way different types of subjective investments can be claimed or denied in different types of interaction. He develops the term 'counter dispositionals' to describe devices that manage the subjectivity of an account, and outlines two ways that dispositions can be managed – firstly, to produce oneself as a normal person, not possessing a disposition to exaggerate, embellish or make unwarranted inferences. This can involve the use of various practices such as 'extreme case formulations' (Pomerantz, 1986), which deploy formulations that include various types of extremity (e.g. 'you always say that', 'I never win'). Edwards (2000) noted that this can create problems for speakers as it leaves them open to accusations of subjective bias, of being disposed to exaggerate. He showed how speakers can counter this hearing by deploying strategies such as softening or ironising an extreme formulation.

The second way of handling subjectivity involves constructing oneself as not the kind of person who would normally make negative or biased assessments, or as someone forced to reconceptualise (usually by some force of events or circumstances) what they previously thought. A classic example is the types of racist disclaimers that Potter and Wetherell (1987) identified – 'I'm not a racist, but …' where the remainder of the turn is devoted to outlining practical reasons why racial equality cannot be achieved – it is a conclusion reluctantly arrived at by someone not disposed to conclude that kind of thing. This type of disclaiming is what Edwards terms a 'counter dispositional' – concluding something despite one's own disposition to believe the opposite. It also relates to Potter's (1996) notion of 'stake inoculation', which refers to a phrase designed to inoculate the speaker from being heard as having a stake or investment in the matter at hand.

The second broad way of 'managing dispositions' covered by Edwards relates to the ways that one's vocal delivery can display one's subjective stance. There is a growing body of work exploring the relationship between features of delivery and the actions being done, e.g., Wiggins' (2002) research into the gustatory 'mmm', Hepburn's research into crying (2004) and Stokoe and Hepburn's (2005) examination of complaints and reports about noisy neighbours. Edwards also explores new technology for studying the phonetic and intonational features of speech, and demonstrates the basis for his transcription gloss 'plaintively' by including readouts of the amplitude and pitch trace of the utterance, along with some cautions about the over-reliance on such technology in isolation from other important features. He notes that objective features of talk are checkable in other ways, for example by examining their uptake from the co-interactants. As Goodwin and

Goodwin (2000) suggest, we should be careful about understanding each utterance in the context of the sequential action in which it is placed. So a key question here is whether there is anything about participants' uptake that will cash out the analyst's hearing of the utterance (however technically informed that may be) as plaintive.

Part of the general focus of Edwards' research is a concern with what psychology is or can be, for the different institutional and mundane environments in which it appears. This is part of discursive psychology's agenda of taking psychology out of the head and instead considering its role where it pervasively appears – in interaction. Potter and Puchta (Chapter 6) share this focus, and develop it by exploring the role played by a variety of psychological categories, formulations and orientations in market research focus groups: more specifically, perceptions, opinions, beliefs and attitudes (POBAs). This fits into the broader tradition of investigation discussed earlier, which aims to show how methods commonly adopted in research can be instrumental in producing psychological 'objects' as their outcome (e.g., Antaki, 1999; Lee and Roth, 2004; Potter and Hepburn, 2005b).

Potter and Puchta show that focus group moderators attend quite elaborately to their own stance towards the products they are eliciting views about. Moderators are at pains to show that they are indifferent to whether participants assess the products and their packaging in a positive or negative way. They display a lack of knowledge about the products and display informality in their conduct of the group through various modes of delivery and lexical choice. Potter and Puchta also show how words like 'think' and 'opinion' play an important role in the focus group by allowing participants to evaluate products without major accountability issues. If one's stance is that one is merely giving one's opinion, one isn't required to justify it as factual.

Hence Edwards and Potter and Puchta show the analytic purchase to be had from rejecting the idea that the lexicon of words for mental states refers to corresponding mental objects. Nikander (Chapter 3) develops this further with talk about emotion, showing how it is deployed in interprofessional meetings populated by an interesting mix of medical and social care workers in Finland. The meetings are designed to make decisions affecting the lives of elderly people. They focus mainly on how much financial support should be given to elderly clients living at home, and whether a client ought to be placed in long-term care. As Nikander shows, the decision-making process in these meetings is not one that easily lends itself to the display or invoking of emotion. To do so would be to relinquish normative requirements for professional and rational judgement.

Nevertheless, as one might expect, emotion terms and categories do make their way into such an environment – in particular, their framing in terms of personal bias and their contrast to 'the facts', which equate with written documents. Nikander also shows that invoking 'concern' does some useful work for the participants. As Potter and Hepburn (2003) showed, concern constructions are a useful way for callers to a child protection helpline to display an appropriately cautious and objective stance. Similarly, in team meetings, Nikander explores how 'concerned feelings' of both the interactants and professional third parties are invoked as a way of calling for specific types of professional intervention. Third-party concern constructions also involve footing, where the feelings of another 'very concerned' professional are invoked, allowing the speaker to sidestep descriptions of their own feelings in the pursuit of various actions.

Nikander also shows that emotionally framed descriptions and categories can perform useful activities – e.g., the description of a carer as someone who is 'caring with joy' turns him into someone worthy of extra financial help. She concludes that there may be practical usefulness to this type of work in allowing professionals to be more reflexive about decision making, and to allow more open debate about what decision making of this type should involve.

The controversial topic of paranormal ability or 'psi' is the focus for Allistone and Wooffitt (Chapter 4). 'Psi' refers to information that can be attained outside normal sensory channels. Allistone and Wooffitt note a problem for parapsychologists – that although the accumulation of experimental evidence clearly shows very statistically significant 'hit rates', suggesting the existence of psi, there is nevertheless a strong experimenter effect, in that some will get much higher, some much lower, 'hit rates' or 'psi conduciveness' than others. This is despite the fact that the parapsychology experiments in question (the autoganzfeld experiments) are conducted in a 'double blind' situation, where neither experimenter nor participant is aware of the stimulus being transmitted to the participant. In a bid to make sense of this, Allistone and Wooffitt begin to look closely at the interaction between experimenters and participants in parapsychology experiments, as the findings suggest that there is something about how the experimenter and participant interact that affects hit rates. Allistone and Wooffitt show that there are different styles of interaction that relate to how affiliative the experimenter can be.

While the first four chapters deal with some of the classics of a broad range of psychological research – shared knowledge; perceptions, opinions, beliefs and attitudes; emotions; and descriptions of consciousness – Augoustinos et al. (Chapter 5) focus on apologising – a speech act. Speech acts are also typically fitted into a cognitive psychological perspective – for example, apologies are related to individual sincerity. By contrast, the interest here is in understanding apologies as collective, where the felicity conditions cease to be individual phenomena. Analysis also reveals the roles played by claims to empathy, emotional suffering, guilt and personal growth.

The question at issue – should the Prime Minister of Australia apologise to the Indigenous people of that country for the dispossession and genocide of large numbers of their predecessors? Many Australian people emailed a newspaper website to give their views on this question. Augoustinos et al. took a subsection of those emails, the ones that replied that John Howard *should* apologise, to examine the multiple ways in which 'apologising' can be constructed and deployed. They found that the most common way in which the activity of apologising is represented in these emails is as something that is not related to assuaging the guilt of contemporary Australians, but simply a matter of empathy for the emotional suffering of others. The benefits of apologising were typically framed in terms of the personal growth and psychological health of the Indigenous peoples, as opposed to broader issues related to economic disadvantages and human rights.

Augoustinos et al. then examine a political speech given by John Howard himself, where he argues that such an apology would be wrong and unfair to the present generation of 'white' Australians, as it would imply an admission of guilt. Howard sets up a contrast between the practical goals – working with the health, housing, education and employment needs of Indigenous peoples – and the symbolic – apologising. Rather than seeing practical and symbolic as compatible goals, Howard constructs them as mutually exclusive, allowing him to both appear compassionate while simultaneously adopting his anti-apology stance.

Augoustinos et al. outline conceptual approaches to the topic of apologising which tend to explore it in a more descriptive way and seek underlying causes such as cultural values or individual beliefs and attitudes. They contrast this with a discursive take, in which the goal is to examine the variety of functions that apologising might have in different interactional contexts. They argue that the latter approach allows greater sensitivity to the multitude of tasks and constructions in which apologies can be involved.

This chapter therefore usefully exemplifies one way to examine nonconversational data such as political speeches or emails. Augoustinos et al. take a broader look at the way issues are constructed out of oppositions and contrasts, and the implications of this, in Howard's speech. They also show the way that apologies can be constructed as coming from the individual, rather than the state. In the emails, they show how people can construct apologies as not necessarily implicating the apologiser in guilt or blame.

Rather than seeing mental terms and descriptions as reflections of mental states or events, all five authors develop a focus on the work performed by such terms and descriptions in their various interactional contexts. In doing so, all five chapters build challenges and possibilities for the future development of both psychology and discursive research that build up around the issues for people living their lives. We explore the possible usefulness of such an approach to psychology in our conclusions to this volume. Meanwhile, Part II develops this theme of psychology in action, among other more institutional concerns, and with a particular focus on clinical interaction.

Talking cure   A common theme of the chapters in Part II is analysis of various therapeutic and diagnostic environments – for many the classic arena for the production and utility of the same types of professional and psychological terms and theories that we have encountered in Part I. Work on therapy and counselling has been able to specify some of the standard features of sequences of counselling interaction, the role of some of the counsellor's activities, techniques of information elicitation, and the role of problem formulations (e.g., Buttny and Jensen, 1995; Peräkylä, 1995; Silverman, 1997). Discursive psychology has been used to study the rhetorical relationship between problem formulations, emotion ascription and descriptions of activities, and issues of blame in relationship counselling (Edwards, 1995; Potter, 1996). Heritage and Sefi (1992) have highlighted some dilemmas that arise when health visitors offer advice to recent mothers.

But how can interactional analysis start to identify what therapy is? It certainly can't appeal simply to the roles (e.g., therapist, client) of those in the therapeutic environment. Will it be able to specify therapy in the therapist's own terms, e.g., to illustrate the operation of transference or projection? Antaki et al. (Chapter 9) tackle these broader questions by way of an examination of a therapist's formulations of a client's talk.

Formulations can be useful as devices that advance a particular interpretation of the words of another – an invented example: 'so you are saying that all white people can't dance'. As such they can serve as useful indicators of shared intersubjectivity (Garfinkel and Sacks, 1970) – by formulating another's words we show or check our understanding of them. Antaki et al. highlight the way that such formulations can function in a therapeutic setting. CA researchers such as Drew and

Heritage (1992a) have shown us that formulations are frequent in institutional settings, where they can package various types of useful actions, such as achieving neutrality in news interviews, provoking debate in a radio talk show, or manipulating negotiations to one's own advantage. The key thing is that the formulation can package some kind of reading or presumption, which can perform useful actions for different people in different settings. A formulation also projects some kind of response – preferably confirmation or agreement – from the speaker.

Studies of therapy talk have shown that a formulation can provide a therapeutic orientation. Hence the client's reported troubles or issues are reflected back to them in a way that renders them therapeutically tractable, for example by constructing the client as somehow in control of their problem, rather than controlled by it. But Antaki et al. are not content with this explanation. A central question throughout the paper asks to what extent CA will have to make use of therapists' concepts; specifically – how can we be sure that a formulation is doing therapy, as opposed to something more mundane? Antaki et al. suggest that we can't simply appeal to the fact that the formulation (or other utterance) occurred in a therapy session, as this would entail an appeal to roles – that everything issuing from the mouth of a therapist constitutes therapy, purely by definition of their role as therapist.

By way of resolving this issue, Antaki et al. set about contrasting the formulations in their therapy with the existing literature on formulations. This is one important way to disambiguate the activities in the therapy session. By showing how the therapist's formulations claim knowledge about the psychological deficiencies of the client, Antaki et al. provide us with one way of understanding what characterises therapeutic interaction, and how it gets done. They therefore conclude that a conversation analytic approach can help us to understand what therapists are doing that differs from ordinary conversation.

While Antaki et al. focus on the role of formulations in therapy, and how this can reveal the operation of therapy through formulations of psychological deficiencies, Speer and Parsons (Chapter 10) examine the role of carefully formulated hypothetical questions in psychiatric assessments of clients referred to a gender identity clinic. Speer and Parsons begin by identifying some of the broader concerns of clients in this unique context – to persuade the psychiatrist that they are 'true transsexuals' worthy of the free treatment that is offered to a selected few patients from each of the UK Health Authorities. They also examine psychiatrists' concerns – to evaluate whether the clients are suffering from any mental health problems, and to avoid 'irreversible mistakes' by assessing whether patients will be suitable for surgery. Speer and Parsons note that psychiatrists routinely employ hypothetical questions in this context, one illustrative example being 'suppose you couldn't go any further with treatment, what would you do?' They examine the role of such questions in the context of the psychiatric assessment.

Speer and Parsons start by noting that hypothetical questions are carefully formulated in such a way as to make their hypothetical status very clear, and to present the hypothetical scenario as something outside of the control of the psychiatrist. In this sense, they encourage clients to engage in two rather improbable actions – to detach from their investment in getting the surgery, and to pretend for a moment that the psychiatrist is not the gatekeeper to that surgery.

Having examined the formulation of hypothetical questions, Speer and Parsons go on to look at their uptake. Not surprisingly, the clients find the actions they are being asked to perform a bit troubling, and their responses all have elements of dispreference about them – e.g., delays to answering, hedging and false starts. While the questions all ask what the client would do, all respond with a description of how they would feel. These initial responses are treated as inadequate by the psychiatrists, and follow-up questions reveal that they are evidently seeking confirmation that the clients would continue to live in the female role.

Speer and Parsons therefore show that hypothetical questions can be doing radically different business according to the institutional context in which they are uttered. They close with a discussion about whether these hypothetical questions are the best way for psychiatrists to proceed in an environment where they are also the gatekeepers to surgery, and where they are constantly being second-guessed by their clients.

MacMartin and LeBaron (Chapter 8) take a similar interest in the role of formulations in therapeutic interaction, with a more explicitly discursively psychological focus on actions performed by descriptions of cognitive distortions or 'thinking errors' in videotaped group therapy sessions. The sessions are with men who are on parole for sexually deviant crimes in the US. Their analysis explores how thinking errors are discursively managed when group members, including the therapists, give and receive feedback about them. An example of a commonly identified thinking error used in the therapy sessions would be 'poor me', where the offender may depict themselves as picked on, hurt, or in need of love and support. Both therapists and offenders orient to the difficulty of displaying knowledge about the mental states of others (which is, by the therapist's own definition, a thinking error) through strategies such as hedging and modalisation (e.g., 'you're ashamed ... and that sort of thing').

Drawing on discursive psychological notions of stake and interest, MacMartin and LeBaron show that by invoking thinking errors, a therapist can perform a stake accusation – calling into question an offender's stake in producing prior or current accounts of his crimes. They also explore how therapists can construct thinking errors as interested or disinterested actions, with different implications for assessing the offenders' therapeutic progress. This neatly illustrates how cognitive distortions are useful rhetorical devices for getting the business of therapy done. Their analysis also shows the implications of the therapists' production of the presence or absence of stake, interest and agency in offenders' accounts.

The theme of clients' troubling identity issues in clinical interaction continues as Pomerantz et al. (Chapter 7) examine a corpus of videotaped medical consultations for instances where patients are seeking confirmation from their doctor that their symptoms are not associated with a serious medical condition. They track the careful way in which patients attend to issues such as their own lack of medical expertise relative to the doctor's, or to troubling identities that may accompany such serious concerns about health. They also show how patients attend to their own identity as a normal patient, in a context where 'hypochondriac' or similar might be hearable. For example, patients report evidence that refutes the likelihood of their self-diagnosed serious condition by displaying their knowledge of symptoms of that condition that they do not have. This allows them to be heard as knowledgeable about the medical condition in question, capable of reasoning clearly and sceptically about it, so not the kind of person who would rush into thinking the worst, while at the same time raising the serious medical condition as an issue for the doctor's consideration. Pomerantz et al. suggest that this state of affairs may lead to problems in the consultation, where the doctor hears the patient's dismissal of the candidate serious health problem as representational of the patient's view on the matter, rather than as something more subtle that may attend to available noxious identities or the doctor's expertise.

All the contributions to Part II therefore focus on specific features of interaction in clinical settings. All pay special attention to how clients and professionals display their concerns and orientations in the unfolding features of interaction. This insight into the concerns and orientations of participants allows some of our contributors to develop ideas about application, and to begin to see how problems arise in clinical interaction. We will draw out and develop these ideas in our final chapter.

Talking competence   The discursive approach developed through-out this book considers practices involving psychological, social and institutional terms, themes and orientations and their relation to a diverse range of professional–client interaction. One feature of such interaction is the asymmetries of knowledge that arise between professional and client; for example, clients typically know about issues related to their own lives and problems, professionals typically possess the professional expertise to advise or counsel on those issues and problems. Chapters in this section develop these ideas with an additional focus on interaction concerning young people within specific institutional contexts – a child protection helpline, a school counselling session, a centre for autistic schoolchildren, and school group-evaluation sessions. The chapters in this section develop important conclusions for our understanding of the construction and treatment of young people and their 'competence' in institutional settings.

While previous research has portrayed the adult–child relationship as prototypically asymmetrical (Aronsson and Evaldsson 1993), asymmetry is seen as a collaboratively achieved phenomenon in CA and DP studies. The focus has been on how asymmetrical relationships can be located within specific instances of talk and how evidence and credibility are sequentially achieved or discounted (see also Drew, 1991; Hutchby, 1996b; Linell, 1990). This suggests that the building of evidence and credibility may involve the deployment of differential knowledge states, access to resources, privileges to participation rights, and claims to participant status.

There is a small amount of research in CA and DP that develops these insights in relation to adult–child interaction (Aronsson and Cederborg, 1996; Bonauito and Fasulo, 1997; Edwards, 1997; Hepburn, 2000, 2005). Here the focus is on how children are *treated* as possessing or lacking perspectives and competences. These studies have considered both the interactional and the wider social consequences of seeing young people's competencies in this way. CA work in particular has been able to show how young people's relations with adults often require certain styles and levels of competence and credibility (Hutchby and Ellis, 1998), and how institutional interaction (e.g., in parent–teacher meetings, kindergartens and hospital clinics) can be employed to frame and constrain children's social competence (Danby and Baker, 1998; Silverman et al., 1998).

The chapters in this collection have a similar focus on how asymmetry may be achieved or discounted, and on the possible mismatch between the institutional requirements of the various settings and sensitivity to the interactional rights and competences of young people. For example,

Cromdal et al. (Chapter 11) draw upon a corpus of classroom inter-action in which peer evaluation is being encouraged in a small group of thirteen- and fourteen-year-old students. This move to more egalitarian assessments reflects recent changes in the national curriculum in Sweden, which includes the introduction of 'problem based learning' (PBL), which aims, by various means, to give students more control over their own learning. Unfortunately evaluation of fellow students does not appear to be a popular move with the students themselves. Cromdal et al. explore the displays of reluctance by the students, par-ticularly to engage in negative assessments of their peers. They also start to document the teacher's moves to instigate and encourage the peer assessment, and his management of the students' resistance. Cromdal et al. raise some issues for the future development of PBL, in particular the issue of individual evaluation, in an approach committed to the sig-nificance of the group in the learning process.

The interaction of professional with young people is continued by Alessandra Fasulo and Francesca Fiore (Chapter 12). Fasulo and Fiore examined eight videotaped 'therapy hours' from a centre specialising in the treatment of people with various degrees of autism. Focusing on careful analysis of therapeutic interaction with two boys, one aged thirteen, the other ten, Fasulo and Fiore found that by focusing on linguistic appropriateness, engaging in continuous questioning and evaluation and by favouring particular topics, therapists reduced the participation and interaction of the autistic young people in their care, despite the overall goal of improving the young people's social skills. They suggest that this is because therapists were working with idealised notions of conversation, both in the available literature and in their training and instruction programmes. Fasulo and Fiore suggest that the logic of everyday talk not only allows for orderly interaction, but also provides for participants' mutual recognition as 'a valid person'.

Buttny and Kellog Rath (Chapter 13) take as their topic a meeting between a female returning high school student and her family, and various staff from the school. How problems are formulated in this context is crucial, and the importance of careful descriptions of people and events in this context is stressed. Buttny and Kellog Rath show the strategies that the co-director employs in seeking to elicit possible prob-lems with the student mother's return to a school at which the father of her child and her own brother are both still present.

Buttny and Kellogg Rath conduct a detailed analysis of interactional cues, including body movements such as eye gaze and head nodding. They show how delicate and troubling issues are both produced and engaged with in the meeting, and how formulating a candidate problem with a query is a useful device. The co-director employs this device particularly where participants' engagement with problem talk appears minimal or even evasive. The device elicits more focused engagement with the co-director's candidate problems from the mother and her family.

Finally, Wiggins and Hepburn (Chapter 14) focus on how asymmetries of competence are collaboratively negotiated with regards to children's eating practices. Using two data sources – audio-recorded interactions within family mealtimes and calls to NSPCC helplines – they examine how children and adults manage the delicate issue of feeding children an appropriate amount of food. This involves constructions of a child's 'appetite' and 'satiety', and often children themselves are treated as having greater 'access' to such knowledge. Conversely, however, it is the adults who are normatively treated as being able to discern such knowledge from children – through reference to verbal or physical behaviour (such as spitting out food or being around to see the child's 'appetite' declining). The implications of such negotiations are far-reaching, not just in terms of developing 'appropriate' eating practices, but in relation to issues of force-feeding and claims of child abuse. As with previous chapters, the institutionality of the interaction – either a family mealtime or a telephone call to a child protection helpline – is produced within the talk itself. The speakers display certain expectations and responsibilities, such as who should provide evidence for potential child abuse and who is entitled to know about their young child's satiety needs.

The chapters in Part III therefore pull together examples of interaction in which children and adults are treated as differently competent in various settings. In doing so, they build on the earlier parts of the book and focus on specific areas of practical relevance, such as how the status of young people is produced and resisted on a moment-by-moment basis. The issue of practicalities and DP research more broadly is then discussed in our final chapter.

Part I

Psychology in action

2   Managing subjectivity in talk

Derek Edwards

Introduction

One of discursive psychology's key concerns has been the ways in which talk manages subject–object relations, or mind–world relations (Edwards, 1997). Early interest focused on factual discourse (e.g., Edwards and Potter, 1992; Potter, 1996), the 'object side', but this was already part of a general interest in respecifying psychological topics such as memory (Edwards and Middleton, 1986; Edwards, Middleton and Potter, 1992) and attitudes (Potter and Wetherell, 1987), as practices performed in discourse and social interaction. The 'object side' issue was how, in producing versions of things and events, speakers (or writers of text) build the factual status or objectivity of what they are saying. That is to say, we examined how descriptions and accounts are produced as reflections of the things they are about. The 'subject side' is an integral part of those same practices of description and accountability. By working up the subjective status of an account, generally somebody else's account, its objectivity is undermined. Subjective or 'subject side' accounts are ones that reflect a speaker's 'stake and interest' in a topic (Edwards and Potter, 1992).

It is important to emphasise that these are not inferences drawn by the analyst, that a given speaker or stretch of talk *actually is* subjective or objective. Rather, these are matters *attended to in the talk itself*. In the argot of ethnomethodology, they are members' concerns. The analytic task for discursive psychology (DP) has been to examine how, on what occasions and in the service of what kinds of interactional practices discourse handles and manages its objective and subjective bases. Increasingly, the major analytic resource for this project is conversation analysis (CA), although there is also a relevant linguistic-pragmatics literature on how stance, subjectivity, etc. are encoded in language, for example by the use of modal verbs (*ought, would, must*, etc.) and various subjunctives and conditionals. My aim in this chapter is to update our understanding of how subject–object relations are managed in talk-in-interaction, foregrounding how the 'subject side' is handled, and incorporating some recent empirical studies and work in progress.

To begin, we pick up the trail using a classic example from earlier discussions of 'stake and interest'. It is the infamous utterance during the 1963 Profumo trial, by 'call girl' Mandy Rice-Davies, when being cross-examined about her sexual relations with various British government ministers including John Profumo and Lord Astor, and also a member of the Russian military. The dialogue went something like this (from Edwards and Potter, 1992: 117).[1]

Extract 1

```
Counsel:        Are you aware that Lord Astor denies any
                impropriety in his relationship with you?
                  (0.8)
Rice-Davies:    Well he would wouldn't he
Jury, etc.:     ((prolonged laughter))
```

The point of Rice-Davies's response was that Astor had a clear motive to lie. Rather than taking that denial as objective (a reflection of factual reality), the force of her reply is that it should be taken as stemming from the subject side – a reflection of Astor's stake or interest in the matter. In factual discourse generally, establishing fact may require controlling for stake.

The Rice-Davies example is useful in that it contains another feature that was developed in subsequent DP work: the use of the modal *would* to formulate a *disposition* to act or talk in a particular way. The everyday reasoning here is related to 'script formulations' (Edwards, 1995, 1997). Where there is a standard, predictable way of behaving, whether for anybody in that setting or for a particular person who generally acts that way, then whatever they do in accordance with that cultural or personal 'script' (in this case, Astor's denial of impropriety) can be attributed to a *disposition* to talk or act that way. Again, the effect is to 'subjectivise' Astor's testimony, rendering it a reflection of him (his interests, tendencies or motives) rather than the truth.

DP has extended its analytical interest in how the 'subject side' is managed, beyond the operation of stake and interest in factual discourse, toward how psychological states generally, including dispositions of all kinds, are attended to as part of talk's situated practices (Edwards, 2004; Edwards and Potter, 2005; Potter and Hepburn, 2003). This includes extending the study of dispositional uses of modals such as *will, would* and *going to* or *gonna*, as in 'I'm not gonna hit an old lady' (Edwards, 2006a). However, I will focus here on two general, related themes: (1) how people handle their accountability for what they say in terms of dispositions to say it; and (2) how manner of vocal delivery, including intonation, laughter and other non-verbal features of talk, handles a speaker's subjective stance. The following sections review some work on those themes.

Managing dispositions to say things

The original DP theme for subjectivity (e.g., in the 'DAM' summary: Edwards and Potter, 1992) was stake and interest, mainly in the sense of self-interest. But stake and interest are only part of a very broad range of kinds of investment that people may claim or deny, with regard to the content of what they say. More broadly, there is a range of common-sense kinds of tendencies or *dispositions* to act or talk in particular ways, where dispositions can be emotional, cognitive, epistemic, moral, situational or character-based. Retaining an interest in subject–object relations, I include here a range of ways in which speakers may show that they are *not disposed to get things wrong*. Dispositional ways of getting things wrong include being prone to tell tall stories, being prone to exaggerate, being prejudiced, and being paranoid or disposed to moan or complain. These are examples of research topics for DP where the task is to see how they work, not as indications of a speaker's actual veracity or bias, but as actively managed practices of social interaction. I focus here on two general ways in which people may be at pains to manage subject-side dispositions: (1) by showing themselves as not disposed to make too much of things (e.g., to exaggerate, draw extra-ordinary inferences, etc.); (2) by showing themselves as reluctant to say negative things (e.g., to complain or criticise, or adopt a prejudiced position).

Not disposed to say too much

Various studies have taken up a theme first developed by Harvey Sacks regarding the practice of 'doing being ordinary' (Sacks, 1984). Often this amounts to displaying oneself as not prone to tell tall stories, nor to experience and report extraordinary events, nor over-interpret mundane events as extraordinary: 'You cannot have a nervous breakdown because you happened to see an automobile accident. You cannot make much more of it than what anybody would make of it' (ibid.: 427). Subsequent work by Jefferson (2004) built on Sacks's observations of an 'at first I thought ... and then I realized ... ' device for the presentation of extra-ordinary witnessings. An initial case was the recurrence, in witnessings of what turned out to be the assassination of President Kennedy, of accounts such as 'I heard a noise that I thought was a backfire of one of the motorcycle policemen' (ibid.: 134). Wooffitt (1991) found systematic use of the related device 'I was just doing mundane X, when extraordinary Y happened' in reports of supernatural experiences.

One major thing that these devices do is manage subjectivity in the course of relating a potentially dubious factual account. They attend to the notion that what is being claimed is/was in the world, and not in the speaker's head or imagination, nor in any disposition to tell a tall tale (see also Edwards and Fasulo, 2006, on uses of the expression 'to be honest'). Rather, the reporter is brought off as disposed to see ordinary things, and to assume ordinary explanations. These and related devices can be called *counter-dispositionals*, in that they provide ways of managing a report's potential subjectivity, including its stake or interest. In implying a disposition to see things as ordinary, for example, a speaker counters the notion that they might be disposed to see, imagine or infer those things that they are claiming to have witnessed. Indeed, the very use of the device displays a sensitivity to normal, rational accountability not only there and then at the time of the witnessing, but here and now on the occasion of its telling.

Another range of practices, somewhat echoing what is involved in recounting extraordinary experiences, involves saying things in extreme ways: that is, the use of what Pomerantz (1986) termed 'extreme case formulations' (ECFs for short). ECFs are descriptions and assessments that include extreme, ultimate or end-of-the-continuum expressions such as *never, always, brand new, everybody, the best* and *nobody*. They maximise the quality or state of affairs to which they are attached, generally when there are grounds (as with recounting unusual experiences) for expecting an unsympathetic hearing. A subsequent study of ECFs (Edwards, 2000) explored how their users handle the 'subject side' possibility, relevant when using ECFs, of being heard to exaggerate, go to extremes, or again, as Sacks put it, 'make much more of it than what anybody would make of it' (Sacks, 1984: 427). So ECFs provide another context in which speakers may work at being not disposed to get things wrong: 'ECFs are factually brittle, in that an extreme or universalizing statement ("I know nothing," "nobody comes here," "you always say that") risks easy refutation by a single exception, invites being taken nonliterally, and may be treated as an index of the speaker's attitude (subjectivity) rather than as a straightforward description of the world' (Edwards, 2000: 352).

Three ways of handling the subject side of ECFs were identified: (1) the use of 'softeners', where extreme expressions are qualified, often under some kind of challenge;[2] (2) the use of ECFs *as* expressions of investment, where subjective investment, rather than undermining truth or objectivity, is part of a display of sincerity, genuineness or affiliation;[3] (3) ironic and other 'non-literal' uses of ECFs, in which, again, the extremity of ECFs is used as a resource, rather than a threat to their objectivity. Ironic uses and their receipts are often accompanied by laughter but, in any case, all these ways of handling subjectivity are produced interactionally.

Extract 2 is a brief example (see Edwards, 2000: 366). Mary (M) and Jeff (J) are a couple in their first session of relationship counselling. A counsellor is also present.

Extract 2: DE-JF:C1:S1:9–10

```
1 M: →  'cos ↑ you think I'm the wor:st ↓person on this
2        ↑ plan[↓et. (.) At the mo]ment. = ((plaintively))
3 J:         [ ↑No ↓I do:n't,   ]
4 J:     =That's not fai:r, no- (.) I ↓don't,
5 M:     °That's what you've been telling me.°
6 J: →  Hheh heh.
```

Mary's turn at lines 1 and 2 deploys the ECF 'the worst person on this planet' in an ironic characterisation of Jeff's opinion of her. The irony is signalled initially by the relativising, counterfactual quotative '↑ you think', with its individualising, contrastive emphasis on '↑ you'. But irony is also conveyed by the ECF's sheer implausibility as factual description; there are presumably worse people on the planet than Mary, even in Jeff's eyes. The softener 'at the moment' (line 2) comes just after she starts to hear Jeff's overlapping denial (line 3). The irony of Mary's ECF is hearable in how she vocalises that assessment: it is mostly delivered at the top of her normal pitch range, and is plaintively delivered – I will return to the details of that vocal delivery in the second part of this chapter. The irony is picked up in Jeff's denials (lines 3–4) and laughter (line 6). Note some significant details here: Jeff's denial is not outright (e.g., 'I never said that'), but attends precisely to Mary's ECF as excessive ('that's not fair'). Further, his laughter (line 6) is minimal and constrained, sounding more like an appreciation of Mary's heavy irony, rather than ridiculing her distress; he is offering a bit of laughter with, rather than at her.[4]

Not disposed to be negative

Another context for subjectivity-handling expressions, in addition to showing oneself as not disposed to make too much of things, is displaying oneself as reluctant to make negative inferences, or to talk on the basis of prejudice rather than observation or sound judgement. There is some overlap here, in that showing oneself as 'not disposed to be negative' may also involve the use and softening of ECFs. As we have noted, factual claims can be grounded by offering them as *counter-dispositional*: as reluctantly arrived at, or even precisely counter, not only to what others may think, but also to one's own presumptions and biases (Edwards, 2003: cf. Potter, 1996, on 'stake inoculation'). It is a way of denying that you believe what it suits you to believe, or what you believed before you looked – that is, of attending to a possible accusation of pre-judgement or prejudice.

Extract 3 is a fragment from an interview conducted by Margaret Wetherell in New Zealand, at the time of a controversial rugby tour by the then apartheid-practising South Africa. It is taken from Edwards, (2003).

Extract 3: Interview 2: 20

```
 1 R:  Uhm (1.2) I would li:ke to see apartheid done
 2     away with
 3        (1.0)
 4 R:  but can anybody come up with
 5     a- [a (.) positive way of saying 'This is how=
 6 I:      [Mm mhm
 7 R:  =it can be done'
 8 I:  Mm mhm
 9 R:  It's all very well to turn round and say 'Give
10     em a vote'
11 I:  Yes
12 R:  I mean the majority of them (1.0) don't know
13     what a vote is
```

The target expression is 'I would like to see' (line 1). The notion being offered is that the interviewee is not promoting the retention of apartheid out of any kind of preference or liking for it but, rather, his recommendations are counter-dispositional. He would *like* it done away with, if only that were realistic. Apartheid, then, is a solution reluctantly arrived at.[5] Note how the production of R's conclusion as reluctantly and rationally grounded is contrasted with how he characterises advocates of full democracy: their recommendation to 'give em a vote' is something they, somewhat unaccountably, 'turn round and say' (line 9).

Another rich arena for displays of reluctance to be negative is when people are making complaints (which, again, often involve the use of

ECFs: Pomerantz, 1986). Complainers generally attend to their motives or grounds for the complaint, as an integral part of the complaint's production (Drew, 1998). In addition to building the complaint's objectivity (its evidential basis, corroboration, etc.), this involves attending to its possible subjectivity. Complaints may be built as not stemming from any disposition on the complainer's part, to complain or moan (Edwards, 2005). Indeed, there is a collection of commonsense ways of lexicalising such dispositions: *moan, whinge, harp on, go on and on*, etc., just as there are words for other dispositional reasons for speaking (*racism, sexism, paranoia, boasting, axe-grinding*, etc.). The sheer existence of these terms indicates subjectivity-management as a members' concern.

Complaints involve some kind of grievance or transgression, often against the complainer, which immediately makes relevant the complaint's possibly motivated, or dispositional, basis. Yet 'subjectivity' is not simply a threat to a complaint's factual grounding. It may also enhance factuality and seriousness, and be oriented-to in that way by recipients, by signalling how aggrieved, long-suffering, and *non*-disposed to complaining the complainer may be. Making a complaint is not a matter, therefore, of simply deleting or playing down its subject-side basis but, rather, of handling and managing it to best effect. Ways of handling the subject-side of complaints (see Edwards, 2005) include: (1) announcements, in which an upcoming complaint is projected in ways that signal the complainer's stance or attitude; (2) laughter accompanying the complaint announcement, and/or its subsequent delivery and receipt; (3) displacement, where the speaker complains about something incidental to what would be expected to be the main offence; and (4) uses of lexical descriptions such as 'moan' and 'whinge' that formulate subjectivity, investment and a disposition to complain. Extract 4, from a domestic telephone call between Lesley and Joyce, includes an 'announcement'.

Extract 4: Holt:C85:4:2

```
1 L: →   °Oh:.° .hh Yi-m- You ↓know I-I- I'm broiling about
2        something hhhheh[heh .hhhh
3 J:                    [Wha::t.
4 L:     Well that sa↓:le. (0.2) at- at (.) the vicarage.
5           (0.6)
6 J:     Oh ↓ye[:s,
7 L:           [.t
8           (0.6)
9 L:     u (.) ihYour friend 'n mi:ne wz the:re
```

Lesley's expression 'I'm broiling about something' announces an upcoming complaint, the substance of which is not yet provided in the extract. As Drew (1998) notes with regard to this sequence, the announcement formulates the complainer's sense of grievance, which is a canonical component of complaints:

Reporting in this way their emotional response – their sense of grievance – enables complainants to characterize how far the other's behavior has caused offense. In this respect it may be noted that these expressions of indignation are formed as first person assessments, for example, as 'I was so angry,' 'w'l tha tee:d me o::ff,' rather than as generalized assessments (in the form 'it was so . . .'). (Drew, 1998: 311)

Edwards (2005) examines the same extract, focusing particularly on the way Lesley delivers her announcement:

The term *broiling* metaphorically signals a particularly strong reaction to an event that turns out to be a person saying to her at a vicarage jumble sale, somewhat teasingly, 'hhello Lesley, (.) ↑still trying to buy something f'nothing' . . . [The] extract contains, already in the announcement section, some orientation to the possibility that Lesley might be heard to be making rather much of a small event. Specifically, there is the laughter in line 2. Combined with the metaphor 'broiling', this is hearable as Lesley announcing an upcoming complaint whose possibly ironic, even comical features, and her proposal not to be taking it too seriously, are projected in how the announcement is delivered. Lesley . . . manages to provide a sense of . . . being truly aggrieved, while not making too much of it. Again all of this is accomplished, or at least projected, along with the further ironic remark 'Your friend 'n mi:ne' (line 9), prior to the complaint itself being told. (Edwards, 2005: 11)

I will return to the use of laughter and other vocal inflexions later in this chapter, but first let us note something about the term *moaning*, not only as a concept that invokes a person's *disposition* to complain, but as a term used in talk-in-interaction. Here are four separate examples from Edwards (2005).

(1) Les: .hh She wz moaning on about m-me:: an:' (.)
            m:oaning on about him'n ohh

(2) Ann: it's ↑just ev'ryday thi:ngs she's moaning about.

(3) Ann: I >thought'w'l< if I go out she prob'ly gonna
            start moa:nin' about somethin' ↑else.

(4) Mac: he wz (.) ↓moaning about som'ing else I can't
            ↓remembe:r,

In each case, and typically, the object of the verb *moan* is something vague or indefinite (examples 2–4), or absent altogether (example 1).

The effect is of an essentially *intransitive* kind of complaining, an activity done by, and indexical of, the complainer, rather than something caused by a specifically complainable event or circumstance. The phrase 'start moa:ning' (example 3) works in the same way as 'moaning on' (example 1), implying a sustained activity being embarked upon, rather than a specifically targeted complaint. Attention is drawn away from whatever specific object or activity was complained of, to the activity of complaining itself, and the complainer's disposition to complain. Whereas complainers work to objectify their complaints, and work against any notion that their complaining might be dispositional, reporters of complaints, and in particular complainees, can counter them by doing just the opposite: working up their subject-side dispositional basis such that complaints become whinges or moans.

Intonation, voice quality and laughter

Analysis of some of the features examined in the previous section was postponed for treatment here. In actual talk-in-interaction, lexical descriptions and assessments are produced inseparably from *how they are spoken*. Through manner of vocal delivery, speakers display subjectivity or stance with regard to what they are saying but, unlike with lexical content, this is only partially or grossly represented in transcripts, while analysis itself is based on the audio recordings. Despite that, the Jefferson system transcripts used for CA do provide substantial details of interaction-relevant vocal delivery that are absent from standard typists' transcripts, and have provided the basis for detailed studies of the interactional uses of laughter (Jefferson, 1985), and various extensions to the system to include features such as body movements (e.g., Goodwin, 1986; Heath, 1986), applause (Atkinson, 1984), and crying (Hepburn, 2004). Further additions have been usefully incorporated into CA from phonetics (e.g., Kelly and Local, 1989; Couper-Kuhlen and Selting, 1996; Ogden, 2001; Hellermann, 2003). There is space here for only a glimpse of how vocal delivery displays subject-side or disposition-managing features of talk, but this is an area of increasing analytical importance and convergence between CA, nonverbal social interaction, DP and linguistics.

Intonation and subjectivity

Returning to extract 2, we focus now on intonation, and in particular Mary's pitch movement in lines 1–2.

Extract 2 Revisited

```
1 M: → 'cos ↑ you think I'm the wor:st ↓person on this
2        ↑ plan[↓et. (.) At the mo]ment. = ((plaintively))
```

As figure 2.1 shows, Mary's intonational movement during the expression ' 'cos you think I'm the worst person on this planet' travels close to the top and bottom of her talking pitch range during this session. There is marked pitch movement on *you* and on the ECFs *worst* and *planet* (which I take to be an extreme equivalent to 'the whole world'), which is also where her vocal emphasis is subjectively heard.[6] The transcription gloss 'plaintively' (line 2) characterizes the relatively quiet, but highly modulated manner of Mary's talk at this point. 'Poor little me' would also describe it quite well, normatively and subjectively. Clearly, any descriptive gloss of that kind interprets and categorises Mary's speech, like all descriptions do, in a defeasible, potentially objectionable and indefinitely extendible way. What the amplitude variations in the speech pressure waveform and the pitch trace do is show at least part of the basis on which such interpretative impressions are founded, and on which Jeff's hearing, as well as mine, must be based (cf. Local and Walker, forthcoming).

Still missing from the graphs, of course, is Mary's particular voice quality, even if we were to add further details such as a spectrogram and speech formants (which are also available using the software that produced figure 2.1), along with facial expressions and body movements. However, the point of figure 2.1 is that speech carries, in its vocal quality and manner of delivery, a range of somewhat measurable and analysable, but in any case hearable, features via which the speaker conveys subjective stance or 'attitude' toward the content of what they are saying. The key, however, is not pitch height and movement in themselves, but their sequential placement within an unfolding social interaction, and with regard to talk's content: 'pitch height does not function as an isolated, decontextualized display. Instead it becomes visible as a specific, meaningful event, by virtue of the way in which it is embedded within a particular sequence of action' (Goodwin and Goodwin, 2000: 242).

There is a growing body of work on phonetic and intonational features of speech that seeks integration with CA's approach to talk as the sequentially organised production of social actions (see, for example, Couper-Kuhlen and Ford, 2004). Some of that work links sound patterns to 'attitude' and emotional expression in everyday talk (Local and Walker, forthcoming), and aims to ground interpretative glosses of the

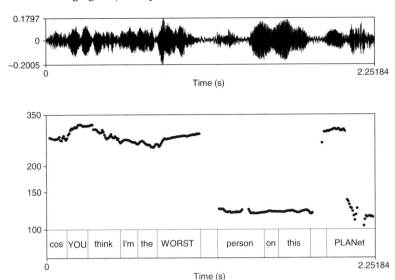

Figure 2.1 Speech pressure waveform (upper graph) and pitch trace (lower graph) for the worst person on the planet.

meaning of participants' vocal delivery and reactions (e.g., Freese and Maynard, 1998; Goodwin and Goodwin, 2000) in measurable phonetic features of talk. Much of the wider literature on emotional expression, however, relies on normative linguistic examples or psychological experiments (e.g., Cowie and Cornelius, 2003) rather than studies of interactional, everyday talk.

The problem remains, even in studies that integrate phonetics, gestures and a CA approach to talk, of how non-verbal expressions and speech characteristics should be analytically described. That is to say, the descriptive language used by analysts is largely, and properly, the range of normative, vernacular expressions available to anyone for describing attitudinal and emotional states. But these are, in the first place, the terms of reference for defeasible, alternative, action-oriented, members' accounts. Furthermore, vernacular languages differ in their 'emotionology' and other psychological vocabularies (Lutz, 1988b; Edwards, 1997), so it is not clear how the description of talk's 'attitudinal' content, outside of participants' own descriptions, should best be done. Interestingly, Local and Walker (forthcoming) suggest that, when emotional or attitudinal states are formulated by participants themselves in the course of social interaction – that is, when they say things such as 'you sound happy' – these formulations may occur in the absence of any measurable acoustic features of the other person's speech, to warrant them.

Voice modulation and subjective expression

Speakers may also modulate their vocal delivery as a conventionally understandable index of a particular subjective, experiential stance on what they are reporting. Stokoe and Hepburn (2005) describe a phenomenon they call 'intonational mirroring'. When neighbours complain about each other, or report suspicious activities (for example, a possible case of child abuse), one of the things they report on are vocal noises, particularly parents shouting and children crying. Through voice quality, coordinated with their talk's lexical content, the reporter can signal a subject-side stance or 'take' on the matter. For example someone whose neighbour had complained about her children's noise produced a counter-complaint about the complainer's own noisiness: '>all of a sudden< (0.4) ban:g bang bang'. The initial phrase '>all of a sudden<' was delivered hurriedly (as shown by the markers > and <). The second part, 'ban:g bang bang', was given increased amplitude and emphasis, mirroring the banging noises themselves. In contrast, her own direct-reported disciplinary comment to her children, 'don't °play°', was reported notably quieter (marked by the degree signs), with the lower volume located precisely on the contentious activity '°play°'. The volume drops again when quoting her children's response: '(°well° (0.3) we were ↑on'y playin.' (ibid.: 653).

One interesting feature of Stokoe and Hepburn's analysis is how these kinds of features of vocal delivery, along with the talk's content, were relevant to the talk's major interactional business and setting. It helped signal whether they were making a complaint (e.g., they were irritated by all the noise), or else expressing a concern (as in a report of child abuse). The wider relevance of intonation mirroring is shown across differences between the two corpuses of data used in the study: neighbour complaints on the phone to a mediation centre, and a collection of child abuse helpline calls. Voice modulation, and vocal mirroring, permit various kinds of alignment and misalignment with, or subject-side stance on, the activities being reported.

Extract 5 is a brief example from one of the child abuse helpline calls (ibid.: 666). The tilde signs ~ (in line 9) mark the start and end of 'wobbly voice', which is talk on the verge of crying (Hepburn, 2004).

Extract 5

```
1 CPO:    D.hh all ↓ri:ght then so e- w- ↑what was your
2         concerns a↓bout these children.
3 Cal:    R:ight. Erm I think it's er:: (0.2) jus one
4         o' their childre:n, (0.2)
5 CPO:    Mm:[:.]
6 Cal:       [E:]m:: (0.2) I think she's bein locked in a
7         room:, (0.3)
8 CPO:    Tch ri:gh[t,]
9 Cal: →           [E ]n she- an her ~crie::s~ (0.3) are
10        really distressin:.
```

The authors note that 'The caller's voice becomes "wobbly" ... or tremulous at *exactly* the point where she is formulating the noise' (Stokoe and Hepburn, 2005: 658), and cite other examples – 'cry: ing, = an ~screa:ming, ~ °khhum°h' – where wobbly voice, emphasis, elongation and extra aspiration (breathiness) were notably characteristic of the child abuse reports. Given that children crying might also be the basis of a straightforward noise complaint, the specific vocal inflexions found in the child abuse reports helped specify *that kind* of crying as abuse-relevant, rather than irritating and complaint-relevant. The accompanying description 'really distressin:' (line 10) further specifies the nature of the cries via their effect on the speaker's mental state (Potter and Hepburn, forthcoming b), rather than via a description of the crying itself. So the object-side of the account (the reported crying) is characterised for the practical purposes of the report (describing abuse to a help line), in terms of its subject-side effects (distressing), and via its precisely located vocalisation (wobbly voice and rise-fall modulation on '~crie::s~'). Through indexing how the talk's context should be empathically heard and understood, this kind of subject-side reporting and voicing offers a kind of re-experiencing of the events themselves, for the benefit of the person hearing the account, that can stand in place of any more concrete evidencing of what actually happened. It renders contentious events inter-subjective, as just precisely what they are reported to have been.

In a very different kind of interactional context, Wiggins (2002) explores vocal features of food appreciation during family meal times: specifically, the occurrence of 'gustatory *mmm*s', defined as '(a) accompanying eating or talk about food and drink (or both) and (b) hearably evaluative in a positive direction' (ibid.: 315).[7] Wiggins notes that 'intonation and sequential features of *mmm* are seen as essential to the construction of pleasure as an immediate and spontaneous, but descriptively vague experience. The gustatory *mmm* also expresses a particularly embodied sense of pleasure' (ibid.: 311). The key feature of the analysis is that these ostensibly spontaneous bodily expressions of pleasure figure, not as direct non-verbal indications of speakers' current bodily and mental states, but as occasioned, functional tokens of social interaction whose interpreted status *as* direct, spontaneous, bodily signals is precisely what they are used socially to convey (cf. the status of emotional expressions in narrative accounts: Edwards, 1997, 1999). As Wiggins notes, people do not generally emit gustatory noises with each mouthful of food. Gustatory *mmm*s are therefore akin to descriptions and evaluations, in that they are optional, varied, relevant, functional, and to be examined on a 'why this now?' basis. They occur as conventional, precision-timed and sequentially occasioned tokens of social interaction (cf. laughter in Jefferson, 1985, and the 'change of state token' *oh* in Heritage 1984, 1998). Rather than subjective experience lying outside of, beyond, or behind the 'surface' of talk-in-interaction (cf. Edwards, 2006b), we find it here under active management within talk-in-interaction itself, integrated into the interactional flow of meaningful sounds, signs, words and actions, and yet used precisely for its status – that is, its conventional, semiotic status – as embodied expression, spontaneous and somewhat beyond words.

Extract 6 provides a simple example of Wiggins's analysis, in which gustatory *mmm*s are shown to occur, not merely as randomly vocalised expressions of bodily pleasure, but as interactionally relevant utterances precision-timed at transition relevance places (TRPs – Sacks et al., 1974).

Extract 6: SKW/D2b–M4 (132–142) (Wiggins, 2002: 319).

```
1              (6.0)
2 Anna:        a sausag:e ↑Simon
3 Simon: →     mm↑m:: (0.4) >no thank you<
4 Michael:     uh- (.) uh::
5              [>(anybody else want) cranberry ↓sauce<
6 Jenny:       [°yeah (0.4) I'll get-°
7 Simon: →     mm↑m[m
8 Jenny:           [I'll have a ↑little bit of cranberry
9              sauce (.) °please- >thank you<°
10 Michael:    >°there you ↑go°<
11 Simon: →    mm↑mm: (0.6) nice
12             (2.8)
```

Wiggins notes that the *mmm*s' precision-timed placement within the conversational flow signals Simon's orientation to the talk, and also his inability to contribute more fully to it: 'his *mmm* on line 3 displays to

Anna that he is attending to food currently being eaten, given that this is articulated first, and followed by a brief pause. The repeated and emphasised *mmm* expressions (lines 7 and 11) continue to demonstrate his engagement with the food. By drawing attention to his consumption in this way, he is also signalling to other speakers that he is unlikely to talk in more depth. This is particularly supported by the speeded up "no thank you" on line 3' (Wiggins, 2002: 319).

The most thoroughly explored vocal inflexion, within studies of talk-in-interaction, is laughter (e.g., Jefferson et al., 1987; Glenn, 2003). I do not propose to review that work here, except to note its relevance to the theme of *subjectivity management*. We have seen some brief examples of laughter in the extracts already reviewed. Again, the key feature of these studies is the way that laughter works inside talk-in-interaction, and with regard to talk's content and sequentially organised social actions. It is a phenomenon far larger than just a spontaneous response to wit or humour, even without taking a Freudian view of the topic (Billig, 2005). Let us briefly consider again the opening lines of extract 4.

Extract 4 revisited
```
1 L: →   °Oh:.° .hh Yi-m- You ↓know I-I- I'm broiling about
2        something hhhheh[heh .hhhh
3 J:                     [Wha::t.
```

Lesley is announcing an forthcoming complaint about how she was slighted at a vicarage jumble sale by a man of whom she and Joyce, to whom she is speaking on the telephone, have had previous acquaintance. Rather than signalling that she has just said something funny, Lesley's laughter in line 2 is part of a range of features of her talk that project and handle just how seriously she (and later Joyce, in affiliation with Lesley) is taking the matter. The laughter manages the notion that Lesley may be making too much of a small thing. It proposes a subject-side characterisation of her as essentially cheerful, not given to complaining, while also setting up the forthcoming story as somewhat entertaining. While her words speak of the seriousness of the offence ('I'm broiling about something'), her immediate laughter, just at that point, signals not merely that it is not so bad after all, but rather, that she is disposed to make light of it. This echoes Jefferson (1984a) on how laughter can be used to make light of matters in troubles-telling; Hepburn (2004) notes the opposite effect with crying. In interactional terms, Lesley is providing Joyce with cues as to what kind of story is to be told, and how to hear and react. Somewhat counter-intuitively, laughter produced as part of a complaint can have the effect of enhancing rather than diminishing the complaint's seriousness and objectivity, precisely by displaying the complaint as counter-dispositional; the complainer is not disposed to make heavy weather of it (Edwards, 2005).

Conclusion

Analysing how speakers handle 'subject-side' considerations, as a practical concern when speaking, is part of a general analytical preoccupation with how subject–object relations are managed in everyday talk. Often we find subject-side and object-side accounts in opposition, where subjectivity of various kinds (stake, prejudice, ulterior motives, etc.) is treated as a threat to a report's objectivity, reliability or truth. Sometimes they work in unison, particularly where motives and other dispositions are offered as running counter to the speaker's claims – *counter-dispositionals* – but also where the proposed disposition is something such as sincerity, honesty or a tendency to speak plainly. Counter-dispositionals are themselves dispositionals, but ones that run counter to the speaker's assertion that whatever they are saying is true or real. So, as we noted for complaints, a complaint's objectivity can be undermined by building the complainer's disposition to moan or whinge, or its objectivity can be enhanced by providing a counter-disposition (e.g., being long-suffering, stoical, generous-spirited, happy, etc.). What we have called 'stake and interest' (Edwards and Potter, 1992) is a particular kind of dispositional consideration relevant to factual claims; 'stake inoculation' (Potter, 1996) is a counter-dispositional practice in which the producer of a possibly dubious factual claim prefaces it with a self-characterisation as predisposed to see things differently.

The general domain in which these practices can be located is that of everyday rational accountability, considered as a speaker's ordinary, pervasive orientation (Garfinkel, 1967). This is in contrast, say, to how people might justify themselves when formally called upon to do so, such as in a court of law or an interview, although those cases are also readily analysable as further cases in point – that is, special cases of how rational accountability is interactively managed in talk. As Pomerantz (1984b) has shown, reasons and bases for saying things are analysable as sequentially organised, actual and occasioned practices performed in the course of speaking. This is quite different from their usual status in psychology, where reasons for speaking figure as theorised mental entities lying behind, beyond or causally prior to actually speaking; or indeed in psychotherapy, where reasons and bases for saying things may figure as matters to be inferred, on some expert basis, from what people say and do not say.

Looking at reasons and bases for saying things as a *practical speaker's concern* means that we are not asking the psychological question, 'Why do people say things?' Rather, we are asking: 'What are the practices by which people handle the idea that they may be saying things for a reason?'[8] Although this contrasts with the 'psychological' question, psychology's way of asking the question has its own practical, and studiable, occasions. It is, after all, part of talk's everyday commonsense accountability that people may avow or attribute reasons for saying things, and psychology decontextualises and reifies that notion, as a matter of mental states lying behind talk. Psychotherapy, for example, is analysable as a set of practices-in-talking in which precisely that kind of accountability is systematically acted out and brought off (see, for examples: Gale, 1991; Morris and Chenail, 1995; Siegfried, 1995; Fasulo, 1997; Antaki, 2001). The pervasive, everyday relevance of 'reasons for speaking' arises out of the facts that: (1) nobody need say anything, or anything in particular; and (2) something being the case is never a sufficient reason for saying it (although it may well be offered *as* the reason). Nevertheless, there are special arenas of social life where doubt and dispute, or motivated bases of saying things, are themes endemic to the setting – not only psychotherapy and counselling, but also court rooms, police interrogations, and various kinds of family and neighbourhood mediation. These are also arenas that are currently under investigation for how subject–object relations feature as essential considerations in how those institutional settings work (Edwards and Potter, 2001).

A familiar objection to discursive psychology and conversation analysis, among other studies of language-based practices, is that their focus on talk, or discourse, omits important things such as the broader contextual setting and the nature of embodied experience and subjectivity (e.g., Parker and Burman, 1993; Hollway and Jefferson, 2000). There is a sense that language, or talk-in-interaction, is to be found only at the surface of things, and that inferences of a different kind need to be made, in order to get at what is going on below the surface. Nobody is claiming that discourse is all there is. However, the rush toward theorising about context and subjectivity is being done without close attention to what is available on the surface. The surface turns out to be unexpectedly rich (Edwards, 2006b) – I acknowledge my rhetorical use of the counter-dispositional 'unexpectedly' – and full of members' orientations to the relevance of the setting, along with the active management of subject-side considerations relevant to what they are saying. In our experience of the physical world, from which we derive the metaphors 'surface' and 'depth', going below the surface of things merely reveals more surfaces to examine – whether under the sea, beneath the skin or under the skull. As Wittgenstein (1958) cogently argued, and also Garfinkel (1967; cf. Coulter, 1990), and in a different way the perceptual psychologist Gibson (1979), the surface is what members themselves are actually seeing and dealing with. To the extent that subjectivity is part of social life, and relevant to language and social interaction (the practices of inter-subjectivity), it has to be made available in mutually understandable ways. There are no private languages. Increasingly, the study of talk-in-interaction reveals the richly detailed and orderly 'surface' workings of social interaction, including gesture and voice quality as well as lexical language. It is here that we find contextual relevance and (inter-)subjectivity under active management in the course of social practices in ways that are essentially, and necessarily, publicly performed, and by dint of that, and *in terms of* that, recordable and analysable.

NOTES

1. The segment of dialogue is taken from the 1989 feature film *Scandal*, directed by Michael Caton-Jones, which dramatised these events.
2. ECF softeners are analysed for the interactional work they do: 'ECF softeners work by (a) providing for a sequential response to a challenge; (b) indexing the speaker as reasonable, taking account of empirical realities, not making excessive claims; and (c) retaining the generalizing work that ECFs perform while being immune from easy rebuttal by countercases' (Edwards, 2000: 359).
3. For example, L and C are talking about C's young daughter Megan in the aftermath of a family bereavement:

```
1 C:     She's been very he:lpful
2          (0.2)
3 L:     Oh: ↓good. An' she's ↑comp'ny for you isn'[she.
4 C:                                                [Oh she i:s.
5          Ye[s.
6 L:       [Grea↑:t [↓comp'ny.
7 C: →              [Definitely ye[:s.
8 L:                              [Mm[:n.
9 C:                                 [Ye::s,
```
(Holt:88U:2:4:10–11, from Edwards, 2000: 362)

With the ECF 'definitely yes' (line 7), C upgrades her own prior 'Yes' (line 5), highlighting not only what Megan is like, but also the act and extent of affiliation between L and C. The choice of 'definitely' rather than, say, 'perfect (company)' attends directly to the *certainty of the assessment* (subject-side) rather than of the qualities being assessed in Megan (object-side).

4. All of these analytical remarks are based on hearing the audio recording, and some are only partially embodied in what the transcript shows. Intonation and voice quality are topics picked up later in the chapter. On the analysis of laughter *at* versus *with*, see Glenn (1995), and Jefferson (1984).

5. Interview data are not optimal for studying the practices of everyday talk, given that interviewing caters for interactional practices of its own. In this case, the speaker may be orienting to the interviewer's presumed sensibilities on these issues, as a social science researcher otherwise unknown to him, or indeed to the interviewer's talk, actions and reactions before and during the interview.

6. It is pitch movement rather than amplitude (volume) per se, that generally corresponds to subjectively heard rhythm and emphasis (Cruttenden, 1997). Note, for instance, the heavy amplitude through '-son on this', which is not heard nor marked in the transcript as stressed.

7. Gustatory *mmm*s are distinct in their intonational contour (typically longer, and with greater and more varied pitch modulation) than other conversational uses of 'mm' (Gardner, 1997), and in their sequential placement and interactional consequences.

8. Cf. Sacks on how to study comprehension and intersubjectivity: 'instead of saying "Let's find a way of seeing whether people understand what somebody else says," we've asked "Is there some procedure *people use* which has as its product a *showing* that they heard and understood?"' (Sacks, 1992 vol. II: 30–1, emphases added).

3   Emotions in meeting talk

Pirjo Nikander

This chapter continues the discursive respecification of psychological notions elsewhere in this book by looking at the rhetorical and situational use of emotion categories in institutional decision making. Using videotaped data from meetings between social and health care professionals, I examine how members in interprofessional teams either invoke, describe and display their own feelings or ascribe them to other people: their clients or other professionals. The chapter shows how reference to emotions, embedded in ongoing narration and description, functions as practical discursive resources for institutional action and non-action: as part and parcel of the process whereby decisions are negotiated, rationalised and justified. The aim of this chapter is thus to move psychology from the realm of cognitive processing by placing emotion discourse firmly into the social, interactional arena.

In the first part of the chapter 1 outline some earlier work on emotion in interaction as well as empirical studies on meeting interaction and decision making that my own analyses build on. After introducing the data and the setting in which they were collected, I then proceed first to look at the discursive uses of concern constructions in meeting talk. I will argue that ascription of concern to other people in talk – *third-party concern constructions* – functions as a recurrent means of establishing direction for practical decision making. In the second part of my analysis, I examine the delivery of emotionally framed descriptions inside longer narrative sequences. I also show how departures from neutralism are sometimes treated as a breach of sound professional practice. Throughout, the chapter underlines and demonstrates the action-oriented nature of emotion categories and the interlinked nature of psychology, institutions and situated interaction.

The action-oriented nature of emotion categories

Organisational and institutional meetings are easily thought to belong to a realm of rationality, neutral information delivery and balanced deliberation and decision making. Organisations follow safeguards and procedures that set rules and criteria for decision making, and this ideal of rationality and neutrality is easily jeopardised by 'emotionality' or by reference to personal feelings. The notion of decision making being 'contaminated' by emotions makes naturally occurring meetings material an ideal showcase for the analysis of emotion discourse in (inter) action. Analyses of sequences from meeting data also help challenge simple juxtapositions between the neutral and the emotional, between ideal (academic) models of decision making and actual practice (cf. Mehan, 1984). In short, they help to explore how psychological rhetoric and emotion categories become integrated into the everyday business of decision making in institutions.

Interactional perspectives on emotions in various organisational and everyday settings are not a novelty. They have been developed and discussed in sociology (e.g., Hochschild, 1983; Denzin, 1984; Jackson, 1993; Bendelow and Williams, 1998), in organisational studies (e.g., Fineman, 2000), in cultural studies (e.g., Lupton, 1998), in cultural psychology (e.g., Shweder and Haidt, 2000), in linguistic anthropology (e.g., Lutz and Abu-Lughod, 1990; Goodwin and Goodwin, 2000), and in gender studies (e.g., Jaggar and Bordo, 1989; Wetherell, 1996). As a precursor to interactionally oriented, non-cognitive empirical analysis on the emotions, Wittgenstein, in his discussion on pain, implied that speakers' utterances should not be understood as direct reflections on their inner experiences (1958: paras. 244–6, 448–9). He also noted that reference to one's own private experience or sensations makes descriptions particularly resistant to denial or challenge. Talk about inner experiences, in other words, always implies personal ownership of that knowledge (cf. Sharrock, 1974; Peräkylä and Silverman, 1991; Nikander, 2002).

Continuing the Wittgensteinian philosophy of mind tradition, writers such as Coulter (1979, 1990) and Harré (1988; see also Harré and Gillett, 1994; Harré and Parrott, 1996) have analysed the differential uses of emotion words and emotion vocabulary. The focus of such work is, for example, on the uses of the emotions in various settings and language games, and on logico-grammatical analysis of talk. Other important contributions to research on situated emotion talk from an 'anti-psychologistic stance' (Coulter, 1979: 1) come from anthropology, cultural ethnography (e.g. Lutz, 1988b; Lutz and Abu-Lughod, 1990), and from social constructionism and studies of historical psychology (e.g. Harré, 1988; Loseke, 1993; Gergen, 1994). This research has established the cultural relativity and historical change of emotion vocabularies and drawn attention to the relationship between the use of emotion words and the local moral and social order (e.g., Heelas, 1988; Lutz and Abu-Lughod, 1990; White, 1990; Harré and Parrott, 1996; for a review see Buttny, 1993; and Edwards, 1997). As a result of such key texts, emotions have been recast as social phenomena that need to be studied in practical interactional contexts of attribution, discursive action and accounting.

Hepburn and Wiggins (this volume) have already shown that a key contribution and methodological enrichment to the analysis of emotion categories in talk and texts comes from discursive psychology (Edwards and Potter, 1992; Harré and Gillett, 1994; Edwards, 1997, 1999; see also Potter and Hepburn, forthcoming a). Discourse and conversation analyses have been instrumental in challenging psychological/ cognitive viewpoints about emotions (e.g. Parrott, 2001), and in moving empirical analysis towards the rhetorical deployment and the sequential unfolding of emotion discourse. In his studies on emotion categories in therapeutic interaction, Edwards presents perhaps the most substantial argument for the non-cognitive study of emotion discourse (Edwards, 1997, 1999). His work also continues and extends other analyses on, for instance, how participants use emotion categories while telling 'moral tales', and on how such telling is part of the practical work of retrospective explaining (Coulter, 1979: 132; Baruch, 1981; see also Sarbin, 1988).

Research into emotions in interaction also intersects with detailed analyses of laughter (Haakana, 1999; Osvalsson, 2004), crying (Hepburn, 2004), and hysteria (Whalen and Zimmerman, 1998). In addition, analyses on media texts and accounts by politicians (MacMillan and Edwards, 1999; Locke and Edwards, 2003), on ordinary democracy (Potter and Hepburn, forthcoming a), on age talk and age as a membership category (Nikander, 2000, 2002), as well as analyses ranging from child protection helpline interaction (Potter and Hepburn, 2003) to doctor's consultations (Ruusuvuori, 2005) have helped to further explicate the rhetorical design of emotion talk in different interactional contexts. In sum, discursive research on emotion has already shown that:

Emotion categories are not graspable merely as individual feelings or expressions, and nor is their discursive deployment reducible to a kind of detached, cognitive sense-making. They are discursive phenomena and need to be studied as such, as part of how talk performs social action. (Edwards, 1997: 187)

The meetings data

The analysis that I present below is based on a 42-hour videotaped corpus from interprofessional meetings collected in Finnish elderly care.

The teams in the meetings consist of professionals from the social and health care: of a medical doctor, members of home care personnel, and of social workers, community nurses and a secretary. The practical task for the team members is to make decisions concerning either the level of financial support to elderly clients still living at home or on transitions from the home or from a hospital to an institution providing long-term care (for further details see Nikander, 2003, forthcoming). The meetings are among professionals only. This means that client cases are presented using both interprofessionally compiled computerised documentation and narrative, in-situ detail that members of the team take up as relevant. The team's work thus consists of assessments of elderly clients' life situations, health and coping. This involves interpretation and description based on a combination of different types of information: first-hand observations and narratives based on home visits, documents and medical records and various numerical details like the frequency of home help and other forms of outside support given. In the analysis of these data, I focus on the information presentation phase of the meetings, that is, on stretches of talk where one of the professionals describes an elderly client's case to others present. This phase is typically followed by discussion after which a decision is made.

Although little work has been published directly on emotion discourse in meeting settings, the broader literature on meeting interaction, multi/ interprofessional teams and decision making is immediately relevant to the questions put forward here (e.g., Holstein, 1983; Li and Arber, 2006; Mehan, 1984; Boden, 1994, 1995; Huisman, 2001; Housley, 2003). Given the focus on the information-presentation phase of the meetings, important parallels can also be drawn with studies that examine case or client descriptions as part of the practice in various people-processing institutions (e.g., Sarangi, 1998; Atkinson, 1999; Forsberg, 1999; White, 2002). A further connection can be drawn between courtroom interaction or litigation and the current data. In both, speakers' descriptions and categorisations work to establish what is relevant to the case at hand, what counts as factual and as evidence for or against a specific decision, and – as we are about to see – with the management of professional neutrality (e.g., Pomerantz, 1987; Greatbatch and Dingwall, 1999).

Tainted decisions?

Emotions are routinely conceived of as natural, irrational and potentially beyond conscious control. They are typically associated with the internal, the potentially unwise and the chaotic; as something that has a tendency to leak and get in the way of rational and thought-through actions. Due to this tendency to polarise emotions and rationality, emotions are often treated as something that need to be kept under check and controlled (e.g., Hochschild, 1983; Abu-Lughod and Lutz, 1990; Lutz, 1990; Edwards, 1997). In institutional people-processing settings this further means that appropriate actions and professional interventions are restricted and guided by safety measures, guidelines and diagnostics that support 'objectivity'.

From a discursive perspective, the polarisation of emotion and rationality can in itself be made a topic of study (Edwards, 1997). Do people use psychological concepts like emotion categories to support, justify and establish sufficient grounds for institutional decisions? How do they refer to particularised and contextualised background knowledge in building what is relevant to the case, and how are emotions built into the situated accomplishment of knowledge? And finally, how do speakers invoke a non-marked, non-emotional stance towards the business at hand?

One place to start looking for answers to these questions is with an extract where the very contrast between inner states and outside facts is taken up and discussed by meeting participants. The extract comes from the beginning of a meeting, where a home helper airs some specific questions that concern the principles of the decision-making practice, and the secretary joins her in this.

Extract 1: Meeting 8. Informal home care allowance (4.28–4.54)[1] Speakers: HH = home helper, D = doctor, S = secretary

```
     1   HH:    There are similar people in
     2          the team so (.) .hh we:
     3          are like in the
→    4          same position that we all have
     5          this concern
     6   S:     That's quite ri[ght ]
     7   D:                    [mm]
     8   HH:                   [ So] I mean
     9          the money deal[er sh]ould be
    10   S:                   [yes ]
    11   HH:    someone who only looks at
    12          the papers .hh and doesn't
    13          get any sort of
    14          those like feelings (0.5)
    15          hh concernfee-
    16          I mean we do [also]
    17   D:                  [mm]
```

```
→  18  HH:    sh[are that concernfeeling]
   19  S:        [Right it's up to the presenter
   20           then [when] presenting then
   21  HH:          [right]
   22  S:      the st[ress] may lie [differently ]
   23  D:          [mm ]
   24  HH:                        [That's right]
   25  S:      Views (.) are presented so
   26           that's where it comes in but .hh
   27           who would know the client
   28           better than you
   29  D:      Mm
   30  HH:     mm[m]
   31  S:        [You should ha- be the
   32           professionals of [course so
   33  HH:                        [hh. We
   34           are provided that papers are
   35           in order
```

The exchange happens four minutes into a meeting that makes decisions about financial support to elderly clients and their carers. Prior to these meetings a home visit is routinely made by a member of the team to check each client's current situation and coping, and the same professional then usually presents the case to the meeting. It is this familiarity with the client's background that the home helper takes up as a potential source of bias.

The point of interest here is the way in which the speakers jointly negotiate what can be counted as fact or evidence in the decision making. Note that having 'concern feelings' is strongly contrasted with written documents and papers. The home helper depicts 'looking only at papers' (lines 11–12) as something that eliminates the use of background personal knowledge and feelings. At this point the secretary, who coordinates the allocation of financial help and sits in several teams' meetings within the district, joins in the conversation. She first confirms that cases are presented somewhat differently, and that personal feelings may have a role to play ('that's where it comes in but', line 26). Simultaneously, however, she establishes team members' personal knowledge about their clients as key to the work done ('who would know the client better than you', lines 27–8). The exchange thus underlines much of the discussion on the use of background information and 'facts' in other literature on assessment and decision making. According to the secretary, one's professional stance towards background knowledge helps to keep its influence in check. The home helper, on the other hand, points out that this is possible only when written facts and documents are there to safeguard the team's decision making.

A second thing to note here is that 'having concern feelings' as something that potentially gets in the way of rational decision making is depicted as a common nominator to all team members. The home helper, in other words, does not simply single herself out or avow having such feelings. Instead, concern is put forward as an attribute that has a presence across similarly positioned individual team members (lines 1–5, 16–18). The final point to make is that explicit engagement in discussion on potential bias can *in itself* be heard as a type of rationality. So there is something of an interesting reversal here: explicit talk about the possibility that decision making is tainted by emotion also functions as a public discursive display of good and conscientious professional conduct and of sound reflexivity.

Third-party concern constructions

Extract 1 already opened up something of the dilemma that professionals in the meetings in question face when presenting clients to their colleagues. The extract also included the use of *concern* as an emotion category in their accounts. Continuing on the ways in which concern is invoked in the data, consider the following client description from a meeting making decisions on long-term nursing home placements. Here the speaker, a hospital social worker, presents a female client who is currently in hospital care. The practical task for the meeting is to reach a decision about whether this client is well enough to be discharged home from the hospital, or whether a nursing home is a better option.

Ascribing concern to other professionals

Extract 2: Meeting 4. Nursing home placements (12.32-)
Speaker: HSW = Hospital social worker
Fairfield = a hospital

```
     1 HSW:  Okay the first one is
     2        ((last name + first name))
     3        (0.8) on page what three
     4        (3.8) ((page leafing))
→    5 HSW:  A: (0.8) er never married female
     6        who has come to us in
     7        Fairfield (1.2) in July a:nd
     8        (0.8) wa:s extremely forgetful
     9        had visited a neurologist
    10        (1.2) in a: just a minute
```

```
    11      >I think it was<
    12      Valley special outpatient clinic
    13      or something and from there we
    14      received the first phone call
    15      from the neurologist (1.2)
→   16      he was very concerned about
    17      this (0.8) forgetful person
    18      and she came then (1.2) at some
    19      point to us er hhh for
    20      t-treatment yes the tenth of July
    21      she just a-after
    22      having seen this
    23      neurologist and (0.8) a to:tally
    24      forgetfull pe:rson lived alone
    25      ((goes on with the case
    26      presentation))
```

The extract is a perfect example of how descriptions of states of affairs in meeting talk are not neutral depictions of outside reality, but rather already in themselves project and index specific outcomes and decisions (Huisman, 2001: 71; see also Boden, 1994). Note how the hospital social worker moves between concrete event descriptions concerning the client's situation and professional outside reactions to these. There are routine features to the client description: it starts with the client's name and her current whereabouts. Also included are details about her medical condition and of how she has come to the attention of the hospital. Two points I wish to discuss in more detail are first, the category 'never married female' (line 5) used to describe the client, and second, the use of the emotion term *concern* in conjunction with the occupational category neurologist (lines 15–16). Together these two do some interesting interactional and moral business that projects direction for a decision.

Combining both the marital status and the gender of the client the category 'never married female' in a very economical way indicates that this woman does not have a spouse or children to fall back on in case she is discharged from the hospital. Despite its demographic, 'just ticking a box'–type character, the categorisation therefore already moves the client into a specific cluster of action-worthy cases and indexes that an institutional intervention may be needed.

Later in the extract, this course of action is supported by the use of 'concern'. Here, interesting links can be drawn to observations on the discursive use of 'concern' in other empirical analyses. Looking at calls to a child protection helpline, Potter and Hepburn (2003) note that callers often start their call by describing *themselves* as concerned.

In their detailed analysis of fifty call openings they found concern constructions to manage a range of institutional and practical issues including the authority of the report, the stance of the caller to what is reported, and the neutrality of the helpline officer answering the call (ibid.: 205). They also show how 'concern' is a useful resource for speakers, as it can invoke a subjective state or stance, while also suggesting something objective to be concerned about in the world. What then are the activities done and the role of concern constructions in face-to-face, professional–professional talk, and can parallels be drawn to helpline telephone conversations?

First, unlike the helpline data, concern is invoked here as something belonging to a third party. The social worker does not exhibit her own personal stance to the case at hand. Instead she makes reference to the observations and reactions of a third party, those of a 'very concerned neurologist'. A neurologist is clearly a knowledge-entitling category, one that possesses special medical expertise with respect to 'forgetful persons' (line 17). What is more, the neurologist has also acted on the basis of his professional knowledge: he has himself contacted the hospital and conveyed concern over the client in question (line 12–15). In sum, the co-selection of a third-party concern construction and the category pair neurologist–forgetful person lends further discursive power to the description and projects a potential outcome.

Let us have a look at another example where the concerns and emotions of a third party – this time the relatives' – are invoked.

Ascribing concern to relatives and clients

In extract 3 below, a hospital social worker describes another elderly client who is currently hospitalised. Discharge has been tried but has proved unsuccessful. We join the much longer discussion at a point where the secretary, for some administrative reasons, asks the doctor whether this case should be put to one side and not discussed in this particular meeting. At this point, the social worker comes in with a third-party concern construction.

Extract 3: Meeting 6. Nursing home placements (14.19–15.13)

Speakers: S = secretary, HSW = hospital social worker, N = nurse, Sunnybrook = a hospital

```
1 S:    Does Pete have an opinion
2       on whether we jump
3       the ones in Sunnybrook over
4       now for the moment (0.2)
```

```
           5        [here ((addressing the doctor))
           6 HSW:   [But (.) I'd (.) still (.) like to
           7        (.) add to this that that the relatives
           8        have contacted us
  →        9        and they are really concerned
          10        (0.5)
          11 HSW:   about this
          12        (0.2)
          13 HSW:   about this that the relatives are all
  →       14        tired out that they can't quite
          15        participate any more either (0.2)
          16        in this cause they felt that
          17        that when ((the client)) was .hhh
          18        in October at home and even if
          19        they had this help and the relatives
          20        visited then the being (0.2)
          21        being at home was so unsafe
          22        that here they felt it (0.7)
  →       23        was >terribly< distressing as well
          24        (0.8) they felt it too THE (0.2)
          25        resident herself (0.5.) or patient
          26        herself (0.2) also felt
          27        unsafe but so did
          28        the relatives °so°
          29        (2.0)
          30 HSW:   They of course wish that
          31        this person doesn't have to
          32        cause she's been in Sunnybrook
          33        this long been there like (0.2)
          34        taken .h care of and waited on
          35        that this she'd like not be sent alone
          36        (.) home at this point
          37        (.)
  →       38 HSW:   So this type of a message came
          39        °from the relatives°
          40        a long phone call so
          41        (1.8)
          42 N:     Home care (0.5) probably doesn't
          43        work in her case
          44        any more so
```

The social worker brings in the relatives' point of view partly in overlap with the secretary's turn (line 6). Note how her reference to the relatives' concern is accepted as a legitimate means of putting the client back on the agenda despite the fact that skipping over particular cases has already been suggested. Another point to note is that, in line with some of the observations made by Potter and Hepburn (2003: 211), the invocation of the relatives' concerns also functions as a prefacing move for an account that further outlines specific reasons, details and the background for the concern. The initial concern construction, in other words, functions as a pre-move for elaboration as the social worker goes on to unpack it with an extended narrative that consists of descriptions of the relatives' longer-term caring efforts, their tiredness and their wishes for a better caring arrangement. Within the narrative, concern is upgraded to 'extreme distress' (line 23), and, towards the end, the social worker invokes common understanding towards the wishes of the client and her relatives ('They of course wish that', line 30).

Much more detail could be teased out of this lengthy extract. We can say, however, that framing the information-presentation phase in terms of someone else's observations and psychological reactions, as opposed to one's own, is an efficient way of projecting direction for a decision. After all, third-party concern constructions, as they are used here, never directly index the speaker's own mental processes, but rather, describe someone else's stance and (understandable) reactions to the matter at hand. Despite the discursive distancing provided by the third-party concern construction, note that the social worker in extract 3 still does some further work to separate herself from the description. Summing up her case presentation on lines 38–40, she clearly positions herself as a passive receiver and deliverer of (lengthy) messages from concerned relatives: 'This type of message came from the relatives' (lines 38–9). After this the meeting moves on to make a final decision.

In sum, then, third-person concern constructions help give direction for the team's actions. They discursively furnish clients with characteristics that justify and call for specific types of professional intervention. Third-party concern constructions also build rhetorical distance between the speaker and the description being delivered. They foreground and report other professionals', relatives' or the clients' voices, display their emotional responses while backgrounding the speaker's own. Simultaneously the case presenter's stance towards the matter remains safely on neutral professional ground.

Departures from neutralism

As we have seen so far, suspending particularised personal knowledge and direct emotional framing in the interest of 'impartiality' predominate in these meetings data. On average, the professionals refrain from direct emotional framing, particularly from directly invoking their own personal feelings. Therefore instances where team members engage in extensive use of emotion categories make interesting deviant cases. In the remaining part of this chapter, I wish to discuss a sequence where one member of the team, a home helper, departs from the neutralistic stance, engages in emotionally framed description and displays a partisan stance towards one of her clients. In the analysis of the remaining data extracts, I continue first to lay out the action-oriented use and the rhetorical design of emotion categories and descriptions. Second, I discuss specific turns that mark emotional framing and argumentation as a breach of acceptable professional practice.

The case in question concerns an elderly man who is actively involved in the daily care of his eighty-year-old brother. In addition, he is also partly responsible for another brother of his who is in long-term institutional care. The carer is eligible to a home care allowance and has received a modest monthly sum that the home helper now suggests should be raised. In what follows, I introduce two short sequences of what is a much longer exchange. Extract 4 begins forty minutes into the meeting and starts at the beginning of the home helper's case description.

Extract 4: Meeting 4. Informal home care allowance (0:40-)
Speakers: HH = home helper, S = secretary
Pseudonyms: Fairfield = a hospital

```
       1 HH:     <Then there's> er
       2          ((last name + first name))
       3          I went there <yesterday> and-a
       4          (3.5)
       5 HH:     hh and here the carer is the brother
       6          ((last name + first name))
       7          (1.8)
  →    8 HH:     It was such a (1.8) an extremely
       9          good feeling to make the (0.2)
      10          home visit just because
      11          how this ((carer)) has
  →   12          taken it to his h- (.) heart to care
      13          for these brothers (0.2)
      14          He's had fseveral brothers
      15          in his caref and now one of them
      16          has got a place in Fairfield
      17          (0.2)
      18 S:      Yes
      19 HH:     a permanent [placement and
      20 S:                  [he has
      21          (1.0)
  →   22 HH:     And (0.8) it's (.) with such joy and
      23          with a sincere heart he does this
```

The home helper starts her description in a routine way by identifying both the carer and the cared for, and by stating that a home visit has been made the day before. After this, however, she departs from the routine, and makes reference to her own feelings with regard to the case in question ('It was such a (1.8) an extremely good feeling to make the (0.2) home visit', lines 8–10). This type of opening already projects a particular type of report based on her eyewitness evidence. Her emotional framing embeds the case as something to be heard as a positive, perhaps exceptional narrative about 'our' work in this field.

Note how, as the description unfolds further, characterisations of the carer's altruistic actions are brought in to explain the home helper's emotional reaction. Formulations like 'taking something to one's heart' and 'doing something with joy and a sincere heart' project long-term dispositional characteristics and attributes to the carer. These are not transitory characteristics: the brother is not likely to 'have a change of heart' in the near future. Instead, the longer-term commitment between the brothers is made clear as the home helper makes reference to the fact that the carer has in fact earlier taken care of both of his brothers, but that one of them is now living in an institution. The descriptions and categories used, alongside the prosodic marking that the transcript is not sophisticated enough to do justice to, set the carer up dispositionally and turn him into a social type with specific longer-term attributes (Edwards, 1997; for more elaborate transcription of emotion in situated activity see Selting, 1994; Freese and Maynard, 1998; and Goodwin and Goodwin, 2000).

The home helper's description trades in moral-evaluative discourse that unfolds through the ascription of attributes, actions and emotions related to them. Later on in the discussion, the team moves to discuss the future sum of financial support to the brothers. A home helper in charge moves the discussion toward formal decision making by asking the team and the home helper for final views on the matter.

Extract 5: Meeting 4. Informal home care allowance (45.00–46.09)
Speakers: HHC = Home helper in charge, HH = home-helper, S = secretary
Pseudonyms: Fairfield = Hospital

```
1 HHC:    So what are we going to thin- (0.2)
2         decide what do you all think
3         (.)
4 HHC:    Or what do you yourself (0.5)
5         think about this ((addressing the
6         HH who is the case presenter))
7 HH:     Then this ((carer)) also: mm told
```

```
  8                me to inform the meetings
  9                that he also .hh (.) still does (.)
 10                like thi:s brotherhood and
 11                brotherly love so (.)
 12                in a way er (.) like that
 13                (.) now that (.) the othe- this oth-
 14                brother who's there in Fairfield
 15 S:             Mm
 16                (0.8)
 17 HH:            Then every other weekend cause
 18                he misses home so much
→ 19 HHC:          But the mea[ning is to
 20 HH:                       [And he then
 21                every other weekend
 22                (.) brings him home and-a then he
 23                takes care of them both he he
 24                ((general laughter, talk,
 25                and nodding))
→ 26 S:            Lovely
 27 HH:            £hehe so I mean brotherly love like
 28                that I haven't come across£ for a
 29                few years now (.) not like what you
 30                can now see in that house
 31                ((A few lines omitted. Talk about
 32                the carer getting tired))
 33 HH:            They've received the lowest rate
 34                before (0.2) but then this
 35                ((carer)) just said that
 36                couldn't it be .hh raised
 37                like to a thousand and six hundred
 38                marks and I said that I can always
 39                take the message but like I cannot
 40                ((talk cut off))
```

Instead of offering a view on a decision, the home helper pursues her earlier narrative about the brothers. Quoting the carer's wishes, she uses emotion categories like brotherly love and thus discursively works towards and justifies her suggestion on a higher benefit. Note that on line 19, one of the team members tries to come in by reminding the home helper about the task at hand ('But the meaning is to'). This turn clearly marks the home helper's line of argument and narrative as unsuitable or uncalled for in this context. It indicates that an answer is sequentially preferred. The interruption is unsuccessful, however, as the home helper, partly in overlap, pursues her story.

Line 23 marks the climax or coda (Labov, 1972) to the story being told: every other weekend the devoted carer takes his other brother out of the nursing home and takes care of not one, but both of his brothers. The prosodic marking, the emphatic speech style and the laughter signal this as the climax in ways that also call for alignment from the listeners (cf. Selting, 1994). The team members respond and align expectedly by general laughter, nodding, and by explicitly evaluating the story ('Lovely', line 26). After this the home helper sums up her story and further justifies its 'tellability' by its exceptional nature (lines 27–30).

A final point to note on the extract is that having pursued the story and after adopting a partisan and personal stance towards it, the home helper again discursively distances herself from it and denies any ownership over specific demands on the case. Moving to suggest a decision, she instead underlines her own neutrality by using active voicing and by quoting an earlier exchange between herself and the client. With this she minimises her own agency and returns to a position of an even-handed informant of objective facts and messages from the client to the team (*'I can always take the message but like I cannot'*, lines 38–9).

In sum, the extracts on the three brothers' story bring forth interesting points about emotion discourse. First, the analysis underlines that the deployment of emotion discourse inside narrative and rhetoric is one of its key features. Second, we can see that the telling of an emotionally framed story and the emotion terms in it are not one-off descriptions, but rather parts in a chain of an interrelated set of categories and descriptions that together perform interactionally significant rhetorical work. They set up people and their mutual relationships in dispositionally specific ways, turning the carer into a sympathy-worthy and action-worthy client type. Emotionally framed descriptions and typifications are mutually constitutive and they are used to identify, elaborate and make sense of each other. Third, the analysis shows that emotional framing, the use of emotion terms in meetings talk, can interactionally become marked as a deviation from common or sound professional practice.

Psychology, emotion categories and institutions

The discussion in this chapter has made an attempt at bridging cognition and interaction as well as psychology and institutional action by foregrounding the analysis of emotion rhetoric in particular settings. All institutions that deal with assessments, grading and evaluation, or with facts, evidence and practical decisions, are out of necessity preoccupied by notions of neutrality. In such settings, different information and knowledge come into play, as facts are negotiated, assessed and weighed. Among these factors is also the professionals' emotional stance toward clients or the issues in question.

Numerous empirical studies on educational assessments (e.g., Leiter, 1976; Holstein, 1983; Verkuyten, 2000) and on court or litigation interaction (e.g., Sudnow, 1965; Greatbatch and Dingwall, 1999), among others, have documented decision makers' use of background knowledge and analysed the specifics of neutralistic descriptions in interaction. Discursive analysis on emotions in interaction like the one provided in this chapter can contribute to these existing analyses in substantial ways. Since reference to emotion is not restricted to meeting settings, the observations made in this chapter have implications that extend to other realms of decision making and other interactional arenas.

From the analysis above, it seems that ideal psychological models of rational practice or decision making fall short of capturing the complexity of situated discursive action. It is my contention that discursive analysis into emotions in interaction can render visible certain taken-for-granted ideals for decision making and teamwork. Research that focuses on institutional action and emotions can help create a better understanding of the situational uses of emotion discourse as part of institutional description, narratives and interaction. As a result, emotion categories are cast as part and parcel of the rhetorical and practical resources for various professions.

The analysis of emotion categories as part of real-world interactional settings can also produce practical applications. In many institutions, professionals are still encouraged to disregard any background information that may affect their conduct or decisions. It seems, however, that the relationship between emotions and institutions is far more complex, and that emotion discourse and the construction and use of background psychological knowledge are an inescapable ingredient in all assessment and decision making.

APPENDIX

Original transcripts in Finnish.

Extract 1

```
1 HH:      Työryhmässä on samanlaisia
2          ihmisiä että (.) .hh me:
3          ollaan niinku
4          samassa asemassa että tää huoli
5          on meillä kaikilla
6 S:       Aivan nii ju[st]
7 D:                   [mm]
8 HH:                  [El ]ikkä siis
```

```
9              se rahan jaka[ja pi]täs olla
10 S:                     [joo ]
11 HH:         semmone joka kattoo vaan
12             papereita .hh eikä
13             tu minkäännäkösiä
14             sellassia tunteita (0.5)
15             hh huolitun-
16             Mehän täällä [my]öskin
17 D:                      [mm]
18 HH:         jae[taan se huolitunnetta ]
19 S:             [Nii se on esittelijä sitte
20             ku[ka ] taas että ku esitellään asiat
21 HH:           [niih]
22 S:          lailla pai[note]taan eri asi[oita ja   ]
23 D:                    [mm ]
24 HH:                                     [Joo kyllä]
25 S:          Tuodaan (.) näkemyksiä esiin että
26             siinä se tulee mutta .hh
27             kukapas asiakkaan parhaiten
28             tuntee kun te
29 D:          mm
30 HH:         mm[m]
31 S:            [T]eillähän pitäs
32             ammattitaitosia olla [totta kai että
33 HH:                              [hh. Me
34             ollaanki siihen asti ku paperit on
35             kunnossa
```

Extract 2

```
1 HSW:         Okei ensimmäisenä
2              ((sukunimi + etunimi))
3              (0.8) sivulla mikä kolme
4              (3.8) ((monisteiden selailua))
5 HSW:         Tämmöne:n (0.8) eh neiti-ihminen
6              joka on meille tullu
7              Teukkaan (1.2) heinäkuussa ja:
8              (0.8) hyvin muistamaton oli:
9              neurologin vastaanotolla käyny
10             (1.2) öh tota: hetkinen
11             oliks hän >ny sitte<
12             Mikonmaan erikoispolilla
13             vai missä ja tota sieltä tuli
14             ensimmäinen tää
15             neurologin puhelu (1.2)
16             hän oli hyvin huolissaan tästä
17             (0.8) muistamattomasta ihmisestä
18             ja hän tuli sitten (1.2) jhossakin
```

```
19          vhaihessah meille tota: hhh
20          h-hoitoo niin kymmenes seittemättä
21          juuri hän tätä a-aiemmin
22          oli ensin käyny tota: (.) tällä
23          neurologilla ja (0.8) iha:n
24          muistamaton i:hminen yksin asunu
25          ((jatkaa tapauskuvausta))
```

Extract 3

```
1 S:        Onks Petellä joku kanta
2           siihen et hypätääks me
3           nää Mikonmaan olijat nyt
4           täs kohden (0.2) yli
5           [täältä ((kysyy lääkäriltä))
6 HSW:      [Mut (.) mä (.) viel (.) tän
7           (.) lisäisin täst et omaiset
8           on ottanu meihin yhteyttä
9           ja ne on todella huolissaan
10          (0.5)
11 HSW:     tästä
12          (0.2)
13 HSW:     tästä et omaiset on aivan
14          lopussa et he ei jaksais tässä
15          enään olla kanssa (0.2)
16          kanssa mukana ku he koki et
17          et sillo ku ((asiakas)) oli .hhh
18          lokakuussa kotona ja vaikka
19          siellä oli nää avut ja omaiset
20          kävi ni se kotona (0.2)
21          kotona olo oli niin turvatonta
22          et tässä he koki sen (0.7)
23          >kauheen< ahdistavana myös
24          (0.8) hekin koki täMÄ (0.2)
25          asukas itse (0.5) tai potilas
26          itse (0.2) myös sen
27          turvattomaks mut niin
28          omaisetkin °että°
29          (2.0)
30 HSW:     Tietysti toivovat et
31          tämän ihmisen ei enää
32          kerta hän on Mikonmaalla
33          näin pitkään siellä ollu ihan (0.2)
34          niin kun .h hoidettu ja passattu
35          että sitä häntä ei niin kun yksin
36          (.) sit enää kotiin laitettais
37          (.)
```

```
38 HSW:     Että tämmönen viesti tuli
39          °omaisilta°
40          pitkä puhelu että
41          (1.8)
42 N:       Se kotihoito ei (0.5) ei
43          varmaankaan hänen
44          kohdallaan enää onnistu et
```

Extract 4

```
 1 HH:      <Sitten on> tuota
 2          ((sukunimi + etunimi))
 3          kävin siellä ja <eilen> ja-a
 4          (3.5)
 5 HH:      hh ja tässä sitte hoitajana on veli
 6          ((sukunimi + etunimi))
 7          (1.8)
 8 HH:      Oli niin kun (1.8) tavattoman
 9          hyvä tunne olla siellä (0.2)
10          kotikäynnillä sen takia että miten
11          (.) s- (.) syämmen asiakseen
12          tää ((hoitaja)) on ottanu näitten
13          veljesten hoitamisen (0.2)
14          Hänel on ollu fuseampi näitä
15          veljiä hoidossaf ja nyt on
16          yks sitte Teukkaan
17          (0.2)
18 S:       Joo
19 HH:      h [vakipaikalle ja
20 S:          [on
21          (1.0)
22 HH:      Ja (0.8) niin (.) riemurinnoin ja
23          sydämestään hän sen tekee
```

Extract 5

```
 1 HHC:     Mitäs me tässä nytten mie- (0.2)
 2          päätetään mitä te ootte miettiny
 3          (.)
 4 HHC:     Tai miten sulla tuli itellä (0.5)
 5          ajatus ((puhuttelee tapauksen
 6          esitellyttä ammattilaista))
 7 HH:      Sit tää ((hoitaja)) vielä: mm käski
 8          sanoa tiedoks kokouksille että
 9          hän vielä .hh (.) vielä sitten (.)
10          niin tätä: veljeyttä ja
11          ja veljesrakkautta niin (.)
12          sillä tavalla tota niin (.) tekee että
```

```
13          (.) nyt ku tää toi- tää
14          veli joka on siel Teukassa
15 S:       mm
16          (0.8)
17 HH:      Niin joka toinen viikonloppu ku
18          se ikävöi niin kovasti
19 HHC:     Mut tar[kotus on
20 HH:             [Ja se joka
21          toinen viikonloppu
22          (.) ottaa sen vielä kotiin ja sit se
23          hoitaa ne molemmat he he
24          ((yleistä naurua, puhetta
25          ja nyökyttelyä))
26 S:       Ihanaa
27 HH:      £ehheh et sellasta veljesrakkautta
28          minä en oo nähny£ ihan
29          muutamaan vuoteen (.) mitä
30          nyt näkyy siellä talossa
31          ((Muutama rivi poistettu. Puhetta
32          hoitajan väsymisestä))
33 HH:      Aiemmin he ovat saaneet tätä
34          alinta (0.2) mutta sitten tämä
35          ((hoitaja)) vaan sano että
36          eikö sitä vois sitten .hh nostaa
37          vaikka tuhanteen kuuteensataan
38          markkaan ni mää sanon et voihan
39          mä viiä terveisiä mut mä en voi
40          ((puhe jää kesken))
```

NOTES

1. Transcripts in original Finnish are in the appendix.
2. I discuss issues concerning the translation of data extracts, and the transcription layout in Nikander, 2001, Appendix 1. Transcription notations are on pages 292–3.

4 Negotiating consciousness: parapsychology and the social organisation of reports of mental states

Simon Allistone and Robin Wooffitt

Introduction

Parapsychology is concerned with a class of subjective psychological experiences which seem to suggest that humans have anomalous communicative abilities: the facility to interact with other humans or the environment without the use of the normal five senses. Experiences such as telepathy (mind-to-mind communication) and psychokinesis (mind-to-matter interaction) are said to be anomalous because there appears to be no biological or physical mechanisms by which to account for these ostensibly paranormal phenomena. (Introductions to and overviews of parapsychology can be found in Edge et al., 1986; Irwin, 1999; and Radin, 1997.)

In the parapsychological literature, the term 'psi' is used to refer to the as yet little understood processes which, it is proposed, underpin the variety of extra-sensory phenomena. Psi is assumed to be a function of the brain. Consequently, parapsychologists are extremely interested in a range of cognitive and mental phenomena which may be related in some way to the operation of psi, such as volition, intuition, states of consciousness, dream states, imagery, and so on. It is felt that if psi does exist, then its effects may be detected in or influenced by precisely these kinds of psychological entities or processes. Examination of, say, the relationship between consciousness and extra-sensory phenomena may reveal more about psi and how it works.

For example, there is evidence to suggest that psi is more likely to occur when people are in some form of relaxed or altered state of consciousness. There is anecdotal and experimental evidence that people are more likely to experience psychic phenomena when asleep, or in some form of meditative state.

The ganzfeld experimental procedure was developed to try to provide a more formal test of the relationship between psi phenomena and altered states of consciousness. It is based on the idea that, when it occurs, psi is a very weak signal, and that our brains can only detect it when normal brain activity is reduced, much in the same way that we can only detect the gentle sound of a tap dripping in a distant bathroom when the house is silent.

The ganzfeld is basically an ESP experiment. Typically, there are three participants: an experimenter, an experimental participant (a volunteer member of the public) and a sender, sometimes a friend or relative of the participant, sometimes another experimenter. The participant is seated by themselves in a comfortable chair in a quiet room. Their eyes are masked so that light is diffused evenly over the retinal field. They wear headphones. Prior to the start of the experiment, they are played a relaxation tape, and when that is complete, they hear only white noise. At this point, the participant is in a highly relaxed state and is experiencing a mild form of sensory deprivation, circumstances which are intended to replicate the altered states of consciousness which, anecdotally, often accompany spontaneous psi experiences.

In another room the sender sits in front of a video monitor. At the point at which the participant's relaxation tape is coming to an end, the sender is shown a video clip, which has been chosen randomly by a specially designed computer system from a database of similar length clips. (To minimise the chance of experimenter manipulation or sloppy experimental practice, it is routine for the entire procedure to be controlled by computer software; this means that the experimenter is unaware of the clip shown to the sender. It is also for this reason that the procedure is referred to as the *auto*ganzfeld.) The clip is repeated a number of times during a half-hour period. During this time the sender is asked mentally to project images from the clip to the participant. This is called the sending period. During the sending period, the participant is asked to report verbally whatever images come into their mind. This is called their mentation. The mentation is audio recorded at the time. The experimenter can overhear the mentation via headphones and makes a written record of the images, impressions and sensations reported by the participant. At this stage, however, there is no communication between the participant and experimenter.

At the end of the sending period, the experimenter initiates contact with the participant via the headphones, and then begins the mentation review, in which the experimenter goes over the images and sensations reported by the participant to remind them of what they reported, and to encourage further recollections or expansion on particular images prior to the judging phase. The final stage of the experiment is the judging phase. After the mentation review, the participant is shown the target clip which was the focus of the sender's attention and three decoy clips randomly selected by computer. On the basis of their imagery during the sending period, the participant has to guess which of the four clips was the target.

By chance, then, participants will guess right once every four trials. However, numerous ganzfeld trials have reported a statistically significant above-chance hit rate, usually around one in three (for example, Bem and Honorton, 1994; Bierman, 1995; Broughton and Alexander, 1995; da Silva et al., 2003; Honorton, 1985; Morris et al., 1995; Parker et al., 1998) or even higher (for example, Schlitz and Honorton, 1992). Because similar above-chance results have been reported by different investigators working in laboratories across the world, some have argued that the autoganzfeld methodology offers a replicable demonstration of psi phenomena (Radin, 1997; see also Utts, 1995). For this reason, the autoganzfeld methodology has attained a significant and controversial status in parapsychology within the past twenty years (Bem et al., 2001; Milton, 1999; Milton and Wiseman, 1997; Schmiedler and Edge, 1999; Storm, 2000; and Storm and Ertel, 2002).

Parapsychologists are interested to explore the everyday and uncontroversial psychological processes which occur during the autoganzfeld procedure, for this reason: if psi is operating during the experiments, then, according to the logic of the experimental procedure, it is at least possible – if not likely – that psi is occurring during the mentation, when the sender is trying to project mentally images from the target video clip and the sender is reporting their experience of their own consciousness. For parapsychologists, then, the participants' report of their imagery during the sending period could offer valuable clues about the way psi works and interacts with established cognitive processes and states of consciousness.

The mentation review, then, is an important part of the experimental procedure, as it provides an opportunity for participants to expand upon their imagery, for example, by describing their imagery and impressions in more detail, or to mention imagery which was unreported during the mentation, or to correct an error in the experimenter's written record. In this sense, parapsychologists are primarily interested in the outcome of the mentation review: further reports of the experience of consciousness during the sending period of the experiment.

But this is the point at which the mentation review also becomes interesting for discursive psychologists who draw from conversation analytic research techniques, and other researchers interested in the relationship between mind and interaction. Whatever further information is elicited in the review does not simply materialise in a social vacuum, unmediated by verbal interaction, available for analytic scrutiny by parapsychologists. It is generated out of a variety of everyday communicative practices – describing, turn taking, the production of questions and answers, the management of repair and clarification – all of which will be mobilised with respect to the requirements of experimental contingencies and expectations associated with the autoganzfeld procedure in particular, and (para-)psychology laboratory experiments in general.

This may be significant. Studies of talk in workplace or institutional settings suggest that the way in which turn-taking procedures (and other routine communicative competencies) are adapted to allow speakers to perform organisationally or institutionally relevant tasks can impinge upon the shape of utterances which are subsequently produced. This is particularly clear on occasions in which the participants engage in a fairly limited range of interactional activities, such as those associated with formal and semi-formal interviews (Suchman and Jordan, 1990; Widdicombe and Wooffitt, 1995; Wooffitt and Widdicombe, 2006). These and other studies have shown that the respondents' utterances are shaped by, and oriented to, the interactional context in and for which they are produced.

The implications for parapsychologists is clear: what is said during the mentation review may be significantly related to its interactional and organisational properties.

In this chapter we report some preliminary observations from a study of experimenter–participant interaction during the mentation review phase of a series of autoganzfeld experiments conducted at the Koestler Parapsychology Unit at the University of Edinburgh during the 1990s. Our analysis here focuses on some of the broader normative orientations which demonstrably inform the conduct of the participants, and we show how these normative expectations underpin the experimenters' and participants' activities. In the final section of the chapter we examine some of the sociological and parapsychological implications of minor departures from the routine procedure of the mentation review.

Orientation to procedure: accomplishing the work of the experiment

To recap: the mentation review is based on the participant's verbal report of events in their consciousness during the period the target materials were being screened. During the review the experimenter goes over the images and sensations reported by the participant to remind them of key moments, or to encourage further recollections or expansion on particular images or sensations. The following extract illustrates some recurrent features of mentation review interaction.

Extract 1: 01–47 E1/F

'E' is experimenter, 'P' is the experimental participant. The fragment code indicates which experimental trial the fragment is taken from, which of the three participating parapsychologists acted as experimenter in this particular trial, and the gender of the participant.)

```
 1 E:   h next you saw a ha:mmer (0.6) and then a bright (.)
 2      white light. hh some words or letters (0.2) see? (0.2) oh:,
 3      h couldn't make out what the rest of it was (1) hh next you saw a roll
 4      of (.) cut-out gorillas, (.) hh and they were black and they were all
 5      standing in a row
 6 P:   uh hn
 7 E:   and they were all the sa:me (0.8) hh next you had the impression of a
 8      glow: lamp hh (0.2) and then a paper train and it was an old-fashioned
 9      kind of train, hh (yeah) 'n it was er running along with its carriages, h
10 P:   [uhhn ]
11 E:   [a:::: ]nd they were eh red with the black roofs on top. (0.8)
12      hhh next a spiral shape (0.5) and the pipes h (1.4) pipes in the mist of
13      a mountain.
14 P:   (k)hhu hhuh huh=
15 E:   =hhh [ha::nd
16 P:        [hh (.) yeah
17      (0.6)
18 E:   ((continues))
```

In extract 1 the experimenter introduces a range of items (the participant's report of a sensation or an image): a hammer, a bright light, some words or letters, cut-out gorillas, a glow lamp, a paper train with red and black carriages, a spiral shape, and pipes in mountain mist.

There are various ways by which experimenters can introduce an item during the review. The main components seem to be the report of the item, the modality of perception/knowing ('saw', 'sensed', 'heard') and a temporal marker which connects that item to the flow of the original mentation ('next', 'and then'). These can be combined in various ways. For example, from extract 1:

```
[item]
    'some words or letters (0.2) see? (0.2) oh:,'
['next'] + [item]
    'next a spiral shape'
['and then'] + [item]
    'and then a bright (.) white light'
    'and then a paper train'
```

```
['next'] + ['you saw'] + [item]
    'next you saw a ha:mmer'
    'next you saw a roll of (.) cut-out gorillas,'

['next'] + ['impression'] + [item]
    'next you had the impression of a glow:lamp'
```

There is one other item preface not illustrated here: variations on ['you said'] + [item]. For example:

Extract 2: 01–18 E1/M:4

```
E:  oka:y, hhh (.) and then you said a song ca:lled (0.4) pink pig slats?
P:  °ah(hh)° pink pig (flats,) °yeah°=
E:  =>okay,<
    (1.5)
E:  a:nd °uhm:,° (0.2) you had a- a feeling of a feeling of things pa:ssing
    ((continues))
```

Experimenters adopt a stepwise progression through the mentation images. After each item of imagery is introduced there is a 'slot' in the interaction in which the participant may provide further information. This orientation to the purpose of the review, and the kind of participant activity which could occur in this sequential location, is manifest in the way in which the experimenter will momentarily withhold moving directly to the next item. So in extract 1, there is a 0.6-second gap between the items 'a hammer' and 'a bright white light' (lines 1 to 2), a similar-length gap between 'spiral' and the first mention of the pipes (line 12) and a one-second gap between 'words and indistinct letters' and 'cut-out gorillas' (lines 2 to 4).

Some participants expand upon every item. These 'high recipiency' participants, though, are rare, and although most participants do at some point offer new information about an item, it is routine for participants to 'pass' on the opportunity to provide further information in these sequential locations. There are various ways in which this 'passing' may be managed. Participants can remain silent after the item has been introduced (in extract 1, for example, in lines 1, 3, 7, 11); alternatively, they can use minimal response and acknowledgement tokens such as 'mm', 'un hn' and 'yeah' (for example, in lines 6, 10 and 16).

It is here that we detect the first evidence of the participants' orientation to a normative framework which underpins the verbal activities which constitute the review. Irrespective of the actual level of recipiency displayed by the participant, the experimenter's activities are designed to maintain the forward interactional movement of the mentation review. So, the experimenters avoided the negative ramifications of what in ordinary conversation could be deemed as potentially disruptive, that is, a total lack of recipiency from a co-interactant regarding the relevance of what the current speaker is saying. The mechanism by which this negation of potential difficulty, as well as the forward interactional movement of the mentation review overall, is affected, can be found in a tacit assumption sometimes evident in non-institutional talk, namely that in specific instances the silence of a co-interactant is equivalent to agreement with whatever the current speaker has said.

As well as constituting the basis by which a specific interactional difficulty (lack of co-interactant recipiency) is overcome, the stepwise transition between review items also throws into relief other aspects in the experimenter's talk that highlight their orientation towards the institutional task of carrying out the ganzfeld procedure. We can begin to illustrate these issues by reflecting on 'you said' prefaces and their occurrence as forms of trouble identification and repair initiation.

For example in lines 6–7 of extract 3 the experimenter states 'I'm not sure what you said next I think it was hole', forecasting a level of uncertainty as to the veracity of the candidate hearing of the item.

Extract 3: 01–09: E3/M

Double degree signs are used to indicate talk or sounds that are extremely quiet.

```
 1 E:   O:ka:y (0.6) hh first one wuz: uh::, (.) h uh sense of heat or
 2      melting, (1.4) .thh then::: deep and distant
 3      (1.0)
 4 P:   °°mhm°°
 5 E:   (.tk) uniform:, (1.3) hh dark shadow:: (1.8) waves: (1.3)
 6      deep dark tunnel (1.7) spots of light (1.3) °°hhh°° uh::, and then I'm
 7      not sure what you said next- >I think it was< ho::le
 8      (0.6)
 9 P:   mm(.) °I think so°
10 E:   °o::kay° (.) hhh then ever (.) ever decreasing circles:?
11 P:   mm,
12      (0.6)
13 E:   °o::kay:,° (0.7) (tk)hh uh: space:: (1.0) °h°stroking, (0.5) so:ft
14 P:   (°°mhm [m°°)
15 E:        [°m-m-° bubble (.) cloud, (1.7) diffus:e (0.5) hhh and then:,
16      shadows in::::- I'm not sure what you said °is° i°°thi-°° >it sounded a
17      bit like<shadows in a: >in a< clipped; (.) sce:ne:
18 P:   °mm,° (0.5) eclipse I think?
19 E:   oh an eclipse: (.) o:kay, (2.6) h aw:ri:ght, (0.6) uh::, slow:: (1.0) h
20      penetrate (1.3) constant (1.3) h bubbling, =swirling, =growing, (2.0)
21      flames (1.1) h rapid movement =reaching =upwards, (1.7) lava, (1.5)
22      engulfing (1.8) h undulating (1.6) h whirlwind, (.) rapidly moving
23      way:, (.) further and further (1.0) h blue, (1.2) h absorption (1.3)
24      sinking (.) or floating,
25      (1.2) ((sound of pages being turned?))
26 E:   h pa:tterns (0.5) °m°cycles (.) °or° circles. (0.8) hhh(a) (1.1)
27      RA:Ndom (1.3) e::ven (2.1) h meandering (1.5) S: pee:d (0.9) °h°
```

```
28    swirling, = shaking, = moving, = round and round. (.) spin (1.0) h
29    change of direction (1.1) a::nd then that was °so::: when I came in,
30    was there any̲thing else? uh
```

Similar work is done at lines 16–17, with the experimenter actually abandoning an item ('and then shadows in') to provide several doubt implicative elements of talk. These include lexical indicators pertinent to both the experimenter's own difficulty with recording the item ('I'm not sure what you said') and the candidate hearing of the item ('it sounded a bit like shadows...'), as well as marked perturbations evident throughout the delivery of the item. In both instances, the experimenter implies activities specific to him as an experimenter, both during the prior viewing period and with regard to the mentation review. It can be seen how 'what you said' is positioned in contrast to what the experimenter has potentially heard the participant say. The doubt implicative elements not only imply that the experimenter-as-the-overhearing-audience has been making a record of the prior talk, but also that some level of inconsistency might exist in this record.

That the participant's ownership of what was said in the viewing period is important during the mentation review is built into the fabric of the review: at the outset the experimenters explicitly state that it affords the opportunity for participants to correct (if necessary) the experimenter's record of the mentation. The question of the participant's ownership of what has been said during the viewing period is reinforced by the implication that he or she can potentially act as the canonical authority should the experimenter's account differ in any way from their own recollection of the viewing period. In this way, it can be seen how the experimenter's orientation to procedure regarding the overall management of the mentation review is not only reflected in how they deal with those mentation review items that are flagged as being potentially problematic, it also begins to shape the participant's role within the whole procedure, irrespective of whether they respond or not.

A further aspect of the overall orientation towards procedure can be seen if we examine how the experimenter deals with those items that have been oriented to as being potentially problematic, subsequent to any response by the participant. If we deal with the sequence across lines 16–19 of extract 3 first, it can be seen that in response to the candidate item 'shadows in a clipped scene', the participant offers a clarification of what was said, correcting 'clipped scene' with 'eclipse' (line 18). Having received this clarification, the experimenter produces what Heritage (1984) has identified as a change of state token, 'oh' (line 19), before repeating the newly clarified term 'eclipse'. The experimenter has thereby displayed both that he has heard the participant's clarification as being different from his own candidate version, and that he accepts the veracity of the subsequent correction. Added to this, the experimenter then moves on to the next review item, despite the fact that this clarification has been potentially mitigated by the participant's own doubt implicative talk, 'eclipse I think'.

We take it here that the trouble in need of participant repair was the exact wording of the utterance initially heard as 'clipped scene'. After the participant responds to the experimenter's doubt implicative talk, the experimenter moves on to the next item, indicating that the potentially problematic issue has been satisfactorily addressed and resolved. There is no further discussion of this item, despite the participant's own doubt implicative formulation. This in turn suggests that the experimenter is orienting to the wider requirements of the ganzfeld procedure, ensuring that the mentation review maintains its forward movement.

A similar situation can be seen in the sequence across lines 6–10 in extract 3. Here, the experimenter offers a candidate version of an item, 'hole'. The participant's 'mm (.) °I think so°' is treated as a minimal confirmation by the experimenter's 'okay'. Moreover, the experimenter does not unpack the hearably mitigating 'I think so', but moves on to the next mentation review item. Rather than exploring in a little more detail whether or not 'hole' was in fact what the participant thought he had said, the experimenter displays an orientation to procedure by continuing on with the mentation review.

This robust forward movement in the face of a mitigated participant response is also evident during the mentation reviews of other experimenters, thereby highlighting the general applicability of what we have designated as an orientation to procedure. In the next extract, it can be seen how the experimenter maintains the interactional movement of the mentation review with a participant who displays minimal recipiency.

Extract 4: 01–41: E1/F

```
 1 E:    h now you see::: (.) a heavy:: outline for:: (.) a second (3.1) h and
 2       then all you see: are BUTtons on a shirt >and< buttons are going
 3       do:wn. (1.1) h >the im-< the image of an (.) lid of a ja:r: and you
 4       could see the rim of the jar (2.3) °hh° again (.) those faces scattered
 5       all over your vision your fa- >those faces< h (0.5) and see that the
 6       bottom of your vision (.) a chee:se (.) a shape like the underside
 7       of an octopus with suction cups
 8 (P:)  (°hh°)
 9 E:    h (.) a dro:p again sli:ding down. (1.1) and again the fa:ces sliding:,
10       (1.9) sliding across your vision (0.7) and a gi:rls face: (.) grinning
11       e:villy (0.7) h a big pumpkin shape (1.5) 11 eyelashes (.) h you would
12       see: the eyelashes first and then you would see the eye opening and
```

```
13        closing and looking round, (.) h it seemed to be a good looking eyes
14        (.) >goo lu-< a pair of good looking eyes and a perfect face(.) hh and
15        now you can see a cigarette or a stick coming out the face (1.5) h I
16        couldn't understand this (.) h dancing (.) and then something
17        coming out of a beards: (.) >u- out of< man's fa:ce (.) a bea:rd coming
18        out of a man's face?
19 P:     °uh: don't think so: (.) don't know°
20 E:     °>okay<° (.) h da:ncing on something coming >of a<out of a man's
21        face, maybe it was the stick again. (1.6) h °°kay°° PIano ke:ys in a
22        circular fo:rma:tion (0.8) all bunched up in the >middle<(.) °hh° a
23        bi:g me:dal (.) va very natural (.) >kind of< imagery (0.6)h the
24        outline of a ba:t
          ((continues))
```

Across lines 1–15 there is no participant recipiency at all, despite the stepwise format of the experimenter's talk. At lines 15–16, the experimenter then introduces an item that elicits a slightly expanded response. This response, however, displays an even higher level of mitigation than those seen in extract 3, since the participant downgrades an already ambivalent statement of 'don't think so' with an overt claim to a lack of knowledge, 'don't know' (line 19). Despite this, the experimenter chooses not to pursue a more definitive response.

In the Edinburgh ganzfeld trials, three parapsychologists took the role of the experimenter, and there is evidence that each attended to the normative expectations attendant upon the experimental procedure. Extract 4 suggests, however, that there are some variations in approach.

Despite the fact that in this instance the participant declines to expand upon the review items, the way in which the experimenter moves on is very similar to how the experimenter in extract 3 moved at line 19, when the participant had provided some form of upgrade. Once again the experimenter receipts the participant's response with 'okay', before producing a repetition of previous talk, although in this case it is a reformulation of the previous review item that the participant declined to expand upon, rather than a repetition of what she has said.

In doing so, the experimenter could perhaps be heard to place the participant's unwillingness or inability to expand within a context of acceptable actions appropriate to the mentation review. That is, the repetition and reformulation of the prior item appears to present 'dancing on something coming out of a man's face' (line 20) as a valid review item, despite both the disparity between the experimenter's candidate suggestion 'a beard coming out of a man's face' (lines 17 and 18) and the subsequent statement, and the necessarily vague nature of the term 'something'. But whatever interpretation of the experimenter's actions subsequent to the participant's declination to expand, extract 4 shows how differences in the actual conduct of each experimenter during the mentation review can be included within the overall orientation to procedure.

A similar orientation to procedure can be seen when there is greater participant participation in the review procedure, although once again it is evident that such an orientation does not preclude changes in approach by the different experimenters. Indeed, in the following extract, we can see variations in how both the experimenter and the participant approach a specific mentation review item. The experimenter delivers an item at lines 4–5, which, whilst referencing the temporal framework of the ganzfeld procedure overall ('and then there was', line 4), also displays a marked degree of perturbation that is tacitly indicative of some level of doubt regarding the item. In this instance, it seems the reason for the experimenter's displayed doubt regarding this item is the fact that in mentioning the nationality of the person seen during the viewing period, there is the possibility that some form of xenophobic or racist connotation could be inferred, rather than any problems regarding the item's veracity. There then follows an extended period of silence (line 6), following which the participant declines to expand on the item. Unlike the instance in extract 4, however, the participant does not simply claim a lack of knowledge regarding the item, but instead produces an overt display of disbelief in terms of the item being attributable to her ('YEAH?', line 7). For her part the experimenter, rather than following the relatively straightforward movement on to the next review item identified in previous extracts, actually begins to pursue an expanded response from the participant.

Extract 5: 01–52: E1/F

```
 1 E:   >there was< a gri:d (.) some sort of a gri:d
 2      (.)
 3 P:   uh huh
 4 E:   h and then there was: a, an- (0.7) a:r(u), (0.3) arabian? person
 5      laying on the grid.
 6      (1.2)
 7 P:   YEAH?
 8      (0.8)
 9 E:   >you said< ay:rab people.
10 P:   ah;. yeAH?
11 E:   °yeah.°
12 P:   °°aw:right,°° =°>(p)hh<°
13 E:   >hh< °huh° hh I'M NOTˆmaking it [up you reallyˆsaid] ˆit =
14 P:                                   [ uh huhuhu        ]
15 E:   =>(u)HH<
16      (0.2)
17 P:   a-Hehe [he:hahaha [heheheˆhe =
18 E:          [hhh       [hhh
19 E:   =and then you had another impression
20      of a black ho:rse? ((smiley voice))
```

Following the participant's initial response to the item, there is a brief pause at line 8 before the experimenter reformulates the item, specifically locating the nationality of the person described in the item as being the contentious term. There then follows a short sequence in which the participant's repeated display of doubt (line 10) is met by the experimenter's confirmatory '°yeah°' (line 11), which in turn elicits '°°aw: right°°' (line 12), a receipt token which exhibits the participant's willingness to accept the veracity of the item. Having established the participant's somewhat moderate agreement, the experimenter goes on at line 13 to indicate that she is in no doubt as to what P said during this particular section of the viewing period, stating 'I'm not making it up you really said it'.

Consequently, it can be seen that whilst some review items are connected to displays of doubt on the part of the experimenter that could tacitly be linked to some mistake in the written record or a mishearing of an original piece of mentation, experimenters treat others as being unquestionably correct. Equally, in terms of the experimenter's orientation to procedure, we can see that rather than pursuing the matter any further, the experimenter in this case aligns to the participant's laughter by introducing the next review item with a 'smiley voice' pronunciation (line 20). In this way, the impact of both differing degrees of doubt regarding review items and the variation in response from the participant in terms of their actually doubting the item are managed within the overall format of an orientation to procedure.

The subtle interplay between the orientation to procedure and a shift in approach dependent upon the type of mentation review items being delivered is also visible in the next extract (a section of which has already been reproduced as extract 2).

Extract 6: 01–18: E1/M

```
 1 E:   hhh okay when you erm: (.) started out you talked about the eh
 2      white noise making you thin(.)k of trains and pla:nes
 3 P:   [yeah ]
 4 E:   [hh   ]hh but you were seeing a book.
 5      (2.5)
 6 E:   h[hh
 7 P:    [yeah
 8 E:   and then you had an old lady who was passing with a walking stick,
 9      (.)
10 P:   y[eah
11 E:    [hh >y sa-< had an image of an indian dancer?
12      (0.8) ((P swallowing))
13 P:   yeah
14 E:   and then the old lady was walking towards you (0.5) hhand then I
15      believe you said you: heard a song called (.) tw: (.) ˆtwigs and seeds?
16 P:   yeah
```

```
17 E:   oka:y, hhh (.) and then you said a song ca:lled (0.4) pink pig slats?
18 P:   °ah(hh)° pink pig (flats,) °yeah°=
19 E:   =>okay,<
20      (1.5)
21 E:   a:nd °uhm:,° (0.2) you had a- a feeling of things
22      pa:ssing
        ((continues))
```

The participant initially provides agreement tokens for each item that the experimenter delivers (lines 1–13). Two items are then introduced using the 'you said' preface (lines14–15, and line 17).

The format of these prefaces includes those elements outlined above. The experimenter says 'I believe you said' (lines 14–15), thereby acknowledging the conditional status of his record. He also invokes a temporal framework that directly links the current talk to the order of the mentation ('and then', line 14), but also provides a candidate version of the item (line 15).

In this instance, an extra level of detail is included as part of the candidate version, in that the experimenter specifically identifies the item as a song, and the participant immediately agrees with these details. A similar procedure occurs during the next review item (line 17), although in this case the participant's recipiency at line 18 has an expanded format, since he also repeats the name of the song. In both cases, once recipiency has been gained, the experimenter provides her own receipt token, 'okay' (lines 17 and 19), and then moves on to the next item.

In both instances, the experimenter can be heard to match the participant's confirmation of the details of the preceding review item with a confirmation of her own. Given the doubt implicative elements associated with 'you said' prefaces, this can be heard as the experimenter indicating both that she has heard the participant's agreement and that it has done enough work to mitigate her prior displayed doubt regarding her own candidate version of the item. We could also link this matching of recipiency with further (second-speaker) recipiency to the nature of the review items being discussed, since it could be argued that the veracity of a specific song title (as opposed to a piece of music that 'sounded like' something) has a limited set of options regarding whether or not a candidate version is right or wrong. Although the fact that in both cases the participant has apparently confirmed the veracity of the experimenter's candidate versions does not necessarily close down further avenues for discussion regarding these items, we can see that the experimenter treats as adequate the 'answer' to the question raised by the doubt implicative elements of the 'you said' preface.

In considering the experimenter's treatment of the participant's responses as 'adequate' in terms of the information that is being sought for during the mentation review, we can also see in extract 6 a more implicit aspect of the orientation to procedure displayed by the experimenters. In both instances in which the experimenter raised the question as to the actual song title, the participants' subsequent confirmations are met by the response token 'okay' (lines 17 and 19). But it is interesting to note that there is a marked difference in the way in which the experimenter moves on to deliver the next item. For the review item reported as the song 'twigs and seeds' (line 15), the experimenter immediately produces the 'okay' response token (line 17), then moves on to the next item after an inbreath and a micropause. The rapid transition in the sequence (Candidate Item → Participant Confirmation → Experimenter Acceptance) is indicative of a preferred response, and as such appears to indicate that despite having raised a question regarding the veracity of the item, the participant's answer served to confirm what the experimenter believed the item to be. In contrast, for the review item relating to the song originally presented as 'pink pig slats' (line 17), whilst the experimenter produces a response token that latches to the participant's prior utterance, and thus can equally be heard as a preferred response, there is a pause of 1.5 seconds before the next item is delivered. Although it is difficult to say with any certainty, the fact that the subject's reiteration of the song title produces a 'doubtful' or ambiguous hearing of the word 'slats/flats' can arguably be said to indicate that the actual difficulties which resulted in the review item being introduced with a 'you said' preface remain to some extent unresolved. This being so, we can begin to see how elements of the written record upon which the experimenter bases her presentation of the mentation items are implied in the presentation of this stage of the ganzfeld procedure. Given that the participant's confirmation has at the very least provided the experimenter with two candidate choices for the second song title – that is, either 'Pink Pig Flats' or 'Pink Pig Slats' – the subsequent pause at line 20 can be heard as the experimenter attending to the written document in front of her, updating or amending it as necessary.

Conclusions: discursive psychology and discursive parapsychology

Potter and Edwards (2003a) outline three strands of discursive psychological research. First, there is the study of the psychological thesaurus: the ways in which psychological terms are used to perform work in discourse. Second, there is the study of the ways in which discourse is used to manage implied psychological themes. Finally, there is a critique of the traditional experimental and cognitivist approaches within psychology, and the attempt to establish an alternative empirical paradigm in which psychological topics are recast as features of verbal and textual action. We see our work on experimenter–participant interaction in parapsychology experiments as contributing to this final discursive psychological project, in that we are exploring the wider interactional framework in which a particular community of researchers attend to a specific (and highly contested) form of cognitive activity and mental experiences. In this chapter, we are not concerned with the ultimate status of anomalous communication, nor, indeed, the participants' experience of the phenomena of their consciousness. Rather we are interested in exploring the ways in which the interactional structure of the mentation review, and its normative properties as a component within a parapsychological experiment, inform the activities of the participants and shape the utterances they produce. To this end, we have sketched how the conduct of both experimenter and participant in the mentation review displays an orientation to procedural and normative concerns of the step-wise progression through the imagery recorded by the experimenter during the participant's prior mentation period.

Discursive psychology – and related styles of analysis, such as conversation analysis – offer a radical departure from the methods and established research practices in the cognitive sciences. Consequently, many working in more traditional experimental approaches treat the arguments of discursive psychology with suspicion, and indeed, the social constructionist element to some form of discursive psychology does invite a fairly radical reconceptualisation of the 'proper' topic for psychology. However, discursive psychology and conversation analysis need not necessarily stand as a challenge to traditional cognitive sciences. We can instead explore the degree to which the approach of discursive psychology and conversation analysis intersects with and is complementary to the concerns of cognitive scientists (Wooffitt, 2005a). To conclude, then, we offer some observations on the extent to which the kind of analysis presented in this chapter can make a direct contribution to a range of methodological and substantive concerns in parapsychological work on the ganzfeld.

It is acknowledged within parapsychology that some experimenters seem to be psi conducive, in that their experiments regularly produce evidence of psi, and others are psi inhibitory, in that they rarely if ever find evidence for psi in laboratory experiments (for example, West, 1954: 150–1; Wiseman and Schlitz, 1997). Parapsychologists have consequently wondered what it is that makes some experimenters so successful and others less so (for example, Smith, 2003).

In trying to understand the experimenter effect, some have suggested that it is necessary to consider the kind of interaction between experimenter and participants in their experiments. For example, experimental evidence from ganzfeld and other parapsychological experiments suggests that broadly 'positive' experimenters who believe in psi obtain better results than negative experimenters who do not (Honorton et al., 1975; Watt, 2002; Wiseman and Schlitz, 1997). General discussions of the characteristics of psi-conducive laboratories draw attention to the effect of the experimenter's relationship with the participant (Giesler, 1986; Honorton et al., 1975; Schneider et al., 2000). Finally, the importance of the rapport between experimenter and participants, and the experimenter's 'warmth', regularly informs more general accounts of the ganzfeld methodology (Schlitz and Honorton, 1992; Parker, 2000; Schmeidler and Edge, 1999).

It is here that a CA-informed discursive psychology can help. It offers a formal methodology with which experimenter–participant interaction can be studied. Moreover, analyses of the overarching organisational and normative structure of the interaction can inform our understanding of the sequential impact of other activities. For example, in the following extract we see an example of the kind of experimenter activity which parapsychologists would identify as a form of affiliation or rapport building.

Extract 7: 01–29: E2/M

```
 1 E:    h (0.5)um: a carpet surrounded by people?
 2       (0.8)
 3 P:    °>mhm<°
 4       (0.5)
 5 E:    hh (.) violin (0.2) someone eating the violin,
 6       (0.5)
 7 P:    °>mhm<°
 8       (0.6)
 9 E:    hhh a:nd a giant chessboard with a pig
10       (.)
11 P:    °°hu°°
12 E:    hhhh [hh: was that right?=((smiley voice))
13 P:         [(°he°)        =yeah
14 E:    hyou had some won:derful imagery [(hhh) ˆhuˆhuˆhu: hhh=
15 P:                                     [°(hh hh)°
16 E:    =°fantastic° hhhh o::kay:: °hh°
```

Here the experimenter temporarily ceases the stepwise progression to offer a comment on the unusual nature of the participant's imagery. Note that this comment is positively framed: the experimenter describes the imagery as 'wonderful', thereby noting its distinctive character but also signalling a form of approval. The participant issues a brief single bubble of laughter after hearing back an image about the chessboard and the pig (line 11). Initially, the experimenter treats this exclamation as signalling possible disagreement with her account of the specific item, as she asks explicitly 'was that right?' (line 12). Upon receiving confirmation, the experimenter then offers commentary and approval of the quality of the imagery. The participant offers some further soft breathy laughter (line 15) and the experimenter matches this with her own more marked laughter.

The participant's commentary on his own imagery thus leads to the subsequent departure from the institutional tasks by the experimenter and precedes a period of interaction in which both participants engage in mild laughter about the image. There are, then, two senses in which the experimenter affiliates with or aligns to the participant. She offers a favourable remark about his imagery, but then collaborates in an activity (laughter) which he has initiated. Thus the topic of her utterances, plus the activity of laughter, work to display her affiliation with, and broadly positive attitude towards, the participant's imagery and his response to it. It is noticeable, though, that these affiliative activities are produced as a marked departure from the institutional and normative task of step-wise item progression.

This departure was incrementally established. The participant responded to the presentation of an item with a laughter particle, which is not routinely used to pass on sequential locations in which expansion can occur. Moreover, this was itself ambiguous, in that it could be heard either as the participant's expression of doubt about the accuracy of the experimenter's report of the item or a self-commentary on the strangeness of the imagery. The experimenter's subsequent turn was designed to disambiguate the relevance of the prior, and which set up a context in which her assessment on the nature of the imagery was a relevant next activity. This kind of analysis, then, identifies not only the broad mechanics of departures from the routine procedure of the review, but also allows us to track the trajectory of subsequent turns and their emergence as a spate of recognisably affiliative interaction. If the success of parapsychological experiments depends on the relationship between experimenter and participant, it is necessary to have a formal account of the communicative practices through which that relationship is, at least in part, constituted. And a first step in that endeavour is to provide an analysis of the sequential organisation of the activities which constitute routine procedure for parapsychology laboratories. We believe that a

CA-informed discursive psychology provides the resources to undertake such a task.

ACKNOWLEDGEMENTS

We would like to acknowledge the late Professor Bob Morris and his colleagues at the Koestler Parapsychology Unit for making available the data discussed in the first section of this paper. We are also grateful to the Bial Foundation, Portugal, who provided funding for the research on experimenter–participant interaction, some of which is reported in this chapter.

5 Apologising-in-action: on saying 'sorry' to Indigenous Australians

Martha Augoustinos, Amanda LeCouteur and Kathryn Fogarty

Talk about apologising, about saying sorry, has been at the forefront of national concern in Australia over the past ten years. In April 1997, the Human Rights and Equal Opportunities Commission tabled the *Report of the National Inquiry into the Separation of Aboriginal and Torres Strait Islander Children from Their Families*, a report that generated unprecedented public debate concerning the mistreatment of Indigenous peoples throughout Australia's history. The National Inquiry concluded that the systematic separation of generations of Indigenous children (what came to be called 'the stolen generations') constituted 'a gross violation of ... human rights' and 'an act of genocide contrary to the Convention of Genocide ratified by Australia in 1949' (HREOC, 1997: 27). Among the many recommendations of the report was that 'everyone affected by forcible removals should be entitled to reparation [including] the children who were forcibly removed, their families, communities, children and grandchildren' (ibid.: 29). One specific recommendation for reparation was as follows:

That all Australian parliaments ... negotiate with the Aboriginal and Torres Strait Islander Commission a form of words for official apologies to Indigenous individuals, families and communities and extend those apologies with wide and culturally appropriate publicity. (Ibid.: 36)

Since then, text and talk about the appropriateness of apologising to Indigenous Australians for past injustices has appeared on a regular basis in national and local print media, on television and radio, in organised community meetings and in everyday discussions between ordinary people. Indeed, it is hard to imagine that any Australian has remained untouched by this issue, or has not been involved in the debate at some level over the past decade.

In this chapter we use a discursive approach to analyse how ordinary people, and the Prime Minister of a nation, attempted to make sense of the social issue of apologising to Indigenous Australians for the forced removal of Indigenous children from their families and communities, an issue that was inextricably linked to sensitive matters pertaining to 'race', oppression, history and a nation's expression of collective guilt. A discursive approach to apologising is an empirical approach. It studies actual texts and talk generated in situ by people as they go about their everyday practices of reasoning, negotiation and struggle over sense making. The value of this approach is its ability to draw attention to the multiple, flexible and contradictory meanings of, in this case, apologising-in-action. Such multiplicity of meaning is not surprising given that people produce their talk and texts for rhetorical purposes: to be persuasive, to fend off accusations of 'stake' or interest, to offer inferences about their own and others' motives, and to produce themselves and others as certain types of people (Edwards and Potter, 1992; Potter, 1996). This last purpose is, of course, the subject of a growing body of literature in discursive psychology pertaining to how identities are produced in talk and text (Antaki and Widdicombe, 1998).

Before turning to our own work it is instructive to look at what the sociological and linguistics literature has had to say about the notion of apologising. Our aim here is to contrast these abstract theoretical approaches to understanding apologising with discursive approaches that emphasise the importance of studying such actions as situated social practices.

Apologising in theory

In everyday social interaction apologies are offered for a wide array of transgressions, ranging from the most trivial and banal, to more serious and significant offences. As Goffman (1971: 117) so eloquently put it: 'Whether one runs over another's sentence, time, dog, or body, one is more or less reduced to saying some variant of "I'm sorry".' Apologies then, are basic to society and function to

appease people we have injured, to avoid accusations and/or reprisals, to implicate contrition, and, of course, to elicit acts of forgiving and be freed from guilt ... It is essential to the smooth working of society that there be standard means of admitting responsibility, implicating remorse, and forgiving. (Norrick, 1978: 284)

This conception of apologising which is central to sociological accounts depicts it as a transformative social act that has the power to restore social harmony. In the words of Tavuchis (1991: 7), the restorative potential of apologising lies in its 'capacity to transform unbearable realities through speech'. So, from a sociological perspective, apologising can be seen to be about the re-accreditation of societal membership to those who have offended and the stabilising of precarious social relations.

Furthermore, Tavuchis argued that, in modern usage, to apologise is 'to declare voluntarily that one has *no* excuse, defense, justification, or explanation for an action (or inaction) that has "insulted, failed, injured, or wronged another"' (ibid.: 17). He drew on sources such as dictionaries, writings on etiquette and journalistic accounts for evidence of what the modern apology means. From a sociological stance, then, an apology can be seen as an act that seeks forgiveness and redemption for what is unreasonable, unjustified or defenceless. It may be contrasted with an *account* – for example, an excuse or a defence – in which attention is diverted away from the agent of the offensive action and directed towards conventional categories of causality such as incapacity, accident, ignorance or coercion.

Similar distinctions between apologies and accounts have been made in the linguistics literature, where *apologies* are usually defined as admissions of blameworthiness and regret by the actor or agent, whereas *accounts* attempt to explain away the undesirable event through the use of excuses and justifications. In Speech Act Theory (Austin, 1961, 1962; Searle, 1969, 1976), apologies are defined as paradigm examples of *expressive* illocutionary acts – that is, speech acts that express an emotional state – and according to Searle (1969), apologies are offered for past acts of which one is ashamed. But Searle also claimed that more was at stake than this. Although he argued that the illocutionary point of apologising was to express regret, he stressed that people usually apologise or express regret *to some end*. In particular, he pointed out that apologies are usually made with the hope of being forgiven or freed from guilt.

More recently, Meier (1998) has criticised existing linguistic research into apologies on the basis of its failure to come up with any consistent and generalisable findings about what constitutes an apology, when apologies are warranted and how contextual factors shape apology behaviour. He argued for a research agenda that moves away from description of what an apology is and one which instead focuses on 'identifying underlying cultural values and beliefs as they inform perceptions of linguistic appropriateness' (1998: 227). In plain terms, Meier's call was for a shift of focus towards the 'why' of apology, positing that this should begin with a search for how culture shapes values and beliefs, which in turn shape when and how people produce apology behaviour. Meier's calls for attending to contextual factors that shape apology behaviour treat concepts like 'culture', 'values' and 'beliefs' as underlying cognitive phenomena that somehow produce and determine why, when and how apologies are made. Our discursive approach, in contrast, is one that seeks to examine apologies as situated social actions that derive their cultural meaning and significance for interactants in the specifics of an on-going interaction. We now turn to consider in more detail a discursive approach which has guided our analysis of empirical data of what it means to apologise to Indigenous Australians for past injustices.

A discursive approach to apologising

Discursive psychology offers an alternative to theorising apology. Although this approach shares the linguistic notion that apologising in interaction is functional, and that both the forms and functions of apologising are variable, it differs from linguistics in that it does not aim to generalise the meanings or functions of different apology forms beyond the specific interactional data under consideration. Discursive psychologists take the view that the meanings and functions of apologising are worked up between people in the specifics of an on-going interaction. Furthermore, the only way that an analyst can gain insight into the multiple meanings and functions of apologising is to examine people's talk-in-interaction where apologising is the topic at hand. We should make clear that discursive psychologists would not claim that there are no shared understandings of what it means to apologise. However, they *would* make an a priori intellectual commitment to approach each instance of apologising-in-interaction with the aim of elucidating its local meaning and function, and when this analytic process is repeated over numerous instances of interaction, commonalities as well as differences in the meanings of, and functions served by, apologies are likely to be seen.

An example of this type of research is provided by Robinson (2004) who uses conversation analysis to examine data from naturally occurring interactions such as telephone calls, persons talking during meal times and games, and doctor–patient consultations, to investigate how 'explicit' (2004: 293) apologies such as *I'm sorry* and *I must apologise* are sequentially organised and how this organisation is related to the social action being performed. He showed how apologies *may* perform the primary social action of making a social claim to have caused offence but – depending on the sequential position of the apology – this action is often subordinate to other primary non-apology actions, such as requesting information or projecting a dispreferred response, such as the imminent declining of an invitation. Similar points were made by Maynard (2003), who showed how apologising often functions to forecast bad news in clinical settings, and Hepburn (2004), who identified apologies as a feature of callers' actions when they disrupt on-going interaction with crying on a telephone helpline. Furthermore, Robinson's (2004) analysis provides evidence that where the primary action being performed by an explicit apology *is* a claim to have caused offence, then the preferred response[1] from the co-interactant is some form of mitigation or undermining of that claim. Robinson's conversation analytic study suggests that often when we say 'sorry' we normatively expect absolution (*That's okay/That's all right*) or disagreement with the need to have made the apology, rather than acceptance of the apology per se (2004: 308).

Another example of conversation analytic research on the topic of apologising is Kotani's (2002) study of a naturally occurring conversation – in English – between an English and a Japanese speaker. Kotani showed how neither speaker's use of 'I'm sorry' indicated acceptance of responsibility for wrongdoing; a prime function of apologising according to the sociological and linguistic perspectives. Instead, Kotani showed how the Japanese speaker's use of 'I'm sorry' functioned to express gratitude and indebtedness to her interlocutor, whereas the English speaker's use of 'I'm sorry' formed part of an account that mitigated against there being any interpretation of fault on her part.

If we accept the discursive psychological proposition described earlier that apologising is a situated social action, then we can begin to contemplate the range of functions that apologising might serve, and the meanings that it has in social interaction. As already alluded to, apologising-in-interaction also implicates matters of identity. The act of apologising allows for inferences to be drawn about the identity of the person making the apology, and this should alert us, as analysts, to the possibility that people might be doing a range of different things when they say sorry. This may include making reparation, but might also include other social actions, such as being polite or presenting oneself in a favourable light.

We now turn to our own analysis of what it means to say sorry to Indigenous Australians for the forced removal of children from their families and communities. We draw our data from two specific sources: first, emails written to a newspaper website on the appropriateness of apologising to Indigenous Australians, and second, the Australian Prime Minister's opening address to the Reconciliation Convention, at which he justified his refusal to offer a national apology to Indigenous people. Although our data are not conversational or, strictly speaking, interactional in nature, these texts nonetheless demonstrate how people struggled to make sense of the act of apologising; how they constructed what it meant to apologise in instances of public communication – in this case, emails posted on a newspaper website and in a set-piece political address. Specifically, we want to examine these instances of public discussion about what it means to apologise in order to explore the sorts of understandings of the act of apologising that people regularly drew on in these contexts, and to what ends. We are interested in exploring how people go about doing apologies in the sense of how they argue an apology should be considered appropriate and why. How is apologising constructed as an appropriate or inappropriate response in relation to a variety of other possible acts in this context, such as denying, rationalising and so on? What strategies, manoeuvres and rhetorics organise talk and texts about the appropriateness of apologising, in this instance of a national apology to the Stolen Generations? In doing so, we will explore the ways in which this issue generated heated debate over what an apology *should* mean to Indigenous and non-Indigenous Australians.

Public reasoning in action: letters to a newspaper website

In this section we examine email texts that supported a national apology in order to show the different meanings imputed to the act of apologising, as well as demonstrating the discursive resources that were repeatedly mobilised to build these meanings. The emails were drawn from a set of thirty-five pro-apology responses sourced from The Australian Online Survey, a website controlled by News Limited. Under the general heading 'The stolen children: APOLOGY', this site invited readers to 'Have your say' on the issue of whether 'Australians [should] apologise for the treatment of Aborigines'. The site also provided information on responses to the online survey: 48 per cent of respondents had voted 'Yes', and 52 per cent 'No'. 104 responses were available for perusal at the site, with 69 being representative of the 'No' case, and 35 representing the 'Yes' case. For the purposes of analysis, the texts were corrected for spelling and any names appended to responses were removed. In other analyses we have examined the email texts that argued *against* apologising, and those findings are reported elsewhere (LeCouteur and Augoustinos, 2001). However, in support of a discursive psychological approach to apologising, we want to show that even amongst the email authors who argued *in favour* of apologising, the meaning imputed to the act of apologising was not fixed but could be seen to vary, even within the one email text.

Emails in support of a national apology

According to the sociological and linguistic theories of apologising outlined earlier, the meanings imputed to apologising in the pro-apology texts should have emphasised the collective responsibility and guilt of 'white' Australians for past injustices perpetrated against Indigenous peoples. Somewhat surprisingly, only four emails in our data-base drew on the explicit argument that all Australians – past and *present* generations – should bear collective responsibility and guilt for the assimilation practices of successive governments. One of these emails is presented below:

Y1:   My answer yes means that the Aboriginal people deserve an apology and that should come from the Australian nation as a whole. We are all products of our past and collectively – not personally – we share a certain amount of guilt for what has transpired. The purpose of the apology should be to bring the issue to the fore. To recognise it for its injustice; to make amends where possible; and to move on into the future. But never to forget.

In this text an apology is constructed as both acknowledging the past injustices perpetrated against Indigenous Australians and accepting collective responsibility and guilt for these wrongdoings. However, the most common meaning imputed to apologising in the pro-apology texts was that apologising serves important social functions such as *expressing sympathy* and understanding, but *not* of accepting responsibility, blame or guilt. As we will see, such a construction served significant rhetorical functions in its contrast with the Prime Minister's arguments for refusing to offer an apology (see below). Examples of this type of construction can be seen in the following texts:

Y16:   Yes we should all say sorry! By saying sorry we are not admitting personal guilt; we are saying that we recognise the abuses of the past, and that we abhor what happened ... We say sorry to acknowledge this sad part of Australia's history.

Y28:   Saying sorry does not implicitly mean acknowledging one's own guilt – it is an acknowledgment that another has been wronged, an expression both of sympathy and empathy, as well as the first step to righting that wrong.

Y32:   Australians have misinterpreted the word 'sorry'. When used in context of the circumstances, it is not an acceptance of guilt or our personal connection with the acts.

Y35:   Saying sorry has absolutely nothing to do with admitting guilt.

Another meaning imputed to apologising in the pro-apology texts was that an apology is a 'practical' solution to a complex social and political issue: a small gesture of goodwill that required little effort on the part of the Prime Minister and the nation as a whole:

Y3:   So, if this is the one day in an entire year where we give an apology from our nation, would it really be that hard?

Y11:   The Aboriginal people have been treated extremely badly and I, as an Australian, love my country and want to be proud of it. We owe them at the very least an apology.

Y15:   Surely saying 'sorry' can't be such a difficult task. If such a small and humble action can have a large effect on the emotional healing of a group of people ... then LET'S DO IT.

In their study of contemporary racist discourse, Wetherell and Potter (1992) observed how several *self-sufficient rhetorical arguments* were regularly deployed in the service of justifying oppressive social practices. Although racist discourse is not the focus of this chapter, the self-sufficient rhetorical argument 'You have to be practical' is visible in these extracts. The practical utility of apologising is contrasted with the small effort required to do so. Note that there is no implication of personal or collective responsibility, accountability or guilt within this construction of what it means to apologise.

As well as being a practical response, apologising was also constructed as an act of politeness and decency; as a social norm that is central to everyday social interaction when another person is aggrieved in some way. Refusing to apologise was depicted as a transgression of this customary norm:

Y2:   It's a simple courtesy. By custom, we express sympathy in another's sorrow. Many Aboriginal people are still living in their sorrow. We can help, just a little, by saying sorry. Perhaps then we will be better able to work together in trust, to seek solutions to the problems of a dispossessed people.

Y31:   We would expect the same.

Note that this construction of apologising enables the question of responsibility for the offence to be sidestepped. Here, apologising is not so much a matter of admitting an offence, but of demonstrating good manners. It also provides a neat illustration of how identities are built up in talk and texts. People who are courteous are positioned as being committed to social harmony; they are benevolent and respectful of others. Indigenous people are positioned as experiencing 'sorrow' and 'problems' that 'we' (non-Indigenous) people can 'help' them 'seek solutions to'. Notably, 'we' are not constructed as the cause of their problem, but as people whom, having demonstrated our sympathy for them, they can 'trust', and with whom they can 'work together'.

The constructions of apologising outlined thus far were often accompanied by the related argument that confessing to the past was a necessary first step in moving forward as a nation. Central to these textual constructions was a therapeutic metaphor of healing. A public apology was represented as the first step in a collective process of healing, without which old 'wounds' and 'scars' would periodically resurface. This *healing the past* argument is illustrated in the examples below:

Y27:   We are now presented with a unique opportunity to confess the past (whether or not we had any direct part in it), seek the forgiveness of both God and the people who have been wronged. Then we can be free of the past, once and for all, and get on with the future, free of any accusation.

Y28:   Australia has before it an opportunity to show we are big enough to correct the mistakes of our forebears and move forward as a truly reconciled nation, knowing that history will judge us as a country that had the maturity to treat the scars of its past in such a way that they could begin to fade, not rise up again to become ugly welts on our nationhood.

In other instances, the emphasis was more directly aimed at the power of an apology to provide emotional healing to Indigenous people. Consider this earlier example once again:

Y15:   Surely saying 'sorry' can't be such a difficult task. If such a small and humble action can have a large effect on the emotional healing of a group of people ... then LET'S DO IT.

In examples like this one, the focus of descriptions is on the psychological and emotional damage caused by the forced removals of Indigenous children, not on other issues that are potentially relevant, such as issues of basic human rights, or issues to do with continuing discrimination and disadvantage in, for example, areas of economics, criminal justice, education and health. By constructing Indigenous peoples' suffering as a matter of psychological and emotional damage, issues to do with their on-going social, political and economic oppression are avoided. Thus, the argument runs, if Indigenous peoples can be healed by the act of apology, then there is no reason why they should not assume an equal place in society. Framing apologising as a matter of emotional healing does not cause major disturbances to existing power relations. Rather, it emphasises the benefits of apologising for both the givers and the receivers. Typically, these benefits are constructed in terms of personal growth or psychological well-being.

To sum up our analysis thus far we can see, in these emails, everyday reasoning practices which suggest that apologising, or saying sorry, can mean a range of things. Although apologising can take on the meanings imputed to it by sociological and linguistic accounts, it can also be seen as a mere expression of sympathy and empathy, a norm of social politeness, or a practical solution to a complex problem.

The Prime Minister's address to the Reconciliation Convention

So far we have analysed some of the sense-making practices drawn upon by members of the public in relation to one of the most significant social issues faced by Australians at the turn of the century. We now turn to an analysis of the arguments deployed by Prime Minister John Howard in a major political address at the Reconciliation Convention (1997). As shall be seen, by constructing apologising to mean an admission of guilt, the Prime Minister was able to make a national apology seem wrong and unfair to present generations of 'white' Australians. Construing apologising as an admission of guilt also enabled the Prime Minster to contest and undermine versions of history that give weight to the suffering experienced by Australia's Indigenous peoples at the hands of past generations of 'white' Australians.

The Reconciliation Convention was held to review the process of reconciliation between Indigenous and non-Indigenous Australians up to that time and to set achievable goals for the future. Howard's address demonstrates a range of rhetorical strategies that effectively repudiate the notion of collective guilt, and therefore reparation, on the part of white Australians, which in turn has the effect of making an apology seem unnecessary and unfair to present generations of white Australians. Although we do not have the space to consider the entirety of Howard's speech (see Augoustinos et al., 2002), we focus here on two particular sections that demonstrate some of the discursive resources that Howard mobilises to justify not making an apology, and at the same time give consideration to the meanings that are being imputed to the act of apologising.

No guilt, no apology: apology as admission of guilt in political rhetoric

At the outset of his address, Howard constructed definitional boundaries around the nebulous concept of reconciliation, drawing on formulations that legitimised his government's approach to this sensitive issue: an approach that came to be known as 'practical' reconciliation, and one that stood in distinction to formulations of reconciliation that were premised upon the central importance of making a public apology to Indigenous peoples. Throughout the speech, Howard constructed the reconciliation process as constituting three fundamental objectives: (1) raising Indigenous living standards; (2) acknowledging history; and (3) working together. Having proclaimed his optimism about the reconciliation process in Australia, Howard identified what he perceived as 'threats to reconciliation'. In the passages below, he argues that reconciliation will not work when the emphasis is on 'symbolic gestures' (P2) or if it is based on 'national guilt and shame' (P3).

P1:   But this optimism, my friends, about the reconciliation process cannot be blind. We must be realistic in acknowledging some of the threats to reconciliation.

P2:   Reconciliation will not work if it puts a higher value on symbolic gestures and overblown promises rather than practical needs of Aboriginal and Torres Strait Islander people in areas like health, housing, education and employment.

P3:   It will not work if it is premised solely on a sense of national guilt and shame. Rather we should acknowledge past injustices and focus our energies on addressing the root causes of current and future disadvantage among our Indigenous people.

This extract sees Howard constructing a version of reconciliation that denies the need for a national apology and, simultaneously, undermines alternative versions that are used to argue in favour of apologising. In P1, he specifically emphasises the importance of being realistic and in P2 he sets up an oppositional contrast between 'symbolic gestures' and 'practical needs', arguing for the greater importance of the latter. The importance of practical needs is, of course, difficult to counter since it is undoubtedly the case that Indigenous peoples' needs in 'health, housing, education and employment' are of utmost importance, and central to any strategies aimed towards reconciliation. Note, however, the way that Howard positions this priority as oppositional to symbolic needs, effectively constructing the practical and the symbolic as mutually exclusive. Clearly, a symbolic gesture such as a national apology for past government practices should not in any way preclude redressing the social disadvantages faced by Indigenous peoples in housing, health, education, etc. Howard had repeatedly used this emphasis on a practical approach to reconciliation to differentiate his view from that of Indigenous leaders, most of whom consistently represented a national apology as a symbolic *prerequisite* to reconciliation. Howard's setting up of the practical and the symbolic as either/or contrasts (rather than as compatible goals) works to justify and legitimate his position on the issue of a national apology. Although he does not make any specific reference to the issue of an apology in this extract, it is implied in P2 and P3 in the references to 'symbolic gestures' and 'national guilt and shame', which can be seen as euphemisms for an apology.

From the current chapter's perspective of what it means to apologise, Howard's statement in P3 that reconciliation 'will not work if it is premised solely on a sense of national guilt and shame' is significant. Feelings of guilt and shame about past wrongdoings are constructed as negative, unnecessary and unproductive feelings that should be avoided. In contrast to the pro-apology emails, where saying 'sorry' is presented as *not* implying guilt, here, 'sorry' *means* an admission of guilt.

Implicit in the phrase 'acknowledge past injustices' (P3) is the notion that present generations should not be blamed for the mistakes of past generations. This was Howard's favoured justification for refusing to apologise: an apology implies guilt and shame; present generations should not be burdened in this way because they are not responsible for things that happened in the past. So strongly associated are these elements in the argumentative structure that invoking any one of them inevitably calls up the others. Again, as in P2, Howard's solution here is to focus on the practical (redressing 'current and future' disadvantage) rather than on the symbolic (an apology). An explicit contrast between the past and the present/future is also set up in P3. Reconciliation will not work if it is based on the shame and guilt associated with past injustices; rather we should focus on the here and now and, of course, the (inevitably better) future. Howard's address is firmly oriented towards the present and the future rather than the past. Again, this practice is implicitly linked to the commonsense argument that 'you cannot change the past'. In P3, too, Howard emphasises categorisation at the level of nation (a practice he deploys throughout the speech). If we are all Australians together, who could possibly want to engage in a type of reconciliation that would produce 'national' guilt and shame? By implication, Howard suggests that invoking such feelings would be divisive and undermining of national unity, pitting white Australians against Indigenous Australians.

No guilt, no apology: contesting Australia's history

Although Howard's speech can be understood as a piece of political rhetoric that justifies and legitimates his government's policy on reconciliation (a 'practical' approach), it is also a speech where he can be seen to be engaged in the on-going struggle over contested versions of Australia's history. The HREOC (1997) report on the Stolen Generations was, after all, a scathing criticism of past policies of successive state and federal governments, describing the practices of forced removal of Indigenous children from their families, communities and culture as acts of genocide. Howard had, on several occasions prior to the completion of the report, declared his antipathy to what he described as the 'black armband view of history' (Hall, 1998), an account of Australia's past that explicitly recognises the dispossession and genocide of Indigenous peoples during British colonisation and the entrenched institutionalised racism of this history. Throughout the speech, Howard made an apparent concession by stressing the importance of openly acknowledging the (historical) injustices perpetrated against Indigenous peoples, representing this as 'the most blemished chapter' in Australia's history. We will see, however, how he subsequently works to discount and minimise this history. In the passage below, for example, he attends specifically to the issue of an apology, of saying sorry to Indigenous peoples for the past practices of forced removal of Indigenous children.

P1:   ... Personally, I feel deep sorrow for those of my fellow Australians who suffered injustices under the practices of past generations towards indigenous people. Equally I am sorry for the hurt and trauma many people here today may continue to feel as a consequence of those practices.

P2:   In facing the realities of the past, however, we must not join those who would portray Australia's history since 1788 as little more than a disgraceful record of imperialism, exploitation and racism.

P3:   Such a portrayal is a gross distortion and deliberately neglects the overall story of great Australian achievement that there is in our history to be told, and such an approach will be repudiated by the overwhelming majority of Australians who are proud of what this country has achieved although inevitably acknowledging the blemishes in its past history.

P4:   Australians of this generation should not be required to accept guilt and blame for past actions and policies over which they had no control.

In P1, Howard both expresses his personal sorrow and states that he is sorry for the feelings of hurt and trauma felt by Indigenous peoples ('Personally, I feel deep sorrow', 'I am sorry') rather than offering an apology on behalf of the nation. This expression of personal sorrow, as opposed to the offering of a national apology in his official capacity as Prime Minister, attends to Howard's own positive self-presentation as a compassionate man who has empathy for those who have suffered from past injustices. It allows Howard to head off claims that he is mean-spirited and unfeeling toward the Stolen Generations. Although the statement he employs here, 'I am sorry', could be heard as an apology, it is significant that Howard does not apologise for government practices and policies, but for the *possible psychological* consequences of those policies for Indigenous peoples ('the hurt and trauma many people here today may continue to feel'). This echoes the *apology-as-healing* metaphor outlined earlier in the pro-apology email texts, but in this instance it is called into service to bolster the opposite argument: that a national apology is impractical for the purposes of remedying past hurts caused by past generations (what good would it do anyway?) as well as being an unfair burden of guilt to place upon present generations of non-Indigenous Australians.

The dichotomy that Howard establishes between the personal and the collective, the private and the public, becomes a critical basis from which he rationalises and justifies his decision not to offer an apology on behalf of all Australians. There was significantly more at stake for Howard in offering a national apology as opposed to a personal one. A national apology openly acknowledging and embracing the collective guilt of the nation also opened the way for the rewriting of Australia's official history, a history that Howard was not prepared to surrender. In P2 and P3, Howard explicitly challenges the 'black armband view' of Australia's history, describing the story of Indigenous dispossession and oppression as a 'gross distortion'. He deploys a series of extreme descriptive dimensions such as '*disgraceful* record', '*gross* distortion', '*deliberately* neglects', to represent this as an abnormal version of Australia's history. Howard uses these extreme case formulations (Pomerantz, 1986) to distance himself from this version of history and to set it up as an oppositional contrast to his own preferred version: 'the overall story of great Australian achievement'. The abnormality of these alternative versions of Australia's history is also accomplished through the use of the device of the contrast structure (Smith, 1990). A contrast is created between fact and fiction, between the 'realities of the past' (P2) (Howard's version of history) and a 'gross distortion' (P3) (the black-armband view). Moreover, this distorted portrayal is further undermined as illegitimate by the attribution of interest or motivation. It is a version that 'deliberately neglects' the positives ('great Australian achievement') that exist in 'our' history (P3). In other words, it is not a factual version; it is an interested one.

Note also how Howard indexes Australia's history of 'imperialism, exploitation and racism' euphemistically as 'blemishes' (P3: a description he had also used previously in the speech) in a way that works to counter characterisations of Australia's history as racist. In Howard's version of history, injustices perpetrated against Indigenous peoples are represented as flaws or stains that tarnish an otherwise great story of a nation. By refusing to give weight and significance to Australia's racist history, Howard is able to justify his unwillingness to accept

responsibility on the part of the nation for past injustices and con-
cordantly to justify why a national apology is not warranted.

After two years of resisting HREOC's recommendations, and under
increasing pressure from backbenchers in his own government, the
media and Indigenous leaders, Howard eventually moved a parliamentary motion expressing his 'deep and sincere *regret* that indigenous
Australians had suffered injustices under the practices of *past* generations' (emphasis added, Hansard, 26 August 1999, p. 9205). It is
noteworthy that in this statement, Howard used 'regret': a word that has
no implications of responsibility or guilt. Moreover, this statement of
regret did not satisfy Indigenous leaders and groups, most of whom
regarded the words 'apology' and 'sorry' as fundamental, not only to
acknowledging historical wrongdoings, but also to expressing guilt and
remorse for these injustices. In April 2000, the government's formal
submission to the Senate Inquiry into The Stolen Generations disputed
the existence of a 'generation' of stolen children, arguing that since only
10 per cent of children had been removed from their families, this did
not constitute a generation. In effect, the government's report amounted
to a denial of the existence of the Stolen Generations (Manne, 2000).

Conclusion

In this chapter we have argued for a discursive approach to understanding apologies and apologising. In contrast to standard sociological
and linguistic accounts, such an approach highlights, and treats as an
analytical resource, the flexible and often contradictory ways in which
the business of apologising gets done in everyday interaction.

The practical relevance of discursive research on apologising would
seem to relate to the significance of the action in everyday life. Apologies
matter to people; it is noticed when they are not forthcoming, and
inferences and attributions of relevant actors are inevitably made – this is
the case regardless of whether the apology involves the mere mumbled
recognition of an accidental contact or a formal statement that
acknowledges the institutionalised injustices of national policy. It is
important to know about the ways in which the act of apologising is
made sense of and argued about in ordinary interaction but we also need
to examine the fine detail of the (typically) messy business that is
apologising. Discursive approaches are designed to shed light on just
this sort of detail; they treat variation and contradiction in argumentation and accounting as a prime analytic resource. As our data set indicates, apologising can be constructed variably as either a personal or
collective act, as free from guilt or guilt-ridden. Such approaches are

thus perfectly placed to permit exploration of the nuances of alternative versions of apologising in specific instances of real-life interaction.

Future directions for discursive research into apologising might involve the examination of naturally occurring instances of apologising in institutional settings. As Barkan (2000) in particular has noted, calls for restitution and reparation by aggrieved minority groups have led to an increasing willingness of at least some nation-states to apologise for historical injustices. The notion of restorative justice in western nations has also led to significant changes to the legal system, where meetings between victims and perpetrators of crime are taking place as part of new moves worldwide towards recognised systems of restorative justice. Such institutional contexts are fertile settings for the detailed analysis of how the business of apologising gets done for significant historical and interpersonal transgressions.

NOTE

1. 'Preferred response' refers to the conversation analytic meaning, whereby the structural design of a turn at talk invites one response in preference to another (e.g., an invitation prefers an acceptance to a declination). It does not refer to the psychological motives of the actors (Hutchby and Wooffitt, 1998: 43–4).

6   Mind, mousse and moderation

Jonathan Potter and Claudia Puchta

This chapter is about the ways that psychology appears in, and is used in, the process of research. More particularly we will be considering the way psychological terms, orientations, constructions and displays are manifest, and practically drawn on, in market research focus groups. This study reflects a broader concern with what psychology is *for* in the different practices, everyday and institutional, intimate and public, in which it appears. The interest here is to contribute to the literature on method as an interactional and discursive accomplishment and at the same time to contribute to the broader literature of discursive psychology. We will start with some comments on the general approach of discursive psychology and then consider research on the interactional accomplishment of research methods.

Discursive psychology

Discursive psychology (henceforth DP) has been developed in a series of studies, demonstrations and overviews, and been refined through debates with a varied range of cognitive and social psychologists, critical discourse analysts, ethnomethodologists, sociolinguists and ethnographers. Edwards (1997) and Edwards and Potter (1992) are foundational texts; Edwards (2005) and Potter (2003) review and summarise DP; Hepburn and Wiggins (2005b) and the current volume collect together recent DP-inspired studies. DP has a rather different object than most of the different traditions that have characterised psychology. It focuses on psychology as embedded in interaction, and as something that gives interaction sense and coherence. Ultimately the topic of DP is psychology from the participants' perspective.

DP is distinct from superficially similar perspectives on topics such as folk psychologies, mental models, person schemata, social knowledge, social representations or theories of mind (Gergen and Semin, 1990; Heider, 1958; Hewstone, 1989; Leslie, 1987; Moscovici, 1984). As Edwards and Potter (1992) have shown, this way of thinking about psychology starts with a perceptual cognitive picture that has person understanding as a form of individual perception and processing. A mental model or theory processes information delivered via perception of other people. Rather than trying to get inside the person as these perspectives do, DP is addressing the psychology that is there for participants as they talk to one another, coordinate their actions, argue and complain, flirt and reassure. It asks questions such as the following. How are dispositions and intentions made hearable in interaction? How is familiarity and emotion shown? How are 'attitudes' involved with actions such as criticisms and compliments? Rather than seeing the task as that of attempting to open up the mythic black box where psychology has been thought to be hiding since Descartes and Locke developed their arguments, it is focused on what Edwards (2006b) calls the 'rich surface' of language and social interaction.

The focus on interaction has led discursive psychologists to draw on the findings, methods and insights of conversation analysis, which provides the most sophisticated available approach for the study of talk-in-interaction. DP also draws on constructionism derived from sociology of scientific knowledge. This highlights the epistemic and reality-productive elements of discourse, and the way these epistemic and psychological issues intertwine. For example, a description of an event can be constructed in such a way that it produces the speaker's own stance as, say, appropriately neutral. Indeed, DP has shown the way that descriptions of 'mind' and 'reality' are pervasively mutually implicative.

Up to now DP studies, and closely related work at the boundaries of CA and ethnomethodology, have concentrated on one of the following six interrelated and overlapping themes.

1. They have studied the procedures through which the psychological implications of talk are managed. For example, they have investigated the way different motives are established and how memories are discounted as flawed (e.g. Edwards and Potter, 1992; Lynch and Bogen, 2005; Watson, 1983).
2. They have researched the way the thesaurus of psychological words is used to do different things in different settings. For example, it has considered the use of terms such as 'anger', 'opinion' and 'noise' (e.g. Edwards, 1999; Myers, 2004; Stokoe and Hepburn, 2005).
3. They have done studies that respecify topics that are central to cognitive research perspectives such as social cognition, cognitive psychology and cognitive science (including scripts and schemata, categories, attitudes and beliefs, perception, theory of mind, the unconscious, emotions – e.g., Auburn, 2005; Billig, 1999; Edwards, 2006b).

4. They have considered psychological 'displays' of various kinds, where psychological states are 'embodied' (Kitzinger, 2006) in the manner of delivery of talk or associated items such as 'gosh', 'uuum' (in the context of food) or sobs and sniffs (Hepburn, 2004; Wilkinson and Kitzinger, 2005; Wiggins, 2002).
5. They have examined the way psychological methods operate in practice and in particular the way they constitute their objects and produce them as the property of individuals (e.g., Antaki, 2006; Puchta and Potter, 2002; Schegloff, 1999). More on this theme below.
6. They have started to consider the relation of psychology to institutions, exploring the way activities in therapy, education, courts and so on are constituted by specifically psychological business, and how institutional objects are constituted as psychological or not (e.g., Edwards and Potter, 1992; Potter, 2005; Potter and Hepburn, 2003).

These themes are not intended to be definitive and completely comprehensive; rather they highlight some of the developments that have been most central. The focus of this current chapter will be mix of themes 1, 2, 4 and 5. It will consider some of the ways that psychological terms and orientations are used in market research focus groups, and the way they are part of constituting the structured organisation of those focus groups. Before that it is helpful to survey some of the recent work that studies social research as interactionally accomplished.

Studies of the accomplishment of research techniques

As our sophistication in studying interaction has increased, so it is possible to develop a richer understanding of the interaction that goes on in social research instruments such as surveys, assessments, interviews and focus groups. In one of the first pieces of its kind Suchman and Jordan (1990) studied interaction in survey interviews. One finding was that questions asked often departed from standardised question formats as interviewers worked to manage local pragmatic issues. And they argued that question delivery will always require ad hoc and local negotiation, subverting the ideal of standardisation. This work on surveys has been considerably extended by Houtkoop-Steenstra (2000) and contributions to Maynard et al. (2002).

Some of this work has focused specifically on issues of psychological relevance. Schaeffer and Maynard (2005), for example, consider interactive aspects of question delivery in standardised surveys, highlighting a range of shortcomings with the idea that pauses are indicators of the time respondents need for 'cognitive processing'. A further group of studies has highlighted the way that interaction in assessment interviews, qualitative interviews, questionnaires or focus groups is consequential for the psychological objects that are produced by the methods (Antaki, 1999; Antaki and Rapley, 1996; Koole, 2003; Lee and Roth, 2004; Maynard and Marlaire, 1992; Potter and Hepburn, 2005a; Puchta and Potter, 2002; Schegloff, 1999).

The contribution here will be particularly focused on the role of psychological notions, orientations and constructions in market research focus groups.

Market research focus groups as topic

The materials and some of the background analysis to this chapter come from a project considering interaction in market research focus groups in the UK and Germany. In a series of papers we have studied a range of moderator actions including question design (Puchta and Potter, 1999), constructing opinions as objects contained within individuals (Puchta and Potter, 2002) and receipting participants' contributions (Puchta et al., 2004). These actions along with broader issues about the way moderators shape the talk of participants are discussed in Puchta and Potter (2004), which also introduces some of the issues developed in this chapter. This work was influenced by, and partly builds on, studies by Myers and Macnaghten (Myers, 1998; Myers and Macnaghten, 1999).

This chapter will take as its topic materials from a focus group run in the UK on hair products. As is common for groups of this kind, the participants sit on low comfortable chairs around a table which has some snack food, coffee cups and ashtrays on it. The session as a whole lasts about an hour and a half. The moderator sits with her back to the video camera that records the whole group for the clients. See figure 6.1. The moderator informs the group members that there are further researchers behind a one-way mirror also behind the moderator. Groups of this kind are video recorded as standard – such records are part of what is purchased by the company or organisation that commissions the group. Part of the skill of moderating is to produce interaction that focuses on the commissioning bodies' interests.

Moderators characteristically start groups of this kind with a general introduction covering what the participants should expect and what the topic of the group is. The introduction here is typical in the themes it covers. The extract below is from about half a minute into the introduction. The moderator (henceforth FGM) has said she will 'explain

Figure 6.1 Introducing the group

what we are doing', emphasising that it will be 'straightforward' and
noting that 'companies before they do anything':

Extract 1: Hair products

```
1 FGM:    Want te (0.2) .hh make su:re that they're doin
2         the right thing before they spend lots of money
3         on it, (0.2) .hh er:m an so they research m:ore
4         or less anything.
5         (0.2)
6 FGM:    That they're thinking of doing. Er:m: (0.8)
7         tk.hh A:Nd the way they >do that< is te (0.2)
8         hi:re som'dy like me an give me all 'o their
9         ideas. =To °kin've (.) trot round the country an (.)
10        show people like you an see what you think o' them.°
11        .hhh I'VE GOt idea:s for: new products and new
12        packaging (0.3) u:m to show you, this morning,
13        .hh u:m (0.4) I work for an independent company,
14        (0.3) I do:n't work for:: erm (0.2) ((swallows))
15        >the people that came up with all this stuff an I
16        didn't come up with any of it.< I didn't do any
17        of the packaging and I didn't think of the products.
18        .hhh an BASically what that means is >I don't care
```

```
19       what you're saying.<
20       (0.3)
21 FGM:  U:m so you can be: very rude about things, (.) if
22       you want to be, (0.2) um an you can be very (0.5)
23       complimentary about things if you want to be an
24       it doesn't make .hh any difference to me at all.
25       Um the important things from my point of view
26       is that you tell me what you think. .hhh We've
27       got nine of you here, (0.2) °um° hh wh(hh)ich is
28       .hhh record.
29       (0.2)
30 FGM:  Um tur:nout. .hhh AN:d >that's basically (cuz)
31       hopefully you all have different opinions about
32       things so (0.2) again don't be poli:te. Um if
33       you disagree with what someone's saying then
34       (.) argue °with them.°
35       (0.6)
36 FGM:  KAY?
37       (0.4)
38 FGM:  Should be straightforward,
```

We will address a number of themes that arise in this introduction, focusing on elements that are relevant to our issue of different ways that psychology becomes involved in interaction.

1.   *Moderator stance and interest*

A basic theme in DP has been the pervasive attention paid by people to issues of *stake* and *interest* (Edwards and Potter, 1992). This is closely related to the issue of the *stance* that they have to a particular claim or object (Potter and Hepburn, 2003). Moderators attend to these matters because of their potential for affecting the contributions of the participants.

This is a major theme in the extract above, where the moderator is introducing what will go on in the group. Note the emphatic and contrastive organisation of lines 13–19. One the one hand:

```
I work for an independent company,
```

And on the other:

```
I do:n't work for:: erm (0.2) ((swallows))
>the people that came up with all this stuff
an
I didn't come up with any of it.<
I didn't do any of the packaging
and
```

```
I didn't think of the products.
.hhh an
```

Note the emphasis on 'independent' (not the same company who makes the hair products), and note the repetition in the description of what the moderator did not do. All of this is cashed out with the following upshot:

```
BASically what that means is >I don't care
what you're saying.<
```

This might seem overdone and redundant. But this is an unfamiliar environment for the participants, who might well be confused about the relation of the moderator to the product ideas. We can hypothesise that experienced moderators who run groups week in and week out have a strong sense of what confusions can arise and how they can be reduced.

The management of stance and interest is not only addressed with this rhetorically formatted contrast, it is also handled in the detail of the descriptive language. Part of this is the use of pro-terms. The 'company' whose 'ideas' are to be discussed is 'they' (lines 1, 2, 3, 6 and 7); that is, not 'we', 'our' or similar pro-terms that would link the moderator and the products. One of the roles of pro-terms is the delineation of stake and stance. Another aspect is FGM's descriptive categories for the products – 'all this stuff' (line 15), for example, can be heard as somewhat distancing and dismissive, particularly in the context of the series of denials of involvement. The 'all this' displays a lack of care of discrimination and 'stuff' is a category that displays a lack of concern or precision or knowledge and projects the more explicit psychological disclaimer that follows.

In terms of DP, and particularly theme 1, what we are seeing here is the moderator managing her displayed stance on what will be talked about: she is indifferent to whether it is seen as positive or negative. This is stated explicitly, and in extrematised form on line 24:

```
it doesn't make .hh any difference to me at all.
```

By using the extreme formulation the moderator displays her investment in the claim (cf. Edwards, 2000). This builds on the earlier formulation (lines 18–19), 'I don't care what you're saying.' That is, she does not have a stake in it, and will not have an adverse reaction to criticism of the products.

In terms of a broader DP of institutions (theme 6) the moderator is constructing her role as indifferent to participant assessments of products, packaging and so on. In interaction terms, participants will not need to be cautious about assessments (they can be 'rude' or 'complimentary' – lines 21, 23) and they should not expect moderator turns such as affiliations or accounts, or displays of upset in relation to these assessments. The moderator is thus working to deactivate the pervasive stake and interest orientation of the participants and constructing her relation to the product as formal and organisational rather than personal and invested.

2. Moderator knowledge

One of the basic features of human life is that people are treated as knowing things. People show what they know in what they say in a range of more or less explicit and inexplicit ways. Constructionist and discourse researchers have highlighted the different ways in which descriptions are accomplished as literal and credible (Potter, 1996); conversation analysts have been more focused on rights and responsibilities of epistemics and the way they are bound up with the interaction order (Heritage and Raymond, 2005). These two themes have a range of overlaps (see Hutchby and Wooffitt, 1998: ch. 8).

Epistemics are involved in market research focus groups in a wide range of different ways. One feature we highlighted in our previous work is the importance of the participants' understanding of the moderator's knowledge for the trajectory of the group. In particular, we noted that asking the moderator questions about the product can cause problems. Apart from generating a possible problem for any participants who might disagree with moderator claims, this unhelpfully moves the focus away from participant to moderator views. We suggested that moderators tend to construct themselves as experts on market research but somewhat naive about, or at least uninterested in, the product itself.

We are not going to devote much space to it here. However, note that the various components of the introduction that manage stance and stake do a double duty in also showing an appropriate lack of knowledge of the product. Not working with the company, or coming up with ideas, suggests an apt lack of knowledge of their nature and detail. Likewise descriptive formulations such as 'all this stuff' (line 15) are outsiders descriptions, avoiding any strong familiarity or concern. And the moderator's characterisation of being given all her ideas to 'trot round the country' (line 9) with avoids presupposing familiarity or understanding.

In general, then, the moderator is managing her knowledgeability (theme 1) and in doing so contributing to an interactional organisation in which she is unlikely to be asked about the nature of the product (theme 6).

3.   *Displaying informality*

So far we have focused on the management of psychological implications and the way in which the institutional organisation of focus groups is produced. We can also consider the role of the moderator's psychological display in generating appropriate interaction in the group. Before we do that there are some things it will be helpful to clarify.

In Puchta and Potter (2004) we distinguish between two broad kinds of accounts. On the one hand, there are accounts that offer descriptions – 'this mousse works well *as it is not sticky*'; on the other, there are accounts that focus on epistemic issues and particularly limitations of claims – 'I find it hard to judge this mousse as *I have not used it much*'. Descriptions are often what moderators are after, and may be encouraged using a range of practices. In contrast, epistemic accounts are typically unhelpful and unwanted – we found that they are treated as 'account clutter' to be headed off if at all possible.

How can the moderator generate an environment that encourages descriptions but discourages epistemic account clutter? Part of what the moderator does is offer a formulation of how the interaction should unfold: 'don't be polite' (line 32) and 'argue' (line 34). However, she also works to generate an environment that discourages account clutter through her style of speech and lexical choices. Although we know that this moderator starts her other groups in a very similar way the opening sounds spontaneous as if she is making it up as she goes along (certainly not learned or recited). Note also the use of idiomatic and slang terms ('trot round the country', 'all this stuff'), and informal enunciation ('kin've', 'o' them', 'cuz', 'kay').

Our general point is that the moderator encourages informality not only by telling the participants that they need not act formally (they don't need to be polite, they can argue) but by *displaying* her own stance to the interaction as informal and not rule bound. Such a display is not dramatic like the shouting of anger or the sobbing of extreme upset. However, it is perfectly suited to the practical task of generating what we might colloquially call a relaxed atmosphere and what we might more technically describe in terms of lexical choice, delivery and accountability.

4.   *POBAs and the mental lexicon*

The American market researcher Naomi Henderson coined the acronym POBA for the Perceptions, Opinions, Beliefs and Attitudes that focus groups are intended to study (Henderson, 1991). On the face of it this is a rather odd collection of psychological objects. Opinions,

Table 6.1

Desires	Actions	Mental objects
want (lines 1, 23, 26)	complimentary (line 23) rude (line 21) polite (line 32) argue (line 34)	thinking (line 6) ideas (line 9, 11) think (line 10, 17, 26) opinions (line 31)

attitudes, perceptions and beliefs are all terms that have a somewhat uneasy dual life in everyday technical social science settings. Moreover, if we consider the literature on focus group moderation and analysis it is not hard to make the list longer – thoughts, feelings, instincts, views, and more. Maybe POBATFIV is a less snappy acronym.

A more traditional psychological perspective would treat these terms as objects of study that are mentally encoded, or at least psychologically bounded in some way. The DP approach here is to bracket off any putative referential specificity of these terms – they may or may not refer to mental objects of some kind, in more or less technical or everyday practices. Instead it is concerned with the practical use of terms from the mental lexicon.

If we examine extract 1 we can see a range of terms that might conventionally be treated as psychological in the sense that they are words for desires, mental objects or actions. As a first analytic move we can loosely categorise them (see table 6.1).

However, this exercise suggests a neatness of the separation of these categories and of psychological and non-psychological words that becomes hard to justify when we consider the specifics of this talk. For instance, given much of lines 1–10 is describing what the commissioning company does, and much of 11–17 is describing what the moderator does, and much of 18–38 is describing what the participants should do; it is not is not clear that the specific words should be treated as psychological. It would be possible to consider in detail the literary construction of the commissioning company, and the role of this construction in the practice of moderation. A central element in the DP project is considering how descriptions are organised to perform practices. However, given the space, let us just concentrate on the terms for mental objects.

Thinking. The term thinking here could not easily be taken as a simple cognitive referent given its application to a rather loosely specified commissioning company. The term works well in this context to specify something like a loose plan or objective that may not come to fruition. Also, thinking suggests something conceptual and creative, thought up.

Crucially, it presents the work that has gone into the materials that the focus group participants will discuss as being provisional. It therefore presents the participants' task as appropriately important – thinking is something that can be changed.

Ideas. The word 'ideas' complements 'thinking', of course. Again, it would be hard to take 'ideas' here as having a simple cognitive referent. They are treated as objects that can be given to the moderator and shown to group members. This notion too suggests conceptual content. It too suggests something that is provisional and can be changed. This again constructs the role of the participants as practical and appropriate – they are involved in a process that can influence something.

Think. The word 'think' is used in two different ways here. The use on line 17 ('I didn't think of the products') is similar to 'thinking' above. The point here is the moderator stressing her non-involvement, particularly her non-involvement with the creation of the products. The occurrences on lines 10 and 26 are classic POBA uses. That is, the moderator is after 'what you think' of the products. 'Think' is nicely open – it can involve evaluations, but is not restricted to that. Moreover, it is not necessarily something that has to be worked at or calculated or assessed (although it does not exclude that). Although 'what you think' appears a very open request it is interesting to consider what it nevertheless discourages. One of the features of POBA questions that we identified in our broader analysis was that they are not easy to respond to in two ways that are very troublesome in focus groups, namely with 'don't knows' or with questions for the moderator. It seems to be hard not to have any thought about something, and thoughts are personal in a way that means the moderator should not be expected to improve on them. So if we think about 'think' in terms of a relatively open generation of responses, which nevertheless heads off some problem responses, we can see its practical value in the setting.

Opinions. This is another classic POBA term. The term 'opinion' perhaps suggests a more developed or more publicly stated position than 'think', although the *Oxford English Dictionary* (1989 edn) defines the former in terms of the latter: 'what one thinks or how one thinks about something'. The definition highlights an aspect of 'opinion' that is particularly relevant here: 'resting on grounds insufficient for complete demonstration'. That suggests something that by definition is not fully accountable. It is talk that participants can offer with less threat of being asked to provide a full justification (see Myers, 2004, for an extended and highly pertinent discussion of opinion talk in the context of focus groups). Put another way, opinions provide a sympathetic frame for participants to offer a range of their own 'views' (thoughts, perceptions, etc.). Characterising participants' talk in this way encourages its production. There is a further element to this. POBA talk, including opinion talk, is typically presented by moderators as something straightforward. POBAs are items that can be delivered immediately – they do not have to be worked out. We will develop this below. However, even in this extract we can see the moderator working up the task as easy and uncomplicated. Note the way the moderator ends this package of instructions with this emphasis on the task for the participants being straightforward (line 38).

What we have tried to do in this discussion is highlight four different ways in which psychology plays a practical and interactional role in the work of focus group moderation. While these have picked up theme 1 (the psychological implications of talk), theme 2 (the psychological thesaurus) and theme 4 (the display or embodiment of psychology), taken together they contribute to the emerging interest in the way psychological practices are partly constitutive of institutional practices. In the next section we will develop this analysis.

Thought in practice

The following extract comes from about fourteen minutes into the group, after the moderator has spent a bit of time with an exercise learning the participants' names (F6.2 etc. mark the position of the figures).

Extract 2: Hair products: first thoughts

```
1 FGM:      The result is astonishing.=with new organics
            ((F6.2))
2           styling elixir, .hh you'll have perfect control
3           with only a few drops, but no one will know you've
4           used a °↓styling produ:ct.°
5           (1.4)
6 FGM:      So.  ((FGM scans group))
7           (2.2)((FGM scans group))
8 FGM:      ↑First thou:ghts on that.
9 Ann:      What- what is it.
10          (0.2)
11 Ann:     Is it a gel, (0.2) or a (.) mou:sse, or a
12          (1.0)
13 Liz:     'Tsa [new prod]uct.=
14 Ann:          [Jsst a- ]
15 Ann:     =New:- [ a new hair ] right.=A new product.
16 Liz:            [huh huh huh]
17 Peg:     T'jsst like a spray is it.
18          ((40 seconds omitted))
19 FGM:     Others' ther- ↑first ↑thoughts?=Ella ↑first
```

```
20                  ↑thoughts ↑on ↑this?
21                  (0.2)
22 Ella:    Mghm* (0.4) w'll my fir:st thou:ght when it
            ((F6.3))
23          said you could use a few drops is (0.3) yeah.
24          ri:ght.
25                  (0.2)
26 Ella:    Ahh↑[uhh!(0.3)                     ]
27 Various:     [((quiet laughter))]
28                  (0.3)
29 Ella:    Cos when- ye know when you get- read the back of
30          the mousse thing and it says do a little golf
            ((F6.4))
31          ball. An you get this (a[mazing) (3.0)]
            ((F6.5))
32 Various:                         [ ((Loud laughter)) ]
33 FGM:     >H↑uh h↑uh< using a nhetball's whorth.
34 Ella:    Yheah [exhactlyh. H↑ah.h       ]
35 FGM:         [>h ↑uh h↑uh h↑uh h↑uh<]
36 Ella:    .hh I'm like ↑mm. .hh er:m (0.3) so a few
37          drops: [ was my     ] fir:st thought. and the
38 FGM:            [((coughs))]
39 Ella:    second one w's .hh (0.4) if it's soft to the
40          touch an doesn't look like you've °used a styling
41          product,° (0.5) °then how° (0.2) °can it work.°
42 FGM:     Mh[m:? ]
43 Ella:      [(°Ma]ke) se:nse.° [(I m'n)]
44 FGM:                          [Yeh?   ]
45                  (0.4)
            ((* marks FGM clearing throat))
```

There is a lot going on in this sequence. What we will do is take up DP themes 2 and 4 and develop them further with material that offers more participant uptake, and therefore a possibly more nuanced analytic purchase. Let us start with some brief further comments on theme 4, psychological display, and move on to a more detailed consideration of theme 2, the psychological thesaurus.

Reading as psychological display

We have already noted something that might be glossed as 'informality' as one kind of 'psychological display'. Another sort of display comes in the first four lines of extract 2. The moderator is doing reading. That is, she is using a recognisable reading inflection. This goes along with her holding up a board on which the product description is written (figure 6.2 suggests that at least some of the participants can read the

Figure 6.2 Moderator reads 'astonishing'

description that FGM is reading out). The combination of board and inflection makes it very clear that the moderator is reporting something rather than offering her own opinions of the product. As we have noted above, showing that they are naive with respect to, and independent from, the product is something that helps establish the characteristic organisational pattern of a market research focus group.

Up to now this phenomenon has been understood using Goffman's different footing categories (Goffman, 1981 – for interactional approaches to reported speech see Holt, 1996; Wooffitt, 1992). One thing that this very emphatic display of reading does is present the words uttered as not those of the speaker, who acts as relayer of views rather than origin. The management of footing, then, is inter alia the management of the speaker's own involvement and accountability. By using the reading voice and the board the moderator makes it clear that she is not responsible for the words. This heads off problem actions such as asking her about their meaning or quality. More broadly it reproduces the important moderator distinction between marketing expertise and product naivety.

First thoughts, gestures, and the psychological thesaurus

We have noted above that 'think' is one of the typical POBA terms that are used in focus groups. The term 'thoughts' is closely related to this (the *OED* has an item of mental activity, a thing that is in mind, an idea or notion). Let us make a few observations about the moderator's use of 'thoughts' and the participants' uptake.

First, note what happens before the first use in the extract (and the group) in line 8. The moderator ends the reading from the card by putting the card down, pausing and then saying 'so' with terminal intonation. At the same time she scans the group. All of this seems to suggest that some contribution on the part of the group members is being encouraged – although none is forthcoming. It is after further delay that the moderator asks for 'first thoughts on that', which generates an immediate response.

We have already suggested that moderators treat POBA items as things that can be delivered immediately. In this case, the construction '*first* thoughts' highlights this immediacy – what is wanted is not 'thought through', calculated, or refined. Furthermore, the emphasis on *first* thoughts may generate a particularly safe environment for responding as any item offered need be defended as only a first thought.

If we consider what the participants' offer there are a number of interesting features of lines 8–17. Ann starts with something that has the grammatical form of a question, although it is not delivered with questioning intonation, nor is it answered (directly). Liz's contribution on line 13 superficially seems like an answer – however, the emphasis on 'new' suggests more a collaborative 'reasoning' about the product from the description. The request for 'first thoughts', then, generates questions and observations about the product's nature. The moderator lets this run for some time, thereby treating it as appropriate for the research task.

After this interaction appears to run down and become repetitive the moderator repeats the first thoughts request, this time specifying first 'others' in general (that is, members who have not contributed), and then selecting a particular group member, Ella, who has not yet contributed to this particular discussion.

```
Others' ther- ↑first ↑thoughts?=Ella ↑first
↑thoughts ↑on ↑this?
```

It is not clear from the video if Ella has shown signs of wishing to contribute that the FGM has picked up. Whatever the case, having been specifically selected by the moderator, she works up to an elaborate response. This is beautifully complex and prefaced with a clear orientation to the 'first thought' construction of the question:

```
w'll my fir:st thou:ght when it said
you could use a few drops is (0.3)
yeah. ri:ght.
```

Ella specifies the particular element of the description (note 'when it said' not 'when you said', showing the success of the moderator's footing management) and characterises her first thought as an ironic agreement (i.e., a disagreement). The irony is delivered hearably through the intonational contour. Note that Ella follows it on line 26 with an extended and inflected laughter particle which sets off quiet laughter across the group. It may be that, although the irony was clear, the action Ella was doing with it was not yet so – it might have been complaining, for example, for which laughter would have been inappropriate. Ella's own laughter, therefore, acted as a guide.

Ella then explicates her ironic response to the 'few drops' description by reporting what happens with mousse. This is presented in scripted terms as something that happens in a standard way. The description starts verbally with 'it says do a little golf ball' and is followed through with an expansive circular gesture. This occasions loud laughter from the group members, and the moderator follows the laughter with a formulation of the sense of the gesture as 'using a netball's worth'. (We can speculate that the moderator may formulate the sense of non-verbal elements of the interaction such as this to clarify them to the research users whose video record provides only a restricted view.) Ella agrees with the FGM's formulation and both laugh. Figures 6.3–6.5 illustrate this. Figure 6.3 is where Ella is saying 'first thought'. Figure 6.4 is where she is saying 'little golf ball' – she is making a small shape in her palm with the fingers of her other hand. Then figure 6.5 shows part of the expansive circular gesture as if she has a very large ball on her lap – this still accompanies the word 'amazing'.

We have spent a bit of time on Ella's contribution here as it shows the value and flexibility of asking for 'thoughts' in this setting. Ella offers a precisely constructed description of a problem with mousse specifically raised by part of the blurb read by the moderator. She characterises this as her first thought, developing it with a non-vocal, but highly intelligible, enactment, receipted by the moderator, who both shows her shared understanding of what Ella is saying and showing and makes the sequence more clearly intelligible to the production workers who are watching behind the one-way mirror and who will watch the video of the interaction.

Some social psychologists have suggested that gesture is a form of 'visible thought' (Beattie, 2004). What we see here is a combination of talk and gesture being used to satisfy the request for a 'first thought'. Whether any of this was or even could be 'going on in Ella's mind' at the moment of hearing the product blurb, it is deftly appropriate to the work of the focus group when it is delivered. The gesture, the words and the 'first thought' are all part of a public and intelligible piece of interaction. Although psychologists and market researchers might treat POBAs as

Figure 6.3 'First thought'

Figure 6.4 'Little golf ball'

Figure 6.5 'Amazing'

mental entities of one kind or another, and although it may be a practical shorthand to do so for some purposes, perhaps the design of new forms of hair mousse, the POBA language is working here *precisely* because of its public and visible nature.

Practices of moderation and psychology

In this chapter we have documented a number of ways in which psychology and discourse are inextricably bound together. It has attempted to explicate psychology from an interactional perspective. This has involved remained agnostic with respect to the nature, status or absence of psychological states and entities enclosed within any of the participants. Instead the focus has been on how 'psychological' phenomena are live in the practices we see here.

Theme 1 – psychological implications

We have shown how the moderator manages the psychological implications of her talk, in particular she constructs a uninterested stance on the product, stressing her lack of stake in its origins, quality or success. At the same time she constructs her knowledgeability carefully, emphasising her knowledge of market research procedures but her lack of knowledge of the product itself.

Theme 2 – the psychological thesaurus

We explored the way the moderator uses a range of items from the psychological thesaurus, in particular the way she uses POBA terms in questions for the participants. Our analysis focused on *think, opinions,* and *first thoughts*. These items can be parts of questions that are hard not to not respond to – they are items that participants should be their own expert on, and they are less susceptible to discounting as flawed than factual or knowledge items. They are also relatively open items – although they tend not to occasion 'account clutter', they occasion a range of descriptions including, loosely speaking, features such as questions, observations and non-vocal displays.

Theme 4 – psychological display and embodiment

We considered the way the moderator displayed her psychological state. We illustrated this both with the moderator's construction of informality and with her footing as the relayer of others' views. Both of these displays have practical consequences for conduct within the group – the displayed informality encourages participation but discourages account clutter; the footing as relayer sustains the separation of moderator from company, making it clear that personal views are not being delivered. Note that this psychological display is in the service of producing the normative organisation of the market research focus group; we are not suggesting that there is some specific feature of this moderator. Rather, the psychological displays are generic features of producing the organisation.

Theme 5 – research methods in practice

The analysis of this chapter has further specified the specific procedures through which different elements of focus groups are produced. In particular it has considered the way psychological terms, orientations and constructions are drawn on in the practices of the group. As we noted above, we have developed this interest with these materials much more elsewhere. This blurs into theme 6.

Theme 6 – discursive psychology and institutional organisation

One of the things we have tried to do here is show the way that psychological terms and orientations are drawn on to produce the distinctive business of the setting. In this case, the management of stance, interest and knowledgeability, the displays of informality and 'just reading', and the use of POBA language (opinions, thoughts) are all coordinated together to generate the distinctive structural organisation of the focus group.

Let us end this chapter with some general observations about the nature of psychology and the applied potential of work of this kind. First, psychology. What we have tried to do here is highlight how psychology and interaction may come together. That is, we have tried to explicate the way phenomena that are traditionally thought of as psychological – motive, knowledge, ideas and so on – are parts of interaction. This is what is distinctive in discursive psychology – it focuses on the way these things are part of discourse practices rather than how they are individual or mental objects. What we have done here is just the briefest sketch of the range of discursive psychology themes and how they might come together in one setting. Each would be the stimulus to a full study.

With respect to application, we have written extensively on this topic elsewhere (Puchta and Potter, 2004). One of the things we noted in previous work was that the stipulations in how-to-do-it manuals for focus group moderators were sometimes out of line with the practices of highly skilled moderators. For example, although manuals may emphasise that moderator questions ought to be simple and one-dimensional, in practice a range of elaborations was used, particularly in topic initial questions (Puchta and Potter, 1999). For reasons of this kind, we suggested that application might be more effective if it took examples of good practice and attempted to explicate their operation. This might allow moderators to take a more strategic approach to their actions. In effect, we were hoping that moderators could turn practices into strategies (see Hepburn, 2006 for further discussion of this approach). Note that in this case, focus group researchers might offer a more depth or psychodynamic approach to 'first thoughts' that would emphasise irrational dynamics or subjective meanings. First thoughts might be treated as relatively uncontaminated by rationalisation or social processes, for example. Our analysis does not show such classically psychological interpretations to be wrong – it is precisely and systematically agnostic to such things as its starting position (Potter and Edwards, 2003). However, it does offer a more interactionally guided account of what POBA constructions of this kind may be doing and ultimately studies that highlight conversational pragmatics in this way may raise challenging questions for cognitive or psychodynamic accounts (Edwards, 1997).

Our interest here has been rather different. If there is an applied focus to this chapter it is a critical one. We have highlighted the limitations of individual and cognitive understandings of psychology in favour of understandings that are interactional and jointly constructed. Its use is a positive and negative one, cautioning against particular kinds of psychological picture and offering an image of psychology in practice that is dynamic and collaborative.

Part II

Professionals and clients

7 When patients present serious health conditions as unlikely: managing potentially conflicting issues and constraints

Anita Pomerantz, Virginia Teas Gill and Paul Denvir

Introduction

Patients not only describe their symptoms during medical visits, they frequently present possible explanations for those symptoms (Gill, 1995, 1998; Raevaara, 1998, 2000; Stivers, 2002; Gill et al., 2004; Gill and Maynard, 2006). Although patients often display uncertainty about their candidate explanations (Gill, 1998), they typically portray them as reasonable, and at least somewhat likely, possibilities. For this study, we analysed instances in which patients offered serious health conditions (a heart problem, appendicitis) as candidate explanations for symptoms and portrayed those candidate explanations as unlikely to be the case, as improbable, while also implicitly or explicitly directing the doctors to investigate and confirm that they were indeed improbable.

This study is part of a larger project of analysing the range of practices that patients use when they present medically serious conditions as candidate explanations. For this project, we examined a subset of those practices: those used on occasions in which a patient presented a serious health condition as an unlikely candidate explanation. We selected this phenomenon because we were intrigued by the following observations:

1. Patients did not simply raise the spectre of serious health conditions as candidate explanations; they spent considerable effort displaying sceptical stances toward those candidate explanations, often by presenting reports that served as evidence for the improbability of the candidate explanations. We wondered what potentially conflicting issues and constraints the displays of scepticism were designed to address and how the discourse was designed to deal with those issues and constraints.

2. In each of the instances, patients used rather elaborate packaging to raise the 'unlikely' serious health conditions. In two instances the

patients offered extended narratives, and in two instances the patients presented other less serious health conditions as additional candidate explanations. We wondered what issues and constraints the elaborate packaging was designed to address and how the discourse was designed to deal with those issues and constraints.

3. In each instance, the patient designed his/her presentation with either some ambiguity about, or minimisation of, how much concern he or she was experiencing. Additionally, patients sometimes shifted their stance with respect to how much concern they claimed or displayed. We wondered what interactional tasks were accomplished with the modulated claims and displays of emotion.

4. As mentioned in point 1, each patient spent considerable effort in portraying the candidate explanation as unlikely, or even quite unlikely. One inference that the doctor could have drawn was that a highly unlikely candidate explanation, one just about ruled out, would not warrant his or her attention. However, we observed that each patient succeeded, if not on the first try then on a second, to direct the doctor's attention to consider and/or address the candidate explanation. We wondered what strategies the patients used to direct the doctors' attention to the candidate explanations.

Our central claim is that the ways in which patients presented the 'unlikely' serious candidate explanations for confirmation were designed to deal with a number of potentially conflicting issues and constraints.[1]

The patients presented serious health conditions as unlikely candidate explanations by reporting that particular symptoms they experienced were atypical of the serious health condition and/or by reporting that symptoms associated with the serious health condition were absent. They incorporated their presentations in sequences and turns which were designed to address a number of potential conflicting issues and constraints that attend this type of activity:

1. Presenting the serious medical condition as a possibility *while also* presenting oneself as a sensible person who does not immediately embrace worst-case scenarios;[2]

2. Presenting oneself as able to make sense of one's symptoms and reason about the likelihood of possible explanations *while also* exhibiting an orientation toward patients' and doctors' differential rights to claim medical expertise;

3. Directing the doctor's attention to investigating and reporting on the serious medical condition *while also* portraying the candidate explanation as quite unlikely, which carries the implication that it need not be investigated.

Data

We reviewed thirty-five videotaped medical consultations in two collections. The first collection contains consultations conducted in the early 1990s at an ambulatory clinic associated with a teaching hospital in a large city in the eastern United States. The second set contains consultations from the early 2000s in a Family Medicine practice associated with a medical centre in a mid-size city in the eastern United States. Among those thirty-five cases, seventeen patients raised at least one candidate explanation, explicitly and/or implicitly, about at least one of their medical complaints. Within these, we identified three clear instances in which a patient sought confirmation that some reported symptoms were not associated with a serious medical condition.

Analysis

For each of the three consultations examined below, we first discuss the discursive practices that the patient used in presenting a serious medical condition as an unlikely candidate explanation. We then analyse how the practices represent at least partial solutions to conflicting issues and constraints operating in that local context.

Consultation 1

The patient was an African American woman in her early fifties; the doctor was a young white male resident. Although the patient had a regular doctor at the medical centre, on this occasion she sought medical care from the same-day clinic at the medical centre. In response to the doctor's request for the reason for the visit, the patient described two complaints: pressure in her lower stomach and pains in her chest. After describing the symptoms associated with pressure in her lower stomach, she presented several candidate explanations, including appendicitis, which she framed as improbable. A bit later in the consultation, the patient raised appendicitis as a candidate explanation a second time.

Patient's first presentation of appendicitis as a candidate explanation

How the patient created an opportunity to raise candidate explanations The patient offered a series of candidate explanations in an early phase of the visit: in the slot provided by the doctor's soliciting her reason for the visit and after she presented the symptoms associated with her first complaint. In response to the doctor's solicitation of the medical complaint (lines 1–2), the patient described a symptom, pressure in her lower stomach, which she claimed was severe enough to hinder normal walking (lines 3–7). She then offered another symptom, a little stinging when she urinated (lines 11–12), which is a symptom commonly associated with a bladder infection. In that interactional environment, the patient offered 'bladder condition' as a first of several candidate explanations (lines 14–15).

Consultation 1a

```
 1 Doc:   Uh why- wh:y are you um at the clinic today=what seems
 2        to be the [problem.]
 3 Pt:             [(W'll) I] ha- I have this pressure in my uh
 4        lowuh stomach,
 5        (1.0)
 6 Pt:    And uh: slightly (stiff) I cain't (0.7) you know (.)
 7        (kinda) can't hardly walk like I shou:ld.
 8 Doc:   Mm hmm,
 9 Pt:    You know,
10        (1.0)
11 Pt:    When I go to ba:throom (um) uh (1.7) it's u:h (1.5)
12        (like/that) stings a little,
13 Doc:   °Mm [ hmm°    ]
14 Pt:        [(And uh)] (1.0) it may be a bladder
15        condition=I've had dat before,
16 Doc:   You've had that [bef- (tha]t's)
17 Pt:                   [An' then ]
18        (0.7)
19 Pt:    I thought it was my appe:ndix=I (don't/wouldn't) know
20        I d- guess (I) wouldna' la:st this long=I woulda' h-
21        had (0.2) woulda' had tuh be here before now.
22        (0.2)
23 Pt:    I don' know=an' den .hh I hadda' lot of ga::s.
24 Doc:   °Mm [hmm°]
25 Pt:        [You] know but it's (0.2) seem to be die:in'
26        down >but I m-< I still have this pai:n inna lower
27        s:tomach.
28 Doc:   Right.
29 Pt:    An it's severe,=you see how the walkin'
30 Doc:   Mm h[mm]
31 Pt:        [ H ]mm .hh
32        (.)
33 Pt:    An' u:m den I had uh pains in my chest
```

In partial overlap with the doctor's acknowledgement of, and display of interest in, the patient's report of the history of bladder condition (line 16), the patient presented a second candidate explanation, appendix, along with reports of circumstances that argued against its likelihood (lines 17–21). The presentation of this candidate explanation is our focus here. In getting no audible response during a brief gap (0.2 seconds) in line 22, the patient commented on appendix as a candidate explanation ('I don' know' in line 23) and then implicitly presented a third candidate explanation, gas.

How the patient raised the candidate explanation while orienting to potentially conflicting issues and constraints   Immediately following the description of her symptoms and before presenting appendicitis, the patient framed bladder condition as a likely possibility and one that was not particularly worrisome (lines 14–15).[3] The practice of presenting multiple candidate explanations, including at least one for non-serious medical conditions, can be seen as a solution to the potentially conflicting concerns of presenting a serious medical condition as a possibility *while also* presenting oneself as a sensible person who does not immediately embrace worst-case scenarios. Had the patient presented 'appendix' as her first or only candidate explanation, it might have been interpreted as her viewing appendicitis as a likely explanation. Hence she might have risked being seen as obsessed with a worst-case scenario (Halkowski, 2006). In this case, the patient presented herself as a person who was not obsessed with the worst-case scenario by raising the likely and less serious explanation of a bladder infection prior to presenting the possibility of appendicitis.

The patient displayed some scepticism about the candidate diagnosis, appendicitis. The patient distanced herself from appendicitis in several ways. First, she presented it as a past thought ('I thought it was my appe:ndix' in line 19), and hence took a less committed stance than she would have had she reported it as a current thought. More importantly, she provided evidence that argued against the explanation. She reported two aspects of her experience with the symptom that provided grounds for its improbable status: the duration of the pain was longer than the duration expected for appendicitis ('wouldna' la:st this long' in line 20) and the level of pain was not as severe as would have been expected for appendicitis ('I woulda' h- had (0.2) woulda' had tuh be here before now' in lines 20–21). In producing these grounds for the improbable status, the patient displayed herself as somewhat knowledgeable about appendicitis, at least with respect to expected duration and severity of pain.

The patient presented herself as able to reason about the likelihood of appendicitis *while also* displaying an orientation to the parties' differential rights regarding medical expertise.[4] When the patient presented appendicitis, she offered it as a report of a 'thought' and followed that with a claim of uncertainty, through which she positioned herself as less committed to it as a possibility: 'And then (0.7) I thought it was my appe:ndix I don't know' (lines 17–19). When she offered a reason for the improbability of 'appendix,' she marked it as merely a guess: 'I d-guess it wouldna' la:st this long.' (lines 19–20). When she offered a further reason for the improbability, she again added a claim of uncertainty: 'woulda' had tuh be here before now. (0.2) I don' know.' (lines 20–23). By presenting the candidate explanations as a matter of uncertainty, the patient displayed her orientation both to the doctor's entitlement, and to her lack of entitlement, to claim medical expertise.[5]

Even though the patient portrayed the candidate explanation as unlikely, which might have implied that it need not be investigated, the patient directed the doctor's attention toward investigating it. The displayed uncertainty may be a way to prompt the doctor to attend to the likelihood of that candidate explanation in order to reduce the patient's uncertainty. In addition to possibly directing the doctor's attention through the use of uncertainty markers, the patient employed a second practice for directing his attention. She narrated a sequence of symptom experiences that implied that she considered *gas* as yet another candidate explanation that she then ruled out.[6] In ruling out this benign candidate explanation, the patient implicitly directed the doctor to consider explanations other than gas for her symptoms (Gill, et al., 2004).

How the doctor responded to the patient's candidate explanation   The doctor responded to the patient's presentation of appendicitis in a noticeably different way than he responded to the patient's presentations of the other candidate explanations. While the patient was raising bladder condition as a candidate explanation and was reporting her history with the condition, the doctor engaged in large, slow nods. The nods seem to indicate that the doctor was considering, and perhaps supporting, a bladder problem as a possible cause. The doctor marked the patient's history with the condition as potentially significant by partially repeating it in line 16 ('You 've had that bef-'). When the patient raised appendicitis as a candidate explanation and presented evidence that implied it was unlikely, the doctor performed two sets of small, quick nods. These nods appear to be minimal acknowledgements, registering receipt of the patient's report and encouraging her to continue. When the patient raised gas as a candidate explanation and ruled it out, the doctor engaged in larger, slower nods and verbally acknowledged the patient's report with "Right" (line 28).

The patient could have read the doctor's differential employment of either large, slow nods accompanied by verbal acknowledgements or small, quick nods with no verbal acknowledgements as revealing a different level of receptivity to the various candidate explanations she raised. By responding with large, slow nods and verbal acknowledgements to bladder condition as a likely cause and to gas as an unlikely cause, the doctor conveyed receptivity to the patient's presentations of those candidate explanations. In contrast, the doctor's small, quick nods were ambiguous or non-committal regarding the doctor's receptivity. Given the doctor's ambiguous or noncommittal reception to the patient's presentation of appendicitis as a candidate explanation. the patient might not have known whether or not the doctor would attend to appendicitis as a possible diagnosis as he gathered diagnostically relevant information.

Patient's second presentation of appendicitis as a candidate explanation

How the patient created an opportunity to re-raise the candidate explanation   After the patient presented 'pressure in her lower stomach' and 'pains in her chest' as two problems for which she sought medical attention (Consultation 1a, lines 3–4, 33), the doctor set the agenda by proposing that they discuss each medical problem separately (not shown here). He began closed-ended symptom queries related to pressure in her lower stomach. In asking about symptoms related to urination (see below), the doctor seemed to have been investigating the possibility of a bladder infection, as urination problems are associated with bladder infections. In lines 82–4, it appeared that the doctor was moving to close the line of inquiry tied to a possible bladder infection. In the interactional environment of the doctor's apparently closing his inquiries associated with the pressure in her lower stomach and possibly moving to inquiries related to chest pain, the patient, with no gap, jumped in to again present appendicitis as a candidate explanation (line 85).

Consultation 1b

```
75 Doc:  .hh U:h (0.2) any burning when you urinate?
76       (1.0)
77 Pt:   M:aybe a little (   )
78       (1.0)
79 Pt:   Maybe (   ) (0.2) I don' know.
80       (0.5)
81 Pt:   until I (1.0) (s'posed to) u:rinate in a cup like
81       [an' ] 'en they take the [uh]
82 Doc:  [Yeah]                   [Ye]ah I- I'll take a look at
83       your urine i- in a little bit and we'll see if that's
84       what's (.) what's goin' on=
85 Pt:   =I jus' hope it wasn't no appendix.
```

```
86 Doc:  Okay.=
89 Pt:   =Was what I was worried [about. ]
90 Doc:                          [Tha- th]at seems to be your
91       major concern whether (.) whether
92       it's [an appendix.]
93 Pt:        [(              ]    )
94 Doc:  [°Yeah°]
95 Pt:   [An' I ] had uh (0.2) cesarian (.) too=
96 Doc:  =°Mm hmm°
97 Pt:   With eight children
98 Doc:  °Okay° (.) well we'll- we'll sort it out when I examine
         you we'll see uh (.) u:h (0.5) i- if that's a
99       possibility
```

How the patient re-raised the candidate explanation while orienting to potentially conflicting issues and constraints   While on the first occasion the patient framed appendicitis as 'improbable', on the second occasion she focused on expressing emotions of concern and worry, using a combination of past and present tense in describing the emotions. In reporting her worries and concerns ('I jus' hope it wasn't no appendix') to reintroduce appendicitis, she took advantage of her entitlement to know and report her own feelings while respecting the medical expertise and entitlement of the doctor to make diagnoses. Inasmuch as doctors direct their attention to stated concerns and worries of patients, the patient used her right to express her emotions and concerns to reintroduce appendicitis such that the doctor might conduct his medical investigation with that in mind and provide the confirmatory diagnostic assessment that the patient was seeking.[7]

Consultation 2

Patient 2 was a white male in his late thirties or early forties; the doctor was a young white female resident. The patient reported that four or five weeks before the medical visit, he experienced symptoms, including cramping, tightness, burning, a 'gas bubble' sensation, and heartburn, in his chest and back. Through the way he presented his symptoms, he raised the possibility that some of them could portend heart trouble, but in each case he also implied that this was unlikely. Nevertheless, he sought the doctor's confirmation that the symptoms were not indicative of a heart problem.

How the patient created an opportunity to describe a series of symptom incidents that implied candidate explanations   Patient 2 raised the spectre of a heart problem in a sequential place in the consultation that was similar to the place that Patient 1 raised the possibility of appendicitis: in the slot provided by the doctor's soliciting the patient's medical business (Robinson 1998, 2006).

Consultation 2a

```
1 Doc:   Suh c'n yih tell me=little bit about (.)
2        what- brings yih here t'day-
3 Pt:    .hhh Oka:y ah::m tss- (0.3) °tsstory bee-
4        (.)>meen awy-< ih- th' story begins a while
5        ba:ck uh::m
6        (0.3)
7 Doc:   °That's fine,°
8        (0.7)
9 Doc:   °°(Yeh)°°
10 Pt:   Started with::: (.) uh:m (.)>I w'z drinkin'<
11       I drank one a' those power drinks?
```

Whereas the sequential environments were similar, each patient used the slot somewhat differently. Whereas Patient 1 used it as an opportunity to first describe her symptoms and then explicitly present her candidate explanations, among which was appendicitis, Patient 2 used the slot to indicate that he would answer the doctor's question by telling a story (lines 3–5). Once the doctor positioned herself as a recipient ("°That's fine°", line 7), the narrative format gave the patient the opportunity to describe his experiences and inferences over multiple turns without significant interference until he produced the upshot of the story. As we will see, this provided him with a way to introduce material that might otherwise have been difficult to introduce in a question-answer series (Stivers and Heritage 2001), such as his sense-making processes as he experienced and interpreted his various symptoms.

> *How the patient raised the candidate explanation while orienting to potentially conflicting issues and constraints*   The patient narrated three episodes of symptoms. In the first episode, he reported on symptoms that occurred four–five weeks before the consultation. In describing the episode, the patient employed symptom descriptions that implied digestive, muscular and heart problems, and further implied that the latter was unlikely.

Consultation 2b

```
10 Pt:   Started with::: (.) uh:m (.)>I w'z drinkin'<
11       I drank one a' those power drinks?
12       (0.6)
13 Pt:   °Red Bull whatever they are now°
14       (0.3)
```

```
15 Doc:  °Okay,°=
16 Pt:   ah:m that evening (0.3) fih like (.) my:
17       lef' si[:de
18 Doc:        [u-How lon'=go w'z thi[s?
[[lines 19-28 deleted]]
29 Pt:   Uhm I fel' like my lef' side of my (.)
30       chest like a- (.) mah had a k- cramp?
31       (1.0)
32 Pt:   °Here,°
33       (0.4)
34 Pt:   °'n tha' w'z fine it didn' la:st, ih w'z
35       very brief, .hhh Ahm ih >fel' like ih was<
36       (.) un- und- the muscle almos' >fel' like ths<
37       (0.2) ths right here.
38       (0.3)
39 Pt:   °Thet the mu[scles (right) ]
40 Doc:              [Tha' w'z right] after you had
41       the drink?
42 Pt:   Thit- tha' w'z- later on in the evening
```

In linking his symptom temporally to his consumption of a beverage (a 'power drink', lines 10–11), the patient raised the possibility that the digestion of the drink might be at the root of his symptom. However, in identifying (both verbally and through gesture) the location of the symptom as occurring on the left side of his chest, he also raised the potential of heart trouble.[8] Additionally, the patient's characterisation that the symptom felt like a 'cramp' and his report 'It >fel' like ih was< ... the muscle almos' (lines 35–6) suggested overworked muscles in the chest area. Thus, three potential candidate explanations were implied by the patient's symptom descriptions.

The patient offered his assessment of the cramping episode as 'fine' (line 34) and provided evidence for not considering the symptoms worthy of concern: it 'didn' last' and it 'w'z very brief' (lines 34–5). Thus he used the *absence* of a symptom usually associated with a cardiac problem, persisting pain, to explain a lack of concern over that incident. In reporting that the cramp 'didn' last' and 'w'z very brief', he under-scored the potential relevance of a cardiac problem while simultaneously portraying it as unlikely (see Stivers, 2002).[9]

In the second episode within the narrative, the patient reported symptoms in a way that re-raised the spectre of heart trouble (tightness in his chest) and digestive problems (burning on both sides).[10]

Consultation 2c

```
48 Doc:  °°Okay°°
49 Pt:   .hh Uh:m following that over the next (0.2)
```

```
50        uhw week er so (0.3) .hh there was a, a slight
51        tightness: (1.2) in the middle (0.3) my chest,
52        (0.8)
53 Pt:    No pain, (0.3) nothing else
54        (.)
55 Pt:    uh:m .hhh then I noticed on the right, en lef'
56        side right approximately right about here .p.hh
57        slight burning?
58        (0.9)
59 Pt:    But again (.) no pain no pains in the arm no
60        shortness 'v breath
```

Again, the patient portrayed a heart problem as unlikely by reporting
that symptoms typically associated with cardiac problems were absent
('No pain, (0.3) nothing else' in line 53 and 'But again (.) no pain no
pains in the arm no shortness 'v breath' in lines 59–60).

After describing a third episode of symptoms,[11] the patient reported
that he had engaged in extended and vigorous sports activities (lines
73–6) and did not feel any discomfort during it (line 78).

Consultation 2d

```
72 Pt:    But .hh no other symptom' beyon' tha:t uh:m
73        (0.2)I've played, sports I play volley ball
74        (0.3)
75 Pt:    eh: yesterday I played outside doubles fer (.)
76        .hh three hours,
77        (1.0)
78 Pt:    Didn't fleny discomfort, (.) during tha:t,
79        (0.2)
80 Doc:   Okay,
```

The patient provided further evidence against the likelihood of a heart
problem by reporting the outcome of these activities, which he later
characterised as a test: exercising strenuously did not cause any discomfort, as it would have had he had a heart problem (line 78).

Several practices incorporated as part of the patient's presentation may
be seen as solutions to potentially conflicting issues and constraints. First,
in describing the various episodes of symptoms that he experienced, the
patient implied he had considered or was considering multiple candidate
explanations, including relatively benign ones (digestive and muscular
problems) in addition to a serious one (heart problem). In doing so, the
patient managed to raise the possibility that his problem could be serious
while also presenting himself as a reasonable person who does not immediately embrace worst-case scenarios (Halkowski, 2006).

Second, in each of his symptom presentations the patient presented
evidence that argued for the improbability of a heart problem. In doing so,

he raised a serious medical condition as a candidate explanation *while also* positioning himself to be seen as sceptical of it and portraying himself as someone who knows what to look for and what to disregard vis-à-vis his symptoms and who can anticipate what might be relevant to the doctor.

Third, in describing the various symptom episodes, the patient implied the serious candidate explanation through reports of symptoms that he experienced (and did not experience), rather than explicitly offering the candidate explanation and/or asserting a causal link. In doing so, the patient presented himself as able to make sense of his symptoms and reason about the likelihood of possible explanations *while also* exhibiting an orientation toward patients' 'entitlement to knowledge in the realm of first-hand experience' and lack of entitlement to reason about the causes of the symptoms (Gill, 1998: 345).

How the patient sought a confirmatory diagnostic assessment while managing potentially conflicting issues and constraints While relating the episodes in his narrative, the patient did not actively seek, or specifically allow opportunities for, the doctor to offer her own view on the cause of his symptoms or indicate whether or not he was correctly interpreting them. However, after reporting his exercise 'test', he shaped his next contribution in a way that tentatively gave the doctor an opportunity to provide a diagnostic assessment. He reported that he had been eating spicy food and was experiencing heartburn that went untreated for lack of medication (lines 83–6). In speculating about a connection between this event and his symptoms ('en I wonder 'f (.) that's part'v (it) er not' in line 88), he made relevant the doctor's confirmation/disconfirmation of the speculated gastro-intestinal cause of his symptoms; however, he did not require it such that it would be hearably absent if not provided (see Gill, 1998; Gill and Maynard, 2006).

Consultation 2e

```
82 Pt:   en it- if it makes a difference (0.7) prior (.)
83        to: (.) even before that I w'z deet'n lots'v
84        uh:m (.) hot stuff (.) 'n getting s'm heartburn,
85        .hh didn' have inning take fer it so ah dis (.)
86        dealt with it.
87        (0.2)
88 Pt:   En I wonder 'f (.) that's pert'v er not but
         (2.1)
90 Pt:   >So 'm 's curious w't-< (.) should I be concerned
91        uh more of a heart? (0.4) [issue?   ]
92 Doc:                            [ih Su:re.]
93        (.)
```

```
94 Doc:  [Sure I]
95 Pt:   [Or  is] it something e:lse,
96       (0.4)
97 Doc:  °Sure wil° (.) Wi'll work through that.
98 Pt:   O[kay]
99 Doc:   [Uh:]:m (0.2) .k.hh °Uh:° number a' questions
100      about (0.2) about yer symptoms
```

The doctor did not respond to the patient's utterance in line 88 as a solicitation, she remained silent, sitting still and gazing at the patient. After a two-second silence, the patient more overtly solicited the doctor's assessment of heart trouble as a candidate explanation. Marking the query as the upshot of the narrative (via 'So', line 90), the patient named the candidate explanation for the first time, explicitly indicating the problem to which he had been obliquely referring throughout the narrative ('heart issue.').

While officially putting the candidate explanation on the table, he gave ambiguous signals regarding the degree of concern he had about the possibility of having experienced a heart problem. On the one hand, seeking the doctor's diagnostic assessment and using the formulation 'should I be *concerned* uh more of a heart (0.4) issue' (rather than 'Is it more likely to be a heart issue') could have been understood as reflecting a concern on his part about the potential of heart trouble. On the other hand, he managed to downplay his concern by (1) framing the question as motivated by curiosity ('>So 'm 's curious') and (2) by naming the condition in a general way (heart 'issue') without reference to a 'trouble' or 'problem'.

The patient's ambiguity regarding his level of concern may be seen as a solution to conflicting issues and constraints. Framing the serious health condition as a 'concern' solicited the doctor's attention to it; however given that the patient portrayed himself as someone who knew what to look for and what to disregard vis-à-vis his symptoms and hence as sceptical in this case, he needed to present himself as not *too* concerned about the serious health condition or he would undermine his stance of scepticism.

Consultation 3

The patient was a white woman who appeared to be in her sixties and the doctor was a young white female resident. Although the patient had seen a number of doctors at the medical centre in the past, the patient had come to the same-day clinic at the medical centre. It is not clear whether the patient made this appointment to talk about any particular health problems; most of the consultation revolved around updating the doctor about the status of the patient's existing health problems. At one point, she reported having experienced a pain on the right side of her chest and offered a heart problem as an improbable candidate explanation for this symptom.

How the patient created an opportunity to tell about a symptom episode   The opening of this consultation did not follow the usual routine in which, after greetings and identifications, the doctor solicits the patient's reason for the visit (Robinson, 1998, 2006). In this visit, the patient burped upon entering the examination room, then remarked that she had been burping a lot lately and began to puzzle about why it had been happening. The doctor started exploring the patient's burping with a series of symptom queries, one of which inquired about chest pain: 'you having any chest pain with this burping?' (line 1). After the patient denied the symptom (line 3) and the doctor accepted the response (line 6), the doctor began what appeared to be the start of another symptom query, 'Have' (line 8). At this point, the patient came in with a latched utterance in which she sought permission to tell the doctor about an incident, 'You wanna' hear somethin'' (line 9).

Consultation 3a

```
1 Doc:    °Okay° .h you having any chest pain with this burping?
2         (0.7)
3 Pt:     Not usually.
4 Doc:    N[o. ]
5 Pt:     [( )]No
6 Doc:    =°Okay°
7 Pt:     ((hiccuping sound))
8 Doc:    Have=
9 Pt:     =You wanna' hear somethin'=
10 Doc:   =Sure.
```

Essentially, the patient made a bid to interrupt what had been shaping up as a series of symptom queries about her burping to initiate talk about a matter of interest to her.

How the patient prefaced and reported the symptom episode while orienting to potentially conflicting issues and constraints   After securing interactional space to tell about the symptom episode, the patient did not immediately talk about the episode. Rather, she provided two kinds of prefaces that displayed her orientation to potentially conflicting issues and constraints.

In the first preface, the patient claimed uncertainty about the correctness of her as yet unstated stance or views ('I- I don't know whether I'm wrong er what', line 12).

Consultation 3b

```
9 Pt:    =You wanna' hear somethin'=
10 Doc:  =Sure.
11       (2.0)
12 Pt:   I- I don't know whether I'm wrong er what. hh
Doc:     Okay
```

By acknowledging to the doctor the potential incorrectness of the views she was about to put forward, the patient displayed an orientation to the patients' and doctors' differential rights to claim medical expertise. The patient implicitly positioned the doctor as the person who would rightly judge the status of her views on the symptom incident about which she would be reporting. In this way, she highlighted the disparity in their respective rights to make inferences or theorise about the cause of symptoms (Gill, 1998). In positioning the doctor as the medical expert and herself as uncertain, she also provided for the relevance of the doctor's assessment of her views after she completed the telling. Additionally, by claiming uncertainty about the correctness of her views, she positioned herself to be 'informed' by the doctor rather than disagreed with in the event that the doctor's views differed from hers.

In her second preface to describing the symptom incident (see below), the patient sought confirmation about the correctness of her knowledge about the warning signs of heart problems. The patient indicated her knowledge of heart symptoms by describing her different reactions to pains on her left side (lines 16–17 and 21) versus pains on her right side (line 23), and she sought the doctor's view as to whether her reactions were appropriate. The positioning and syntax of her solicitation ('I don't worry', line 23, 'Am I supposed to?', line 25) suggested that she was focused on confirming the correctness of her assumption that right-side chest pains generally were not regarded as symptoms of a heart problem. (As we will see shortly, it is with respect to that assumption that the patient cast her candidate explanation of symptoms as thoroughly unlikely.)

Consultation 3c

```
12 Pt:   I- I don't know whether I'm wrong er what=
13 Dr:   =Okay
14 Pt:   I have a heart problem [ okay ]
15 Dr:                          [Mm hmm] right
16 Pt:   Now hhh usually (0.2) when I (0.2) feel a heart pain-
17       [er ch]est pain on this si[de ] ((points to chest, left))
18 Dr:   [°Mm hm°]        [°Mm] hm°
19 Pt:   .hh u::h
20       (1.0)
21 Pt:   I worry.
```

```
22 Dr:   °Mm hm°
23 Pt:   On this side((points to chest, right)) I don't worry=
24 Dr:   =Okay
25 Pt:   Am I supposed to
```

In displaying her knowledge of typical warning signs of a heart problem, the patient presented herself as an informed and appropriately attentive heart patient who routinely made sensible inferences about different types of chest pains, including dismissing right-side chest pains as not heart-related. However, in seeking confirmation, she also displayed an orientation to the doctor as the expert who could officially assess the correctness of her typical reasoning.

In response to the patient's seeking confirmation of the correctness of her knowledge, the doctor started describing the usual symptoms that accompany a heart problem. Then, instead of positioning herself as a recipient of further information about typical warning signs, the patient manoeuvred to tell the doctor about the symptom episode. By asking the doctor if she knew her reason for asking ('Y'know why I'm askin'', line 31), the patient implied that she had something more to tell and, in so doing, redirected the conversation to tell about the incident.

Consultation 3d

```
31 Pt:   Y'know why I'm askin',
32       (0.2)
33 Pt:   The other (n)day, (.) .hh (.) the other even[ing]
34 Doc:                                             [°Mm ] hm°,
35 Pt:   I was sittin' watchin' televi[sion an' I got such a
36 Doc:                                [°Mm hm°,
37 Pt:   (.) .hh really (.) bad pain [right here] ((right side))
38 Doc:                               [°Mm hm mm  ] hm°
39       (.)
40 Pt:   Y'know
41       (.)
42 Pt:   .h An' then h a pain shot down my arm.=
43 Doc:  =Mm hm,
44 Pt:   .hh An' I thought (0.2) if I didn't know any better
45       I'd swear somethin was goin' on with my heart [y'know]
46 Doc:                                                 [°Mm hm°]
47 Pt:   .hh But (.) I didn't tend I didn't worry too much h
48       [like   I    say    I   on]ly worry (0.2) on this
49 Doc:  [Cuz it was the right side.]
50 Pt:   side.=
51 Doc:  =°Right°
```

As in her preface, the patient's description of the symptom episode displayed her orientation to conflicting issues and constraints. The patient described the pain as very similar to left-side heart pain – it was severe ('I got such a .hh really (.) bad pain', lines 35 and 37) and it shot down her arm; thus, in both its severity and its similarity to the typical warning signs of a heart problem, it warranted further attention. The patient then reported that, at the time she experienced the pain, she considered the possibility that her pains were heart-related but largely rejected that explanation: 'If I didn't know any better I'd swear something was goin' on with my heart', lines 44–5. By using a direct reported thought (Holt, 1996), she provided evidence with which the doctor could see for herself that even at the time of the pain the patient both had considered the candidate explanation of a heart problem and also was sceptical that it was the case. In making reference to 'knowing better', and by confirming that she worries when the pain is on the left side (lines 47–8 and 50), she suggested that, based on her knowledge, she largely dismissed the notion that she was experiencing a heart pain. She thus presented heart problem as a candidate explanation that was both worthy of consideration and highly unlikely, making the doctor's assessment relevant while showing that she does not embrace worst-case scenarios.

In short, the patient managed the conflicting issues and constraints of directing the doctor to consider the explanation while also establishing herself as a sensible person. She did this by taking a sceptical stance and portraying her reaction to this particular right-side chest pain as an exception to her usual way of reacting to right-side chest pains. This particularly severe right-side chest pain deviated from the typical right-side chest pains that she routinely dismissed to such an extent that she actually entertained the possibility that it was a heart pain. The severity of the pain, along with its similar characteristics to the warning signs of a heart problem, provided a warrant for raising the matter, even though she continued to treat it as improbable. Though the patient reported that she routinely dismissed right side chest pains, she treated this exceptional pain as an occasion for seeking special reassurance from the expert voice.

The tension between casting the serious health condition as a possibility warranting the doctor's attention while displaying oneself as a knowledgeable and sensible person also is evidenced in the patient's display of concern or anxiety. The patient reported her own reactions to the symptoms as 'I didn't worry too much' (line 47). While she downgraded the degree of worry with 'didn't worry *too much*', she also preserved some degree of worry in this formulation. She rode a fine line between preserving a measure of concern (and thus, medical relevance) and displaying the reasoning she had done to all but dismiss the concern.

Discussion

In this chapter, we have examined some practices that patients used when they elected to present serious medical conditions as candidate explanations. Some practices that we identified are:

- Presenting the serious condition as one of several possible explanations and/or reporting evidence against the likelihood of the serious condition are solutions to the dilemma of how to raise a serious candidate explanation *while also* portraying oneself as a reasonable person who does not embrace worst-case scenarios.
- Reporting evidence against an explanation in the form of reports of the presence or absence of symptom experiences is a solution to the dilemma of how to present oneself as knowledgeable enough to make sense of one's own symptoms and to reason about one's health *while also* orienting to doctors' and patients' legitimate domains of expertise.
- Displaying some modulated degree of concern or worry is a solution to the dilemma of how to direct the doctor's attention to investigating the potential of a serious medical condition *while also* portraying the explanation as unlikely, which could imply that it need not be investigated.

In short, presenting the serious condition as one of several possibilities *and* displaying scepticism and uncertainty via experiential reports *and* modulating one's displayed degree of concern are solutions to the dilemmas of how to raise a serious candidate explanation *and* show that it warrants the doctor's attention *while also* portraying oneself as a reasonable patient who does not embrace worst-case scenarios *and* who respects the differential spheres of expertise between patients and doctors.

In the remainder of this section, we will address the relevance and potential use of this research. We believe that the primary audience that would benefit from our analysis is comprised of health-care providers. Patient-centred health-care providers are committed to listening to and understanding the theories, interpretations and concerns of their patients. However, this is not always an easy task, especially when patients present explanations that they then argue against, when they seem to be concerned about the possibility of having serious health conditions yet also present themselves as largely unconcerned about those possibilities, and when they hint about or allude to serious health conditions but do not explicitly state them (Lang et al., 2000). We think that our analysis can help health-care providers to disentangle fairly complex discourse, which on face value seems puzzling or contradictory, and make better sense of that discourse.

There are two implications of our research that we would like to offer to health-care providers. First, it is important to appreciate the complexities involved for patients in presenting serious candidate explanations. While it is inevitable to attempt to interpret the patients' state of mind from their discourse (Have they ruled out that candidate explanation? Are they concerned about this candidate explanation?), it would be a mistake to overlook the interactional issues and constraints that shape the discourse. When a patient portrays the serious candidate explanation as highly improbable, that may be as much, or more, a product of self-presentational issues than a reflection of the patient's views. The delicate and complicated ways in which patients present these serious candidate explanations create challenges in interpreting and hence responding to these types of presentations.

The second implication is that, if patients are to present serious health conditions as candidate explanations, they need sufficient interactional space to package the explanations in ways that allow them to deal with the multiple issues and constraints that emerge. These complex tasks seem to be nearly impossible to accomplish in an environment driven largely by queries from the healthcare provider. If patients are to present their serious candidate explanations, at least in the configurations we have examined here, they need to secure a certain amount of interactional 'space' to do this work. The interactional space is a joint accomplishment of both participants. The healthcare provider needs to allow the opportunity for the patient to present an extended version of events or narrative from the patient, and the patient needs to have the resources and feel they have the right to detail what needs to be told to have the picture understood as they wish.

It is our hope that through our identifying some of the practices that patients use, health-care professionals might be better sensitised to some of the issues and constraints that bear on patients' presentations of serious health conditions as candidate explanations and to recognise the complex work that patients perform to handle these constraints.

NOTES

1. This approach to discursive phenomena is similar to, and compatible with, the approach taken by Billig et al. (1988). In responding to patients' presenting serious health conditions as candidate explanations, doctors also display an orientation to conflicting constraints (Gill and Maynard, 2006).
2. This point particularly complements Halkowski's (2006) finding that patients present themselves in ways that would enable them to be seen as 'reasonable' patients. Halkowski found that patients can do this via narratives in which

they report that they first considered rather mundane possible causes for their symptoms ('at first I thought') before considering more serious possibilities.

3. The understanding of bladder condition as both likely and not particularly worrisome was achieved, in large part, in the patient's reporting that she had a history of the condition ('I've had that before'). In reporting the history, the patient provided grounds for its likelihood inasmuch as bladder infections recur and her prior experience might mean she would be more likely to be able to identify it again. In reporting the prior occurrences in a matter-of-fact manner, she implied that having a bladder condition was not a particularly newsworthy or serious event.

4. The patient displayed an orientation to differential expertise when presenting each candidate explanation. When presenting bladder condition, she incorporated an uncertainty marker 'may' ('It may be a bladder condition') and supported the likelihood of the candidate explanation by drawing on her experiences ('I've had dat before'), which is the kind of expertise that patients are entitled to claim (Drew, 1991; Heath, 1992; Gill, 1998). When presenting gas, she reported her symptom experience and relied on everyday logic for an understanding of the basis for ruling it out.

5. In presenting 'appendix' as a very tenuously held idea, the patient not only displayed deference to the doctor's expertise. She also maintained a stance that would not have to be strongly disagreed with if the doctor were to conclude that appendicitis was improbable.

6. The patient ruled out *gas* as a candidate explanation by describing a symptom history that argued against it as the cause. She reported that the gas was subsiding but the symptom remained ('I hadda lot of ga::s' 'You know but it's (0.2) seem to be dy::in' down but uh- I still have this pai:n inna lower s:tomach'). Understanding the candidate explanation as ruled out requires the use of everyday causal reasoning: the presence of a causal agent should produce the effect, and the absence of the causal agent should result in the absence of the effect.

7. In a later phase of the consultation, the doctor informed the patient of his diagnostic conclusions. He referred back to the patient's concern about appendicitis, gave multiple reasons for ruling it out, and reassured the patient not to worry. It is likely that the extent to which he reassured the patient was a response, at least in part, to the patient's invoking worry and concern to reintroduce appendix as a candidate explanation.

8. As Stivers (2002: 312) has argued, such specificity in symptom presentations can be 'diagnosis implicative'. For example, 'a parent can mention that their child has a "barky" cough to index croup, green nasal discharge to index sinusitis, or white or yellow spots on the child's throat to index strep throat'.

9. Stivers (2002: 321–2, lines 31–4) shows how a parent uses the same device to suggest that her child no longer has strep throat.

10. See Halkowski (2006) for a discussion of how the patient's formulation 'noticed' (line 55) works to counter undesirable inferences.

11. In the interest of space, we omit a discussion of lines 61–71, in which the patient moved the narrative to the present and reported that he sometimes experienced a gas bubble which was of short duration.

8 Arguing and thinking errors: cognitive distortion as a members' category in sex offender group therapy talk

Clare MacMartin and Curtis D. LeBaron

Sexual offending remains a serious social problem. Because of significant psychological repercussions for many victims and the high rates of offender recidivism, there is a pressing need for research on the effective treatment of sex offenders (Johnston and Ward, 1996). The most common form of intervention consists of cognitive-behavioural therapy incorporating concepts of relapse prevention (Murphy and Smith, 1996). Typical targets of treatment are aspects implicated in the origins and maintenance of sexual offending: offenders' deviant sexual preferences, their lack of empathy for victims, and cognitive distortions (Marshall, 1999). In this chapter, we present discursive research on the treatment of offenders' cognitive distortions.

Cognitive distortions represent one facet of problematic cognitive processes theorised to underpin offenders' criminal behaviour; denial or minimisation of sexual offences, problematic attitudes toward women and children, and crime-supportive attitudes have also been identified (Marshall, 1999). Abel and his colleagues (e.g., Abel et al., 1984, 1989) employed the term 'cognitive distortions' to describe those offence-relevant beliefs of child molesters that serve to justify and maintain their conduct. The literature suggests that offenders support sexist beliefs about women, likely view children in sexualised terms and endorse attitudes supportive of the sexual entitlement of males (Ward et al., 1997). Clinicians and researchers stress the importance of such distorted thinking and maladaptive beliefs in the facilitation or justification of sexual offences (Johnston and Ward, 1996). Cognitive-behavioural therapy assumes that, in order for sex offenders to alter their behaviour, they must change the way they think. The present study of videotaped group treatment investigates talk about cognitive distortions as a therapeutic resource.

The conceptualisation of cognitive distortions in the clinical literature on sexual offending builds on theory and research in social cognition.

147

People as social perceivers are assumed to be cognitive misers who are limited in their capacity to process social information (Fiske and Taylor, 1984). Information-processing strategies include short cuts resulting in confirmatory biases and other attributional errors associated with stereotypes and prejudiced thinking. The employment of such short cuts by sex offenders is viewed by cognition researchers as adaptive and normative, in the sense that non-offenders also routinely use these short cuts; however, the content of biases in offenders (e.g., the legitimacy of having forced sex with women) is considered mal-adaptive and deviant (Johnston and Ward, 1996). It has been argued that the social cognition literature on stereotype change provides useful advice about therapeutic strategies for changing sex offenders' mal-adaptive beliefs (ibid.).

The notion of the social perceiver as motivated tactitian (Fiske and Taylor, 1991) has more recently replaced that of the cognitive miser. Johnston and Ward (1996) reviewed the work on affective and moti-vational factors in social cognition (e.g., Showers and Cantor, 1985) and related it to treatment for sexual offending. Whether a person uses processing short cuts or effortful but more accurate cognitive strategies is presumed to depend in part on his or her affective needs, goals and motives, and on the demands of the specific tasks. When they experi-ence intense positive or negative affective states, offenders are assumed to rely on the more primitive cognitive heuristics available for decision making; research suggests that relapse prevention is best supported by interventions helping offenders learn to cope effectively with negative affect and life stressors (Johnston and Ward, 1996). Cognitive distor-tions are conceptualised both as perceptual limitations that have causal status in the commission of sexual offences and as strategic, post hoc rationalisations used to justify offences. For example, the literature suggests that offenders may not only be poor at interpreting women's negative cues (which are designed to prevent or stop unwanted sex) but that offenders also strategically ignore these cues in the interest of meeting their own needs (Craig, 1990).

Discursive psychology has criticised mainstream psychology, includ-ing cognitive and social psychology, on many grounds (e.g., Billig, 1996; Edwards, 1997; Edwards and Potter, 1992; Potter 1996; Potter and Wetherell, 1987). For example, both language and cognition are theorised differently under discursive psychology, than under conven-tional cognitive psychology, where perceptual cognitivism dominates theory and application, including the cognitive-behavioural treatment of sexual offending. Discursive researchers view cognition, not as a collection of technical inner processes and mental entities, but as a discursive phenomenon constructed and oriented to in people's talk and texts (Potter and Edwards, 2003a). In adopting a constructionist view of language and social life, discursive psychologists eschew the naive realism bound up with positivist investigations of biased or accurate mental representations of reality. Cognition and reality, and evaluations of them as distorted or accurate, are reformulated as discursive constructions (ibid.). In line with ethnomethodological conversation analysis, discursive psychology respecifies psychological concepts such as attitudes (Potter, 1998; Potter and Wetherell, 1987), attributions (Edwards and Potter, 1992), cognitions (Edwards, 1997) and emotions (Edwards, 1999) as discursive categories used by participants in actual talk-in-interaction. We extend the project of discursive psychology by examining how cognitive distortions are employed as categories in talk in group therapy for sex offenders. Our research does not demand that we endorse the ontological status of the cognitive processes and products presumed by cognitive-behavioural frameworks to precede and underwrite sexual offences. Rather, we examine how participants (therapists and offenders) use cognitive distortions as rhetorical resources in therapy interactions.

Discursive-psychological research has recently been conducted on sex offender group treatment in the prison system in the United Kingdom (Auburn, 2005; and Lea and Auburn, 2001). Auburn and Lea (2003) criticised the notion of cognitive distortions as individualistic mental entities, concluding that cognitive distortions are analysts' categories that have been abstracted from sequences of talk. However, these authors acknowledge that the academic rhetoric of cognitive-behavioural therapy may not entirely reflect what therapists do in actual practice. Auburn (2005) analysed devices of narrative reflexivity whereby offenders could discount inferences that their narratives about their offences contained cognitive distortions. Orientation to cognitive distortions was inferred on the basis of offenders' construction and repair of factual descriptions of their offences to display their accountability for their crimes. However, in Auburn's British corpus, cognitive distortions rarely appeared as identifiable categories in talk. In contrast, our research analyses explicit talk *about* offenders' cognitive distortions and perceptual limitations.

Three theoretical features (see Potter and Edwards, 2001) help us contrast our discursive research on cognitive distortions with more conventional approaches (e.g., Abel et al., 1989). First, we treat discourse about cognitive distortions as situated: it is both occasioned and rhetorical. By 'occasioned' we mean that discourse is embedded in a particular context as part of some kind of sequence that makes the discourse relevant. For example, a therapist's reference to an offender's distorted thinking may be occasioned by that offender's previous talk about suicide. Discourse is also pervasively rhetorical (Billig, 1996). A factual description of an offender's cognitive limitations may be designed to argue that he has a high risk of reoffending and to counter an alternative version that would minimise his dangerousness. This brings us to the second theoretical feature of discursive research, which views discourse about cognitive distortions as action-oriented. Concerns about fact, interest and accountability dovetail with a focus on the actions performed by descriptions of offenders' cognitions as members' concerns and activities. A therapist's description of an offender's apparent lack of insight regarding his victim's resistance during an offence acts as an assessment of his need for ongoing treatment. Finally, our discursive research on cognitive distortions is constructionist: discourse about offenders' mental states *constructs* certain versions of the world that do certain things. An offender's description of his suicidal thinking is part of his larger claim that he has been falsely accused of a new crime while on probation. Such discourse is also *constructed* from particles, words, figures of speech, descriptions, narratives, etc. that we study to see how such talk is built to perform actions.

Method and materials

We analysed sessions of videotaped discourse of weekly therapy sessions involving two court-appointed therapists and six men on parole for sexually deviant crimes in the United States. We investigated cognitive distortions ('thinking errors' in the lexicon of this particular sex offender group) as participants' categories. By using the term 'thinking error', participants cast cognitive distortions, not as aberrant features of offenders' cognitive profiles, but as mistakes that can, presumably, be corrected. Our focus was on the practical orientation of descriptions of thinking errors or perceptual deficits. Relevant segments of talk about thinking errors and perceptual deficits in six sessions of group therapy were identified and transcribed following Jeffersonian conventions (Hutchby and Wooffitt, 1998). Pseudonyms were used for therapists and offenders. Our analysis was informed by discursive psychology (e.g., Edwards and Potter, 1992) and conversation analysis (e.g., Hutchby and Wooffitt, 1998).

This group's therapy programme, outlined in a client workbook, requires that an offender provide full disclosure of his offences, including his thoughts and feelings during the offence and his interpretation of his victim's feelings and behaviour. Details of such disclosures are recorded as written homework assignments. Each week, offenders take turns reading their homework so that therapists and other offenders can critique it toward eventually approving it. If the group does not vote to approve, an offender must revise his written disclosure. Revisions ensue over the course of successive sessions until all members are satisfied with the offender's version. In group therapy, participants sometimes challenge thinking errors identified in written disclosures read aloud or in spoken talk about current issues; arguments consisting of or orienting to such challenges constituted the focus of our analysis. These programme features are common to many cognitive-behavioural interventions for sex offenders in North America (Marshall, 1999).

The client workbook states that 'thinking errors determine psychopathology'. Specifically, the idea is that criminal thinking causes crime. Part of therapy requires that offenders learn to identify their offending cycle, which consists sequentially of trigger events, thinking errors, negative feelings, deviant urges, offending, and thoughts and feelings after the offence. A glossary of nineteen common thinking errors is listed in the workbook (e.g., 'Power Play' refers to attempts to dominate and control other people). In this chapter we explore arguments in sex offender therapy talk about whether certain thoughts can be categorised as problematic and whether the nature of the trouble is ascribed to motivated and/or unmotivated cognitive processes. Our analyses use extracts from one therapy session to show how such categorisations involve therapeutic concerns about *agency*, *accountability* and *stake*, three notions central to discursive psychology.

Presentation and analysis of data

Agency, accountability and stake in descriptions of cognition

Discursive psychology is concerned with how reports are rhetorically designed to attend to the agency and accountability of persons in the reported events; reports also attend to the accountability of a current speaker's actions, including those performed through the activity of reporting itself (Edwards and Potter, 1992). Following Edwards and Potter, we find there is an important relationship between the accountability of persons *in* therapeutic talk about thinking errors and the accountability of persons producing such talk. Edwards and Potter also discuss dilemmas of stake. A speaker may work to maintain his or her own vested interest without appearing to be doing so: if that vested interest becomes transparent in such talk, its credibility can be discounted as the product of stake or interest. Such dilemmas can be managed by doing various kinds of attribution through reporting.

In our brief review of the social cognition literature on sexual offending, we described theories and research on both the limitations and motivations associated with offenders' cognitive processing. Our study documents how researchers' issues in the academic literature are: a) respecified as participants' concerns in actual therapeutic talk about offenders' thinking; b) enrolled as rhetorical resources designed to mark offenders' therapeutic progress and to impact on their current and future conduct. We highlight interactions in which offenders and therapists argue about whether offenders' thinking is distorted and what the basis of that distortion is. Cognitive distortions, then, are something that must be discursively negotiated and accomplished in the course of therapy.

Matters of stake and interest are critical in this institutional setting. One episode in our analysis (extracts 1 and 2) features argumentation about whether an offender's current thinking is normal or distorted (and, therefore, an object of therapeutic intervention). Offenders' presentation of their current thinking as normal may display their therapeutic progress. But offenders are required to take responsibility for their offences and to show self-awareness by acknowledging cognitive distortions associated with both past and current conduct. They must also admit when they cannot see how their thinking is distorted. Another episode in our analysis (extract 3) concerns argumentation about whether an offender is currently able to see his past thinking as distorted. Offenders must present as genuine in both their ability and inability to identify their thinking errors, and be committed to correcting them.

In these two episodes, thinking errors are treated variably by therapists in terms of the amount of control offenders are assumed to exert. Thinking errors can be described as indexing either motivated or unmotivated cognitions. Motivated cognitions involve strategic rationalisations used in a manipulative way by offenders to deny deviance and responsibility or to justify offences. For example, an offender who threatens to commit suicide if he is jailed is described as engaging in controlling conduct designed to minimise his agency and accountability for his actions (including, possibly, his commission of a new sexual assault). Unmotivated cognitions involve automatic perceptual deficits over which offenders are presumed to have little control. For example, an offender who is unable to specify how his victim resisted during his past assault of her is described as a man currently incapable of manifesting such insight even if he wishes to do so.

Suicidal thinking: agency and the automaticity of cognition

Extract 1 involves Carl, an offender who has told the group that he must go to another town to answer a new sexual offence allegation brought against him by a woman Carl allegedly assaulted. Carl insists that he has been falsely accused. Earlier in this session, therapist Mike notes the fear in Carl's voice when he talks about the prospect of being jailed again. Carl recounts how petrified he was the first night he was jailed for his previous sexual offence, and how he is currently afraid of the police. Mike describes Carl's fear as 'pretty natural' (he is a sex offender on felony probation and ought to fear the police); however, Mike also tells Carl this fear is something that he must find a way to control. Mike invites Carl to confront his fear by imagining the worst-case hypothetical scenario (being handcuffed and put in jail) and by then offering the best way of coping that he can think of in that scenario. Other participants include Sara (Mike's co-therapist) and Ethan (another offender).

Extract 1: Tape A4 1994 6.15 37:16

```
 1 Carl:   I'd try ta kill myself.
 2         (1.0)
 3 Mike:   Okay ↑that's not a real good
 4         ex(H)A(H) [ Mple  ] ↓of
 5 Sara:             [In yer ] in yer
 6         [Pee Oh's ] office with the handcuffs on=
 7 Ethan:  [*Whoa::h*] ((*smiley voice))
 8 Sara:   = yer [gonna tr]y to ↑kill [yerself?]
 9 Carl:         [ No::   ]           ['f they ]=
10         lock me up an' ev'rything
11         I'd find some way to kill myself.
12         (1.1)
13 Carl:   That's what I would ↑do. (0.3)
14         ↓I've thought about that even this past week.
15         If I was to get any-↑ANY ↓time
16         I've thought about it (0.4)
17         If I was to get locked up again the petrif-
18         the night I had that first night (0.4)
19         if I was to get locked up again (.)
20         .hh I'd try tuh find a way to ↑end my ↓life.
21         (0.4)
22         That's what I would ↑do. (.)
23         ↓And I'll stick by that.
24         (0.4)
25 Mike:   Mm [hmm]
26 Carl:      [ I ] will ↑kill ↓myself.
27         I'd rather be ↑dead (0.4)
28         [(>↓than end up<)]
```

```
29 Mike:  [Okay.               ] (0.3)
30        Well ↑that's one option, (0.9)
31        Gimme a↓nother option.
```

In almost choric fashion, group members treat Carl's suicidal talk (line 1) as problematic. After a one-second pause, Mike's turn-initial 'Okay' (line 3) displays minimal receipt of Carl's response and pre-figures the shift to Mike's evaluation of that response as unacceptable. Mike's understatement, '↑that's not a real good ex(H)A(H)Mple' (lines 3–4), categorises Carl's suicidal talk, not as a serious threat, but merely as a poor exemplar of the candidate response of excellent coping that Mike had encouraged. This utterance involves laughed-through delivery, which softens Mike's criticism, treating Carl's answer as outrageous and not to be taken seriously. A similar display of incredulous levity is found in Ethan's 'Whoa::h' (line 7) uttered while he smiles. His exclamation overlaps with Sara's response. Her challenge of Carl's suicidal talk undermines the credibility of his threat by questioning the feasibility of killing oneself while handcuffed in the presence of correctional officers (lines 5, 6, 8). Her question makes available inferences that Carl is being overly dramatic to manipulate the sympathy of the group or is otherwise being unreasonable about his options.

Carl faces a dilemma in responding. If he minimises the seriousness of his prior suicidal talk, he risks being viewed as insincere, which would erode the credibility of his protestations of innocence regarding this new allegation. But if he insists too emphatically that he will indeed kill himself in the scenario posed by Mike, Carl's rationality can be challenged on the grounds that restrictions on his liberty will afford him few opportunities to carry out his plan.

Carl resists others' challenges in variable ways. First, he addresses Sara's implication that his suicide plan is not reality-based by engaging in self-repair: he rushes (line 9) to clarify that he would attempt suicide at some future point and in some location, not necessarily during the meeting in his probation officer's (PO's) office (lines 9–11). Second, Carl resists inferences that he is being impulsive and inauthentic by underscoring the automaticity and consistency of his suicidal thinking. It is this particular action that we wish to foreground in our analysis. On line 14 Carl declares: '↓I've thought about that even this past week'. This utterance, with its use of the upgrader 'even', suggests that his suicide threat is not a one-off retort blurted in the heat of the moment but rather is a sustained pattern of thinking. The extreme case formulation (Pomerantz, 1986) 'any time', with 'any' emphatically uttered and repeated (line 15), portrays the automatic, perseverative character of his suicidal thoughts and their connection to fear (the self-aborted 'petrified' on line 17, which Carl had mentioned when describing his feelings during his prior experience in jail). Carl's fear was normalised earlier in the session by Mike; here, the self-reported automaticity of Carl's thoughts, which are tied to understandable emotional reactions, minimises Carl's agency and the deviance of his thinking.

Mike resists this version. The acknowledgment token 'Okay' (line 29), in overlap with Carl's talk, prefaces a move away from the topic of suicide to next-positioned matters (Beach, 1993) that are pivotally signalled by the disaffiliative discourse marker 'Well' (see Schiffrin, 1987). Instead of displaying concern about Carl's suicide bid, Mike categorises it as 'one option' (line 30), the prosody of which further emphasises his casual stance. Mike then demands an alternative option from Carl (line 31). Mike's reference to suicide as open to amendment builds on the hypothetical reasoning displayed in Carl's prior talk in the form of the conditional verb tense (lines 1, 11, 13, 22, 27) (see Edwards and Potter, 1992, on the rhetoric of argument). By encouraging other options, Mike stresses Carl's agency and simultaneously invites more constructive actions than suicide.

'Power Play': suicidal thinking as motivated cognition

The session continues with Carl and others discussing how Carl might cope with jail time, should he be arrested. Extract 2 consists of a portion of Mike's subsequent feedback to Carl in which Mike identifies Carl's suicidal talk as indicative of a thinking error called a 'Power Play'.

Extract 2: Tape A4 1994 6.15 45:00

```
 1 Mike:  I mean in ↑this ↓group we talk about
 2         giving help °and receiving help.°
 3         ↑We talk a↓bout, (0.5)
 4         whether yer a citizen er a criminal. (0.2)
 5         An' I think? (0.6) to be honest with you:,
 6         i:f (.)they ↑put the cuffs ↓on you,
 7         'n' the first thing that pops into yer ↑head ↓is
 8         'I'm gonna ↑kill ↓myself'
 9         ↑that's ↓criminal ↑thin↓king. (0.7)
10         Yer just sayin', (0.3)
11         'We:ll, (.) ↑you ↓Power Played me
12         you put ↑cuffs ↓on now I'll do the better one.
13         (0.5)
14         I'll turn my ↑cap↓tors:, (0.5)
15         into: (.) rescuers. (0.5)
16         >(Y'know)< I'll? (0.3) I'll ↑sui ↓ci:de,'
```

```
17        an' then that turns anybody who would wanna
18        re↑strain ↓you an' hold you ↑do:w↓n (0.4)
19        into somebody who has to ↑care ↓for you:
20        a:nd, (0.4) uh:: (.) provide ↑med↓ical support
21        an' ev'rything like ↑tha:↓t.
22        >°I mean the°<-↑yer just ↓turnin' the ↑ta↓bles
23        on 'em.-It's a big time ↑Power ↓Play.
```

Mike's response orients to normative group practices (lines 1–2) whereby he reminds Carl of the legitimate bases for providing and receiving feedback. The group parlance, 'giving help °and receiving help°', is packaged in terms of shared practice as a kind of consensus formulation (Edwards and Potter, 1992) using the first-person plural: 'in ↑this ↓group we talk about'. This frames Mike's upcoming feedback, not as a personal attack, but as a recognisable offer of help. Mike's speech continues with an oratorical repetition on line 3 ('We talk a↓bout') of the phrase appearing on line 1, here used to introduce two kinds of mutually exclusive identities available to group members: 'whether yer a citizen er a criminal' (line 4). Mike then delivers his opinion, starting with the modalisation 'I think' which is followed by a stake inoculation (Edwards and Potter, 1992): 'to be honest with you:' (line 5). In signalling his next utterance as motivated by a norm of truth-telling, Mike counters a possible charge that his upcoming challenge is insensitive to Carl's prior admission of his fear of imprisonment, a self-disclosure that Mike invited.

Mike uses rhetoric of argument ('i:f (.) they ↑put the cuffs ↓on you', line 6) to challenge Carl. The use of this format retains the hypothetical character of both the situation and Carl's reaction to it, underscoring Carl's agency in choosing the dysfunctional response of suicide and allowing for a more functional choice instead. Criminal thinking is invoked to refute further Carl's prior minimisation of his own responsibility in the production of suicidal thinking, which Carl had argued for in extract 1 on the basis of the uncontrollability of his own thoughts. Mike uses active voicing to categorise these automatic suicidal thoughts as criminal: 'the first thing that pops into yer ↑head ↓is "I'm gonna ↑kill ↓myself" ↑that's ↓criminal ↑thin↓king' (lines 7–8). He uses the first-person pronoun to animate the contents of Carl's thoughts. In the wake of Mike's earlier reference to the choice about whether to behave as a citizen or as a criminal (line 4), this reference affirms Carl's responsibility for his implicit adoption of a criminal identity. The automaticity of Carl's thinking is acknowledged in Mike's description of a suicidal thought that 'pops' unbidden into Carl's head (line 7). But the linking of such impulsivity to criminality counters an alternative version that would defend Carl's suicidal response as an understandable and uncontrollable reaction to the prospect of unfair incarceration.

Mike uses reported thought again to unpack the manipulation inherent in Carl's suicide threat (lines 11–16). Mike thus undermines the version implied by Carl that his suicide threat is an innocent reaction to a false accusation and the prospect of being victimised in jail. The dispreferred opening of Carl's thinking error as constructed by Mike (' "Well" ') serves to project its disaffiliative character in the form of rebellion against the correctional system's exercise of power: ' "↑you ↓Power Played me you put ↑cuffs ↓on" ' (lines 11–12). The verb 'Power Played' suggests that, from Carl's point of view, there is no difference between the correctional system's use of power and his own in terms of legitimacy. The law of the jungle implicitly rules. We note the second-person reference ('you') to refer to the correctional authorities as the recipients of Carl's accusatory talk, which identifies them as the intended targets of his strategy. The employment of the future tense, ' "I'll do the better one. (0.5) I'll turn my ↑cap↓tors:, (0.5) into: (.) rescuers. (0.5) >(Y'know)< I'll? (0.3) I'll ↑sui↓ci:de" ' (lines 12–16), builds on Carl's own use of it (extract 1, line 26). Carl's suicide bid is thus described as premeditated revenge. The strategy behind the suicide attempt is located in a string of unfolding actions in which Carl is held responsible for the jailers' shift from restraining Carl to caring for him.

Mike's shift to the use of the second person (line 18) signals his move from active voicing of Carl's thoughts to Mike's therapeutic evaluation of them as deviant (lines 17–21). Mike then summarises the gist of Carl's thinking error: 'yer just ↓turnin' the ↑ta↓bles on 'em.-It's a big time ↑Power ↓Play' (lines 22–3). The adjective 'just' reductively emphasises this as the only reasonable interpretation of Carl's suicidal talk. The adjectival phrase 'big time' stresses the magnitude (and the obviousness) of this form of cognitive distortion.

Mike's categorisation of Carl's suicidal talk as representing distorted (and criminal) cognition serves an important therapeutic function. Having invoked the identities of citizen and criminal as contrasting options that offenders are free to adopt or reject, Mike can frame Carl's suicidal thinking as a strategically motivated form of criminal thinking which becomes implicitly linked to a criminal identity that Carl has the freedom to resist. Mike's talk in this portion assumes that offenders can select functional or criminal ways of thinking (along with the conduct and identities that respectively underwrite them). Cognitive distortions are treated as under the will of the offender to monitor and replace with more adaptive thoughts. Indeed, a bit later in this session, Mike exhorts

Carl to live by the ideas of the group, avoiding any 'Power Plays' when he leaves town to respond to the new allegation. Such moves as Mike's treat cognitions as moral choices rather than reflex-like perceptions that offenders cannot help but use.

What complicates our analysis is the pedagogical character of Mike's argument. Mike uses the second person to *tell* Carl what he is thinking, to evaluate the deviance of his thoughts and to make available inferences about his continued need for treatment. Telling someone what he is doing can perform the attributional work of blaming, but in a subtle way that resists undermining because such talk is always accountable as a mere effort to enlighten someone. In explaining to Carl how and why his talk reflects distorted thinking, Mike makes available the inference that Carl may be unaware that his thoughts are deviant. Thus Carl is not necessarily treated as a Machiavellian person actively trying to manipulate the therapy group members in the same fashion as his hypothetical manipulation of his would-be jailers. Rather, he is positioned as someone who needs to be informed about his thinking on the grounds that he lacks the self-awareness to understand its problematic nature. This positioning of Carl by Mike (as naive 'student' of his own cognitions rather than as a hardened criminal) opens up a space for rehabilitation. Thus Mike emphasises Carl's agency while simultaneously casting Carl as unknowing. In the next section, we further explore the action orientation of talk about limitations in offenders' perceptual abilities.

'You can't see that right now': perceptual deficit as unmotivated cognition

In extract 3 below, Mike gives feedback to another offender, Alfred. Earlier in his discussion of his offence, Alfred acknowledged that his victim cried and wanted to stop having sex, reactions that he ignored. In accord with the homework questions Alfred must answer, the group has asked him what he did during the course of his offence to evoke such responses in his victim. The group has also asked Alfred to identify forms of subtle resistance that his victim displayed. Alfred appears perplexed by these questions. In a lengthy speech, Mike tells Alfred he needs to be 'real scared' that he doesn't 'have a clue' about why a girl starts crying in the middle of having sex with him. Extract 3 consists of a subsequent portion of Mike's interaction with Alfred. Mike formulates the nature of Alfred's current perceptual limitations and assesses their implications.

Extract 3: Tape A4 1994 6.15 1:19:00

```
1 Mike:     What is a man capable of
2           if he doesn't know when he's hurting someone.
3           (1.5)
4           He's capable o' hurtin' people right and ↑left
5           ↓and not even being a↑war↓e of it. (4.0)
6           What is a man capable of if he can't tell
7           when someone's resisting him. (1.6)
8           He's capable of doing things to ↑peo↓ple
9           that they don't wanna have ↑done ↓to them. (3.1)
10          Real scary. (1.4)
11          So what's yer [↑prob↓lem why'rn't]=
12 Stan:                 [ .hghghghghgh       ]
13             [ hghghghh      ]
14 Mike:     =[why'ren't you ] able to see this thing.
15          (2.6)
16 Alfred:  °I::::::. (1.9.)
17          (Uh: maybe) (0.3.) didn't wanna see it at that
18          time.°
19          (1.4)
20 Mike:    How come you can't see it right ↑no↓w
21          'cause you ↑wanna ↓see it. (0.8)
22          In this ↑group (0.2) ↓you would be
23          consider:ed, (0.5) a suc↑cess
24          ↓if you could see why she cried. (1.0)
25          Yeah (but) there's a big ↑pay↓off
26          for you to see it
27          but still you can't see why she was crying.
28          You ↑can't ↓explain that to us right now,
```

Mike's speech contains multiple references to Alfred's current limited insight into his victim's distress. Much of Mike's talk appears directed to discounting an inference made available by Alfred's lack of understanding. To profess ignorance regarding one's sex partner's reactions is to suggest that one was unaware of her withdrawal of consent to sexual activity. In this sense, Alfred's cognitive limitations may be seen to reflect the absence of mens rea, or guilty mind, which is an element required to show that a crime has taken place. Explicit orientation to Alfred's cognitive deficit runs the risk of minimising his accountability because he was incapable of accurately interpreting his victim's words and actions as a refusal. However, Mike's oratory upholds Alfred's responsibility for monitoring his own perceptual limitations, the dangerousness of which is highlighted.

Mike uses the hypothetical question opening 'What is a man capable of if …?' twice in extract 3 (lines 1, 6) to conjecture about the on-going danger to society posed by Alfred's cognitive limitations. The recycling of this question builds on two undisputed manifestations of Alfred's lack of awareness, that he was hurting his victim during the offence (line 2) and that she was subtly resisting him (line 7). However, Mike's question confronts these troubling facts, not in terms of their impact on Alfred's past victim, but in terms of their implications for future victims. Mike's questions (lines 1–2, 6–7) employ the present tense 'is' and third-person categories ('man' to refer to a generic offender and 'someone' to refer to a hypothetical victim). A script formulation (Edwards, 1994) of a dangerous offender is created, which de-individuates Alfred in terms of how he is likely to be seen by others, including potential victims. Mike's script formulation constructs the generality of Alfred's perceptual limitations and the on-going and pervasive threat he currently poses to women. Unlike other possible situations in which a description of someone's ignorance may characterise that person as benign, Mike's description of Alfred's perceptual inability (to interpret others' reactions and to acknowledge his own dangerousness) is used to emphasise the frightening risk he poses to society. Extreme depictions of perceptual limitation and of danger are thereby mutually implicative.

Lengthy pauses at the end of each of Mike's questions (1.5 seconds and 4.0 seconds on lines 3 and 5 respectively) may open up slots for responses from Alfred that are not produced. Perhaps the third-person format of the questions does not explicitly foot him as an intended respondent. Mike answers his own questions, constructing replies that stress both Alfred's dangerousness and his unawareness of this fact. Mike's first response describes the generic 'man' as being 'capable o' hurtin' people' (line 4). The inclusion of the noun 'people' emphasises Alfred's dangerousness by referring to multiple hypothetical future victims. The phrase 'right and ↑left' (line 4) stresses the scope of harm, which projects the expectation that harm of such magnitude should be easy for the offender to detect. The limitations of the offender's cognitive ability to assess his own extrematised potential for harm are underscored through the inclusion of 'even' in the clause 'and not even being a↑war↓e of it' (line 5). Mike's second response describes the generic sex offender as 'capable of doing things to ↑peo↓ple that they don't wanna have ↑done ↓to them' (lines 8–9). The absence of hedging in this construction portrays the offender's potential victims as clearly non-consenting.

Emphatic constructions of Alfred's dangerousness and of his inability to see it are foregrounded with more pauses. A 3.1-second pause (line 9) after Mike's second reply is followed by Mike's assessment of the upshot of the generic offender's dangerousness, 'Real scary', after which there is a lengthy 1.4-second pause (line 10) during which Alfred could presumably take the conversational floor. When he fails to respond, Mike asks Alfred to provide an account for his on-going perceptual limitations. The use of present-tense verbs in 'So what's yer ↑prob↓lem why'rn't =why'ren't you able to see this thing' (lines 11 and 14) constructs Alfred's limitations, using perceptualist language ('see'), as a current concern.

Alfred's response resists this formulation. After a 2.6-second pause, he attempts a reply on line 16 using an elongated 'I'. The elongation reserves a turn space, demonstrating Alfred's commitment to produce an explanation while simultaneously displaying difficulties in that production. One difficulty may be that an admission of ignorance, in the form of an 'I-don't-know' reply in this slot, would constitute further evidence of Alfred as perceptually flawed and dangerous. After a 1.9-second pause, Alfred answers: '(Uh: maybe) (0.3.) didn't wanna see it at that time' (lines 17–18). The modalisation 'maybe' helps ward off rejection of Alfred's answer on the grounds that his inability to assess accurately his victim's past behaviour may also be diagnostic of his inability to assess his past thinking. His answer thus constitutes a qualified stake confession (see Potter, 1996). Alfred suggests that his past perceptual deficit could be strategically motivated by denial, whereby in the past he minimised his culpability by deliberately misrepresenting rape as consensual intercourse. The past tense verb 'didn't wanna' and the temporal reference 'at that time' describe this deficit as a past flaw rather than an on-going deficiency. An temporal contrast is set up implicitly between Alfred's past and present motivations: his lack of willingness 'to see it at that time' and his willingness now to understand his conduct and his victim's reactions.

Alfred's attempt to contrast past (distorted) cognitions and current (accurate) ones fits with other analyses we have conducted on noticings of cognitive distortions and their receipts in these data (MacMartin and LeBaron, 2006). Such a contrast ideally demonstrates therapeutic progress; the offender can display self-awareness in the present about his conduct in the past when such insight was absent (see also Auburn, 2005). However, Mike's response (lines 20–8) rejects Alfred's answer as inadequate. Mike recycles his question explicitly, using the present tense to repair Alfred's depiction of his lack of insight as a past problem: 'How come you can't see it right ↑no↓w' (line 20). Mike suggests that Alfred's failure to show insight into his victim's distress is not attributable to resistance or denial on his part. Mike treats Alfred's desire for insight as indisputable (' 'cause you ↑wanna ↓see it', line 21). This is argued on the basis of group norms of therapeutic success ('In this ↑group (0.2) ↓you would be consider:ed, (0.5) a suc↑cess ↓if you could <u>see</u> why she cried', lines 22–4) and the stakes involved ('there's a big ↑pay↓off for you to s<u>ee</u> it', lines 25–6). Mike treats Alfred's lack of awareness, not as the product of motivated denial or strategic manipulation, but of an unmotivated inability (even disability) on his part: 'but st<u>ill</u> you can't s<u>ee</u> why she was crying. You ↑can't ↓expl<u>ain</u> that to us right now' (lines 27–8). The contrastive conjunction 'but' (line 27) sets off Alfred's wish for such insights from the fact of their absence. Given the high stakes in being able to demonstrate awareness about his crime, Alfred's lack of insight can be explained only in terms of cognitive limitations he still must overcome. The reference to his inability to provide an adequate explanation 'right now' (line 28), when he clearly has an interest in doing so, suggests that Alfred still has considerable distance to cover in therapy with respect to addressing his perceptual deficits.

Summary

We examined how concerns about offenders' agency, accountability and stake in the production of cognitive distortions were emphasised and minimised in therapeutic arguments while offender accountability was nevertheless maintained by therapists. In extracts 1 and 3, both offenders argued for the normalcy of their current thinking, albeit in different ways. In extract 1, an offender managed inferences about the impulsivity and deviance of his suicidal talk through his description of suicidal thoughts as an automatic and consistent pattern of thinking tied to a reasonable fear of being jailed. In extract 3, the offender attempted to contrast his past perceptual limitations with his current self-awareness. In both cases, the therapist challenged offenders' moves. In extract 2, he described suicidal thinking as a type of motivated cognition whereby the offender was strategically planning to manipulate correctional authorities. Suicidal thinking was accepted as an automatic cognition but one co-extensive with the agency of the offender who was responsible for choosing to adopt a criminal identity in threatening suicide. In extract 3, the therapist argued that an offender's cognitive distortion was not restricted to the past (in the form of a strategic minimisation of culpability) but rather consisted of a current unmotivated inability to perceive the harmfulness of his crime and his victim's resistance during it.

Despite the different kinds of thinking errors invoked in extracts 2 and 3 (motivated and unmotivated respectively), both offenders were instructed by the therapist about their thinking errors and were hence treated as potentially unaware of the problematic aspects of their current thinking. Of note also were the flexible ways in which notions of offender agency (or its absence) could be enrolled in therapeutic interactions. For example, Alfred was described as dangerous because of his inability to read others' reactions to him; nevertheless, the therapist's interventions displayed the expectation that Alfred demonstrate agency (and associated self-awareness) in another form, by accepting the fact of his cognitive deficit and vigilantly monitoring it and his conduct.

Discussion and conclusion

Arguments about cognitive distortions or perceptual deficits constitute a therapeutic resource in sex offender group therapy talk. Of importance is how matters of agency, accountability and stake figure in orientations to thinking errors as motivated and unmotivated. We examined how the categories of cognitive distortions and perceptual limitations are flexibly enrolled in arguments performing an assortment of actions. For offenders, such actions include resisting accusations of deviance, demonstrating compliance with treatment goals and marking their own progress in therapy. For therapists, such actions include invitations to offenders to adopt functional (rather than criminal) identities and assessment of offenders' risks of reoffending.

The cognitive-behavioural model of treatment calls for the cooperation of the sexual offender; recognition of cognitive distortions implies an offender's willingness to assume the task of managing his deviance (Winn, 1996). Our chapter documents how an offender's description of the automatic nature of his suicidal thinking is employed to argue that such thinking is a reasonable response to an unfair accusation (extract 1); a therapist's arguments about offenders' problematic thinking construct offenders as potentially unaware of the erroneous nature of their cognitions, whether those cognitions are described as manipulative and controlling (as in extract 2) or as perceptually limited (as in extract 3). Offenders are thus positioned as needing therapy. In both cases, these arguments: a) construct an implicit identity for offenders as learners (i.e., as capable of being rehabilitated); and b) affirm offenders' responsibility for monitoring and amending their problematic thinking.

Our analyses offer a number of theoretical and empirical contributions to discursive psychology and to the study of sex offender therapy. First, unlike previous discursive research on sex offender therapy (Auburn, 2005), our study analyses cognitive distortions as explicit categories in talk. Second, the ways in which thoughts are described and the rhetorical uses to which thought descriptions are put turn out to be as flexible and variable as emotion discourse, and in potentially similar ways: thinking can be described as normal or pathological, as the precipitant of events or as a reflex-like reaction to them (see Edwards, 1999, on emotion discourse).

The analytic focus of discursive psychology on fact construction and its concerns with agency, accountability and stake can be fruitful for the study of sex offender therapy because such therapy in practice addresses offenders' responsibility and motives. Future research could study other tasks of treatment beyond the identification of cognitive distortions, such as acknowledgment of the offence cycle, development of relapse prevention plans and the management of offender denial (see Winn, 1996). Discursive research also has practical relevance for the investigation of process issues in therapy. This topic has been neglected in the treatment of sexual offenders and in cognitive-behavioural therapy more generally (Serran et al., 2003). Recently, quantitative studies involving observer ratings of videotaped sex offender therapy sessions have identified therapist characteristics correlated with behaviour change in clients (Marshall et al., 2002, 2003). For example, Marshall et al. (2002) reported that therapists' empathy and warmth, along with directive and rewarding actions, were significant predictors of reductions in victim blame, minimisation of offences and denial of responsibility in offenders. Discourse analysis of challenges of offenders' cognitive distortions provides a qualitative means of examining therapeutic processes, not in terms of statistical linkages between inputs (i.e., therapist variables) and outputs (i.e., client variables) but in terms of micro-analysis of moment-by-moment interactions. Therapist style, the contents of intervention, and client characteristics (as evidenced in offenders' receipts of interventions) would be studied in an integrated fashion as discursive achievements involving members' matters.

Our participants' concerns about intentionality, and the freedom to choose how to think and behave, map onto researchers' concerns in the field of social cognition. One problem with normative depictions of biases in information processing is that they may imply that social perceivers are not responsible for the prejudiced outcomes of decisions based on such biases. On this view, a social perceiver is at the mercy of cognitive limitations whose automaticity minimises that perceiver's agency and, therefore, accountability. However, Fiske (1989) has argued that intentionality and responsibility can readily be ascribed to the perceiver who is considered active (though not necessarily conscious) in deciding where and how to devote his or her cognitive resources; intent exists when the perceiver has options. This stance resonates with our findings. Therapists sometimes argue for the existence of offenders' options regarding their thinking and behaviour. In their orientation to relapse prevention, these arguments emphasise offenders' capacity to choose to think like citizens or criminals, and to monitor their own perceptual deficits and their effects. Our research on cognitive distortions provides insight into how the possibilities of therapeutic change are constructed in the actual talk of sex offender therapy.

ACKNOWLEDGEMENTS

This research was partly supported by a Social Sciences and Humanities Research Council of Canada Postdoctoral Fellowship awarded to the first author.

9   Members' and analysts' interests: 'formulations' in psychotherapy

Charles Antaki, Rebecca Barnes and Ivan Leudar

Discursive psychology's interests in respecifying the traditional phenomena of psychology is well exemplified, we think, in the way that conversation analysis (which is a mainstay of discursive psychology) can illuminate psychotherapy. This chapter is about two things: what conversation analysis has to say about psychotherapy as an interaction, and what it has to say about psychotherapy as psychotherapy. We want to see what we can say about what therapists are up to: how they achieve what seem (to us) to be their therapeutic objectives.

In looking at therapy that way, we are in what is sometimes called 'applied CA'. That is to say, we are certainly going to be looking very closely at the exact exchange of talk, and relying on the accumulated insights of CA to see how it works. But, unlike the utterly unmotivated looking of 'basic' CA, we do have our eyes open to the institutional work that the talk is likely to be carrying out. Moreover, we are conscious that, in therapy talk, we have something about which institutional representatives themselves have stories to tell: what Peräkylä and Vehviläinen call 'stocks of interactional knowledge' (Peräkylä and Vehviläinen (2003). In these circumstances, a CA account can be corrective (it may prove the therapists' account wrong, even on their own terms), or it might be illuminating (it might show they are right, and provide detail), or it might reveal something unsuspected but meaningful to the therapists (again, in their own terms; we leave aside those things that CA reveals about the interaction as an interaction as such, and in which a therapist would have no special interest).

But it leaves an important question hanging, and we want to address it in this chapter. The question is: when CA does its work on therapy talk (be it corrective, illuminating or revelatory), to what degree must it use therapy's own concepts, even to get going at all? Our answer is that it ought not, and that it should stick to its guns; but that in doing so it must, reasonably enough, have access to what any member of the culture

166

would know about what words mean, and the implications they have. Therapy theory is, we would say, no direct help to CA, but CA is, or can be, helpful to therapy theory, at least in what it says about therapists' practice.

We shall illustrate the argument with a look at parts of one longish extract from a psychotherapy session. We shall describe part of the extract using ordinary member's terms: that is, how we think it might be described by anyone who has passable expertise in what we characterise as educated British culture. We want to home in on a certain apparently recurrent feature in the extract: what we might, in ordinary terms, describe as the therapist's 'offering back to their client a brief version of what he has just said'. That is, where the client has described some state of affairs, or described some feeling, and the therapist summarises it or paraphrases it. Here is an example:

Extract 1: JP/Ronnie 7/7/98[1] You didn't get enough response
(all extracts are from the same four-minute stretch set out in the Appendix)

```
1 C:    ye:s, I ↑thought (0.6) £ >ek< with- with money I think I-
2       I- thought I could pull it off, because if I c- £ (0.8)
3       if I just had-clients coming in, (1.1) >y'ner<=they
4       would have (.) re:financed it as I went al↑ong
5 T:    r:ight,
6       (0.5)
7 C:    erm:, (1.4) >but ah- er- bu' th-< they just didn't come in.
8       (1.0)
9 T: →  you ↑didn't get enough response to your ↓ads.
```

'You didn't get enough response to your ads' is a version of what her client, Ronnie, had just been saying. In a moment we shall say more in detail about these formulations (as we shall call them, following Garfinkel and Sacks' (1970) initial observations, and Heritage and Watson's (1979) later highly influential account). Now we just want to rehearse the basic question in front of us. We shall be seeing a number of moments in which a therapist formulates what her client says: will a CA analysis help us understand what that formulation is doing for the speaker *as a therapist*? If it does, then to what extent will CA have to make use of members', or therapists' concepts? We mean: to what extent will the CA story have to mobilise concepts which any cultural member would see straight off, like 'offering a psychological interpretation'? Or those which only therapists (or those using a knowingly therapeutic discourse) would spot, like 'resisting transference'? In answering this question we shall be using CA's accumulated insights into *formulating* as a social action, so let us provide a potted history.

Formulations

Formulations, as a general feature of any talk, were noticed by Garfinkel and Sacks (1970) as ways in which a speaker could offer another their understanding of the situation-so-far, allowing the other to ratify it (or not) and thereafter proceed with the conversation on that basis; they saw formulations, in a sense, as allowing speakers a public display of agreed intersubjectivity. Heritage and Watson (1979) systematised the observation as an adjacency pair, that is, a first part which projects an agreement in a second part. In other words, they noted that if one speaker formulates what has just been said, then the other speaker is expected to take the opportunity to acknowledge that formulation, and indeed to ratify it. Here are examples of formulations of the gist of what the previous speaker has said, and then of an implication, or consequence of it, in an 'upshot':

Extract A (from Heritage and Watson, 1979: 132) Gist formulation (arrowed) (I= interviewer; S–Slimmer of the Year). Note that line lengths have been altered.

```
1 S     When I was at college I think I looked like a matronly
2       fifty. And I was completely alone one weekend and I got
3       to this stage where I almost jumped in the river. I just felt
4       life wasn't worth it any more - it hadn't anything to offer
5       and if this was living I had had enough.
6 I→    You really were prepared to commit suicide because you
7       were a big fatty.
```

Extract B (from Heritage and Watson, 1979: 134) Upshot formulation (arrowed) (I= interviewer; R= respondent)

```
1 I     If occasion -if occasion 'rises again will you take similar
2       action?
3 R     Well we have never hesitated so far to er take action where
4       er freedom is being abused.
5 I→    So there might be another occasion on which you will use
6       the law against unions.
7 R     Not necessarily against unions but against any body or
8       which has become over mighty er and is abusing its
9       responsibilities er if that happens to be a trades union so be
10      it but we're not I repeat not er looking out er for trouble to
11      bash the trades union er the unions have their proper role to
12      play and I believe that to be not in the political field
```

The fact that formulations allow the current speaker to select some parts of the prior speaker's words, ignore others, add spin, and present the package in a form that projects agreement makes them a powerful discursive tool. Heritage and Watson's systematisation of the phenomenon gave researchers what became a much-used resource, and it is now commonplace to see CA work identify, as part of some further analysis, a speaker's formulating the gist or upshot of some selected aspect of the previous speaker's words, and this being ratified (as is normatively preferred) or resisted by that speaker. We might note, as it were in parenthesis, that the term 'formulation' has also expanded in usage to cover a multitude of descriptive practices, especially in the wider realm of discourse analysis, but we shall stick to the adjacency-pair sense of the term here, so as to profit from what Heritage and Watson identified as its two specifically directive editorial features: their claim to find the new description in the words of the previous speaker, and the presumption that this new description is to be agreed with.

Where do formulations appear? Heritage had suggested in 1985 that '*Although it* [i.e. formulating] *is relatively rare in conversation, it is common in institutionalised, audience driven interaction* [where it] *is most commonly undertaken by questioners*' (Heritage 1985: 100). More recently Drew (2003) has probed why this might be the case. In looking through a corpus of non-institutional telephone talk, he reports that that so-prefaced formulations are indeed comparatively infrequent in ordinary conversation. This suggested that they were doing some institutional job, and Drew surveys four different settings to see whether it was always the same one. He finds that when used by a radio talk-show host, a formulation may propose a tendentious reading of what the caller has said, prompting or obliging them to have to argue their case (although we should note that Hutchby (1996–9:53) finds that callers can also use them 'benignly', to extract what is relevant to the show's interests); by news interviewers, it may be a neutral alternative to an 'oh' news receipt, and so serve the need to appear impartial while clarifying issues for the broadcast audience; and in industrial negotiations, though ostensibly reporting the other's position, a formulation might also manipulate it to one side's own advantage (Drew, 2003).

Interestingly from our point of view, Drew's fourth institutional setting is therapy, but unfortunately (for us) he chooses a case where it is the client, not the therapist, who is doing the formulating. Nevertheless there too he finds the formulation doing specific work (checking the implications of what the therapist has said), adding to the general picture that emerges: formulations can be a vehicle for achieving an institutional objective, and that objective differs according to the specific institutional requirements in operation. A news interviewer needs to squeeze the most newsworthy juice from their interviewee, and to do so while seeming impartial, but the industrial negotiator needs to reach agreement in a dispute. Both use the format of a formulation to advance a presumptive version of the other person's talk, but the interests that the presumption serves vary from setting to setting.

Formulations in therapy

With this view of formulations as advancing an institutionally relevant version of the other speaker's words, but serving the specifics of each separate institutional setting, we turn to see what CA and CA-influenced researchers have made of them. Although there is very suggestive material in Sacks' (1992) own early lectures on an adolescent boys' therapy session, the first explicit account of therapy formulations appears in Davis (1986). She crystallised the idea that formulations were a way in which the therapist could advance the therapeutic agenda by recasting the client's troubles in the language of therapy. Indeed her point was that such a move was better termed *re*formulation, given the change it proposed. Since then the theme has been elaborated to show (among other things) that upshot formulations might be more serviceable for therapy (Hak and de Boer, 1996); that formulations allow the therapist to 'suggest that the patient's answers index an underlying mental pattern' (Peräkylä and Vehviläinen, 2003, p 739); that they can choose to tilt the formulation towards the problem expressed in the client's talk or towards its putative solution (Phillips, 1999); and that the adjacency pair format gives clients the opportunity (at some cost) of resisting the therapist's move (Madill et al., 2001; Antaki et al., 2004). Davis' basic observation, nevertheless, remains the core idea: a formulation is a conversational device which expects the confirmation of a therapeutically oriented paraphrase of the client's talk.

At this point we pause. We have skipped over a crucial point. A formulation is indeed a conversational device which expects the confirmation of a paraphrase. But how do we, as analysts of social action in general (not as people trained in therapeutic practice with its special interests), know that the paraphrase is one that is *in the service of therapy*? It is no good to say that it is so because it issues from the therapist. Not everything the therapist says during the session necessarily does an institutional job, or not necessarily the apparently obvious one (for a persuasive account of the variety of ways in which institutional objectives are reached, see Drew and Heritage, 1992b).

To say that the formulation is being wheeled out in the service of therapy is of course for conversation analysts to use their ordinary members' intuitions of what a therapeutic intervention ought to look like. Davis sees the formulation as transforming ordinary miseries into therapisable ones, and she has no trouble persuading us that this is so, without having to recruit any therapist to vouch for her reading. Among the others, even though we know that at least two authors are trained in therapy, none needs therapeutic authority as such to make their claims about what is going on.

It is either the case, then, that therapeutic moves are so obvious that we need no theoretical guidance to spot them; or that conversation analysts' identifications of therapeutic moves have never been properly warranted and may well be wrong. But if they are wrong, in what sense are they wrong? Not, perhaps, in seeing general features of adjacency-paired formulations (as, for example, that they project agreement), because that is a normative claim, based in part on the brute frequency of agreements and more importantly on the troubles shown in dis-agreements, if and when they come. Nor are conversation analysts wrong in interpreting specific deployments of formulations, such as, say, that a particular formulation comes after a troubles-telling, and rephrases it to focus on something within the individual's control. That is a matter of understanding what people do with language. So it must be in the very last step: that paraphrasing misery in just such a way *is* therapy, or part of it.

Can that last step be wrong? It may be, and this is where there is a potential conflict between therapy theory and CA. In their own internal debates, the therapeutic community must always see their descriptions trumping those of CA. Therapy theory may always – since it is therapy's business, after all – say that such and such a step in a session (for example, a formulation), whatever it looked like to the untrained eye, was not in fact therapeutically motivated, or, if it was, then not because it was a formulation. What CA sees as doing work as a formulation might, according to this hypothetical view, really be something quite different: it might be 'confronting the client's hidden fears', ' inter-preting the client's unspoken desires' and so on.

The stand-off between CA and therapy theory cannot, we think, easily be resolved along Peräkylä and Vehviläinen's (2003) sympathetic lines of convergence. Recall that for Peräkylä and Vehviläinen, CA can per-form a service to therapy – it can correct their accounts of what thera-pists do, or add detail, or discover new practices. But correction of therapy theory's descriptions of practices can only happen if they are operationalisable; and elaboration and discovery might, as we men-tioned above, simply be dismissed by therapists themselves as irrelevant to the description of therapy that they find most useful. The solution to the stand-off is, we think, a division of labour, and an acceptance of the incommensurability of the two discourses. CA is speaking to a general audience who will share its members' view of what probably counts as therapy. Therapy theory may or may not agree, and is rightly unembarrassed to say so, having expert rights to redescribe, in its theoretically grounded terms, what CA sees in its own.

It is worth setting out that polar opposition in such stark terms so that we can see where some common ground might lie in the middle. If the therapist agrees that a move is indeed part of the therapeutic practice, then they might be interested to see just how it works. But CA does the work first, without reference to formal theory or what Peräkylä and Vehviläinen call the therapeutic stocks of interactional knowledge; that would, as we have argued, be a distraction.

Some comments on the sequential use of formulations

We approach our own data, then, with the central idea in mind that formulations, by virtue of selecting out some aspect of a client's talk, or drawing out some implication of it, and putting it to the client in a form that expects confirmation, can be a resource for therapists to do therapeutic work, as ordinary members understand it. What we want to do is offer a reading of two sorts of work that formulations do, and show how they do their jobs by virtue of their sequential placement and their internal design. We shall add a small variant to the accumulated CA story, but we shall get to that later.

Data

The full extract is given in the appendix, and might be glossed as follows. We are listening to a one-to-one session conducted by an eclectic, humanistically based therapist. The client, 'Ronnie', has been talking about his impatience, and is finishing off an illustrative story from his work life. He started up a leisure facilities company which needed clients to come in to 'refinance it as it went along', but these clients didn't appear. Even if they had, he says, it wouldn't have been enough, as the business really needed a very large initial investment which would repay only over a long period. The therapist, 'T', suggests that it needed patience. Ronnie demurs: not just patience, but money. The demand wasn't there. Others had tried this kind of business before, but it hadn't worked. He acknowledges that before embarking on the scheme he should have 'done his homework'. The therapist observes that preparation is important. She then offers an interpretation of his behaviour as stemming from his self-gratifying impulsiveness.

That is one, fellow-ordinary-members', account of the extract, and it necessarily smuggles in various analyses of what is going on (we say, for example, that Ronnie is 'finishing off a story', that the therapist 'suggests' something, that Ronnie 'acknowledges' it, and so on). We accept it for the sake of a first pass, and will correct or refine it as becomes necessary as we get on with the analysis. We will go chronologically through three cases of formulation in our appended data. In doing so we shall see how the therapists' words accomplish two, quite different, discursive effects.

Extract 2: Ronnie 7/7/98 You didn't get enough response (partly seen as extract 1 above)

```
1 Ronnie:   ye:s, I ↑thought (0.6) £ >ek< with- with money I think I-
2           I- thought I could pull it off, because if I c- £ (0.8)
3           if I just had- clients coming in, (1.1) >y'ner<=they
4           would have (.) re:financed it as I went al↑ong
5 T:        r:ight,
6           (0.5)
7 C:        erm:, (1.4) >but ah- er- bu' th-< they just didn't come in.
8           (1.0)
9 T:→       you ↑didn't get enough response to your ↓ads.
10 C:       no:. (.) and even if they ↑had've come in, I think I
11          would've ↑still fallen ↑o:ver, (.) because I >didn- havuh-<
12          (.) I hadn't got enough b↑ackup ready-
```

When we saw these data earlier we made the point that 'you didn't get enough response to your ads' was a paraphrase of what the client had said, and so it is. But notice three further things about this paraphrase. Two are to do with where it occurs and one with its internal design.

Sequentially, notice that the paraphrase comes after a full one-second absence of talk. That is a long time, given that the client has finished his turn, completing what he started in line 1, by delivering the second part of a contrast pair (Smith, 1990; Wooffitt, 1992). So the ball is in the therapist's court. Announcements want receipts, and the normative way to do a receipt is to do it quickly and positively. But that is not what the therapist does. The silence signals a dispreferred turn; whatever else it is going to be, it is not going to count as a receipt, as such (it won't be an immediate 'what a shame!' or similar). What she does do after the pause is to give the paraphrase 'you ↑didn't get enough response to your ↓ads'. Given that it comes in the place of a delayed receipt, it comes across as an understanding check, accounting for her silence as having not been a withholding of receipt but rather an opportunity for Ronnie to continue.

What of the design of the formulation itself? It is a neutral gist-formulation of what Ronnie has said. And perhaps that accounts for his normatively standard response, which is an immediate confirming negative, and progress to elaboration of the story on which he is embarked. In other words, the formulation 'works' both as a formulation as such, and also, in its sequential position, as a display that the therapist's previous silence was to be construed as space for Ronnie to continue, not as a receipt withheld.

We might ask at this point whether there is anything here that might speak to the institutional work of therapy (in keeping with our project; that is to say, as an ordinary member might understand it, and without reference to therapy theories as such). One candidate is that in ordinary conversation support for story-telling is done by continuers ('uh-hm' and other such particles) and not normally by formulations. There is something about their core characteristic of offering a reading for ratification that seems to offend against two people's ordinary relationship with each other. As Drew (2003) observes, a non-institutional conversationalist does not ordinarily have to clarify or solicit stronger versions of their interlocutor's story, because in ordinary conversation, the story is not being solicited so as to go 'on the record' (as it is in therapy, as in news interviews and other institutional question and answer routines). So here we have an example of what therapy might not notice about itself, if indeed therapists have any stake in the issue, which of course they reasonably might not.

Let us carry on with Ronnie's story and see how the therapist's formulations develop it. This next extract comes ten lines, or about as many seconds, after the extract above. Ronnie is developing the story, explaining that the failed business had needed a larger initial investment than he had in fact made.

Extract 2: Ronnie 7/7/98 It needed patience

```
22 C:    =it'ws a business that you needed tuh- (.) s'tuv- °put
23       in (.) fifty or a ↑hundred thou:sand (0.8) (tha' you) had
24       (.)
25 T:    °m°
26 C:    erm (.) and then wait for the supply of clients, o [ver
27 T:                                                      [°s-°
28 C:    a sortuv (.) ↑two year period, (.) so=
29T:→    =so it needed patience
30       (1.1)
31 C:    ye:s but it also needed erm- a lot of financial support.
```

Now here there is no latency between the client's turn in line 28 and the therapist's formulation in 29; rather, she latches her formulation as a sentence completion. That in itself suggests something, perhaps that 'her mind is with him', or, more interactionally, as a signal that his story

might be promptly concluded. But we leave those speculations in the air
to notice two more obvious things: the content of the formulation is (to
the ordinary cultural member) distinctly more presumptive than 'you
didn't get enough response to your ads' had been (see line 9 above). It is
much more than a simple gist. It exemplifies the kind of thing that has
been noticed already by CA researchers (the most relevant here being
Peräkylä and Vehviläinen's work on psychoanalysis; Peräkylä and
Vehviläinen, 2003, Vehviläinen, 2003): it finds a psychological account
in the client's words. It does not actually accuse Ronnie of lacking
patience; yet, where his account located the problem in the type of
business ('it was a business that you needed to put in fifty or a hundred
thousand and then wait for the supply of clients'), the therapist's formulation locates it in (someone's) psychological make-up. It needed
patience – implicitly, of course, on Ronnie's part. Perhaps it is this that
accounts for the (normatively) notable delay of over a second before
Ronnie responds, and then only in a mitigated agreement ('yes but ...').
The non-normativeness of this would, in ordinary conversation, strongly
index some degree of what one might call resistance; perhaps in a
therapeutic environment such a term is too freighted with special
meaning to be appropriate, but at least we can say that Ronnie is signalling some sort of non-ratification of the therapist's psychological
account. More than that we cannot say in CA discourse, and here would
be a good example of a point at which we would hand over to a therapist
for psychological interpretation.

Now we come to the last of the formulations we want to look at, and it
is the most complexly designed, faced as it is by the client's repeated
non-ratification of what the therapist is proposing. It starts about half a
minute after the extract above ends.

Extract 3: Ronnie 7/7/98 So there's not enough preparation

```
59 C:    ['n ↑other (bizn'd) tried it an' they've
60       gone broke in in- England
61 T:    yes, (.) yes yes [:
62 C:                     [(the sig- uw- z- th-) (.) hh=>praps
63       z'if=ud=done=ma homework< more I would have
64       found out that- (.) °it wouldn't w-wor [k.° (.) (°s-°)²
65 T: →                                          [so there's
66       ↑not en- ↑not enough preparation beforehand
67       (0.7)
68 ?:    °mm°
69 T:    and not enough erm- (0.6) no- I-↑ think it's= preparation's=
70       =>thi< th't's the key word here.
71       (0.8)
```

Lines 65–6 ('so there's not enough preparation beforehand') show a good example of the Davis (1986) line on formulations as problem-oriented, which, as we have observed, has been a constant through CA's work. What the therapist says could well be glossed as, for example, Peräkylä and Vehviläinen's description of a formulation 'propos[ing] an underlying mental pattern that could possibly explain the patient's prior talk' (2003: 739). But what interests us is just how the therapist brings it off. It is decidedly not like the formulations that have been canonically described by others. It is not, for example, like this one from Hak and de Boer (1996: 93):

Therapist   You appear not to be able to draw a line somewhere, huh, to, you know, it's up til here and not further. Do you recognize this within yourself, that you, when people are requesting something from you, even if you don't know it any more, that you nevertheless will do it?

Where Hak and de Boer's example is full of direct references to the client and their inner states, here we see T bringing off her formulation of the client's story without actually nominating the client directly. Just as in 'so it needed patience' (see above), 'so there's not enough preparation beforehand' is a passive form, obscuring the agent. Nevertheless, it casts it significantly in the present tense – this is something that the therapist is seeing about the situation (and, of course implicitly about Ronnie) *now*, in his therapisable life. We might gloss what she says as 'you don't (currently, generally) prepare for things enough' – but of course that is not what she actually says, and the difference is revealing.

One might see her choice of words as what Bergmann (1992) calls 'discreet talk', or Peyrot's 'oblique proposals' (Peyrot, 1987), a signal that what the other speaker is being accountable for is something negative in the circumstances. And recall that T has already had one brush with Ronnie's resistance (if we can call it that) to her formulation ('so it needed patience' was met with a 1.1 second pause then a mitigated agreement).

Just as with 'so it needed patience', 'so there's not enough preparation beforehand' is met with a silence. After 0.7 of a second, someone does produce an 'mm', but it might be either party (it is not possible to tell from the audiotape). In any case, it is the therapist who is first to come in again intelligibly, and in so doing takes the floor before her 'error' might be made still more visible by Ronnie's continuing silence. It is in this unpropitious environment that we see T abandon the formulation in line 69.

What T does at this point is complex, and worth unpacking, as it seems to do a number of things in the service of (what we would see as) therapy.

Extract 4: Ronnie 7/7/98 So there's not enough preparation (2)

```
65 T:                    [so there's
66      ↑not en- ↑not enough preparation beforehand
67      (0.7)
68 ?:   °mm°
69 T:   and not enough erm- (0.6) ↑no- I- ↑think it's= preparation's=
70      =>thi< th't's the key word here.
71      (0.8)
```

As we mentioned above, the therapist begins line 69 as if it were a continuation of her turn in line 66, retrospectively implying that she had not finished, and so excusing any uptake of her formulation. This may be described as a self-correction in a later turn – an 'embedded correction' (Jefferson, 1983, 1987). It is this danger of the client (again) displaying 'resistance' which, we think, occasions the subsequent development of T's turn. She abandons the way her formulation was shaping – she does not complete what it is that there was 'not enough' of. Instead the speech perturbation 'erm'-, her pause and '↑no-' marks her stopping herself; it is what might be called a 'realisation', an observation to herself as much as to her client (or the invisible overhearer – what Jefferson nicely calls 'talking to God'). The effect of directing her comments to herself (or God), of course, is to excuse (perhaps even disqualify) the client from making any response. That, we think, is orienting to the dangers that he might still be 'on strike'.

Moreover, and still in the service of excusing C from being accountable for ratifying T's formulation, note that what T is thinking is that 'it's preparation that is the key word here' (delivered awkwardly, and with a 'rush-through' (Schegloff, 1988). The phrase 'X is the key word here' would, we can say as members, be very unusual in ordinary discourse. It represents something institutional: to identify a 'key word', in the sense of identifying a psychological state as being a possibly significant candidate in explaining behaviour, requires or claims expertise in 'psychology' or 'human nature' and so on. Although incorporated into on-going talk, lines 69–70 actually shift T into an exposed or explicit form of correcting which provides a place for an account of the sort 'That's the word I was looking for!' This negates the possible reading of the first upshot as incompetent, replacing it with an utterance designed as the result of problem-solving ingenuity. This changes the action in the on-going talk (Jefferson, 1987: 99).

Notice also that T is using something not about her own experience but about C's experience. Now to claim expertise about others' experience is, we suggest, part of what members recognise as 'doing therapy'. So it is 'therapy talk'; but, to return to its sequential placing, remember that it is being set out as a repair of an abandoned effort at formulation. It is 'safer' for the therapist to direct a therapeutically worded observation to herself (or God) than to press on with a formulation that normatively expects ratification.

What we have here, then, is the sight of a therapist having to pay the price of using a device which makes relevant the client's immediate uptake: if it is not immediately forthcoming, that may, as Hak and de Boer put it, 'imply a challenge to the formulator's capacity and competence in monitoring the gists of talk' (1996: 85). The therapist in this extract copes by restarting the formulation, as if it had not yet been properly finished, then immediately abandoning it, incomplete, for something which calls far less urgently for the client's approval. We don't know, of course, whether this is a general practice, but it is at least one way in which the therapist can use the conversational resources at her disposal to get some delicate interactional work done.

The upshot of all this is that formulations can certainly be a vehicle for proposing readings of the client's experience, but their sequential placement shows they can do other things as well, equally in the service of the institutional requirements of the conversation. We might even say that our analysis of the three formulations in T's talk in the extracts above add up to something which would be in Peräkylä and Vehviläinen's (2003) terms, a 'finding' about the practices of therapy. We might argue that we have seen how, in the extract above, 'a therapist copes with exposure of non-ratified formulation' or some such. To do that satisfactorily would need a fuller argument, but even that there is some tentative plausibility to it is testament to how far one can get without us having to check our readings out with a therapist, or with a theory of therapy.

Concluding comments

To conclude, our argument has been that, yes, CA helps us understand what the therapist is doing as a therapist, and without necessarily having looked through therapist's theoretically informed eyes. We've been considering paraphrases, or, in CA terms, formulations. Our first bit of evidence that these are being used institutionally is that the way they appear in these data is not how they appear in ordinary talk; so an institutional reading is indicated. So to go on and investigate just what it is these formulations do is to understand what they are doing for the therapist as a therapist.

In doing so, we have used ordinary members' concepts – because we analysts are members of the culture ourselves, and to have any purchase on that culture's language must mean understanding references to culturally general notions. It would be impossible to do analysis (of any kind) without recognising, 'straight off', what any speaker of the language would recognise, at various 'levels': that the client is reporting a distressing incident; that such and such a phrase is an idiom; that some other phrase is conventionally an exaggeration, or a compliment, or, in the sort of cases we have here, a 'psychological insight', and so on. But it is quite possible (and indeed possible only) to ignore things which are not available to all members of the culture. Our analysis of the deployment of formulations here, though tentative, at least shows us something visible to any member of the culture with time to sit down and work through the detail of a recorded interaction. They will see, like us, that a formulation in therapy can work to offer the client a way of reading his or her words which leads to a therapeutic 'moral' or 'lesson'. And we can also see that it has costs, and can meet client resistance.

We would be uncomfortable with going further and invoking technical therapy concepts (like, say, 'channelling' or 'transference') which refer to theory-bound phenomena, visible or intelligible only to trained personnel. There is a strong ethnomethodological strand in CA which commits it to study only what participants make visible to each other as members (and therefore to the analyst as overhearing member). That, of course, could be seen to be a handicap and a limitation by those with other ontological and epistemological commitments. But if the therapy theorist can offer a public version of the phenomenon (as might be possible with, say, 'active listening') then a dialogue with CA would be possible. There are indications that this is starting to happen, encouraged by pioneering work such as that of Anita Pomerantz with medical professionals (see, for example Pomerantz, 2005.) Both practitioners and analysts would then have a place where they could meet on common ground, and offer complementary skills.

APPENDIX

JP/Ronnie 7/7/98 starting about minute 24

```
1 C:    ye:s, I ↑thought (.6) £ >ek< with- with money I think I-
2       I- thought I could pull it off, because if I c- £ (.8)
3       if I just had- clients coming in, (1.1) >y'ner<=they
4       would have (.) re:financed it as I went al↑ong
5 T:    r:ight,
6       (.5)
7 C:    erm:, (1.4) >but ah- er- bu' th-< they just didn't come in.
8       (1.0)
9 T:    you ↑didn't get enough response to your ↓ads.
```

```
10 C:  no:. (.) and even if they ↑had've come in, I think I
11     would've ↑still fallen ↑o:ver, (.) because I >didn- havuh-<
12     (.) I hadn't got enough b↑ackup ready-
13 T:  yes.
14 C:  but they didn't come in. [(.) so I did realise that- (1.3) ↑er
15 T:                           [°right°
16 C:  >y'ner< they weren't going to come in that fast=it
17     ↑wasn't [a fast turnover business. (.) it wasn't-
18 T:          [°yeh°
19 C:  >it w-↑just-< (.6) er:m- (2.5) it was much more a long
20     ter:m business,
21 T:  yes=
22 C:  =it'ws a business that you needed tuh- (.) s'tuv- °put
23     in (.) fifty or a ↑hundred thou:sand (.8) (tha' you) had
24     (.)
25 T:  °m°
26 C:  erm (.) and then wait for the supply of clients, o [ver
27 T:                                                     [°s-°
28 C:  a sortuv (.) ↑two year period, (.) so=
29 T:  =so it needed patience
30     (1.1)
31 C:  ye:s but it also needed erm- a lot of financial support.
32 T:  and you didn't have enough s-=financial support.=
33 C:  °I didn't have ↑near enough f-financial suppor [t° t-
34 T:                                                 [°↑right°
35 C:  ↑to- (.8) or I could have done it as a sort of like a
36     gro:wing hobby
37 T:  °m°
38 C:  °in° (.) in that ↓way.
39 T:  yes:.
40 C:  er: [m
41 T:      [°>ys<°
42     (1.4)
43 C:  but it didn't work very well in ↑that way either, becuz- (1.0)
44     er:: >well it ↑might have worked< I still had to invest (1.0)
45     a lump sum to sortuv even ↑start it
46     (.5)
47 T:  °m°
48 C:  with- with ↓advertising (.)
49 T:  °m.°
50     (.3)
51 C:  and once (cs)- once I'd ↓borrowed (.) ↑that money,
52 T:  °°m°°
53     (.5)
54 C:  I needed (.3) money to come ↑in.
55     (.3)
56 T:  °°w'uv°°°c↑ourse::,° (.) to keep it °going°,
57 C:  yeh=
58 T:  ↑that's right, ye [s
59 C:                    ['n ↑other (bizn'd) tried it an' they've
```

```
60        gone broke in in- England
61 T:     yes, (.) yes yes [:
62 C:                      [(the sig- uw- z- th-) (.) hh=>praps
63        z'if=ud=done=ma homework< more I would have
64        found out that- (.) °it wouldn't w-wor [k.° (.) (°s-°)²
65 T:                                            [so there's
66        ↑not en- ↑not enough preparation beforehand
67        (.7)
68 ?:     °mm°
69 T:     and not enough erm- (.6) no- I- ↑think it's=preparation's=
70        =>thi< th't's the key word here.
71        (.8)
72 T:     ↑you had an id↓ea, (.) and you wanted to put it into
73        operation,= for ↑various reasons, including >yknow< (.) as
74        you say grandiosity, (.) right?
75        (.8)
76 T:     ↑erm- (.) and ↑er (.) >and t'< something that you ↓love,
77        working (.) with erh- °with water° (.) ° an sea° (.) °an-°
78        °°an every↓thing,°°
79        (.4)
80 T:     *but- iw-* ((*strangled*)) it was the id ↑ea (.) that was
81        so exciting to you, (.) that you- had a- ↑great urge
82        to do it.
83        (.4)
84 C:     y- [yes
85 T:        [without thinking through the practi↑calities:.
86        (.5)
87 C:     th-w'z- y
```

NOTES

The research reported in this article was supported by ESRC grant RES–000–22–0330.

1. We are grateful to Jean Pain for allowing us access to these data, which have been anonymised.
2. From 'praps' to end of his turn is a perfect decrescendo, flattening out at the end.

10 'Suppose it wasn't possible for you to go any further with treatment, what would you do?' Hypothetical questions in interactions between psychiatrists and transsexual patients

Susan A. Speer and Ceri Parsons

Introduction

Psychiatrists, like other medical professionals with a diagnosing or prescribing role, control access to a range of forms of treatment, medication and service that their patient, or their patient's carer, may want access to. This 'gatekeeping' role is particularly acute in settings where a patient's desire for a certain medicine or treatment (e.g., for the drug methadone, or for 'cross-sex' hormones and sex reassignment surgery) may also be interpreted as a symptom of their 'condition' (e.g., heroin addiction, or transsexualism).[1] The UK National Health Service (NHS) Gender Identity Clinic (GIC), is one setting where the psychiatrist's gatekeeping role is renowned.

Practitioners in a GIC deal primarily with patients who self-identify as 'transsexual'.[2] Transsexualism is formally designated in the Diagnostic and Statistical Manual of Mental Disorders (DSM-IV, 1994) as a 'Gender Identity Disorder' (GID). Persons diagnosed with GID are said to exhibit 'a strong and persistent cross-gender identification and a persistent discomfort with their sex or a sense of inappropriateness in the gender role of that sex' (The Harry Benjamin International Gender Dysphoria Association, 2001: 4). Statistically, transsexualism is thought to affect 1 in 11,900 males and 1 in 30,400 females (ibid., 2001: 2). The treatment for the majority of transsexuals consists of taking high doses of cross-sex hormones (Hormone Replacement Therapy), and undergoing Gender/Sex Reassignment Surgery (GRS/SRS) (Green, 2000).

In order to obtain hormones and be referred for surgery, pre-operative transsexuals must be assessed by two psychiatrists at a Gender Identity Clinic. Psychiatrists meet with patients attending the clinic once every three to six months prior to surgery. Follow-up consultations are also held in the months after surgery. One of their principal concerns during the assessment sessions is to decide whether the patient is an appropriate candidate for treatment. They assess the patient according to a pre-defined set of medical criteria and aim to produce a 'differential diagnosis' (that is, to accurately diagnose the type of gender identity disorder and to determine that the patient is not suffering from some other related or unrelated mental health problem).

The internationally recognised Harry Benjamin International Gender Dysphoria Association's *Standards of care for gender identity disorders* (2001) specifies that, before patients can be referred for surgery, psychiatrists must establish that they meet both 'eligibility' and 'readiness' requirements. As part of the eligibility requirement, patients must participate in the 'Real Life Test' (also known as the 'Real Life Experience'), in which they must demonstrate that they are living full-time within their aspired-for gender role for a period of at least a year. This will include at least one year on high doses of cross-sex hormones. To meet the 'readiness' requirement, patients must demonstrate 'further consolidation of the evolving gender identity or improving mental health in the new or confirmed gender role' (ibid.: 7).

One of the principal concerns of transsexual patients undergoing psychiatric assessment at the GIC is to persuade the psychiatrist that they are an appropriate candidate for surgery. Research suggests that some will be resentful for having to see a psychiatrist at all (Green, 2000: 914); they regard the psychiatrist as an 'unwelcome intruder' (Brown and Rounsley, 2003), and find the ritual process associated with the Real Life Test unnecessarily strict, lengthy and humiliating (Reid, 1998). Indeed, the NHS assessment process has been widely criticised by patients who have completed their treatment and who report 'aggressive and rude handling, punitive rules' and 'threats to withdraw treatment' (Burns, 2004a; see also West, 2004).

The contrasting concerns of psychiatrists and patients generate a number of tensions within the treatment context. Commentators have noted that patients, concerned not to delay or risk being refused surgery, are unlikely to report any ambivalence about their chosen gender identity, believing (often correctly) that it will be a 'contra-indication' for surgery. Similarly, they actively resist suggestions that they have a 'gender problem', and simply repeat a stereotyped gender narrative found commonly in 'the published developmental histories of trans-sexuals who preceded them' (Green, 1987: 7–8, 1974; Stone, 1993), claiming, for example, that they have 'always felt' this way – that they are a 'woman/man trapped in a male/female body' (Raymond, 1994: xvi).

Thus, the practitioner–patient consultation has been described as an 'adversarial encounter' (Newman, 2000: 399), which results in a 'cat-and-mouse' game that mitigates against the goals of both psychiatrists and patients. So, for the psychiatrist the issue is 'how can I be sure that this person is a "true transsexual" and not just telling me what they think I want to hear in order to obtain treatment?' For the patients it is 'how can I convince this sceptical psychiatrist that I am a true transsexual, and tell him what I think he wants to hear in order to get my treatment?'

There now exist a number of commentaries and ethnographies reporting on some of the tensions that exist in the assessment and treatment of transsexual patients. One particular account which stands out is Sandy Stone's (1993) compelling response to Janice Raymond's (1979) radical feminist book *The transsexual empire*. Stone (1993: 13) argues:

in pursuit of differential diagnosis a question sometimes asked of a prospective transsexual is 'suppose that you could be a man [or woman] in every way except for your genitals; would you be content?' There are several possible answers, but only one is clinically correct.

Here Stone alludes to some of the tensions generated by the gate-keeping role of the psychiatrist and the institutional demands of the clinic. The idea that patients must provide a 'clinically correct' answer to this question in order to be recommended for surgery (i.e., to state that they would *not* be content if they could not change their genitals), captures something of the way these tensions, and the game of 'cat-and-mouse' referred to above, get played out interactionally. However, there are a number of problems with accounts like Stone's. As is characteristic in this literature, Stone's observations are based on second-hand, retrospective reports on treatment rather than first-hand examples of real-life, real-time consultations between psychiatrists and transsexual patients. Consequently, we have no way of knowing whether the kind of diagnostic question Stone refers to actually gets asked by psychiatrists anywhere in empirical reality. Moreover, if psychiatrists *do* ask such questions, we have no way of knowing how such questions – and the associated interactional tensions they are supposed to illustrate – get played out interactionally. Our aim in this chapter is to use spontaneous, naturally occurring data from an actual treatment context in order to gain some analytic purchase on precisely these issues. Drawing on a single case, we explore how the psychiatrist uses this kind of question to establish the correctness of his diagnosis and the proposed treatment (i.e., that the patient is indeed a 'true' transsexual), and how the patient responds to this kind of question and works to persuade the psychiatrist that they are indeed an appropriate candidate for surgery. Finally we consider whether psychiatrists and patients treat only one possible response as 'clinically correct', as Stone (1993) suggests.

Materials and procedures

The example we analyse here derives from a corpus of materials collected by the second author, which consist of audio-recordings of ninety-five one-to-one, psychiatrist–patient consultations in a UK NHS GIC.[3] This is the largest GIC in the world. Ninety-five per cent of all NHS referrals are dealt with here, and psychiatrists at the clinic see 600 new patients each year. There are four consultant psychiatrists at the clinic, and of these, two were involved in recording their sessions with patients for this study. Each session lasts between fifteen and sixty minutes.[4]

We found six examples of our target hypothetical question in our data. Like the question Stone refers to above, each involves the psychiatrist putting to the patient a *hypothetical* scenario where sex re-assignment surgery is not granted, or where the patient's cross-sex hormone treatment is withdrawn. The psychiatrist proceeds to ask the patient what they would *do* in that situation. These sequences typically consist of structure 'suppose that you could not do/have X treatment ... What would you do?'[5] Each example was delivered by the same psychiatrist, usually in the context of a first or second meeting with a patient.[6] The extract we subject to a detailed analysis below is a representative example from the six we identified across our corpus.[7] This excerpt was transcribed by the first author using transcription symbols developed by Gail Jefferson (2004). We will show how the hypothetical question is built, and how it functions in the psychiatric assessment of transsexual patients. We will end by considering the extent to which this kind of hypothetical question may be deemed a useful or 'successful' strategy in the psychiatric assessment and treatment of transsexual patients.

The interactional organisation of hypothetical questions

The hypothetical questions in our data follow a strikingly similar pattern. Consider our first extract below. The question (marked with → in the left-hand margin) comes at a point where the psychiatrist has spent some time exploring with the patient (who presents as a 'male-to-female' transsexual) how well she passes as female, and whether she has a realistic view of herself in her new role. The patient is in the process of defending herself against the psychiatrist's suggestion just prior to the start of this excerpt that she may still look more like a man than a woman:

Extract 1: T11 Session 2 17.38 – 19.30

```
1 Patient:  I think I'm feminine enough(I know) . hhh
2           (.)
3 Patient:  I mean without ma:jor surgery and (talt)-
4           alterin' my fac:e
5           (1.2)
6 Patient:  I've- this is the face I'm ↑stuck with
7           basica(h)lly(h) [(hh).hhh
8 Psy:                      [Oh ↑yes yes right oka:y .hh
9           uh::m
10          (0.6)
11 Psy:(1)  → .Pt .hh suppo:se, (.) just suppose it- (.) for
12    (2)   → some reason it wudn't be- it wasn't possible for
13          you to go any fu:rther with trea:tment
14    (3)   → what would you do
```

The hypothetical question sequence consists of three parts. The psychiatrist begins, in the first part of the sequence, by inviting the patient to imagine something: 'suppo:se, (.) just suppose' (line 11). As Peräkylä (1993, 1995) shows in his work on the use of hypothetical questions in AIDS counselling, a speaker may begin their turn in this way in order to manage the 'conditionality' and 'epistemological status' of the hypothetical scenario that is about to be described (Peräkylä, 1993: 301ff). In this excerpt, by elongating the second syllable on 'suppo:se', and then restarting, this time adding the word 'just' (line 11), the psychiatrist draws attention to, or 'marks' the special nature of, what he is inviting the patient to do (i.e., it is marked as 'purely suppositional' or hypothetical). In this sense, he is guiding, or instructing, the patient how they should interpret, or read, what comes next, at the same time as 'upgrading' the conditionality of the description (Peräkylä, 1995: 292).

The psychiatrist proceeds in the second part of the sequence to describe the future hypothetical scenario that he is inviting the patient to imagine: 'it- (.) for some reason it wudn't be- it wasn't possible for you to go any fu:rther with trea:tment' (lines 11–13). The self-repairs and perturbations in this excerpt are very revealing. Note the way in which the psychiatrist begins as though to launch immediately into the description of the hypothetical scenario – 'suppose it wasn't possible for you to go any further with treatment'. Instead, however, he initiates a repair on 'it', adding the additional turn component 'for some reason' (lines 11–12). This repair does further work to manage the epistemological status of the forthcoming description and its 'purely suppositional' nature. In particular, the psychiatrist presents the possible reason or cause for the hypothetical scenario he's about to put to the patient as a generalised one that's not pre-established or ordained (by him or by anyone else) in advance. By constructing his turn in this way, he works to remove the imputation that is potentially available to the patient at this time that the hypothetical scenario he is about to describe may become a reality, that it is imminently possible or likely, or that the psychiatrist himself will action that scenario.

The additional repair in which 'wudn't be' is replaced by 'wasn't': 'it wudn't be- it wasn't possible for you to go any fu:rther with trea:tment' (lines 12–13) does additional work to maintain the hypothetical nature of the scenario that is being described. In this case, 'wasn't possible for you' is more distant and conditional sounding than 'wudn't *be* possible for you', which brings the hypothetical scenario further into the realms of possibility, making it appear more immediate and hence more threatening for the patient.

In the third and final part of the sequence the psychiatrist puts a 'wh' question (Schegloff and Lerner, 2004) to the patient – 'what would you do:' (line 14). This furnishes the patient with the information they need in order to determine precisely how they are supposed to respond in relation to the hypothetical situation they have just been asked to imagine. Note that this question has already been projected by virtue of the first and second parts: with 'suppose scenario X' the psychiatrist projects 'then question Y' (see Lerner, 1991: 442ff). It is worth noting that the question could equally run off in the opposite direction as in 'question Y' if 'scenario X' (e.g., 'what would you do if you couldn't proceed to surgery?'). However, the virtue of the former turn design is that it allows the psychiatrist to mark and manage the hypothetical, conditional character of the scenario 'up front', and thus deflect the patients' potential worries that the scenario that he is about to describe may come about. In addition, he marks this as a special class of question in a series of questions, thereby ensuring that he will get a particular kind of *hearing* for the talk with which he is about to be engaged, and that he is talking to a correctly prepared and aligned recipient. It may also be one of a number of ways in which the psychiatrist secures the patient's cooperation in advance of raising an issue that he deems will be of a *delicate* or *sensitive* nature.

To summarise, then, the hypothetical question in this extract has three identifiable parts:

(1) an invitation to the patient to imagine something;
(2) a description of the hypothetical scenario that the patient is being asked to imagine;
(3) a question component which asks the patient how they would act in relation to that hypothetical scenario.

The psychiatrist uses this hypothetical format to present something that could be highly threatening and consequential for the patient's future as though it is inconsequential to the outcome of their assessment: by definition, 'a hypothetical question is one asked out of interest, as the answer will have no effect on the situation' (UsingEnglish.com).

However, here we have a paradox: no matter what the psychiatrist does to manage the epistemological status of the question, framing it as 'purely hypothetical', the institutional and policy context of the clinic environment (and in particular his role as gatekeeper) means that treatment decisions – and specifically decisions about whether or not the patient will proceed to surgery – are something over which he has a great deal of power and control. In this respect, hypothetical questions concerning withdrawal of treatment are not only diagnostic implicative, but they also appear to hold a disproportionate amount of *institutional weight*.

It is worth drawing a contrast here with the way in which hypothetical questions function in the rather different institutional environment of AIDS counselling (Peräkylä, 1993, 1995; Silverman, 1997). In this therapeutic setting, counsellors use hypothetical questions such as the one in extract 2, below, to ask patients who are HIV positive how they would cope if they became ill.

Extract 2: (Peräkylä, 1995: 270)
C1 is the counsellor, P is the client.

```
1 C1:  s::Say::(0.2) we can't say and you can't say,
2 P:    Ye[ah
3 C1:      [but say you did begin to get i:ll (0.8) or say
4          you got so ill that you couldn't kind of(0.2) make
5          decisions for yourself.=who would (0.4) you have to
6          make them for you:.
7          (0.3)
8 C1:  Who do you: (0.2) consider your:
```

The counsellor uses the hypothetical format in order to encourage the client to talk about their fears for the future, and dreaded issues surrounding illness and death. Clearly, in this setting the topic of the hypothetical scenario is also potentially delicate for the patient – it does, after all, invoke the reality of their own potential death when they are not yet ill! However, the chief difference between AIDS counselling and the psychiatric assessment of transsexual patients is that, where in the former setting the counsellor may occasionally be required to tell the patient their prognosis (Peräkylä, 1995: 300–1), they nonetheless have absolutely no control over whether the proposed hypothetical scenario may come about: they cannot influence whether the client's health will deteriorate or whether they will die of an AIDS-related illness, for example. Indeed, no matter what the AIDS counselling patient says in response to the hypothetical question, it will not make that scenario any the more likely. In the gender clinic setting, by contrast, the psychiatrist *does* have the institutional authority to influence whether the proposed hypothetical scenario may come about. In this respect, then, for both psychiatrist and patient, the proposed hypothetical scenario is not hypothetical at all. Instead, patients are highly attuned to the possibility that they may be held accountable for their response to this question, and that their response, along with everything else they say, may have a bearing on the outcome of their assessment.

Additionally, in our data there appears to be a somewhat incongruous relationship between the delicate *manner* in which the hypothetical question is delivered and the comparatively non-delicate *location* in which the question is launched. Thus, even though the psychiatrist does his best to manage the epistemological framework of the question and his role in relation to the hypothetical scenario, he does not prepare the patient in advance for the *topical content* of that scenario (i.e., for the raising of the topic of the possible withdrawal of treatment).[8] Thus, the hypothetical question is not linked explicitly to the prior discussion:

Extract 3: (Start of extract 1)

```
1 Patient:  I think I'm feminine enough (I know) .hhh
2           (.)
3 Patient:  I mean without ma:jor surgery and (talt)-
4           alterin' my fac:e
5           (1.2)
6 Patient:  I've- this is the face I'm ↑stuck with
7           basica(h)lly(h) [ (hh).hhh
8 Psy:                      [Oh ↑yes yes right oka:y .hh
9           uh::m
10          (0.6)
11 Psy:     .Pt .hh suppo:se, (.) just suppose
```

Here the topic of the prior discussion appears to be coming to a close: in this extract (and partly in response to a lack of uptake by the psychiatrist (as in lines 2 and 5), the patient produces what Schegloff and Sacks (1973: 306) describe as an 'aphoristic' formulation which can be heard as summarising the 'moral' or 'lesson' of their perspective. As Jefferson (1984b: 211) notes, 'summary assessments appear to be implicative of closure for a topic, and are recurrently deployed prior to various forms of topic shift'. In this respect 'I've- this is the face I'm ↑stuck with basica-(h)lly(h)' (lines 6–7) 'primes' the next slot for the psychiatrist to launch whatever topic he wishes to raise next. Thus, even though the patient may have figured that something delicate is coming, there is good reason to believe that the topic of their treatment and the possible ceasing thereof is the last thing the patient might expect at this point. Indeed, the question appears to come 'out of the blue'. The patient is thereby put 'on the spot'. In fact this seems to be precisely what the psychiatrist is aiming to do.

Again, compare this with what happens in AIDS counselling, where the counsellors systematically 'prepare their clients for the hypothetical questions concerning the future, by means of careful topic elicitation and topic development' (Peräkylä, 1995: 333). Specifically, counsellors work to ensure that the surrounding talk provides an environment in which 'the possible future situation has already been hinted at, but not yet explicated' (Peräkylä, 1993: 297).

Extract 4: (Peräkylä, 1995: 273)

```
 1 P:   (Can you-) (.) what are the main uhm symptom- (0.5)
 2      what actually does pneumonia (.3) do to you?
 3      (.4)
 4 P:   Once it's ( ) (within your system).
 5 C2:  It gives you a cough,
 6 P:   Yeah.
 7 C2   breathlessness
 8      (3.5)
 9 C1:  Are these things you've thought about before or not
10      really.
11      (2.0)
12 P:   Uh::m (0.2) Sorry what d'you mean- what
13      (lik[e the-)
14 C1:      [All these this discussion we're having
15      about. =Symptoms and things.
16      (0.4)
17 P:   Yeah I had (0.2) I have thought about
18      them,=[(as I said) I thought before: mo:re=
19 C1:        [Mm
```

```
20 P:   =so [that (0.2) err: (1.0) ( ) that I am=
21 C1:      [Mm
22 P:   =thinkin more- (0.4) about them more now because
23      (.6) I'm a little bit more settled in this
24      work (.) [job. And if it's (you sort of)=
25 C1:           [Right.
26 P:   =(        ) (so now: I've got more) time
27      (I) will be-
28 C1:  (      [   )
29 P:         [ (actually) taking a [leave (so)-
30 C1:                              [s::Say::(.2) we
31      can't say and you can't say,
32 P:   Ye[ah
33 C1:     [but say you did begin to get i:ll (0.8) or say
34      you got so ill that you couldn't kind of (0.2) make
35      decisions for yourself.=who would (.4) you have to
36      make them for you:.
37      (0.3)
38      Who do you: (0.2) consider your:
```

In this excerpt the hypothetical deals with the topic of the client's possible future development of an AIDS-related illness (lines 33–5). However, it is the client who first topicalises the 'symptoms' associated with pneumonia (lines 1–2). Pneumonia in HIV-positive patients is commonly indicative of the collapse of the immune system and the onset of 'full-blown AIDS' (Peräkylä, 1995: 274 n.18). Thus the counsellor's hypothetical question is picking up on and topicalising a connection that was first initiated by the *client*. As Peräkylä puts it, 'the counsellor is only making explicit what the patient has already implied' (1995: 275).

So, what might account for these apparent paradoxes and incongruities? In particular, why might the psychiatrist do all this work to manage the epistemological status of the question and his own stake in relation to it, and orient to the hypothetical scenario as a 'possibly delicate' one for the patient, if (a) it is transparent to both parties that the question is not just hypothetical, but that what the patient says in response to it may be used by the psychiatrist to influence whether or not that hypothetical scenario may come about, *and* (b) if the psychiatrist is simultaneously going to undercut the work he does to manage the epistemological status of the question by delivering that question seemingly 'out of the blue'?

One possible explanation revolves around the issue of what business these questions are designed to achieve. Where in AIDS counselling the whole purpose of the hypothetical question is largely to assist the client in their capacity to face up to their fears about becoming ill, in the psychiatric assessment of transsexual patients, the hypothetical question is used in the service of an altogether different set of institutional goals. Specifically, it is used as a diagnostic tool, to assist the psychiatrist in coming to an accurate differential diagnosis.

In order to assure themselves that this is the correct course of treatment for this patient, to obtain a spontaneous response which will provide a valid diagnostic test of the patient's commitment to their aspired-for gender role, and which avoids the patient producing a stereotyped 'textbook answer' (i.e., saying what they think they should say under these circumstances in order to get the treatment they desire), it makes a certain amount of sense to put the patient 'on the spot' and not to let on to them that the question is coming. However, one consequence of this is that, in the here and now, the question serves, first and foremost, the psychiatrist and not the patient. Since patients are usually highly attuned to this, they are faced with a dilemma. For any patient who wishes to proceed to surgery, they must, on the one hand, respond 'on the spot' to this hypothetical situation that has been put to them seemingly out of the blue and do so as spontaneously and honestly as possible. On the other hand, they must be cautious about the question and the diagnostic import of their answer and monitor their response for displays of authenticity and their genuine commitment to their aspired-for gender role.[9] They must also avoid saying anything that might be deemed by the psychiatrist to be a contra-indication for surgery, or which may influence the likelihood that the psychiatrist will take steps to influence whether the proposed hypothetical scenario may come about.

So, how does the patient deal with this dilemma? How does she respond to the hypothetical and work to persuade the psychiatrist that she is an appropriate candidate for surgery? And does the psychiatrist treat only one possible response as 'clinically correct', as Stone (1993) suggests?

The patient's response and the psychiatrist's follow-up questions

The hypothetical question triggers long stretches of talk in which the psychiatrist probes the patient's response and prompts her to elaborate. Space restrictions do not allow us to provide a detailed analysis of the patient's response here. However, what we hope to do in the remainder of this chapter is to give the reader a flavour of how her response runs off, and to reflect on what this response might tell us about the function of hypothetical questions in this particular institutional environment.

Note first of all that the psychiatrist has asked the patient, 'what would you do?' This question could have been designed to make a range of alternative kinds of responses relevant. For example, the psychiatrist could have asked, 'how would you react?', 'how would you feel?', or even 'would you continue living as a woman?' The distinctiveness of 'what would you do?' is that it projects as a relevant next action an answer in which the patient details what they think they would *do* or how they would *behave* if the proposed hypothetical scenario that has just been put to them were to become a reality. By asking her what she 'would' do, the question is inviting the patient to describe something dispositional – to formulate her likely behaviour pattern in the hypo-thetical scenario given what she knows about herself (Edwards, 2006a).

Answering such a question might initially appear to be a straightfor-ward task for the patient. However, the patient's response is noticeably troubled. Consider Extract 5, below, which is an extension of extract 1.

Extract 5: (extension of extract 1)

```
 1 Psy:        what would you do:.
 2             (0.8)
 3 Patient:    (I ha'n't cum)- I ha'n't thought about that
 4             really I'm j's:t
 5             (.)
 6 Psy:        Ok:ay b[ut I I-
 7 Patient:           [(it's gonna be)]
 8 Psy:        I'd like to invite you to: to give it some
 9             thought no:w.
10             (0.8)
11 Patient:    Er:m,
12             (2.4)
13 Patient:    I'd be upse:t, ye:ah very.
14             (.)
15 Psy:        Yes I'm sure you w'[d °yes.°
16 Patient:                       [C'z this is sompthing I
17             really want,
18             (.)
19 Psy:        Ye:s.
20             (.)
21 Patient:    [Er
22 Psy:        [So what would you do:.
23             (1.8)
24 Patient:    Dunn:o
25             (0.6)
26 Patient:    Don't ↑know.
27             (3.4)
28 (Patient): Uh(h)m
29             (.)
30 Psy:        Well I'll put it to you bluntly
```

```
31                    [w'd you continue to li- [live as a woman [or
32 Patient:           [.hhh hhhh               [.hhh          [OH
33                    YES yeah >I'm sompthin' I'm no:w< I'm now a
34                    woman now: >I- this is it I couldn't go back.<
35                      (0.2)
36 Patient:           >Oh no there's no going ba:ck.<
37                      (.)
38 Patient:           °No°
39                      (0.2)
40 Psy:               .Pt °interesting° ri:ght.
41 Patient:           No going back (°no:°).
42                      (.)
43 Patient:           >I w'dn't wanna go back no::w< (would there).
44                      (1.0)
45 Patient:           This is- this is me: I love it I:, this is me:
46                    I've never been so happy in my li:fe.
47                      (.)
48 Psy:               .Hh (.) Ri:ght? hh
```

The patient's response is noticeably delayed (line 2). Moreover, it does not – initially at least – deal with the psychiatrist's question on its own terms (i.e., in terms of what she would *do*). Instead, the patient provides a reflexive comment on her not having considered or even 'thought about' the very hypothetical situation she's being asked about: '(I ha'n't cum)- I ha'n't thought about that really' (lines 3–4).

Of course, it is perfectly reasonable to argue that this patient really 'has not thought' about and 'does not know' how she would respond if the hypothetical scenerio that is being put to her were to occur. However, this kind of response – that is, one that indexes a cognitive inability or lack of knowledge of some sort – turns out to be a very common patient response to this question (for more on this see Speer, forthcoming b). And perhaps it is rather more common than one would expect if one were to attempt to explain patient responses exclusively in terms of cognitive processes.

As discursive psychologists and conversation analysts have shown, the detail of what members say in such 'state formulations' cannot be *reduced* to (that is, they cannot be explained exclusively or primarily in terms of) cognitive processes, or members' desire to describe some internal 'reality'. Instead, members consistently describe cognitive processes as part of *doing* things (Edwards, 1997). Utterances which index cognitive difficulties, lack of knowledge, thought processes and the like operate at an action level, to do interactional, identity implicative work (Beach and Metzger, 1997; Hutchby, 2002; Jefferson, 2004[1984]; Potter, 2004).

What identity implicative work might this kind of response achieve for this patient in this case? First, it works as an account for not answering the question with the kind of answer made relevant by it, and which may thereby be expectable in this position – namely a description of the patient's hypothetical *actions*. Second, it allows the patient to defer answering the question on its own terms – and at least until she has gleaned more information from the psychiatrist regarding what the implications of her response might be. Finally – and crucially – the patient's initial response may inoculate her from precisely the imputation that may be made available at this time, that she is not an authentic candidate for surgery, that she has entertained the possibility of not wanting or having surgery, or that she is a strategist who has rehearsed her response in accordance with some kind of script that is designed to manage just such a question.

Indeed, even while this patient may not have read the Stone quote cited earlier, the trans community is such that patients usually enter treatment with an armoury of research and knowledge about the kinds of questions they may be asked, and already have an idea of precisely what they may be held accountable for. So, in this context, we can tentatively assume that, although it comes 'out of the blue', this kind of question may not come as such a surprise to the patient. By treating the hypothetical scenario as one that they had not previously thought about, or entertained, and by indicating that they are unable to grasp what the question is (apparently) getting at (i.e., that if they could not have surgery, would they give up living as a woman and revert to the male sex?), their response seems designed precisely so as to display that the possibilities contained within the hypothetical question (withdrawal of treatment and/or reverting to the male sex) has not even crossed their minds, and that only one outcome (surgery in order to 'become a woman') preoccupies them. To a certain extent, then, by putting the patient 'on the spot', the psychiatrist may inadvertently assist the patient in providing just this kind of 'spontaneous' and 'authentic' answer.[10]

So how does the psychiatrist respond to these displays, and to the patient's apparent difficulties? One common way in which questioners may respond to their co-interactant's apparent difficulty in formulating a 'type-conforming' answer is to treat that difficulty as caused in some way by something in their just prior turn. One possibility open to the psychiatrist in this case, for example, is to treat the presuppositions contained in his original question as problematic in some way, and to rework his question such that it is easier for the patient to produce a response (something which he could very appropriately do at such a juncture if he wishes to appear tentative and helpful). Interestingly however, the psychiatrist does not (initially) treat the patient's response in this way. Instead, he treats her response in a literal fashion (as evidence for her not having thought about it) and proceeds to invite her to think about it now (at the same time as reflexively commenting on the nature of the action with which he is currently engaged): 'I'd like to invite you to: to give it some thought no:w' (lines 8–9).

The patient now responds in terms of her hypothetical feelings and not her actions: 'I'd be upse:t, ye:ah very' (line 13). However, the psychiatrist treats such feelings talk as self-evident and patently *not news*. Thus he says, 'Yes I'm sure you w'd °yes°' (line 15), and when the patient elaborates with the account 'C'z this is sompthing I really want' (lines 16–17), he simply says 'Ye:s' (line 19), before reiterating his original question *without repairing it*: 'so what would you do:' (line 22), thus implying that it is the patient's response that is inadequate, and not his question. It is only after some lengthy delays, and the patient's two 'don't know' responses (lines 23–9), that the psychiatrist clarifies what the question was apparently getting at: 'w'd you continue to li- live as a woman or' (line 31).

Discussion

Although we have only begun to touch on some of the things that are going on in these data, we do hope to have given the reader a feel for the kind of work that is done with hypothetical questions in this particular institutional context. In particular, we hope to have provided an illuminating illustration of how just one – albeit extended – question-and-answer sequence can offer a window on the kinds of larger-scale issues, agendas and tensions that are associated with the GIC environment and display something of these tensions in microcosm. As we have shown, psychiatrists, patients and trans theorists often write about the interactional problems within the NHS assessment and treatment process (e.g., Burns, 2004a, 2004b, 2005; Reid, 1998; Stone, 1993; West, 2004). However what a fine-grained analysis of hypothetical questions and patients' responses can do is provide grounded arguments about psychiatric practice and about the gatekeeping of gender in medical environments that is based on first-hand examples of real-life, real-time interactions, rather than second-hand, speculative or retrospective reports on treatment.

We have shown that the precise function of hypothetical questions is highly dependent on the interactional environment in which they occur. Indeed, in contexts where the doctor is a gatekeeper, hypothetical questions work rather differently than they have been shown to do in the more therapeutic environments discussed by Peräkylä. In particular, where in AIDS counselling the counsellor has no control over whether the proposed hypothetical scenario may come about (for example, the counsellors in Peräkylä's data cannot influence whether the client will die of an AIDS-related illness), in our data, by contrast, the psychiatrist *does* have the institutional authority to influence whether the proposed hypothetical scenario may come about. Patients are usually highly attuned to this, and to the possibility that their response, along with everything else they say, is, or might be, *diagnostic implicative*. It follows that, if they wish to proceed to surgery, they must continuously monitor themselves for displays of authenticity and for their genuine commitment to their aspired-for gender role. It is this, in part, which accounts for the interactionally 'troubled' nature of their responses.

We want to end by considering the extent to which the psychiatrist's questioning strategy can be considered successful. On the one hand, we could argue that transsexual patients are already very skilled at managing a difficult situation. They respond actively and creatively to the demands of the encounter and manage well within a problematic set of constraints. In this sense, psychiatrists may be losing the 'cat-and-mouse' game and may need to 'up their game' so that patients are not continuously second-guessing them and tailoring their responses and their life narratives accordingly.

On the other hand, although the patient's response to the hypothetical question may appear troubled, this does not necessarily mean that the psychiatrist's questioning strategy is unsuccessful, or that they are bad, hostile, insensitive gatekeepers. Indeed, as we have shown, the psychiatrist may intend to make things difficult for the patient, put them 'on the spot', or make them think that their answers will be inconsequential, in order to avoid precisely the kinds of second-guessing and stereotyped narrative scripts alluded to in the literature, and make an accurate differential diagnosis. Psychiatrists are in a difficult situation here, and it is hard to imagine an alternative means by which they may produce a reliable diagnosis, and without somehow troubling the patient. Even though the psychiatrist's questioning seems hostile, then, we must ask, given the current socio-legal and medical context within which they must work, could the psychiatrist proceed in any other way? If so, how?

ACKNOWLEDGEMENTS

Susan Speer would like to acknowledge the support of the ESRC (award number RES-148-0029) and The British Academy (Overseas Conference Grant OCG 38081). The latter financed dissemination of some of our findings at the International Gender and Language Association Conference, Cornell University, 5–7 June 2004. Both authors would like to thank Victoria Clarke, and colleagues who attended the CA and Psychotherapy Conference at Manchester University, 11–12 June 2004, for their useful comments on an earlier draft.

NOTES

1. It is important to note that we are not wishing to imply a particular connection between transsexualism and drug addiction here.
2. We use the medical term 'transsexual' as opposed to the more political term 'transgender' to describe our research participants, because this research deals specifically with individuals who seek medical treatment to change their sex. The notion of transgender is often used in a political context by transgender activists, specifically in order to avoid medical categorisation.
3. Although it is preferable to make video recordings when dealing with co-present interactions (to access the interlacing of talk and gesture, for example), in this case ethical constraints restricted us to the use of audio only. The first author is currently collecting video-recordings as part of a large-scale ESRC-funded project at this clinic (Speer and Green, forthcoming).
4. Since patients meet with psychiatrists relatively infrequently (every three–six months), none of the patients appears in this corpus more than once.
5. Our interest in these questions stems less from a desire to produce a generalisable sequential rule for the operation of hypothetical questions across contexts than from a concern to unpack what interactional business this distinctive interactional object does for this psychiatrist in this institutional setting.
6. Although both psychiatrists were oriented to the same medical and assessment goals, and to similar interactional business, since they did not use a standardised protocol when assessing patients, it is perhaps unsurprising that just one of them put this particular hypothetical question to his patients.
7. For a more extensive analysis of questions from across the data set see Speer and Parsons (2006), and Speer, (forthcoming a).
8. We use 'topic' here in the vernacular sense of the term as in 'what is talked about' (Schegloff, 1979: 270 n.13).
9. In other words, the patient must treat the hypothetical suspiciously, as a 'test question' for which there may be a right or wrong (or, in Stone's (1993) terms, a 'clinically correct') answer – and one for which they may later be held accountable. They must not only establish for themselves at the outset what the clinically correct answer might be, but if they are to appear authentic and spontaneous, they must do all this and deliver the correct one as though doing so *without thought or design*.
10. Indeed, as soon as it becomes evident precisely what the psychiatrist is getting at, the patient moves to an immediate and emphatic 'yes' response

(lines 32–33). The 'oh yes' marks a change of state (Heritage 1998) and orients toward the problematic nature of the question in that it presumes that such a possibility might even have been considered. The patient also thereby casts their initial difficulties in answering the psychiatrist as having been caused by some ambiguity in the question, and not by some (cognitive, accountable) failure within themselves.

Part III

Youth and institutions

11 'Doing reluctance': managing delivery of assessments in peer evaluation

Jakob Cromdal, Michael Tholander
and Karin Aronsson

As the site of young people's daily affairs, school is the home of peer culture.[1] This is where the social order of the peer group comes to life as part of the mundane interactions between its members. With the recognition of the interactional basis of peer culture (cf. Speier, 1971; Corsaro, 1979; Sacks, 1979; Goodwin, 1980) and its everyday relations to the social orders of the adult world, ethnographers, sociologists and social psychologists alike are facing an interesting set of partly distinct social phenomena. However, while the ubiquity of these distinct social orders in school has been massively theorised (James and Prout, 1990; Jenks, 1997, for a recent development of sociological theorising on childhood), we know comparatively little about the actual practices through which these orders co-exist and mesh with peer group practices as natural features of participants' social lives (Cromdal, 2006).

The study at hand takes as its point of departure ethnomethodology's recognition of social order as a practical accomplishment of members' situated actions. By examining how a group of eighth-grade (13–14-year-old) students engage, together with their teacher, in a demonstrably institutional activity, namely that of self- and peer assessment, we propose to examine merging points between peer culture and the educational order of the school, as they surface in participants' orientations to their own as well as each other's actions during the unfolding event. More specifically, by investigating in some detail the coordinated production of participants' actions, we will demonstrate how students display reluctance in relation to the institutional activity as such. This practice – of displaying reluctance to the formal task – has a bearing on our understanding of peer culture, and its relation to the institution. It also provides some insights into the discursive organisation of emotions. From this observation arises a second theme of inquiry, namely the teacher's attempts to deal with student resistance to the task. Here we comment on some interactional devices through which the teacher can be seen to solicit student assessments. Before proceeding with the analysis, we offer a brief presentation of the educational ideas underlying the practices of self- and peer assessment, as well as their broader encompassing educational programme commonly known as problem-based learning (see, e.g., Boud and Feletti, 1991).

Peer-group concerns and school's institutional goals

For some years now, theories of learning have stressed the active role of the learner as well as the social nature of educational activities (e.g., Forman, et al., 1993; Mercer, 1995; Säljö, 2000). The resulting implementation of this 'collaborative turn' in education entails a gradual shift in the organisation of classroom activities, from teacher-fronted lessons to project-centred work in more or less autonomous student groups. Roughly, the key idea is that students will be active in their acquisition of knowledge, rather than passive recipients of teachers' lectures. What is interesting to note is that such organisation of class-room education recognises the peer group as an important context for learning. Indeed, it can be proposed that such a solution is an attempt to align the peer group with the institutional goals of the school.

Lately, Swedish schools have witnessed a rather thoroughgoing development of these ideas, with the introduction of problem-based learning in primary and secondary education. Interestingly for our purposes, the emphasis on student autonomy applies to the assessment and evaluation of the group's work, which is thought of as an integral part of the learning process. The role of the teacher here is – at least in theory – that of a resource, a consultant, rather than a party to which the group is responsible for its actions. That is to say, it is the task of the student group to decide whether the issues posed have been dealt with in a sufficient manner, and whether all parties have contributed to the work in a satisfactory way.

Needless to say, this is very different from traditional education where teachers alone are responsible for assessment and evaluation of students' progress. One of the implications of this division of labour is a potential clash of competing moral orders: the goals, norms and values of the institution may well prove to be at odds with those entertained by the peer group. Also, the stakes are considerably raised when the group is made to handle the formal assessment and evaluation of its members' progress, as these are matters which may have a bearing on the final marks of the individual students at the end of the school term.

In other words, peer assessment and evaluation are activities in which students are institutionally obliged to comment on and judge their own efforts as well as that of the other members of the group. Needless to say, this can be a socially sensitive task. At stake here is the institutional order of the school as well as the social and moral order of the peer group. This can be seen as a form of 'culture contact' (Mackay, 1975; Speier, 1976), and the practical issue for participants is how to measure up to the potentially conflicting requirements imposed by those social orders. It is precisely such a nexus of conflicting rights and obligations, as they are brought about by the participants as relevant and consequential features of the interaction, that forms the focus of the present study. More precisely, our analyses constitute an attempt to flesh out the locally deployed methods through which participants orient to the evaluation practice *as* a dilemma, and through which they work towards its resolution. And now to some data.

Initiating peer evaluation: turn devices, instructions and collaborative challenges

The present analyses mainly draw on a single extract of talk, taken from a twenty-minute evaluation session involving a group of five eighth-grade students and their teacher. The group has spent the past week working on a project, and towards the end of the period slated for the assignment, the time has come to evaluate the group's work. Our analysis focuses on the early phases of the meeting (its first 3.5 minutes), during which the students are taking turns in evaluating the work of one of the group members, Stina. Such evaluations form a fairly new routine at the school, and the session is set off by the teacher giving the group the following instructions:

Extract 1: Instructions
```
Participants: The teacher (teach), Johan, Emil, Anna, Lisa,
and Stina
1 teach:   e::h well let's see he::re (.) I was thinking that
2          you cou::ld (0.5) e:h evaluate each other.
3          (0.7)
4 Stina:   ehhmpfhh ((sigh + headdrop))
5 Johan:   [↑no↓o:! ((eyes on Stina))
6 teach:   [that is- yes! That is to say how each and every
7          one ha:s worked? (0.5) ((facing the group)) and ↑how
8          each and every one has functioned in these (.)
9          group conversations.
10         (3.8)
11 teach:  I was thinking if we start with that then we go on
12         wi:th (.) ((turning to Lisa)) e:h work.
```

```
13 Lisa:    do we go ↑rou:nd like this Stina me Emil Anna
14          [Johan? ((moves hand around the table))
15 teach:   [ye:s
16 Lisa:    okay!
17          (0.5)
18 Johan:   do we have to s[ay (too)?
19 Emil:                  [well Stina's got [plenty of
20          experience! ((sarcastic voice, turning towards S))
21 teach:                  [ye:s ((to Johan))
22 Johan:   no↑O::?= ((headtilt at teacher, grimacing))
23 Emil:       [   (xx)    ]
24 teach:   =and t[hen we do:] like this (0.5) then we do like
25          this like you take what's been goo:d first (.) and
26          then we take what's been le:ss good.
27          (1)
28 Lisa:    ((facing Emil, ironic voice)) it's so hard I don't
29          know wha- (.) [Emil's been so good so I don't know
30          anything bad to say! Oh! ((raised eyebrows, wobbles
31          her head))
32 teach:                  [we can begin with Sti::::: (.) >we
33          can< begin with Stina. ((the teacher writes
34          (Stina's name?) on a paper in front of him))
```

Let us first focus on the teacher's instructions. The announcement in lines 1–2 sets the agenda for the meeting, making it clear that the business at hand has to do with evaluations. A closer inspection of this initial announcement reveals the teacher's use of a psychological construct: 'I was *thinking* that you cou::ld (0.5) e:h evaluate each other'. Note, that this term, 'thinking', is a rather unforced way of producing an instruction, much in line with the democratic ideals of problem-based learning.

After this, the teacher goes on to clarify that the target of the evaluation is the efforts and participation of each member to the group's work (lines 6–9), rather than evaluating, say, what each of the students has learned. Hence, the teacher can be seen to provide the group with some institutionally relevant instructions as to how to go about the upcoming activity. The two elements featuring in the teacher's talk, *what* is to be evaluated and *who* is to do the evaluation, can be seen as part of the specific organisational framework, namely problem-based learning, which stresses the active involvement of students in the entire process of education. Moreover, this ideology proclaims an aspiration to get away from assessments of learning outcomes (see, e.g., Swanson et al., 1991; Woods, 1994), focusing instead on the process of learning.

We may preliminarily note that the teacher's turn in lines 6–9 is followed by an extended pause, upon which he returns to the overall agenda for the meeting, informing the group that they will do the evaluation for starters, then get back to the project work. Again, the teacher's formulation of the agenda invokes the psychological construct of 'thinking'. However, as before, the psychological construct of 'thinking' does not reflect a cognitive state. The teacher is not engaging in reviewing and sharing with the students his thoughts on the matter of evaluation and how to go about it. Rather, 'thinking' forms a rhetoric and interactional device through which the teacher in a relatively democratic way summons the students to engage in the proposed activity (see, e.g., Edwards, 1999; Potter and Hepburn, 2003; Edwards and Potter, 2005, for some accounts of how cognitive states may be invoked to accomplish discourse work).

However plausible, the above characterisation does not capture the locally sensitive production and reception of the teacher's actions. Let us therefore consider some further interactional details of this exchange. As the teacher starts presenting the agenda for the meeting at the beginning of the extract, Stina looks up from her notebook. Then, as it becomes clear that the incipient activity is about 'evaluating each other', she produces a loud sigh and drops her head in a disgruntled manner (line 4). Upon this, Johan, who has been facing Stina from across the table, immediately produces an objection '↑no↓:' ('↑na↓e:j') (using a markedly rising-falling intonation, which gives this action a hearably frustrated character). In this way, Johan displays an understanding of Stina's actions as disaffiliative with the evaluation project just presented by the teacher. Furthermore, he picks up on Stina's disaffection and produces an allied emotion display. In other words, the two students' turns are matched both on the level of action and affective stance towards the incipient activity announced by the teacher in the opening lines of the transcript. As we will soon discover, what we have here is an embryo to an unfolding collective resistance towards this institutional task.

Returning to the transcript, we may note that Stina's and Johan's protests come out in overlap with the beginning of the teacher's instructional turn in line 6. Upon hearing these protests, the teacher breaks them off with a simple 'yes!', displaying his instructions as much less negotiable than the term 'thinking' might have implied. These instructions serve to unpack the gloss of peer-evaluation: through the turn initial qualifier 'that is', the teacher produces the instructions as an explicit detailing of the matters to be evaluated. It is possible then, to view the teacher's turn as a set of instructions comprising a two-part list of things to be assessed, formulated as questions: 'how each and every one ha:s worked?' and '↑how has each and every one functioned in these (.) group conversations'. Along with this line of reasoning, the items on the list may be seen as procedural questions, i.e., questions that are offered to guide the students' evaluation work. This set of instructions is not allocated to any particular recipient; it is addressed to the group as a collective. Hence, if a student were to self-select and produce a response in line 10, s/he could be heard as not just supplying a potential evaluation of the group's work, but crucially, as *volunteering* an opinion on the matter.[2] In view of the previous disaffiliation with the teacher's agenda, displayed by two of the students in lines 4–5, a voluntary alignment with the evaluation task could be at odds with the displayed stance of these students, and possibly constitute a violation of the seen-but-unnoticed moral order of the group. We will return to this matter shortly.

As none of the students picked up the prior turn, the teacher again formulates the agenda for the meeting, placing a marked emphasis on the word 'start' (line 11) and turning his gaze directly to Lisa, who responds in line 13. However, rather than treating the teacher's turn as a prompt to begin the evaluation, she forwards a procedural inquiry, asking if they are to take turns according to the seating arrangements at the table. The suggested working order is then established by the teacher's confirmation and Lisa's acceptance in line 16. We may note that by suggesting a geographically 'natural' speaking order, Lisa manages not to produce an opinion at this point and, notably, to postpone her own participation in the evaluation work. In lines 18–22, Johan explicitly challenges the task again, first by asking if they really 'have to say' (by implication referring to the verbal production of opinions), then, after the teacher's firm confirmation, by producing another token of distress: a prosodically marked 'no↑O::?' ('na↑E::J?') combined with a backwards head tilt and a contorted facial expression, which lends his protest an air of exasperation. We may also note that Johan's questioning of the task appears after the working order has been established collaboratively by Lisa and the teacher, that is, in a position relevant for the beginning of the evaluation activity. Hence, the exchange between Johan and the teacher in lines 18–22 further delays this from happening.

The teacher's instruction that follows in lines 24–6, is designed to establish a procedure for how to go about the evaluation: you begin with what has been good, then you proceed with the less positive assessments. One idea of such an instruction may be educational: it is important that students learn to assess both positive and negative features of one another's conduct. As such it may be seen as part of a socialisation process, through which students become accustomed to the academic practice of giving and receiving critique.

A final remark on the students' receipt of the teacher's instructions is in place. We already noted that Johan's questioning of the task in line 18 was produced in a sequential position where Stina might have begun the peer evaluation. We may also note that the overlapping sarcastic remark by Emil about Stina's abundant experience (of the group's work, presumably) occupies virtually the same slot. This move opens up for a new trajectory of action, namely one in which Stina may respond to Emil's remark, rather than begin the evaluation activity. Again, the teacher's instruction in lines 24–6 reorients the group to the task at hand.

The pause following upon this instruction creates another slot in which Stina could have begun the evaluation. However, the person to take a turn at talk is Lisa (lines 28–31). While her action is formatted as an assessment of Emil's contribution to the group, it is obvious that it cannot be interpreted as a serious attempt. The entire turn is produced in an exaggerated enthusiastic voice, lending her actions as unmistakably playfully sarcastic, and she finishes off by raising her eyebrows and letting out a delicate 'oh!', wobbling her head at the same time, to give an impression of feigned fascination. In other words, Lisa can be seen to exploit a previously unattended turn at talk (in line 27) to pull off a parodic evaluation of Emil; she is playing at doing peer evaluation, and she is doing so in a sequential environment where that very activity might take place.

To recap, we have discussed some of the interactional means through which the teacher announces the upcoming institutional business of peer-evaluation, providing a range of organisational instructions for how this is to take place, through which he strives to make this activity happen: to make the students engage in the evaluation. We have also noted how in receiving the teacher's actions, the students deploy a variety of means to collaboratively resist the evaluation project, by way of parody, emotive displays, outright objections, passivity and stalling the activity by initiating alternative trajectories of action. Let us now turn to inspect in some detail the participants' ways of managing personal opinions pertaining to their peers' contribution to the group, of their ways of 'doing peer evaluation'. We will focus our analyses on the students' ways of displaying reluctance to the task, and in particular on the delivery of negative assessments of their fellow students' work.

Non-substantial opinions and reluctance work

Recalling the teacher's instructions, the current evaluation task requires the students to identify both positive and negative features of the individual group members' contributions to their joint work. This task then involves students' expected production of positive and negative assessments of their peers, as well as of themselves. Let us therefore investigate how such assessments are interactionally managed, beginning with an

instance of self-assessment. The transcript is taken from an early stage of
the meeting, in which Stina is nominated to go first. It follows directly
upon an unsolicited comment from Lisa, who claimed that Stina had
been working fine.

Extract 2: Stina's self-assessment

```
1 teach:    let's put it like this what does Stina think
2           herself?
3           (2)
4 Anna:     hehe[he
5 Stina:        [about me?
6 teach:    yes.
7 Anna:     hehehe
8 teach:    if you evaluate your [own contribution.
9 Stina:                         [but do I ha:ve to do it?=
10 teach:   =yes.
11          (2) ((Stina looks down then up at the ceiling))
12 Stina:   °oh Gunnar!° [hehehe
13 Anna:                 [hehehe
14 Stina:   ((looking down at the table, gaze moving sideways,
15          increasingly high tonal pitch)) oh well I guess
16          I've worked pretty much like the others it's been
17          about the same I guess (.) ↑yeah?
18 teach:   are you satisfied with your contribution?
```

The teacher's initial remark that Stina should be allowed to speak for
herself hearably nominates Stina as the only legitimate speaker in the
next turn, which is evident in the two-second pause that follows upon
the teacher's turn (and perhaps also by Anna's laughter in line 4). Yet,
rather than producing the expected assessment, Stina initiates a clarification sequence, making sure that what is expected of her is an
assessment of herself. The teacher confirms this, then offers a reformulation, stressing that the requested action is an assessment of her own
'contribution' (line 8), rather than of herself as a person. Before the
teacher's instruction is brought to a completion, Stina replies with an
explicit rejection of the request, asking in line 9 whether she really has to
produce an assessment. Upon the teacher's sustained request in line 10,
Stina disengages from their mutual gaze by looking down at the table
and then to the side and up at the ceiling. She then produces a barely
audible resigned protest, addressed directly at the teacher "°oh Gunnar°'
('°men Gunnar°'),[3] finishing off her turn with strained laughter, with
which Anna aligns in line 13.

Stina then goes on to propose that she has worked about the same as
the others in the group. She prefaces her turn with the Swedish token

'nämen' (which roughly corresponds to 'oh well' in English), then produces a first self-assessment ('having worked like the others'), using the qualifiers 'I guess' and 'pretty much'. She then proceeds to paraphrase this account ('it's been about the same'), again using the qualifiers 'about' and 'I guess'. The turn-preface in line 15 suggests that the following talk is to be heard as produced reluctantly, possibly even against her own will, and that the turn final particle '↑yeah?' ('↑ja?') suggests that she has nothing more to add. Furthermore, by interspersing her talk with this type of hedges and qualifiers, Stina can be heard to produce a personal, yet rather tentative opinion on her own working efforts; an assessment which she may be willing to revise, if necessary.

There is an attitude being staged and publicly displayed here, of Stina being everything but happy about delivering the assessment that is being required of her. This becomes especially evident if we consider the open rejection of the teacher's request in line 9: having tried all other forms of resistance, she can now be heard to reluctantly produce a provisional, and pretty much neutral, assessment of her own contribution to the group.

Clearly, then, Stina's self-assessment seems organised to manage various concerns dealing with speaker subjectivity and recipient design. It is nowhere near an attempt at bragging, and it is carefully tailored not to be heard that way. In general, actions such as self-assessments can be socially sensitive: an overly positive judgement is at risk of being heard as self-praise. Moreover, in the current context, a positive self-assessment could be construed as a negative evaluation of the rest of the group. On the other hand, a strongly downgraded assessment in the present context would suggest that Stina has not fulfilled her duties as a student, and furthermore, would make her potentially accountable to the teacher for letting the group down. Indeed, since the task at hand is to evaluate Stina's contribution to the group, virtually *any* comment that evaluates her efforts in the group can be heard to imply a judgement of the other group members. Against this background, it is interesting to see that Stina's turn in lines 15–17 does not actually assess her contribution in terms of 'good' or 'bad' or any other morally accountable metric; the assessment squarely places her on a par with the other students in the group. Hence, by strictly equalling her own efforts to those of the other students, she manages not to pass judgement on (or to praise) either. We will shortly return to discuss the local usefulness of this collective metric against which individual actions are measured. Let us for now move on to consider the next extract, in which Lisa is prompted to assess Stina's efforts.

Extract 3: Lisa's assessment of Stina

```
1               (7) ((the teacher writes in notebook))
2 teach:   and what does (1) Lisa: say then?
3               (1) ((the teacher makes a note))
4 Lisa:     about Stina? (.) or about myself? ((facing the
5               teacher))
6               (0.5)
7 teach:   about (0.3) Stina. ((looks up at Lisa))
8               (0.5)
9 Lisa:     ((looks down in book)) yeh well that's about
10             ri:ght I guess hehemf (0.5) ((scribbles in book))
11             ↑(hum:hum:hum:
12 teach:  (1.5) ((makes a note, then looks up at Lisa))
13 Lisa:    ((scribbling)) it's the same with all of us all of
14             us has like (.) has like worked equally well
15             [and all that, I think.
16 teach:  [yes (.) nothing positive to say?
17             (0.5)
18 Emil:    no. ((ironically))
19 Lisa:    yeh well that is positive isn't it hehe[he
20 teach:                                                              [uh huh
21             (0.5) ((the teacher makes a short note))
22 teach:  negative then?
23             (2)
24 Anna:   that she was ill yesterday hehe[he! ((looks at
25             Lisa))
26 Lisa:                                                    [hehemf
27             (2) ((Stina smiles faintly and turns her head away
28             from the group))
29 teach:  negative? ((looks at Lisa))
30             (1)
31 Lisa:    °↑du↓nno°
32             (1)
33 teach:  nothing in particular?=
34 Lisa:    =no.
35 teach:  no.
36             (2) ((the teacher makes a note))
```

After making a note of Stina's self-assessment, which serves to terminate the previous exchange, the teacher allocates a new question to Lisa, asking what she has got to say. In light of the previously established order of procedure (extract 1, lines 13–14), according to which the evaluation is to proceed in rounds following the seating order around the table, the teacher's question is hearable as a 'new round-initiator'. However, it does not specify the exact object-to-be-assessed, and Lisa opens up a clarification sequence asking whether she is expected to produce a self-assessment, just like Stina did in the previous exchange.

After this is clarified, the teacher looks up at Lisa, who looks down in her book and produces a qualified agreement: 'yea well that's about ri:ght I guess' (lines 9–10), which she finishes off with a short laugh token. Lisa then aligns with Stina's assessment, pointing out that they all have been working equally well (lines 13–15).

Let us unpack this brief exchange in some detail. Note that Lisa's agreement with Stina's preceding self-assessment is produced as an alternative to a personal assessment of her group mate, showing as it were her reluctance to engage in the evaluation activity. The empirical evidence of her displaying reluctance toward delivering the assessment expected of her is abundant: First, before she starts talking, Lisa suspends eye contact with the teacher, which can be seen as a token of disaffiliation with his request for an assessment of her group mate. Second, her agreement in lines 9–10 displays a hearable distance to, or disinvolvement with, the evaluation task altogether: the initial token, 'yeah well' ('nämen'), suggests that, rather than disagreeing, Lisa could not care less, and the specifically non-precise qualifier 'I guess' ('väl') suggests that she does not necessarily fully agree. Third, Lisa disengages further by using two other vocal expressions, short laughter and humming, while starting to scribble in her book. The former expression is somewhat ambiguous, as is often the case with laughter (Glenn, 2003; Edwards, 2005), but would seem to suggest in this case that Lisa is orienting to the sensitive nature of the situation (cf. Osvaldsson, 2004). The humming seems more straightforward: its precise timing with the onset of her scribbling suggests that she is demonstratively attending to other matters besides the exchange with the teacher. Taken together, Lisa's moves massively index her as reluctant to comply with the assessment task at hand.

The teacher does not visibly attend to Lisa's displayed disengagement with the task. Rather, he makes a short note in his book and looks up at Lisa without speaking. The effect of his withholding of a relevant response results in the turn staying with Lisa (cf. Sacks et al., 1974), and we can see that she goes on to produce an extended account for her agreement with Stina's self-assessment (lines 13–15). Lisa's account invokes (and pretty much echoes) what Stina has already said, namely that they have all worked equally well. This of course is consistent with her previous action, in which she already agreed with Stina's account. Note, however, that Lisa concludes her account with the tag 'I think' ('tycker jag'), which transforms her account into a personal opinion. Since this is exactly what has been asked of her, it can be seen as a way of complying with the teacher's request. Furthermore, it may serve to conclude her part of the assessment.

However, the teacher does not acknowledge Lisa's assessment as complete. Instead, he proceeds by asking in line 16 whether Lisa has in fact nothing positive to say about Stina's contribution to the group. In line 19, Lisa objects to the teacher's treatment of her assessment as neutral, pointing out that her previous assessment was in fact a positive one. The teacher accepts this characterisation (line 20) and asks now for a negative opinion (line 22). The sequential organisation of the teacher's moves in lines 16–22 is interesting: by treating Lisa's first assessment as neutral, he is able to solicit a positive comment, then accepting Lisa's qualification of that assessment as de facto positive, he is able to move naturally over to the next assessment part – the negative opinion. The smoothness of this transition is partly provided for by the previously established assessment procedure: to first comment on the positive aspects of the person being assessed (or rather, her/his contribution to the group), then to produce a more critical assessment (cf. extract 1, lines 24–6).

The silence that follows upon the teacher's question in line 22 seems to suggest that what is asked of Lisa is a dispreferred type of action. Indeed, it is tempting to treat the pause as a token of Lisa's reluctance to produce a negative assessment and the ensuing events lend support to such a reading of the data. Although the teacher's question is clearly allocated to Lisa, it is Anna who takes the next turn and volunteers a jocular complaint, pointing out that Stina was ill yesterday. Clearly, being absent (implied in 'being ill') from the group means that you cannot contribute to its work, and Anna's complaint in fact qualifies as a relevant type of action with respect to the teacher's prompt – a negative assessment. However, it also provides a clearly legitimate reason for Stina's absence and can therefore be seen as a 'safe' one (Sacks, 1992; Edwards 2005). Generally, a student's absence due to illness may be very relevant to group evaluation, and such complaints may be used, for instance, to account for why the group has failed to meet the timeline. At the same time, such complaints do not engender any negative consequences for that member, since all students have an institutional 'right' to be ill and miss school. In the present case, Anna concludes her turn with a laughter token, which is immediately picked up by Lisa, suggesting that the complaint is not to be heard – and in fact is not heard – seriously. Rather, in the absence of any action from Lisa, the allocated next speaker, Anna's contribution can be seen as an attempt to let Lisa 'off the hook' at a socially sensitive point in the interaction.

Anna's volunteering of a jocular complaint at this point in the interaction suggests that the students attend to each other's local concerns and orient to the social sensitivity of the task imposed on them by the teacher. Furthermore, in collaborating to find a way out of this social dilemma, they invoke and orient to an underlying moral order of the group, a form of group solidarity against the institutional requirement of more elaborate and critical comments.

Returning to the transcript, we may note that the teacher does not acknowledge, or in any way orient to, Anna's candidate assessment. Instead, there is a new silence during which the teacher continues to look at Lisa (lines 27–8),[4] then repeats his request for a negative opinion (line 29). Hence, Anna's contribution is disqualified as a response to the teacher's request, and again, Lisa is called on to critically comment on Stina's work. After another hesitant pause she produces a prosodically marked '°↑du↓nno°' ('°↑vetn↓te°'), which displays her reluctance to comply with what is being asked of her. Interestingly, in the next turn the teacher unpacks this 'dunno' as 'nothing [negative] in <u>particular</u>' (line 33), hence treating Lisa's response as in compliance with the task, rather than as another refusal to produce an assessment of Stina. This hearing is corroborated by Lisa (line 34) and confirmed by the teacher in line 35, who then goes on to make a note in his book, thus concluding the assessment activity with Lisa.

In sum, we have seen Lisa drawing upon a range of interactional resources to display her unwillingness to critically evaluate her group mate. The hedged responses, the humming, the disaffiliative bodily orientation and, in particular, the absence of a negative opinion, massively index her as reluctant to engage in the institutional activity of peer evaluation. In other words, the social sensitivity and awkwardness of this activity is brought about and displayed by her actions, and hence available to the other participants in the group. Ultimately, Lisa's assessment of Stina is thus produced collaboratively or even collusively rather than as a ready and spontaneous personal response to the teacher's initial request (line 2).

Our final extract shows some further interactional means through which the students manage to avoid this sensitive task. The interaction in extract 4 follows directly upon the previous transcript.

Extract 4: Emil's and Anna's assessments of Stina

```
1           (2) ((the teacher makes a note))
2 teach:    Emil? ((looks up to face Emil))
3           (1)
4 Emil:     I concur.
5 teach:    <what a bloody boring ↑gro:up!> ((makes a note))
6 Stina:    [hehe hehehehe
```

```
 7 Lisa:    [hehe hehehehe
 8 Anna:    [hehe [hehehehe
 9 Emil:    ((smiles)) [yeah well (.) but it- it wasn- it was
10          just finding facts and answering questions the
11          [first days (.) that's li-
12 teach:   [uh huh
13          (1)
14 teach:   Anna? (.) 'I concur' ((ridiculing voice))
15 Anna:    yeah: (.) I go alo:ng! [he[hehe hehehe
16 Lisa:                          [he[hehe hehehe
17 Stina:                             [hehehe hehehe
18 Emil:                             [hehehe hehehe
19          (1) ((the teacher makes a note))
20 teach    nothing negative [except 'was ill' then?
21 Anna:                     [but we've all done (.) some.
```

Having made a note in his notebook, the teacher looks up and selects
Emil as the next person to produce an assessment, in line with the
predetermined order (extract 1, lines 13–14). He accomplishes this by
simply addressing Emil by name, using a questioning intonation. After
a slight pause, Emil responds, 'I concur' ('instämmer').[5] This very brief
exchange merits some comment. Let us first note that Emil's choice of
lexical term and the minimalised format of his turn expresses something of a formal, bureaucratic or otherwise heavily marked form of
agreement (e.g., to be expected at a formal board meeting). This is not
how people go about agreeing with each other in everyday Swedish
conversation. Secondly, this minimalistic agreement matches the short
form of the teacher's request and its allocation. Furthermore, it is
delivered in a dead serious tone of voice, and it could be argued that
such overdoing of seriousness may serve as a way of introducing a sense
of humor to the statement, or even mockery. Certainly, it is responded
to with a humorous comment by the teacher in line 5. A third feature
to note is that not only is Emil's reply in itself minimalistic, but, in
contrast to Stina's and Lisa's prior contributions, it is produced without any further clarifications or hedges. There is, of course, one significant similarity: in agreeing with the previous assessment, Emil is
drawing on a technique already introduced by Lisa, who in turn
claimed agreement with Stina's assessment. In a way then, the availability of previous assessments provide later speakers with an option to
simply tag along, to align with what has already been said, instead of
producing a unique, personal contribution. In response to Emil's over-
stretched seriousness, the teacher exclaims with exaggerated despera-
tion 'what a bloody boring ↑gro:up!'. This action can be heard as the
teacher's bracketing of the formal event, in that he himself submits a

personal, humorously upgraded evaluation of the group. In so doing, he displays his orientation not merely to Emil's previous turn, but also to the previous students' unmistakable reluctance to produce substantial assessments of their group mates. The teacher's action generates lively laughter from several students (lines 6–8), upon which Emil points out that the past days' work merely involved finding facts and answering questions. Emil's account thus orients to the target of the teacher's complaint, namely the overall absence of critical evaluations. According to this account, there has not been much trouble accomplishing the task as the work itself was rather straightforward. Hence, there is no ground on which critical evaluations of the group's members might be based.

Notably, the teacher does not pursue the issue any further with Emil, but moves over to address Anna. Note that in soliciting an assessment from Anna, the teacher supplies a candidate answer by recycling Emil's previous reply ('I concur') in a markedly ridiculing voice (line 14), thereby challenging her in a teasing manner. He thus orients to the students' avoidance of producing assessments of their own.

In producing a novel, less formal version ('I go along', line 15) of Emil's original response, Anna manages to sidestep several local concerns. For one thing, she manages to reject the teacher's alternative, and with it the ridiculing overtones he has proposed. However, and this is crucial, she still accomplishes the very same action, just not in those exact words. This casts the exchange as an act of verbal duelling, in which Anna manages a swift comeback (rather than responding in a purely defensive way; Tholander and Aronsson, 2002), which again generates much appreciative laughter from the other students. Ignoring the joking, the teacher makes a brief note and summarises Stina's assessment: 'nothing <u>negative</u> except "was ill" then?' This po-faced receipt (Drew, 1987) brings the interaction back on the formal track of peer evaluation, as we can see in Anna's defensive account (line 21), in which she points out that they have all done some work. By shifting back to the formal agenda, the teacher is thus able to (temporally) terminate the joking and solicit an assessment from Anna. This technique of shifting between mundane talk and institutionally focused interaction – as well as between humour and serious business – is successfully exploited by the teacher as well as by several students in the later phases of the meeting. On a somewhat different note, her assessment can be seen as a mere acknowledgement of his prior summing up ('nothing negative', line 28), which again reflects the collaborative – or even collusive – nature of the teacher's monitoring of the peer assessment process.

Concluding discussion

Group evaluation constitutes a meeting point between the educational order of the school and the social order of the peer group. Our investigation has highlighted the socially sensitive nature of peer evaluation and shows, in some interactional detail, how students go about the task of producing (or not producing) personal assessments of their own and their fellow group members' contribution to the joint project. Self- and peer-assessments of group performance emerge, not as spontaneous responses, but as collaborative or at times collusive products of teacher–student conversations.

The most obvious way of obstructing the evaluation project was to question its necessity, or even to deny cooperation outright with the teacher's request for self-assessments of the peer group. However, the very occurrence of the meeting implies an asymmetric distribution of local rights and responsibilities, and the students were not in a position to altogether rebuke the institutional project of group self-assessments. Rather, the students' actions show their attempts to find a socially manageable way of participating in the meeting: of satisfying the teacher's demands, by producing actions that might qualify for peer assessment, yet by making their reservation to the task observable-reportable for all present parties, so as not to violate the shared yet largely taken for granted moral order of the group.[6]

This was overwhelmingly accomplished by the students' various displays of reluctance to fulfil the task, which was often accomplished by various emotion displays, sometimes collaboratively coordinated in the sequential unfolding of talk. Through such displays, students were seen to handle concerns of subjectivity and recipient design. Showing reluctance to the task served to save the speaker from being heard as volunteering an opinion, and we have seen that students would go to some length to avoid that risk. Alternatively, humorous assessments would often be produced by non-addressed parties, to fill the sequential slots in which a student's opinion was expected. Such moves were typically collaboratively supported by laughter from the other students. Another technique for sidestepping the delivery of personal opinion, available to later speakers, was to simply agree with the preceding speaker's assessment.

When forced to produce an opinion, however reluctantly, students' assessments would cast the individual group members as a homogeneous collective ('the same'), in terms of work effort. Indeed, during the early phases of the meeting, students would repeatedly state that 'they have all been working equally (well)'. This was something of a standard form of assessment, and its routine use is reminiscent of a practice that Wieder (1974) labelled 'telling the code'. Wieder's study of a half-way home for drug addicts shows how the residents, when approached by the staff, would overwhelmingly respond by the formulaic statement 'you know that I won't snitch', thus displaying for all present parties that their loyalties were, and would remain, with the inmate collective. The difference in the nature of the two institutional settings notwithstanding, when presenting the teacher with 'we have all been working equally well' as virtually the only form of assessment of the group's work, the students can be seen to be telling the code of group solidarity.

It is perhaps possible to view this practice as a result of the organisation of problem-based learning, which promotes the significance of the group in the learning process. A problem-based learning project begins with the students jointly establishing the goals for their future work as well as the means through which these goals are to be attained. However, the evaluative practice, albeit organised as a group meeting, involves students producing assessments of their group mates' *individual* contributions to the group, rather than merely commenting on the group as a whole. A student producing a negative assessment of a fellow student may be held accountable for this action not just to that particular student but also to the rest of the group. Moreover, the presence of the teacher at the meeting is significant, especially as he has been continuously taking notes of the students' assessments. This may alert students to the stakes involved in commenting negatively on their work and having this judgement documented by the teacher for future grading or other assessments. It is of little surprise, then, to find students orienting to the sensitivity of this task.

It needs pointing out that peer group evaluation presents a range of practical concerns for all the parties involved, not just for the students. Consequently, we have seen how, in pursuing the institutional agenda, the teacher would attend to curricular matters as well as to peer group concerns, for instance by accepting imprecise and non-substantial student comments as de facto valid assessments, or by bracketing the formal agenda of the meeting by producing personal humorous assessments of the group, possibly as a way of taking the tension out of the meeting, or perhaps even to incite or provoke the students to produce personal opinions.

In sum, we have shown how public displays of reluctance serve as practical resources for participants to handle a set of institutional dilemmas.

APPENDIX: SWEDISH TRANSCRIPTIONS

Extract 1 Instructions for group assessments

```
 1 teach:   e::h då ska vi se hä::r. (.) Jag tänkte att
 2          ni skall få:: (0.5) e:h utvärdera varandra.
 3          (0.7)
 4 Stina:   ehhmpfhh ((sigh + headdrop))
 5 Johan:   [↑na↓e:j! ((eyes on Stina))
 6 teach:   [de vill säga- jo! de vill säga hur ha:r var och
 7          en arbetat? (0.5) ((facing the group)) och
 8          ↑hur har var och en fungerat i dom här (.)
 9          gruppsamtalen.
10          (3.8)
11 teach:   jag tänkte om vi börjar med det så fortsätter vi
12          me:d (.) ((turning to Lisa)) e:h arbete.
13 Lisa:    kör vi ↑ru:nt så här Stina mej Emil Anna
14          [Johan? ((moves hand around the table))
15 teach:   [ja:
16 Lisa:    okej!
17          (0.5)
18 Johan:   måste vi sä[ga (också)?
19 Emil:               [Stina har ju [mycket erfarenhet!
20          ((sarcastic voice, turning his head towards Stina))
21 teach:                          [ja: ((to Johan))
22 Johan:   na↑E::J?= ((headtilt at teacher, grimacing))
23 Emil:    [ (xx) ]
24 teach:   =och d[å gö:r] vi så här (0.5) då gör vi så
25          här att då tar man det som varit bra: först (.) och
26          sen tar vi det som varit mi:ndre bra.
27          (1)
28 Lisa:    ((facing Emil, ironic voice)) det är så svårt jag
          vet inte
29          va- (.) [Emil har varit så duktig så jag vet inte
30          vad jag ska säga för dåligt! Åh! ((raised eyebrows,
31          wobbles her head))
32 teach:   [vi kan börja med Sti:::: (.) >vi
33          kan< börja med Stina. ((the teacher writes
34          (Stina's name?) on a paper in front of him))
```

Extract 2: Stina's self-assessment

```
 1 teach:       [om vi säger så här vad tycker Stina
 2          själv?
 3          (2)
 4 Anna:    hehe[he
 5 Stina:       [om mig?
 6 teach:   ja.
 7 Anna:    hehehe
```

```
8 teach:    om du utvärderar din [egen insats.
9 Stina:                       [men må:ste jag göra det?=
10 teach:   =ja
11          (2) ((Stina looks down then up at the ceiling))
12 Stina:   °men Gunnar!° eh [hehehe
13 Anna:                     [hehehe
14 Stina:   ((looking down at the table, gaze moving sideways,
15          increasingly high tonal pitch)) nämen jag har väl
16          jobbat som dom andra ungefär det är
17          väl lika (.) ↑ja?
18 teach:   är du nöjd med din arbetsinsats?
```

Extract 3: Lisa's assessment of Stina

```
1           (7) ((the teacher writes in notebook))
2 teach:    och vad säger (1) Lisa då?
3           (1) ((the teacher makes a note))
4 Lisa:     om Stina? (.) eller om mig själv? ((facing the
5           teacher))
6           (0.5)
7 teach:    om (0.3) Stina. ((looks up at Lisa))
8           (0.5)
9 Lisa:     ((looks down in book)) nämen det
10          stä:mmer väl hehemf (0.5) ((scribbles in book))
11          ↑hum:hum:hum:
12 teach:   (1.5) ((makes a note, then looks up at Lisa))
13 Lisa:    ((scribbling)) det är ju så med alla alla
14          har ju typ (.) har ju jobboat lika bra och
15          [så, tycker jag.
16 teach:   [ja (.) inget positivt att säga?
17          (0.5)
18 Emil:    nej. ((ironically))
19 Lisa:    jomen det är ju positivt hehe[he
20 teach:                                [mm
21          (0.5) ((the teacher makes a short note))
22 teach:   negativt då?
23          (2)
24 Anna:    att hon var sjuk igår hehe[he! ((looks at
25          Lisa))
26 Lisa:                             [hehemf
27          (2) ((Stina smiles faintly and turns her head away
28          from the group))
29 teach:   negativt? ((looks at Lisa))
30          (1)
31 Lisa:    °↑vetn↓te°
32          (1)
33 teach:   inget särskilt?=
34 Lisa:    =nej.
```

```
35 teach:   nej.
36          (2) ((teacher makes a note))
```

Extract 4: Emil's and Anna's assessments of Stina

```
1           (2) ((the teacher makes a note))
2 teach:    Emil? ((looks up to face Emil))
3           (1)
4 Emil:     instämmer.
5 teach:    <vilken jäkla tråkig ↑gru:pp!> ((makes a note))
6 Stina:    [hehe hehehehe
7 Lisa:     [hehe hehehehe
8 Anna:     [hehe [hehehehe
9 Emil:     ((smiles)) [jamen (.) men de- det var ju in- det var
10          ju bara att leta fakta och svara på frågor
11          [första dagarna (.) det är j-
12 teach:   [mm
13          (1)
14 teach:   Anna? (.) 'instämmer' ((ridiculing voice))
15 Anna:    ja: (.) håller me::! [he[hehe hehehe
16 Lisa:    [he[hehe hehehe
17 Stina:       [hehehe hehehe
18 Emil:       [hehehe hehehe
19          (1) ((the teacher makes a note))
20 teach:   inget negativt [förutom 'var sjuk' då?
21 Anna:                   [men alla vi har ju gjort lite.
```

NOTES

1. We would like to thank Alexa Hepburn and Sally Wiggins for generous comments on an earlier version of this chapter. Thanks are also due to the members of two seminar groups at Linköping University: 'the discourse group' and 'the conversation group'. This paper was prepared with financial support to the first author from the Swedish Foundation for International Cooperation in Research and Higher Education (STINT) and to the second author from The Swedish Research Council (VR).

2. A possible objection here might be that conversational lists typically come as three-part constructions, and that participants at talk overwhelmingly orient to this expected three-partedness of lists, as has been shown in several conversation analytic studies (Jefferson; Lerner). Hence, along with that line of reasoning, the pause in line 9 could be analytically accounted for by the students' expectations of a final list component, rather than their hesitation to provide a relevant answer to the teacher's questions. There are strong indications, however, that this is not the case here. Firstly, whereas the rising intonation and emphasis in the final part of the first list component (line 7) makes the teacher's turn hearable as unfinished – and indeed suggests that this *is* a list-in-progress – the second component of the list has a very different

intonation contour: the rising-questioning intonation and emphasis is placed on the first element of this list component (and ↑*how* has each and every one has functioned in these [.] group conversations.) while its ending is produced with a typical final intonation, suggesting rather that the teacher's turn is brought to an end. Further to this interpretation may be added that, in line 10, the teacher seems to orients to the absence of action from the students, as we are suggesting above.

3. This format, 'but + name' is commonly used in Swedish to produce somewhat downgraded oppositional actions, akin to, but not as strong (or weak, rather) as, pleading. A corresponding candidate action in English might be 'oh c'mon', if produced in a 'resigned' kind of voice.

4. It is very hard to interpret Stina's actions here, who smiles faintly and looks away from the group. Let us therefore only tentatively suggest that the smile may be a way of acknowledging the awkwardness of the current situation, where Stina's group mates are being made to comment negatively on her work. Following this line of reasoning, her turning away from the group may be a way of showing that she is not fully attending to what is about to be said about her.

5. The Swedish verb 'instämma' has a formal ring to it, just like 'concur' does in English.

6. Clearly, 'seen but unnoticed' orders of social conduct (Garfinkel, 1967) present researchers with an analytical challenge, as they pose as the topic of inquiry precisely those matters that members take for granted in the ordinary course of affairs. Within ethnomethodological studies, a common technique to find these relevant, yet mostly invisible, orders is to look for deviant cases in which assumed norms and expectations are being accountably violated, as such occasions allow analysts to flesh out the participants' orientations to the underlying norms, as well as their attempts to restore the order. In the present data, such a violation occurs later in the meeting, as Emil presents an overly positive assessment of Stina's contribution, claiming that she in fact has done most of the work. This is immediately oriented by the other students – as well as by the teacher – as a grave violation of the moral order of the student group.

12 A valid person: non-competence as a conversational outcome

Alessandra Fasulo and Francesca Fiore

Putting autism into context

Dealing with a condition such as autism is intimidating if one is not a clinician, especially if the interactions examined are in a therapeutic setting and experts are involved; but we were supported in our research by the significant contributions made in other studies to the understanding of social situations involving people with communicative disabilities, autism-related (see below) or otherwise originated.[1] We shall not attempt an explanation of autism as a syndrome, but will touch upon research that has looked at the social situations which constitute the everyday life of people – especially children – diagnosed with autism.

Existing theories accounting for the most common symptoms of the autistic-spectrum disorder are grounded in extended experimental research (see overviews in Frith, 1989; Baron-Cohen et al., 1993, 1989; Sigman and Capps, 1997) but there is also evidence that changing the nature of the tests, for example by introducing objects familiar to the children, can produce better performance (e.g., in Theory of Mind tests: cf. Astington and Gopnik, 1991). Bushwick (2001) suggested that the unusual behaviour of autistic individuals generates impoverished social experiences leading to insufficient social learning. Some aspects of autistic behaviour, like echoing, eye aversion or repetitive movements, are liable to confound observers' expectations, in particular those related to the interaction order and functioning. Wootton (1999), however, has been able to demonstrate how, even in the case of *delayed echoing* (the insertion of strings of talk coming from a distal context), echoing turns are respectful of transition relevance places, thus avoiding or minimising overlap, and can run in parallel with non-verbal, cooperative activity.[2] In another study by Local and Wootton (1995) assessing prosodic and formal features of 'pure echoing' (i.e., repetition of proximal others' utterances), it is claimed that children's skills with repetition make it a favourite tool to manage interactional tasks, so that many instances of echoing, while in a sense not completely apt, can still assume responsive and sequential fitness.

If nobody can be blamed for being puzzled by sudden rushes of irrelevant activity in the middle of a conversation or a game, strategies for familiarising interactants with the nature of the disturbance can make a great impact on their interactional withdrawal. For example, Ochs et al. (2001), in their pioneering ethnography of high-functioning and Asperger autistic children, compared peer interaction in classrooms where the child and his family underwent 'disclosure' about the disturbance to the whole classroom with situations in which the classroom was not informed (in one case not even the school staff). In cases where the classmates were aware of the possibility of anger-reactions, stereotypical movements and expressions, but also aware of the autistic children's intact abilities and interest in social relations, positive inclusion practices (i.e., involvement and support) were more frequent. Conversely, negative inclusion practices such as 'neglect, rejection and scorn' (ibid.: 416) were encountered more frequently by children whose classmates did not know what to expect, how to react or how to interpret their behaviour. Similarly Schuler (2000), when observing children who had been trained to treat the contributions of their autistic classmates as relevant, however odd-seeming, reported a marked increase in the quality and quantity of the affected children's relevant moves, which in turn permitted richer experiences of participation.

The impairment of pragmatic skills associated with autism cannot be denied, nor is it useful to disregard the specific sensitivities that affect the functioning of social contacts as we are socialised to expect them. Nevertheless, the study of spontaneous interaction allows us to deconstruct the problem into different areas of performance in which individuals with autism show varying degrees of competence, some of which, for instance those concerning turn-taking and sequential implication, are more or less intact even in the most severe cases (Local and Wootton, 1995; Wootton, 1999, Ochs and Solomon, 2004). As with Ochs and Solomon's reflection on the concept of *practice* and with Bushwick's reassessment of the role of *social learning*, the study of autism compels us to examine the functioning of social reality *tout court* and the theoretical tools used to investigate it; looking at autism with interactionist- and ethnomethodologically inspired analytical lenses permits a deeper inquiry into the difficulties of both the affected people and those in their immediate social context.

One of the goals of the present chapter is to show that therapeutic intervention could be strengthened if it were founded on a better awareness of the nature of talk-in-interaction as a system with its own organisation and features. Competence coincides only partially with analytical descriptions of the way conversation works; lay models of 'good' talk typically underestimate the extent to which 'happy exchanges' (Ochs, 1983) not only tolerate but *require* ellipsis, repetition, irregular syntax, turn fragmentation and partial overlap. When training and instruction programmes are founded on idealised and unrealistic models of conversation, they can lead to leakages in the machinery and a waste of resources.

Research site and data set

The interactions examined below were recorded at a Centre specialising in the treatment of persons of varying ages with autistic disorders. The research focuses on two boys, one thirteen and the other ten years old. The data set includes paper-and-pencil observations of the entire Centre's spaces and activities; audio recordings of interviews with the therapists (at the beginning of the data collection, and with a follow-up when the data were under analysis); examinations of diagnostic tests and reports on the target patients; ten video recordings of their weekly therapy, and observational diaries of any recording session. Literature concerning the theoretical approaches informing the Centre's therapeutic activity was also collected.

The boys, whom we will call Marco and Giulio, have both been diagnosed with high functioning autism. Giulio, the younger one, was described as having higher linguistic skills and a wider vocabulary when compared with a typical child his age, though his speech was somewhat manneristic. His social attitude was assessed as good, whereas Marco was reported to prefer the company of adults and to be more anxious with respect to social contacts and new situations. Marco also had more difficulties with morphology and syntax. In both cases, the reports mention difficulties with the non-literal plane of language.

The boys' therapy hours included a regular sequence of activities,[3] each occupying from ten to fifteen minutes, comprising: Work (table tasks which could be performed autonomously or with the aid of a therapist); Free Time (devoted to games like puzzles or pretend play); Time for Talking (where the boys sat and talked with their two therapists); Meal (they consumed a snack in the Centre's kitchen); and occasionally Motor Activities, performed in the outdoor space of the building. On reviewing the complete recordings, we realised that the most promising activity for study would be Time for Talking, not simply because of the obvious predominance of conversation, but because preliminary evidence indicated that participants often found this activity unsatisfactory.

The young patients whom we observed, recorded from the moment of their arrival in the afternoon, appeared at ease in the environment and happy to see their therapists. They also seemed to enjoy the routines predisposed in the Centre: they usually started out with Work, taking out notebooks and boxes from the shelves of the Work room, eagerly pursuing each task. Interaction with the therapists was open, and questions were asked and answered by both parties in the unfolding of the tasks and during passage from one task to the next. During the time dedicated to conversation, though, we observed this fluency and involvement to be reduced: both children expressed impatience toward one of the therapists, and in one case Marco protested, at the end of the allotted time, that he 'had not spoken' yet (though he had in fact participated in the conversation). We realised that the highly structured environment did not work so well when the task was a strictly conversational one, and decided on a selective analysis of Time for Talking interactions.

Time for Talking, talking for what?

The need to dedicate a separate time and space to conversation arises from the need to develop the specific social skills associated with verbal interaction. When asked about the meaning of this activity, one of the two therapists interviewed said, 'it is a methodology to develop theory of mind'. Specifying the objectives, she declared that it serves to 'guide the interest in others', 'widen the topics of patients' interaction', and 'make them aware of their problem and work on what makes them different with respect both to normality and to the other children' (such as the non-speaking children also attending the Centre). In the final interview, carried out a few months after the recordings, the therapists reported a significant increase in the two children's competence compared to what they knew we had observed, this being demonstrated by more frequent initiatives by the more withdrawn patient to communicate his personal experience, and the establishment of a solid personal friendship between the two boys. The second therapist,[4] Luigi, also alluded to the fact that during the time we were collecting our data the interactions were sometimes 'a bit conventional'.

The encounters examined below show how the various objectives of the colloquia collided with each other to the detriment of efficient participation and interactive agency, these being often hampered by an insistence on linguistic appropriateness and the tendency to favour particular topics. We will focus on how a preoccupation with linguistic appropriateness runs counter to the inner logic of spontaneous talk-in-interaction, which not only warrants orderly exchanges but provides for participants' mutual recognition as 'valid persons'. For analytical purposes the different sections below deal separately with aspects that are co-present in most of the excerpts.

Disregarding tellability

The dimension of tellability, in the sense both of orientation to new information and of newsworthiness, is often disregarded during Time for Talking. This is a consequence of consistent attempts to concentrate on a restricted range of topics and to elicit talk regarding widely known matters, matters so elementary as to render difficult any interpretation of what is actually being asked for.

Extract 1

```
 1 Anna:        Let's talk a little bit about family
 2 Giulio:      Oh. Mar[co's
 3 Anna:              [Yes.=>here for example.< Marco,
 4               ((to M)) >look<
 5               >let's do- let's hear Giulio for a second. <
 6               (1.0)
 7 Anna: →       What? is a fa⌊mi[ly ((didactic tone))
 8 Giulio:                      [It's a]l- ↑they are- they are=
 9               ↑they are, uh <Mum, and Dad.>
10 Anna:         A:h. (0.2) >so< it's Mum and Dad,
11               then who else is there, in the fa:[mily.
12 Giulio:                                         [And me:
13 Anna:         And G[iu:lio.
14 Giulio:            [Giu:lio.=((rolling head))
15 Anna: →        =And this is a family, isn't it?
16       →       it's some people who stay <to⌊gether.>
17 Giulio:       Uh.
18               (1.0)
19 Giulio:       But Lina too.
20               (1.5)
21 Anna:         So. ↑Lina is your cou⌊sin.
22 Giulio:       Uh. but she's a relative of mi:ne.
23               ((pointing to himself))
24 Anna:         Ye:s. [she's] ( [   ])
25 Giulio:             [A-]      [it's] a lo:ng family we have=
                 it's [lo:ng.
26               ((looks to A then L, opens arms for 'long'))
27 Luigi:            [((nods smiling to G.))
28 Anna: →       >Everybody's=family< is lar:ge.
```

The conversation begins, after a brief exchange on the logistics of the encounter, with the main therapist, Anna, announcing the first topic of the day (line 1), which one of the children (Giulio) interprets as pertaining to a specific family ('Marco's'). But after seeming to agree with the interpretation, the therapist goes on, selects Giulio as the speaker, and asks him to define what 'a family' is. Anna starts out with the typical intonation pattern of didactic interrogation; Giulio apparently grasps the nature of the question and begins answering in overlap (line 8). Yet the readiness to react does not imply an easy answer: he starts out with 'all' but stops and lists two categorical members, 'Mum and Dad'. The answer is accepted but leads to the prompt to go on. Giulio then adds himself to the list of family members, taking the interrogation to refer to his own family. The therapist wraps up at this point by recycling her former question and providing a general definition ('people who stay together'). Giulio approves and waits: he seems to interpret the preceding sequence as a preface whose purpose is to ascertain whether the meaning of the word 'family' is known to him, so he utters an acknowledgement token and waits for more to come (line 17). Since nothing is added by Anna, he continues his last course of action and adds another family member to the list, for whom the therapist provides the kinship term 'cousin'. Giulio sees this as a correction, so he claims that his cousin Lina counts as family too, and comments on the unusual size of his family (lines 22, 25–6). While the second therapist, Luigi, who had been addressed with a glance, smiles at the comment, Anna again generalises and corrects the non-idiomatic adjective Giulio had used ('long'), saying 'Everybody's family is large.'

Generalisation of patients' experience has been noted by Antaki, Leudar and Barnes (2004) as a didactic move contrastive to the uptaking of personal sides in received accounts, thus constituting an opportunity for conflict if the patient has a different agenda. Here, too, the move seals off pursuit of personal issues and ignores the humoristic nuance of Giulio's turn, conveyed by both tone and gestures. This exchange, like others in this collection, illustrates a tendency to clear conversation of personal content in favour of generic knowledge and school-like correctness of expression (Fiore, 2003).

The proposal of a 'simple' conversational task reveals confusion between lexical competence and conversation. Sheer knowledge about something does not automatically make it a good conversational topic: on the contrary, in the logic of conversation, that which is obvious is precisely what is *not* an appropriate object of talk. It makes the issue of relevance prominent and creates an expectation for the speaker who raises the obvious to display an awareness that that is what they are doing. Giulio's series of moves shows that not only does he perform competently, he also expects his competence to be assumed by the interaction partner. That is why he does not consider the question about family as self-sufficient. Anna, however, treats the boy's pieces of talk as mere samples of speech to be checked for correctness and determinedly stays on a general level in spite of the trouble she has making it generative of dialogue.

A similar example involves a dialogue between Anna and Marco, one day when Giulio was absent, about Marco's imminent passage to high school.

Extract 2

```
1 Luigi:      What school did you choose?
2 Marco:      The schoo:l (s-) (.) school Filippini (.)
3             school Santa Lucia Filippi:ni
4 Anna: →     Mh. That's how it's called?
5 Marco:      Yes ((nods))
6 Anna: →     And what school is i:t?
7       →     what does one do in this scho[ol?
8 Marco:                                   [Santa Lucia
9             FiliPPI:ni ((raises head and looks at A))
10 Anna:      What does one do in the school Santa Lucia
11            Filippini?
12 Marco:     What it's done in other=other school::s
13            they make me wr↑ite,
14 Anna:      They [make you wri-
15 Marco:          [Make me ho:mework
16 Anna:      Do ho:mework,
```

The school topic was selected by Anna, and follows on from Marco's statement, at the end of the previous session, that he was going to change school. After Marco appropriately answers to Luigi about the new school, giving its name and even self-repairing to complete the information (lines 2–3), Anna produces two contributions which run against the norm which favours pursuit of new knowledge. The first is a request for confirmation of the name of the school (line 4), in a form that indexes not mishearing but rather doubt about the correctness of the name just given. To this Marco simply adds confirmation, verbally and non-verbally. This repair sequence not only interrupts the flow of conversation, as with all exposed corrections (Jefferson, 1987), but also endangers its basis by inferring that anything said could in principle be incorrect. (Why cast doubt on information which, in addition to Marco's being its more entitled owner, is given in a complete way?) The second question is also problematic: she presents it in two formulations, with a self-repair apparently heading towards clarity: 'What kind of school is it? What does one do in this school?' As with the question about what a family is, here also is a tricky assumption of simplicity, making the question in fact difficult to answer. Firstly, Marco has not been there yet; and secondly, just as with family, school is school. In his reply Marco is able to show the idle character of the question, answering that they do there what they do in every other school, and then providing a couple of items of common school activities, writing and homework. Anna repeats each item keeping the 'list intonation', as if asking for more, and in repeating the second item she corrects the form (in Italian the correct form is 'make me *do* homework'). Such uptakes appear to indicate that she is not interested in the school particularly, but rather wishes Marco to provide evidence of his capacity to enumerate school activities and to do so correctly.

Both questions are conservative, in the sense that they do not aim to obtain new information but to keep Marco on well-established matters that can be assessed. Such questioning about well-known issues challenges the child's status as a competent speaker while systematically erasing the position of uninformed recipient on the part of the questioner.

Mismatches on 'granularity'

When children introduce a topic of their own, they can be asked questions that appear non-congruent as to their level of specificity. We can call this a 'granularity' problem, following Schegloff (2000). By this word he refers to 'the terms in which the world is observed, noticed, and experienced by members of society in the range of settings in which they live their lives' (2000: 718). As an analytical tack to interaction, granularity is a cue to the 'order of relevance' speakers regard as appropriate to the domain of experience they are talking about.

On speculative grounds, we can state that granularity varies with the degree of expertise in a given domain (and in this sense is probably a useful technique for self-positioning), but also that expectations on the level of granularity mirror an appraisal of interlocutors' general competence and of their interests in perceiving reality. The questions we will discuss, of which a series is shown in extract 3 below, are occurrences of poor expectations concerning the granularity of an on-going narrative.

Marco has been trying for a while to introduce a narrative about a live shark exhibition he visited with his parents. At the onset of the narrative, he is asked about aspects of the experience which are at best collateral to the points of interest Marco found in it.

Extract 3

```
1 Anna:         =Sharks. where? (0.2) in the sea?
2 Marco:        No, Sunday staying in Rome.
3 Anna          In Ro:me. ((to M., nodding))
4               (1.0) ((Anna looks at Giulio but he is soothing
                his lips with a handkerchief))
5 Anna:         At an <↓exhibition.> ((to G.))
6 Marco:        At an exhibition where you saw (    ) of sharks.
7               [...]
8 Anna:    →    Listen, but were they dead or alive?
9 Marco:        Oh::: I've seen the- the tank they are not dead
10 Anna         Ah they were in the tank
11 Marco:       Yes.
12 Anna:   →    How many were they?
13 Marco:       U- uh, sharks are two.
14 Anna:   →    Two. (.) but how bi?g were they?
15              (1.2) ((Marco looks down then to Anna))
16 Marco:       Uh::
17 Anna:        This big? ((extending arms))
18              (0.8) ((Anna stays in the position))
19 Marco:       Uh it did not look like a hammer shark uh:::
20              it was not uh sword shark it wasn't °sword°
21 Anna:   →    Listen Marco.
22         →    was it THis:? big this shark
23              or was it bigger?
24 Marco:       The shark and I don't know
25              (0.8)
26              It was a shark with monster-teeth
```

In answer to inquiries on whether the sharks were dead or alive, their number and size (lines 8, 12 and 14), the therapist picks on a layer of factuality seemingly distant from the more experiential or specialistic level of detail that would make the exhibition a 'tellable'. The boy answers the first question with a protest, 'Oh::: [...] they are not dead', as if the possibility that the sharks were dead would make the event much less remarkable. When asked about size, he starts on a comparison with other types of sharks and big fish (hammerhead shark, swordfish), offering a substantial cue to the order of knowledge he regards as appropriate. The therapist rejects the option of going into a comparative assessment and with an explicit repair of the conversational trend ('Listen Marco') she suggests another way of measuring, based on local gesturing resources. Marco's disappointment is visible in various signs of disengagement: repetition of the topicalised item and refusal to give the answer ('and I don't know'), the turn beginning 'and' being typical of both resignation and rebuttal. Once again he tries to get into a detailed description ('a shark with monster teeth') but in what immediately follows (not reported here) the conversation will be confined, with the involvement of the other child, to the construction of an analogical representation of sharks' length.

As with the ones discussed before, questions of this type do not stem from an interest in the topic of conversation. In fact, not only does the questioner often know the answer already, and the questions are uttered in that artificial tone typical of interaction with incompetent speakers, but they do not address – in fact often do not even wait for – the aspects of the recounted experience that were striking or tellable for the children. By taking control away from the child of the way the story gets told, the entitlement to the experience and the recognition of competence (both conversational and relative to the domain the story is about) are also stripped. Similar moves deflate story-telling of its intrinsic motivation and do not enrich the relationship, besides wasting opportunities for children's exercise in complex linguistic activities. The last extract of the chapter, showing a late reprise of this story, will provide further evidence of the waste of potentialities implied by granularity mismatches.

Sequential threats

Already visible in the former examples is a disregard for the *sequential orientation* of the young patients' talk. By sequential orientation we mean the position of upcoming turns relative to a certain communicative act which they project. Meaning has been shown to be produced incrementally, setting forth the conditions for locating events within spatio-temporal coordinates.[5] This often requires introductory talk – a *preface* – which is also a way to negotiate listeners' availability and/or success in establishing common ground (Sacks, 1992). If no problem arises with the coordinates, the preface is not opened up but met by continuers as an encouragement to proceed with the sequence. In the following interaction, this structure is compromised by repeated interrogation on preliminary information:

Extract 4

```
1 Marco:    And:: I have:: videotape ItaliaUno* ((TV channel))
2           I have seen the sunset of dawn
3 Anna:     The su:nse:t of d[awn (   )
4 Marco:                     [A movie
5 Anna:     From sunset to dawn?
6 Marco:    A film. that I recorded.
7 Anna:     Did you record it?
8 Marco:    Y↑es:
```

```
9 Anna:      >And you are able< to re[cord movies?
10 Marco:                         [Mum did it] =
11           = it's va:mp:ires' stuff.
12 Rosario: No! that was Litt:le Cree:ps.
```

After Marco starts talking about a movie he has seen, Anna repeats its
title with interrogative intonation, and Marco explains what kind of TV
programme it was, namely a movie. But her next turn shows that she
was actually pointing to trouble with the title-form, as she substitutes a
repair request with the offer of a changed wording (not 'the sunset of
dawn' but 'from sunset to dawn'). Marco ignores this and expands his
previous turn, specifying that it was a recorded movie, but again he
meets a repair request from the therapist addressing the expansion ('Did
you record it?'). His positive answer is not accepted, and Anna directly
challenges his ability to perform the action he has just attributed to
himself (this was already implied in the emphasis on 'you' of the former
question). Marco complies briefly and in a low tone of voice, saying that
it was his mother who did it, and with a rush through goes on talking
about the topic of the movie ('vampires' stuff'). This aggressive kind of
repair reminds us of the type of question that Garfinkel asked his students to pose to their interactional partners, a challenge to basic interactional trust (Garfinkel, 1963); here, they are not aimed at achieving
intersubjectivity but at exerting control on the formal correctness or
veracity of the preceding utterances. But because the repair-requests are
addressed to turns establishing premises in order to develop a further
point (something we could call 'revising the premises') they are an even
more serious threat to intersubjectivity than correction/repair in itself,
because the meaning that every utterance gets from its position relative
to what is projected is misconstrued. To paraphrase, we could say that it
is the speaker's 'project' to be unacknowledged, denying him the very
resource for meaning-making in conversation. Again, the boy's minimal
responses and his rush through at the end of the extract, latching his
answer to the subject of the movie he wanted to talk about, is evidence
that such moves are indeed perceived as a disturbance in the communicative process. In support of the claim that such moves are disruptive
of intersubjectivity and perceived as such by their recipients, we will look
at an example in which misunderstandings follow upon questions that
are disrespectful of sequential orientation.

Misunderstandings caused by expected sequential relevance

In many of the examples shown, including the last one, the children
react with impatience to ill-posed questions, as shown by the quickness

with which they try to get rid of the conversational obstacles in order to pursue their sequential point. Sometimes, though, they lend pertinence to therapists' interventions and make sense of them in ways which are compatible with their sequential emergence. Such sense-making operations produce misunderstanding as to the nature of these moves.

In extract 5, Giulio mentions a Christmas tree as one of the items his father has reserved at the general store, and goes on to talk about the toys that are going to be his presents. But Luigi, the second therapist, halts him on this path and redirects him to the Christmas tree. The misunderstanding occurs in lines 6–7 and is triggered by a possible double interpretation of the Italian form 'com'è' which can mean both a request for description ('how is') and a request for reasons ('how come')?

Extract 5

```
1 Giulio:    My Daddy (has ha-) you know what he reserved?
2            at the store he bought me a Christmas tree.
3 Anna:      Ih:: how nice.
4 Giulio:    He bough- he reserved me the STRATOcoce and
5            the rest of Dragonball VEGEtuva
6 Luigi      And how is/how come this Christmas tree?
7 Giulio:    And because he liked it.
8 Luigi:     No but how is it made
9 Giulio:    It's big ours yes. ((shows size by raising hand))
10           ((to M)) look I got the Ci Seventeen ((type of toy
11           in the series)) the android
12 Luigi:    Stop ((leaning hand toward G to stop him))
             ((taking L's hand and pushing it back))
13 Giulio:   And another Vegeta, the [Stratococe
14 Luigi:                            [Ask him if he had done
15           the Christmas tree as well
             ((takes G's hands and points it to M))
16 Giulio:   Did you do: the Christmas tree:?
```

The question in line 6 is prone to misunderstanding *vis-à-vis* expected competence for at least two reasons: in terms of content, because it is a request for a description of a widely known item (Christmas trees before decoration are basically all similar except for their size); and sequentially, because the child's discourse-trajectory was already past the tree and into the issue of toys when the therapist asked the question. So since the tree was not the point of the child's turn, the question would be legitimate only as a clarification request, and not as topic-expansion, and this is exactly what Giulio makes of it. He answers to the (semantically possible) question 'How come?' – i.e., 'Why?' – and explains that his father bought the tree because he liked it. The answer is quick and has a conclusive tone and, as in Marco's turn before, bears a sign of impatience in that it begins with the conjunction 'e' (and). The turn is directed to closing the clarification sequence and going on, but the therapist repairs this understanding and explains 'No but how it is made'. Again, Giulio complies quickly without leaving any opening for the expansion of the topic; nevertheless the answer is apt and, as we were saying, it probably picks on the one possible dimension on which to evaluate a bare Christmas tree ('It's big'). In the continuation of the sequence, Giulio tries to go on with the toy topic, this time looking at his friend and trying to ignore the therapist's vocal and gestural attempts to stop him, but at last, after a brief non-verbal duel with the hands (lines 12–15), he has to give up.

As in many other cases in these sessions, the therapists' actions are informed by their policy of valuing certain topics over others. The Christmas tree relates to one of the therapists' preferred topics, the family, whereas monsters, video games and horror stories are discouraged because they are part of the children's 'stereotypia' and thus symptomatic of their disturbance. Of course, they are also stereotypical of children in a more general sense. It could perhaps be possible to exploit the motivating force of children's best-liked topics in order to direct them into subjects of general interest, without undermining the basic methods of meaning-making.

Let us look at another occurrence of misunderstanding, this time involving Marco. The extract is taken from the same session. After the Christmas tree topic has reached a dead end, Marco has been allowed to introduce his own topic, the shark exhibition we are already familiar with. As illustrated in the comments on extract 3, he successfully bypasses the battery of questions with which his opening is met and gets into describing the different properties of the animals he has seen. The misunderstanding concerns the utterance in line 3, where the therapist responds to the information about the Jackstar shark's teeth with the objection that she does not know him. Marco's best guess is that she somehow expects to be familiar with that individual shark (line 4).

Extract 6

```
1 Marco:   Jackstar is a shark which has ro- round teeth
2          ((makes a round move with his index finger))
3 Anna:    I don't ↑know him
4 Marco:   It's not a name.
5 Anna:    Is it a race?
6 Marco:   It's a race of sharks.
```

The misunderstanding seems to be caused by Anna's rejection of the role of uninformed recipient; she reacts with the typical line she uses when the children bring up their 'stereotypical' subjects, i.e., 'I don't know it'. This time, though, the topic had already overcome censorship and Marco had been encouraged to tell Giulio, the other boy, about this experience. At this point, then, the objection is misplaced, and Marco makes a guess at its sense, reacting as if she did not understand that he was using a categorical name, and by implication affirming that she was *not supposed* to know Jackstar sharks (indeed, this was precisely the piece of new knowledge he was handing over to her). Anna, after a pause, decides to go along with this and asks for confirmation of another candidate interpretation of 'Jackstar' ('Is it a race?').

The misunderstandings shown above are evidence that both children expect their therapists to act in accordance with the normative requirements of mundane conversation; they trust them to do so, and expect to be credited with full speakership by having their communicative plans respected and the newsworthiness of their contributions acknowledged. They can be misled by acts which do less than this, and in trying to come up with answers to the 'why this now?' query lying at the basis of conversational sense-making, they tend to upgrade the acts they receive.

Reaching alignment

The last example illustrates an exchange in which therapist's uptakes of the patient's turns appear oriented by a more 'natural' attitude, one that corresponds more closely to what is observed in symmetric mundane conversation. The 'Time for Talking' session has been just called to a close, but Marco works at its margin to deliver another shark story. Anna accepts this and intervenes straightforwardly and economically, almost only asking for genuine clarifications, providing acknowledging expansions, uttering continuers, or silently waiting during Marco's enthusiastic account.[6]

Marco's account incorporates a clear orientation to intersubjectivity, visible in his efforts at clear pronunciation, mimicry of the shapes of central aspects of the description, and emphasis on the relevant points. He gains agency turn after turn, becoming responsible for the content of his talk and giving feedback to the contribution of the others.

Extract 7

```
1 Anna:      All right. now we go in the other room=
2                 [((Marco claps one hand on the other twice))
```

```
 3 Anna:       [=and we go do the (evaluat[ion) ((to G.))
 4 Marco:                               [NO:! wait,
 5             First I have to do [so:mething. (.)
 6             a <fish.> ((raises hand as in asking to talk))
 7 Anna:       Yeah.
 8             (0.3)
 9 Marco:      The stomach, (.) the stomach of a <↓shark>
10             because he has teeth <points> ((staccato mode; he
              mimes something round with his hands));
11 Anna:       Has POI?Nted? teeth ((taps fingers with folded
              hands as in jaws movement))
12 Marco:      The shark,
13 Anna:   →   What's the stomach got to do with it?
14 Marco:      (             ) in the <skeen,>
15 Anna:   →   The? skeleton?
16 Marco:      No the <SKEt>.=the scren .=
17             =where they show the:=the sharks that (    )
18 Anna:   →   Ah in the <screen?>
19 Marco:      Yes::: ((nodding))
20 Anna:   →   There were some videos=fi- some fi[1:ms.
21 Marco:                                         [LISten,
22             sharks EAt >turtles.<
23 Anna:   →   Yes.
24         →   (0.8)
25 Marco:      Because sharks break them the:, she:,
26             <sh-e-lls> of:: tu=>turtle.<
27 Anna:       The ↓shell.
28 Marco:      The sh-
29 Giulio:     The ↑sh:ell.
30 Marco:      Y::es. the shark ate the turtle.
31 Anna:   →   Mh.
32 Marco:      Oh::, even dolphins they can beat.
33 Anna:   →   Yes ((nodding))
34         →   (0.6)
35 Marco:      Everyone.
36 Anna:   →   Even the men.
37             (.)
38 Marco:      Even men.
```

Marco overlaps with Anna's announcement of the end of the activity to communicate that he *has* to do something, automatically raising his hand to ask for speaking rights. The permission is accorded and he starts the telling in a hurry, beginning with something about the sharks' stomach that involves their particular teeth. Anna corrects the expression (line 11) and at Marco's reprise asks again about the role of stomach. Despite these turns of hers interrupting to some extent the unfolding of the account, they are, compared to her other contributions analysed above, more oriented to intersubjectivity. The first question could be an understanding-check, while the second, about the stomach (line 13), reveals that she is keeping track of the content of preceding turns.

To explain about the stomach, Marco has to mention the video he has seen, but has trouble with the word 'screen'. Anna's candidate-repair (line 15) is met by the child with an effort to come up with the right words, which implies first some repetitions and then a switch to a paraphrase, which is also the best strategy with hearing troubles in general (Schegloff, 1979). Anna's repair requests are not taken by Marco with the dismay we observed in other examples, but instead with efforts toward clarification. Also, his interpretation of the repairs as relevant and originated by genuine lack of understanding is not denied in the therapist's following turns, which on the contrary respond with a 'change of state token' (line 18) and an understanding check (line 20) in demonstration of the success of Marco's repair moves. After the collaborative construction of the information regarding the source of Marco's knowledge (videos), he explains that sharks eat turtles. Anna says 'yes' and waits. Expansion on the information follows about sharks being able to break turtles' shells. Anna replies, repeating one of the words that Marco had trouble with ('shell'), and Marco tries again to say it, but stops in between and looks at the other boy, who cooperates and says it for him (line 29). Marco continues with a 'yes': he confirms their interpretation and starts heading for a conclusion of the shark-eats-turtles concept, in a different phrasal format that expresses wonder for the fact. This is a story of big sea animals, with their different powers, fighting against each other, so the conclusion is built by adding other very powerful shark victims, dolphins. Anna receives this again with an affirmative uptake, verbal and non-verbal, and waits. Marco offers a remark of general value ('everyone practically') to which Anna appends her own piece of knowledge ('even men'), which Marco repeats approvingly.

This narrative evolves as a 'happy exchange', we daresay, with an ending that finds the two participants aligned in a joint conclusion (lines 35–8).[7] Outside the cage of the didactic framework, the listener in this exchange accompanies the speaker toward the point of his contribution, which gradually comes out from the initial confusion. Motivated to share his wonder for the apprehended knowledge, Marco is able to convey both content and evaluation, and, encouraged by continuers, confirmations and pauses, can proceed to an appropriate exit. The repairs are kept to what is necessary and do not test competence; either Anna shows not to understand what Marco is talking about or offers candidates after Marco's word-search, a situation which ordinarily calls for listeners to join in (Goodwin, 1981; see also Giulio's identical reaction in line 29). It is possible to observe Marco's consolidation of agency throughout the exchange: starting with the 'LISten' (line 21), which recruits the recipient into the listener position; going on to the confirmation with which he accepts the item offered to his word-search, showing that he owns the contents the others are contributing to (lines 19 and 30); and continuing until the repetition by which he approves of Anna's own information about sharks beating men (line 38). Marco's turns lengthen and become consequential to one another once Anna has reassured him that he can talk despite the allotted conversational time having ended.

Same people, same day, same room, but the full assumption of the listener's stance has fostered the complementary speaker's role, and permitted both interactants to meet in an area of personal interest, enriched by evaluation and by cooperative co-construction.

Discussion

General educational objectives like correctness of speech, as well as therapy-specific ones like the controlling of conversational topics, have been observed throughout the extracts to conflict with the stated aim of improving children's social skills. The general strategy of the therapists appears based on the core assumption that talk must be elicited by continuous questioning. Especially when such prompts are given in ways which presuppose the questioner's former knowledge of the information asked for – for instance a didactic tone of voice – and are followed by evaluation in third position (Sinclair and Coulthard, 1975), the whole meaning of the interaction shifts from dialogue to interrogation, with a substantial impoverishment of the role of the interrogated participant and of the quality of the relationship. The therapists appear also unaware of the disruptive effect of opening repair sequences within an on-going production.

In previous work on classroom interaction it was observed how the organisational constraints of a classroom, the moral mission of the institution embodied in its tradition of practices, and commonsense assumptions about talk converged to produce an environment in which the natural resources of conversation were to a great extent suppressed (Fasulo and Girardet, 2002). Educational training aiming at enhancing the quality of classroom interaction often involves changing teachers' discursive moves, for instance having them abolish evaluation in third position, and producing contingent queries, suspending – for the sake of participation – correction of misspellings and the like (Orsolini and

Pontecorvo, 1992). Conversational actions are in fact context-creative and, like sharks, can beat all other attempts at context definition: in our sessions, for example, children were often told to tell things to each other (see for example Extract 5, lines 14–15) but the constant uptakes, in the form of questions, repair requests or corrections coming from the therapists, made quite unlikely the selection of the peer as addressee.

The dialogue analysed was threatened on a number of levels fundamental to spontaneous talk-in-interaction: *tellability*, that is, orientation to contents which have some kind of import for at least one participant; *granularity*, the recognition of the level of detail the other can operate at; and *sequential orientation*, the assignment of meaning to turns relative to their position.

Such features are by no means sheer technicalities: they imply full recognition of the speakers' position, through trust in the fact that they know what they are doing, and respect for the communication project that can be read in their sequential construction. Acknowledgment of interactional positions and trust in communicative competence are, in turn, at the bases of social order and shared reality (cf. Garfinkel, 1967; Goffman, 1967; Luhmann, 1968; Todorov, 1995).

In interacting with people who can, for reasons of age or disability, be attributed communicative impairments, it is common to withdraw interactional trust. Foreigner-talk and baby-talk can be reinterpreted as a means to layer the situated identity engaged in the interaction and give over to the other only a diminished *persona*; in a former study on family interaction we described the practice of 'backstage talk' as a safety device with which adults or older members accompanied exchanges with the younger ones, so not to be fully interacting with dubious partners (Fatigante et al., 1998). Apparently, routine contact with people who have communicative disabilities or undeveloped competences does not automatically lead to normalisation of interaction, but can, on the contrary, routinise artificial tones, impersonal topics and simplified contributions.[8] This could be another source of explanation, beside that of contradictory goals, for the artificiality in both tone and content of the examples discussed. However, familiarity with the functioning of talk-in-interaction and with the research findings on pragmatic skills in autism could support the endorsement of a different approach to conversational exchanges. For example, relying on the demonstrated competence in turn-taking and sequential construction, narrative and longer sequences could be allowed to develop instead of privileging the adjacency-pair format. Appreciating the importance of uninformed recipiency would allow the potential of children's pre-existing interests to be exploited instead of censoring them, through relevant questions and use of mechanisms such as the continuers, pauses, 'mirroring repetition' (Lumbelli, 1992) and change-of-state tokens, which all signal attention and interest. Awareness of the context-creative property of conversational moves would lead to avoidance of the discursive features of didactic interrogation. Taken together, the strategies just mentioned may warrant *recognition* which, beside and outside therapeutic issues, is a fundamental requirement of well-being in common life.

APPENDIX

Original Italian versions of extracts:

Extract 1

```
1 Anna:        Parliamo un <pochino>, della famiglia.
2 Giulio:      Ah. di Ma:r[co.
3 Anna:                   [Si]=>ecco ad esempio.< Marco,
4              ((a M)) >guarda<
5              >facciamo- sentiamo un attimo >Giulio-<.
6              (1.0)
7 Anna:    →   Che? cos'è una fa↓mi[:glia? ((t. didattico))
8 Giulio:                          [E' tu]t- ↑sono- sono=
9              ↑sono, eh <mamma, e papà.>
10 Anna:       O:h. (0.2) >allora< sono mamma e papà,
11             e poi chi altro c'è, nella fa[mi:glia.
12 Giulio:                                  [E i:o]
13 Anna:       E G[iu:lio.
14 Giulio:        [Giu:lio].=((dondolando il capo))
15 Anna:   →   =E questa è una famiglia, no?
16        →   sono delle persone che stanno <in↓sieme>.
17 Giulio:     Eh.
18             (1.0)
19 Giulio:     Ma pure Lina.
20             (1.5)
21 Anna:       Allora. ↑LIna è tua cu↓gi:na.
22 Giulio:     Eh. ma è familiare ↓mi:o.
23             ((indicando se stesso))
24 Anna:       S:i. [è] ([   ])
25 Giulio:     [A-] [è' na] famiglia, lu:nga. la no:stra=è [lu:nga.
26             ((guarda A e poi L; allarga le braccia))
27 Luigi:      [((annuisce sorridendo verso G.))]
28 Anna:   →   La >famiglia=di tutti< è gra:nde.
```

Extract 2

```
1 Luigi:    Che scuola hai scelto?
2 Marco:    La scuola: (s-) (.) scuola Filippi:ni. (.)
3           scuola Santa Lucia Filippi:ni
```

```
 4 Anna:  →   Mh. Si chiama cosí?
 5 Marco:     Si ((annuisce ))
 6 Anna:  →   E che scuola é:?
 7        →   cosa si fa in questa scuol[a?
 8 Marco:                            [Santa Lucia
 9            FiliPPI:ni ((alza la testa e guarda A))
10 Anna:     Che cosa si fa nella scuola Santa Lucia
11           Filippini?
12 Marco:    Quello che fa: che fa altre=altre scole::
13           me fa scr(ivere,
14 Anna:     Ti [fanno scri]-
15 Marco:    [Mi fanno] co:mpiti
16 Anna:     Fare i co:mpiti,
```

Extract 3

```
 1 Anna:     =Gli squa:li. dove? (0.2) nel mare?
 2 Marco:    No domenica stando a Roma
 3 Anna:     A Ro:m a. ((a M., annuendo))
 4           (1.0) ((Anna guarda G, ma lui è intento ad
             umettarsi le labbra con un fazzoletto))
 5 Anna:     A una <↓mostra.> ((a G.))
 6 Marco:    A una mostra che si vedevano ( ) degli squali
 7           [...]
 8 Anna:  →  Senti ma erano vivi o morti?
 9 Marco:    Oh::: ho visto la- la vasca non sono morti
10 Anna:     Ah nella vasca stavano
11 Marco:    Sì
12 Anna:  →  Quanti erano?
13 Marco:    E- eh, squali sono due.
14 Anna:  →  Due. (.) ma quanto erano gra?ndi?
15           (1.2) ((Marco guarda in basso e poi Anna))
16 Marco:    Eh::
17 Anna:     Così? ((allargando le braccia))
18           (0.8) ((Anna rimane nella stessa posizione))
19 Marco:    Eh non somiglia allo squalo martello ohh:::
20           squalo di: ah spada non e:ra °spada°
21 Anna:  →  Ascolta Marco.
22        →  era grande coSI':? questo squalo
23           o era più grande?
24 Marco:    Lo squalo e non lo so
25           (0.8)
26           Uno squalo coi denti a mostro
```

Extract 4

```
 1 Marco:    E:: ho:: >videocassetta italiauno
 2           ho visto<.il tra:monto dell'alba:
 3 Anna:     Il tramo:nto: dell'a[lba ( )
```

```
 4 Marco:                           [Un f̲ilm.
 5 Anna:     Dal tramonto all'alba?
 6 Marco:    Un film. che ho registrato.
 7 Anna:     L'h̲ai registrato?
 8 Marco:    S↑i:
 9 Anna:     >E sei capace di< re[gistrare il film?  ]
10 Marco:                       [E' stata mamma] =
11           =è cose di va:mpi:r̲i̲
12 Rosario:  No: quello è pi:cco:li Bri:vi:di.
```

Extract 5

```
 1 Giulio:   Mio papà (ha avut-) lo sai che m'ha prenotato?
 2           alla Standa m'ha comprato un albero di Nata?le.
 3 Anna:     Ih:: che bello.
 4 Giulio:   m'ha comp- m'ha prenotato lo STRATOcoce e
 5           il resto di Dragonball VEGEtuva
 6 Luigi:    E com'è quest'albero di Natale?
 7 Giulio:   E perché gli piaceva.
 8 Luigi:    No ma com'è fatto
 9 Giulio:   E' grande il nostro si. ((mostra grandezza
             sollevando la mano))
10           ((a M)) Guarda io ho avuto il Ci diciassette
11           l'androide
12 Luigi     Basta ((allunga  la  mano  verso  G  per  fermarlo))
             ((prendendo la mano di L e spingendola via))
13 Giulio:   E un altro Vegeta, lo [Stratococe
14 Luigi:                          [Chiedigli se lui l'ha fatto
15           l'albero di Natale
             ((prende la mano di G e indica M))
16 Giulio:   T̲ul'hai f̲a:tto l'albero di Nata:le?
```

Extract 6

```
 1 Marco:    Jackstar è uno squalo che ha i de- denti rotondi.
 2           ((fa una rotazione dell'indice))
 3 Anna:     Non lo con↑osco
 4 Marco:    Non è̲ un nome.
 5 Anna:     É una razza?
 6 Marco:    É una razza di squali.
```

Extract 7

```
 1 Anna:     Va bene. allora adesso andiamo di là=
 2           [((Marco batte una mano sull'altra))
 3 Anna:     [=e andiamo a fare la (valutaz[ione) ((a G.))
 4 Marco:                                 [NO̲:! aspetta,
 5           P̲r̲i(ma) devo fare una [co:sa. (.)
```

```
6                  un <pesce.> ((alza la mano per la parola))
7 Anna:            Eh.
8                  (0.3)
9 Marco:           Lo stomaco, (.) lo stomaco di uno <squalo>
10                 siccome ha i denti <punti> ((scandisce e mima con
                   entrambe le mani qualcosa di tondo))
11 Anna:           Ha i denti a PU?nta? ((batte le dita a mani giunte
                   come nell'unione di mascelle))
12 Marco:          Lo squalo,
13 Anna:   →       Lo stomaco che c'entra?
14 Marco:          (        ) nello <schemmo,>
15 Anna:   →       Lo? (.) scheletro?
16 Marco:          No. lo <SCHEtto>.=lo schemmio .=
17                 =dove fanno vedere gli:=gli squali quelli ( )
18 Anna:   →       Ah nello <schermo?>
19 Marco:          Si::: ((annuendo))
20 Anna:   →       C'erano dei video=fi- dei fil[ma:ti.
21 Marco:                                       [SEnti,
22                 gli squali MAngiano le >tartarughe.<
23 Anna:   →       Si.
24         →       (0.8)
25 Marco:          E perchè i squali li rompe i:, gu:,
26                 <gu-s-ci> di::, ta=> tartaruga<.
27 Anna            Il ↓guscio.
28 Marco:          Il gu-
29 Giulio:         Il ↑gu:scio.
30 Marco:          S::i. La mangiava lo squalo=alla tartaruga.
31 Anna:   →       Mh
32 Marco:          Oh::, Anche i delfini battono.
33 Anna:   →       Si. ((annuendo))
34         →       (0.6)
35 Marco:          Tutti.
36 Anna:   →       Pure gli uomini.
37                 (.)
38 Marco:          Pure uomini.
```

NOTES

1. See studies collected in Goodwin (2003).
2. The child studied in Local and Wootton (1993) and Wootton (1999) was aged 11.4 and was diagnosed with severe autism, with an estimated linguistic age of $2-2\frac{1}{2}$.
3. The Centre is inspired by the theories and procedures developed by Theo Peeters (1998), who proposed a treatment exploiting the tendency of individuals with autism to build their understanding of their surroundings, and to figure out appropriate action, using associations between concrete aspects of the world. The treatment sets up highly structured settings and

tasks in order to enhance patients' operational skills and self-efficacy. However, the conversational techniques analysed are not directly related to the author's approach.

4. We refer here to a first and second therapist because Anna, whom we designate as first, is the one playing a major role in the colloquia, although in principle they have each been assigned a patient and have equal responsibility. She is also the one speaking the most during the joint interviews.

5. Cf. Labov and Waletzky's (1967) *Orientation* section found at the beginning of elicited narratives.

6. On therapists' interventions *vis-à-vis* children's initiatives see Fiore (2003).

7. These are not the very last lines of the sequence, though, because they go briefly into scuba divers as victims of the attacks.

8. Sella, personal communication.

13   Discursive practices in talking problems during a school–family meeting

Richard Buttny and Sandra Kellogg Rath

This chapter examines a meeting between family members and a high-school co-director.[1] The meeting was called for a returning student who was newly a mother. What is interesting about this is how the talk extends into the personal matters of the family, such as: interpersonal relationships with the father of the baby, accountability for the pregnancy and birth control. We look at the discursive practices in formulating problems and in accounting for such versions. In particular, we focus on how participants, at times, orient to and manage these problems as delicate matters.

In talking problems, persons are invariably positioned through their own or other's accounts (Davies and Harré, 1999). How one is positioned can be especially important in institutional contexts, such as a school. Institutional representatives typically have far greater knowledge of institutional norms and practices than lay clients (Gumperz, 1982). We need to examine how this asymmetry of knowledge, access and power plays out in communication events such as meetings or interviews. For instance, a recent study of a high school–family meeting for a teenage mother's return to school found that this student was positioned in contradictory ways, by conflicting category predicates – as being a mother, a fifteen-year-old with friends, needing to do homework (see also Buttny, 2004: ch. 2). Such conflicting positionings were oriented to by participants as a possible problem: for the family as something that could be resolved through the grandmother's help, while for the school as something that may make graduating difficult and may necessitate her transferring schools.

The present study examines a different segment of this same school–family meeting for a returning student-mother. The content of this segment of the meeting reaches further into the private and interpersonal realm of relationships that may pose problems. This is consistent with recent trends in which the boundaries between school and home are becoming increasingly blurred (Bryan, 2004). In the past, the school's primary role was to encourage students in particular areas of study or careers. Today schools are expected to become more involved in students' lives, in what was traditionally thought to be the family realm. Teachers and staff discuss much more with their students; they are now expected to instruct about issues such as sex, alcohol and drugs (Lieberman, 2004; Rayburn, 2004).

Discursive analysis offers a useful perspective to approach such phenomena because it takes the realm of the school and of the family as discursive constructions (Potter, 1996), a 'construction' in the sense that what counts as educational or as personal are not natural categories, but rather are constructed out of participants' activities and appraisals. So a task for discursive analysis is to describe the constructing practices whereby these realms of school and home, and their boundaries, become oriented to and (re-)created through interaction. What counts as appropriate for the school or the home, as part of education or as personal, are matters that are oriented to and worked out in the course of talk-in-interaction. There are social norms or cultural taboos that serve as guidelines and, as already mentioned, these are said to be changing as more demands are placed on our schools. These norms or taboos can be taken as conversational resources that can be invoked, used or ignored in the course of a meeting. As participants move into discussing personal topics, their talk may mark these topics as 'delicate objects' (Silverman, 1997). The advantages of taking a discursive turn is that we can eschew reifying what is appropriate or not for discussion in school. Instead, we treat 'the boundaries' between school and family as a discursive object, as something that participants will orient to in various ways during talk-in-interaction.

Formulating candidate problems during the school–family meeting

The meeting involves a returning high-school student who was away from school to have her baby. She is accompanied by her mother and brother (also a high-school student) and infant child. From the school staff, the co-directors, her homeroom advisor and the social worker are present. This data extract is taken from about two-thirds of the way through the meeting. Thus far the meeting has been comprised of, in broad strokes, initial, congenial 'small talk' about the new infant and related baby stories; then it moved to the task of anticipating problems in the student-mother's return to school (for an analysis of this section of the meeting, see Buttny, 2004: ch. 2). This leads to a discussion of the relationship with the infant's father, who is also a student at the school.

In this school–family meeting, consider how the co-director initially raises the issue of the relationship with the father in the following extract.[2]

Extract 1

(Participants: CD1 = co-director 1, CD2 = co-director 2, SW = social worker, HRT = homeroom teacher, MO = student mother, GM = grandmother, BRO = brother of the student mother).

```
 1 CD1:  >All right so there's< that ↓one (.) issue,
 2       then the second issue is::
 3       the complicated social (.) dilemma in s↑chool (.) between
 4       (1.2) you and ah ((turns to look towards SW))
 5       (1.9)
 6 SW:   Johnny
 7 CD1:  Johnny ((hits hand on table))
 8       (3.8)
 9 CD1:  So (1.4) and ((points to BRO)) then that's for you ↑too
10       how's it for you?
11 BRO:  (°It's fine. °)
12 CD1:  You- you- would it be helpful if:?
13       >I mean< iz- is it impossible I: (1.6)
14       ↑do you ever have a conversation with him °about°?
15       (1.3)
16 BRO:  Once ( [    )
17 CD1:        [>Do you bo- two just avoid the subject?<
18       >↓what do you do<
19       (0.8)
20 BRO:  Really we never talk about it
21       (1.1)
22 HRT:  Yo[u guys are still hanging out though right?
23 BRO:    [The baby (or)
24       (1.2)
25 BRO:  Once in a blue moon =
26 HRT:  = >yeah<
27       (1.7)
28 BRO:  'Cause we work ↑together °so:°
29       (1.1)
30       h[ave the same jobs (and)
31 CD1:   [(    )
32 CD1:  And you were once very close ↑friends
33       (1.1)
34       what is:- what do you think you are now?
35 BRO:  (Well) you can't blame it only on him.
36       (2.1)
37 CD1:  Well you co↓uld, but ↑you don't
38 BRO:  Yeah ya ↑could (but) ↓you can't blame it only on him.
```

While the meeting is not labelled as such, the talk can be heard as doing counselling. Our extract begins with the co-director (CD1) closing down the prior topic and then moving to an agenda statement: 'the second issue is:: the complicated social (.) dilemma' (lines 1–3). CD1 characterises the current state of affairs as a 'dilemma', and then moves to engage the family members in conjointly examining it and related matters. The co-director also had used this same term, 'dilemma', to characterise the first issue that she raised for discussion in this meeting.

Extract 2

```
1 CD1:   >All right< so now:: the dilemma is,
2         there's a lot of issues
3         (1.4)
4         It's very hard (1.2) to go back to school
5         when you have >a little baby< ↑right
```

Our focus here begins with the co-director's formulation 'the complicated social dilemma' (lines 1–3), which involves the returning student-mother, the father, Johnny, her brother and others. In raising this 'dilemma' or problem for discussion, the co-director faces the challenge of probing into the personal realm of the family and their interpersonal relations.

The co-director pursues her formulation 'the complicated social dilemma' by turning attention away from the student-mother and to her brother (BRO). CD1 may be taking some of the focus away from the mother for the moment by involving the brother. CD1 shifts to the brother by 'then that's for you ↑too' (line 9) and pursues this line with the open-ended query 'how's it for you?' (line 10). The brother responds by denying or minimising the existence of problems with the conventional '°It's fine°' (line 11). Interestingly, we will see that CD1's query here is one of the few open-ended questions she asks in the entire meeting. Instead it will be seen that CD1 probes family members by asking about a candidate problem.

In her third-turn response to BRO's answer, 'fine,' the co-director continues to examine the brother's relations with Johnny by wondering about how he deals with a peer who got his sister pregnant. CD1 pursues this by proposing the contrasting alternatives to BRO, 'have a conversation with him' or 'just avoid the subject,' combined with a tag question (lines 14, 17–18). These alternatives are presented as a kind of 'dilemma' which invites BRO to say what he does – to tell his side. Here we use 'dilemma' as a member's term rather than as an analytic concept (e.g., Tracy, 1997).

The co-director exhibits some difficulty in articulating these alternatives, as witnessed by her three false starts and self-repair, 'You- you-would it be helpful if:? >I mean< iz- is it impossible I: (1.6) ↑do you ever have a conversation with him' (lines 12–14), before uttering the initial alternative. CD1 displays these alternatives as delicate objects (Silverman, 1997), that is, as possibly awkward or difficult for BRO to discuss.

As mentioned above, the co-director uses the practice of offering a candidate version of the problem (or possible problem) along with a query to project the family member's response. This practice sequentially suggests that the family member address the candidate problem. At the same time it allows them the flexibility to disagree or explain. Either way it functions to engage the family member in discussing this issue.

A moment later, the co-director again employs this practice of offering a candidate problem formulation to probe the brother's relations with Johnny. CD1 contrasts the past with the present: 'you were once very close friends ... what do you think you are now?' (lines 32–4), the suggested point being that former close friends, who are no longer close, can have a complicated or problematic relationship.

Another aspect of this practice of raising candidate problems is the epistemic basis of the ascription. Is the candidate problem statement (a) something known, (b) a plausible consequence of the current state of affairs, (c) a speculation, or what? For instance, the co-director claims that the brother and Johnny 'were once very close friends' (line 32). For our purposes it is less important how the co-director knows this – first-hand observation, or second-hand report from the social worker, homeroom advisor or other staff – than how this claim is discursively used and how the recipients take it.

The brother resists CD1's versions of his relational problems with Johnny and her implicit positioning of him. Instead of straightforwardly addressing CD1's query and offering a version of his current relationship with Johnny, BRO challenges an assumption behind the query by the response, 'you can't blame it only on him' (line 35). Or in response to CD1's initial dilemma formulation 'have a conversation with him' or 'just avoid the subject' (lines 14, 17), BRO's turn initial 'Really' from line 20 suggests that it is neither of CD1's proffered alternatives. The homeroom teacher (HRT) asserts, 'You guys are still hanging out though right?' (line 22), as a way to collaboratively question BRO's prior avowal that he and Johnny 'never talk about it' (line 20). BRO accounts for the apparent inconsistency between the descriptions 'hanging out' and 'never talk about it' by saying they work together (lines 28–30) yet seldom 'hang out' – as he puts it, 'Once in a blue moon' (line 25).

Lexical choice in engaging in these delicate matters is obviously important: for instance, BRO's use of the indexical 'it' in 'Really we never talk about it' (line 20) or in 'You can't blame it only on him' (line 35) or CD1's seeming deletion of the 'it' at the end of the utterance 'Do you ever have a conversation with him °about°?' (line 14). In CD1's second possible alternative she uses 'the subject' in 'just avoid the subject?' (line 17). Each of these indexical terms references the story of BRO's sister and Johnny without having to say it, and begins to construct the issue as a delicate object (Silverman, 1997).

A problem staff members may face is getting participants to open up and engage in discussing and examining problems. Part of the professional competence of a counsellor is to break through the participants' reticence and resistance (Peräkylä and Silverman, 1991: 467). Participants may prefer to deny or minimise the existence of problems. We have seen this in the above extract. The brother uses resistance practices to the co-director's queries on problem talk *vis-à-vis* Johnny. At most, he offers a minimal account to explain their relationship. BRO mitigates the implied blame hearable behind CD1's query (lines 14–18) and even reasserts this in the face of her challenge (lines 35–8). In minimally going along with CD1's probing of problem talk, BRO also is resisting her candidate positioning of him and his relations with Johnny.

Co-telling improving relations

The co-director turns the discussion back to the student-mother by asking about the candidate problem: 'Do you still feel angry at him?' (line 40).

Extract 3

```
40 CD1:  Do you still feel angry at him?
41       (2.1)
42 MO:   Not as be↑for:e.
43       (1.0)
44 GM:   It's over
45 MO:   Things are >ya know< slowing down everything is:
46       (1.0) you know he's- (.) he's being ↑goo::d (.)
47       he's doing his part ↓you know
48       (1.0)
49 GM:   He's coming ov[er to see the baby
50 CD1:               [This is new?
51 MO:   This is new this is recently =
52 GM:   = Now he's::: ((circular hand gestures))
53       (3.8)
```

```
54 GM:    And:: ((points towards BRO)) they working it
55        a little better since he's been coming over they
```

Notice that '*still* feel angry' (emphasis added) implies the existence of her prior anger. MO's reply confirms this while simultaneously minimising it (line 42). The grammar of emotion discourse takes an intentional object, that is, to be angry is to be angry *with someone*. Anger implicates notions of blameworthiness for that anger (Edwards, 1999). Anger can also be used as a shorthand gloss for the problematic relations between the student-mother and student-father within the school. We will see that CD1 uses the affect terms 'angry' and 'mad' as a way to raise questions about possible problems.

An interesting feature of talking problems is that one can admit to problems, e.g., being angry, while at the same time presenting those problems as less than in the past, as things getting better or improving. The mother and grandmother collaboratively work to minimise the present problems through their favourable appraisals of Johnny in repositioning him.

The grandmother (GM) joins in co-telling about this improvement in relations with Johnny. The grandmother comes in during a pause to aid her daughter by initiating an explanation for the improved relations: 'It's over' (lines 42–4). Again we see the indexical 'It' – in this utterance ambiguously referencing MO's anger, the troubles with Johnny or, possibly, her relationship with Johnny. MO then builds on this utterance in accounting for her diminution of anger. She describes an improving situation, 'Things are >ya know< slowing down' (line 45), and favourably appraises Johnny's behaviour, 'he's being ↑goo::d (.) he's doing his part' (lines 46–7).

As MO appraises Johnny's behavior, beginning each clause with 'he's' (lines 46–8), GM adds a third part to this list with 'He's coming over to see the baby' (line 49). A three-part list confers a sense of completeness and of generalisation – generally, relations with Johnny are improving (Jefferson, 1990). The grandmother starts to add another 'he is ...' description of Johnny, 'Now he's::: ((circular hand gestures))' (line 52), but leaves this incomplete. After a pause GM adds that relations between BRO and Johnny also have recently improved. GM's formulation 'they working it a little better' (lines 54–5) suggests the existence of some prior problems, which BRO did not mention (see prior section). In these co-tellings of problems, the grandmother positions herself as more authoritative, in a sense as speaking for the family.

So in this segment MO's and GM's co-telling works to reposition the mother and her relations with Johnny. There still is some anger, but 'not

as before': Johnny is coming over to be involved with the baby and
relations are improving. In evaluative terms, these changes in Johnny's
actions constitute part of the family's upbeat assessment.

In addition to the family members' co-telling, the co-director needs
to be seen as part of the joint production of talking problems. As we
have seen, CD1 raises the candidate problem of 'still feel[ing] angry'
(line 40), which projects responses from MO and GM as to the status
of the relations with Johnny and the family. A moment later, CD1
probes GM's account of Johnny coming to see the baby by 'This is
new?' (line 50). MO immediately confirms this by repeating CD1's
locution 'This is new ...' (line 51) but as an assertion rather than a
query. While it may seem odd to claim that CD1 partakes in jointly
producing the family's problems, CD1's forming candidate problems,
queries and probes are a constituent part of where the problem talk goes
and how it gets told.

Locating accountability

In light of these accounts of improving relations with Johnny, the co-
director then moves to propose an alternative appraisal of events and
query the student-mother. CD1 asks MO whether she sees the state
of affairs as one which both she and Johnny are responsible for (lines 58–
61). Presumably this version of their both being responsible would be
the optimum appraisal for reconciliation.

Extract 4

```
54 GM:    And:: ((points towards BRO)) they working it
55        a little better since he's been coming over they
56        (2.0)
57 GM:    °And°
58 CD1:   Do you have a way of thinking about it
59        in which you ss::: can see it as something
60        that you and Johnny both made a mistake
61        about [ >I mean< both did, [ both chose.
62 MO:          [((averts gaze))      [((nods head for 3.4 seconds))
63        (1.9)
64 CD1:   >Do you feel that way °about i[t°?<
65 GM                                   [((averts eye gaze))
66        (2.9)
67 GM:    HHh °really-° (1.3) okay it was ↑a mistake
68        on both their par:t? but °hh° it's ↑here:
69        what can we do about it ya know [we gotta keep
70 CD1:                                   [( ) sometimes
71        you're mad at one- you feel like well (.) it's all ↓his fault
```

In producing this appraisal CD1's self-correction and lexical choices here reflect the delicate matters under discussion. Initially she formulates it as 'both made a mistake about', then immediately corrects it to 'both did', then elaborates as 'both chose' (lines 60–1). Clearly the latter two versions, 'both did' or 'both chose', are less judgemental than the initial version, 'mistake'.

In response to the co-director's formulation, 'both made a mistake', MO confirms this version by nodding her head in agreement while remaining silent and averting her gaze in looking down. This fragment is further transcribed to capture some aspects of gaze.[3]

Fragment 1 (from extract 4)

```
60 CD1   that you and Johnny both made a mistake
   MO     _____

61 CD1   about >I mean< both did, [ both chose.
   MO     _____,,,,,,,,,,,,            X_____
62 MO                               [((nods head for 3.4
            seconds with gaze averted))
63        (1.9)
64 CD1   ((to GM)) >Do you feel that way °about it°?<
   MO                  ... X_____
```

CD1's formulation of accountability here may be heard as an optimum version of reconciliation, yet it brings about a noticeably uncomfortable moment for MO. MO casts her eyes down after CD1's formulation 'both made a mistake about'. She remains verbally silent for over 5 seconds while nodding her head in agreement for 3.4 seconds. She continues with her eyes down except for a momentary glance up and then does not look up until CD1 addresses GM. In this sequential context these non-verbal responses can be seen as a display of shame or embarrassment (Goffman, 1967; Heath, 1988).

CD1 orients to the mother's non-verbal responses as delicate matters as seen by her not pursuing a verbal account from MO. Instead CD1 turns the question away from her and to the grandmother for her assessment (line 64). The co-director moves to alleviate the pressure on the daughter by turning to the grandmother and getting her view of this proffered appraisal.

The grandmother too seems taken aback by the question (see fragment 2, below). GM displays a seeming discomfort or embarrassment as she averts eye gaze with CD1 (her eyes turn to the right) during a noticeable silence of 2.9 seconds, followed by a hearable out breath and response cry, 'really', as she casts her eyes down in the course of another pause, 1.3 seconds, as she gains her composure and begins to answer, 'okay it was a mistake ...' (lines 67–8).

Fragment 2 (from extract 4)

```
 64 CD1  ((to GM)) >Do you feel that way °about it°?<
 65 GM                   _____ ,,,((averts gaze))
 66      (2.9)
 67 GM   HHh °really-° (1.3) okay it was ↑a mistake
 68      on both their par:t?
 69      but hh it's ↑here: what can we do about it
          ....X_____
```

GM's responses here (lines 65–8) – eye gaze aversion, hearable out breath, response cry and silences – are notoriously difficult to interpret. Also, the other participants do not orient to them in any observable way as a next-turn proof procedure (Hutchby and Wooffitt, 1998), as, for instance, CD1 did to MO's non-verbal responses by directing attention elsewhere (line 64). However, the sequential context helps us to make sense of what is going on here. GM's flustered responses immediately precede her verbal utterances, and sequentially come in response to CD1's alternative appraisal query. And this follows the prior exchange between CD1 and MO. GM's responses here can be seen in sequential context as the fourth part of an accountability sequence. The sequence begins with CD1's queried assessment to MO, followed by MO's non-verbal concession, then CD1's query to GM, and GM's responses here.

As the grandmother gains composure, she replies with a 'Yes-but' account. GM agrees by paraphrasing CD1's formulation and using CD1's term 'mistake' (line 67). But she continues by citing the fact of the baby being here. She resumes eye contact with CD1 in uttering, 'it's here' (line 68). In light of this 'mistake', this fact, she adds the 'but'-clause in doing the account. GM accounts by the proverbial or idiomatic expressions 'what can we do about it' and 'we gotta keep', presumably 'going', but she leaves this idiom unfinished at the onset of CD1's overlap (lines 68–70). Proverbial or idiomatic expressions often work to close down topics (Drew and Holt, 1988), which we may conjecture, GM would probably prefer to do here.

The co-director comes back to question the grandmother with the problem formulation that it is all Johnny's fault (lines 60–71). Notice the contrast to CD1's prior formulation: they are both responsible (lines 67–8). In doing this formulation CD1 uses the affect terms, 'you're mad at one' (line 71), which is similar to her earlier query to MO, 'Do you still feel angry at him?' (line 40). Each of these versions draws on a discursive affect, i.e., 'mad at' and 'angry at', to position Johnny as the object of this negative emotion or blame. As CD1 puts it in ascribing the hypothetical feeling to GM, 'you feel like well (.) it's all ↓his fault' (line 71). In a word, CD1 is checking to see if GM has lingering problems with Johnny as the one who started these problems by getting her daughter pregnant.

Again we see CD1 using the practice of offering a candidate problem plus a query to prompt the family member to respond. The grandmother responds by denying her blaming Johnny and instead shifts the blame to her daughter (lines 72–4). In shifting the blame to her daughter, GM goes on to offer an explanation why. In her explanation, GM positions her daughter as being irresponsible for failing to use birth control and not consulting with her, while simultaneously positioning herself as 'the type of mother that I am' (line 76–7). GM's rather direct pronouncement of blame may reflect a mother's prerogative that she can be more critical of her own. Also, there is a hearable intensity in the delivery of GM's blame and explanation which is not adequately captured in the transcript and which underscores her stance.

In this section CD1's offering candidate problems with a query changes the trajectory of the discussion from improving relations to matters of accountability. This change, of course, is brought about in a conjoint fashion. It is not simply that the co-director raised these questions, but that the student-mother and grandmother addressed them, elaborated and extended the discussion. GM paraphrases CD1's formulation and uses her appraisal term 'mistake'. So in this sense, CD1 helps co-construct the problems and accounts along with the family participants.

Advising

Discursive problems, of course, call for solutions. Thus far we have seen the co-director primarily probe the family members to get their sense of the (possible) problems in relations with Johnny. In this section we see CD1 moving from locating problems to offering advice. For instance, in response to the grandmother's blame account of her daughter, CD1 draws on GM's raising the notion of taking her daughter for 'birth control' (line 79) to recommending that her daughter use condoms (line 83).

Extract 5

```
70 CD1    [( ) sometimes
71        you're mad at one- you feel like well (.) it's all ⌊his fault
72 GM     No >no no no< uh I cannot blame him=I blame- (0.8)
73        mostly I blame >her< (0.6) because she should've
74        taken care of ⌊herself.
75        (1.2)
```

```
76        and I feel she should've- (1.2) the type of mother
77        that I am=she should've come up to me and talked to me
78        (1.4) an::d if:: (0.6) worse would've come
79        I would've taken her for ↓birth control (1.2)
80        ↓and the baby wouldn't be here.
81        (2.0)
82 GM     >See<
83 CD1    In the future (wear a condom) too?
84        (0.6)
85 GM     ((avert eye gaze))
86        (1.5)
87 GM     h >ya know< it's something that you don't want to think ↑about
88        but when you have [girls ↓you have to h
89                          [((resume eye gaze))
90        (1.9)
91 CD1    Okay so- (    ) ↑and you still have to
92 GM     Yeah I have another one ↓a twelve year old
93        (1.6)
94 CD1:   No but even ↑for her, >you kno[w< =
95 GM                                   [Oh yes:
96 CD1    = it's one thing taking care of one child =
97 GM     = Oh yeah (         )
98 CD1    It's not (0.7) necessary >it's not necessary to have<
99        (1.7) five children while you're trying ↓to (0.6)
100       < get out of school >
101       (2.3)
102 GM:   Well he's been coming over to see the ba::by::
103       and: he's been- they've been tal::k↑ing:: and
104       (2.0) not much of arguing now °and°
105       (6.2)
```

The contrast in lexical choice is interesting here: CD1's 'wear a condom', uses more concrete language than GM's more abstract, generic
term 'birth control'.[4] CD1 draws on GM's category term, 'birth control'
(line 79), as a conversational resource to invoke an instance of this
category, 'condom'. CD1 simultaneously shifts focus from GM's
account of the past, of what her daughter should have done, to plans and
what she should do in the future. CD1's utterance (line 83) can be heard
as advising, though advising formed as a question.

CD1's utterance (line 83) is doubly delicate in that it is not only
offering unsolicited advice but also raising the question of GM's
daughter's birth-control practices with a specific recommendation.
GM does orient to CD1's query as delicate as seen by her seemingly
uncomfortable responses (lines 84–9): her noticeable silence (lines
84–6), eye gaze aversion (line 85), and brief out breath before verbally
responding (line 87) and eventually resuming eye contact (line 89).

These delicate matters are also reflected in the content of GM's response – as 'it's something that you don't want to think ↑about but when you have girls ↓you have to h' (lines 87–88). Again, the use of the indexical terms 'it's something ...' allows GM to avoid explicit reference to her daughter's birth-control usage or sexual activities.

In the co-director's third-turn response (line 91), she again draws on GM's prior utterance as a conversational resource to make her point. CD1 uses GM's locution 'you have to' (line 88) and intensifies it to 'you still have to' (line 91). In effect, CD1 reasserts her prior advice about condom use. Advice projects an appraisal from the recipient as to that advice, i.e., whether the recipient agrees or not with it, intends to follow it, and so on.

Gaining agreement or compliance, or at least avoiding resistance, is an important part of the practice of advising (Vehviläinen, 2001). The co-director builds on the grandmother's introducing the term 'birth control'. CD1 also displays concern that GM understands and agrees with her recommendation. In the grandmother's response that she has another daughter, 'a twelve year old' (line 92), she seems to be elaborating on her prior turn about 'when you have girls ...' (line 88). CD1 moves to correct her understanding and to point out that she is primarily talking about the student-mother (line 94), as she goes on to explain by the extreme case, apocryphal formulation of 'hav(ing) five children' while in school (lines 96–100) (Pomerantz, 1986; Edwards, 2000). Here CD1 draws on the practice of exaggeration in raising a possible problem (Buttny, 2004: ch. 4). By exaggerating the possible consequences, a problem can be raised without it being too descriptive of the recipient's situation – too close to home.

The grandmother's responses in this advising sequence are interesting. GM's initial two responses (lines 87–8 and 92) can be heard as 'competence assertions' (Heritage and Sefi, 1992) in response to CD1's advice. That is, the grandmother elliptically claims to know about what CD1 is advising.

GM makes no unequivocal acceptance of this advice, though as CD1 continues with her explanation, GM does offer 'unmarked acknowledgements' of the advice (ibid.). For instance, following CD1's correction that she is talking about the student-mother, GM displays recognition with an emphatic 'Oh yes:', overlapping CD1's post-positioned 'you know' (lines 94–5). As CD1 continues to explain, GM latches an 'Oh yeah' after CD1's initial clause (lines 96–7). GM's latter two responses appear to be done perfunctorily – an acknowledgement without agreeing – a kind of 'passive resistance' (ibid.) to CD1's direction.

GM remains noticeably silent following CD1's further explanation for the recommendation (lines 98–101). After a 2.3-second gap (line 101), GM does respond by repeating her earlier upbeat assessment of the improved relations between her daughter and Johnny: 'Well he's been coming over to see the ba::by::' (line 102) (cf. line 49). GM elaborates further on this upbeat assessment (lines 102–4). CD1 does not probe this assessment as she did the first time. Instead, the discussion falls silent for around 6 seconds. So GM is able to shift the topic from the advice about her daughter's birth control to a 'bright side' account (Holt, 1993) of the improved relations with Johnny.

Conclusion

An interesting consequence of doing discursive analysis of a tape and transcripts is that you often end up in places that you did not anticipate, you discover things about the participants' discursive realities that you did not realise initially. This happened to us here: our initial sense of the data involved the four main participants' different accounts and positionings of Johnny – a kind of mini-*Rashomon* project. But we came to see the metaphorical notion of the positioning of persons as itself based on particular kinds of communicative activities. The participants' different constructions of Johnny emerge from their different constructing actions. How Johnny was positioned through the talk-in-interaction seemed more compelling than Johnny's positionings. The project then became refined to describing some discursive practices in talking problems about Johnny and related matters.

One discursive practice in particular stands out: the co-director probes the family members, not by questioning alone, but by formulating a candidate problem along with a query. Formulating a candidate problem involves an actual or possible problem. Such problem statements are not made for their descriptive adequacy alone, but for their implications for action. This practice of candidate problem plus query projects recipients to give an account to comment on, explain, or justify their agreeing or disagreeing with the co-director's formulation. As a kind of deviant-case analysis, the co-director does ask an open-ended question at one point, but receives a conventional reply, 'It's fine' (line 11). In light of the inadequacy of such an answer, the co-director moves to using the candidate-problem-plus-query practice to project more focused responses. In addition, unlike a stepwise entry in advice giving found among health visitors (Heritage and Sefi, 1992), here the co-director does not use an initial inquiry but instead initiates with a candidate problem formed as a query.

In formulating a candidate problem, the co-director's speech at times reflects the delicate matters being raised. This orienting to delicacy can be seen through her self-correction of lexical choice in changing from 'mistake' to 'both chose'. There are a number of descriptive terms for describing an event, but each term or lexical choice can carry with it moral connotations (Silverman and Bor, 1991). This orienting to delicacy also can be seen in the use of indexical terms to avoid explicit reference to MO's sexual activities (e.g., 'it'; 'something'), or in shifting focus away from MO when she was visibly uncomfortable. Initially the candidate problem was raised using seemingly neutral language ('complicated social dilemma') which then needed to be probed and unpacked. Another kind of strategy was to exaggerate a possible problem ('have five children'). But such exaggeration or extreme-case formulation can also serve as a way to be delicate in that it seems unlikely to literally apply to the student-mother.

In a prior study of this same meeting examining the first issue (Buttny, 2004), the co-director formulates the problem by the practice of ascribing contradictory positionings, or conflicting category predicates, e.g., being a fifteen-year-old, a student and a mother. The co-director displays less concern about the delicacy of these ascriptions perhaps because such problems are more within the purview of the school, and also are mutually known conditions. This contrasts with the present study, where the co-director relies more on the practice of candidate problem plus query. This may reflect that the co-director is probing into what traditionally have been family matters. Also, the co-director has less knowledge of these relational matters with Johnny and between the mother and daughter.

In engaging the family on these various problems, the co-director faces the task of raising some seemingly personal issues for the family members to respond to. As we have seen, the co-director probes the family members about their feelings (e.g., anger) and interpersonal relationship with Johnny, as well as the student-mother's use of birth control. An important feature of discursive analysis is that these matters – feelings, relationships, or birth control – are not inherently private or personal. None of these topics is explicitly referenced as 'discussable' or as 'too personal' by participants, yet certain features of the talk-in-interaction mark them as such. This is consistent with Silverman's observation that delicate matters are 'locally produced and managed [by the] participants themselves' (1997: 64). For instance, perhaps the most delicate moments of the meeting come in the uncomfortable responses of the student-mother and grandmother in response to the co-director's candidate appraisal that MO and Johnny are both responsible (see fragments 1–2). MO's noticeable silence, eye gaze aversion and head nodding, as it were, speak volumes.

The co-director faces the practical difficulty of formulating the candidate problem to deal with substantive matters, but doing so in a way that the family members will partake in jointly examining. This practical difficulty in counselling is heightened by the fact that this meeting is likely to be a one-shot encounter, rather than a series of meetings.

We saw at times the family members refuse to discuss the topic the co-director has formulated. For instance, the grandmother resists discussing her daughter's birth control plans as seen by her noticeable silence and her topic shift to a bright-side account of relations with Johnny. In addition, the brother offers minimal responses to the co-director's problem formulation by denying the problem and even challenging her assumption. Such reticence and resistance can be heard as reflecting the private or personal matters of family life. While educational practitioners are being called upon to deal with matters that have traditionally been considered within the purview of the home, family members can still resist such inquiries. These changing border regions of school and family will likely continue to be gingerly negotiated. Future research could continue to describe the various discursive practices of ascribing problems in everyday and institutional contexts.

NOTES

1. Thanks to Bernadette Calafell for her comments on cultural aspects of this videotape and to the editors of this collection for their close readings and comments.
2. Extracts 1 and 3–5 follow each other in sequential order.
3. Transcript conventions adopted from Goodwin (1984):

___	(solid line)	The person is gazing at the speaker.
,,,,,,	(commas)	The person is turning away from gaze.
	(blank)	The person is not gazing at the speaker.
....	(dots)	The person is turning towards gaze
X	(an 'X')	The person is resuming gaze.

4. It may be that condom use is more common among high-school students than other forms of birth control.

14 Food abuse: mealtimes, helplines and 'troubled' eating

Sally Wiggins and Alexa Hepburn

Introduction

Feeding children can be one of the most challenging and frustrating aspects of raising a family. This is often exacerbated by conflicting guidelines over what the 'correct' amount of food and 'proper' eating actually entails. The issue becomes muddier still when parents are accused of mistreating their children by not feeding them properly, or when eating becomes troubled in some way. Yet how are parents to 'know' how much food is enough and when their child is 'full'? How is food negotiated on a daily level? In this chapter, we show how discursive psychology can provide a way of understanding these issues that goes beyond guidelines and measurements. It enables us to examine the practices within which food is negotiated and used to hold others accountable. Like the other chapters in this section of the book, eating practices can also be situations in which an asymmetry of competence is produced; where one party is treated as being a less-than-valid person (in the case of family practices, this is often the child). As we shall see later, the asymmetry can also be reversed, where one person (adult or child) can claim to have greater 'access' to concepts such as 'appetite' and 'hunger'. Not only does this help us to understand the complexity of eating practices; it also highlights features of the parent/child relationship[1] and the institutionality of families.

Approaching eating practices in this way rests on certain assumptions that are characteristic of discursive psychology (DP; see chapter 1 of this volume). For instance, we do not claim to prescribe what actually *is* the right amount of food for children to eat, or how parents should exert control (or not) over their child's eating habits. To do so would be to prioritise our own interpretations over those of the participants. Instead, we use DP to examine *how* eating practices are constructed and made relevant in interaction to perform different tasks (e.g., Wiggins, 2001; Wiggins and Potter, 2003). For instance, we can consider how psychological concepts of eating, such as 'tastes' and 'appetite', are constructed and used in everyday practice, as here-and-now, account-able activities. Thus we take a very practical approach to examining eating issues, focusing on how eating is 'achieved' and in particular, how people deal with managing the quantities of food for children's consumption.

We begin our investigation by considering how children's feeding practices have been a concern for developmental psychologists (amongst others), in terms of classifying and interpreting different styles of con-sumption behaviour and parenting practice. We then use two sets of data to show how DP can help us to examine the subtle negotiations of food between parents, children and those concerned about the possible mistreatment of children. We also consider the institutional business going on in both sets of data – feeding and caring for children, and determining cases of abuse – and how these are interwoven with the management of eating practices. Finally, we close with some notes about the 'usefulness' of this kind of analysis.

Feeding children as a parental concern

Within developmental branches of psychology, parental control of, or influence over, children's consumption has been widely researched (e.g., Drucker et al., 1999; Carper et al., 2000; Cullen et al., 2001). Yet surprisingly little research actually looks at eating in situ (Gable and Lutz, 2001; Harvey-Berino and Rourke, 2003; Park et al., 2003). Work that does do so typically uses an approach involving the coding of specific behaviours. For example, Koivisto et al. (1994) have made use of the BATMAN coding frame ('Bob's and Tom's Method for Assessing Nutrition', Klesges et al., 1983) which classifies behaviour such as 'food request' and 'refusing food'. In a similar way, Hays et al. (2001) noted the various behavioural strategies used by mothers to encourage their children to eat. This research is important in that it focuses on the specific situations in which food is managed, rather than with more generalised theories, for example about 'parenting styles' and their influence on children's eating habits (e.g., Spruijt-Metz et al., 2002; Kremers et al., 2003; Faith et al., 2004). However, the classification of strategies in this way conceals the variety and detail of activities that are managed during a mealtime. It also relies heavily on researchers' interpretations of what 'refusing food' may actually consist of, and does not tell us how such activities are collaboratively produced. We argue, therefore, that a more situated and detailed focus is necessary to begin to understand the complexity of parent–child interaction around food.

The control over the amount of food consumed by children also recurs as an important element in psychological research (e.g., Carper et al., 2000; Robinson, 2000; Tiggemann and Lowes, 2002). For example, Birch (1990) has argued that parents often believe that children would not be able to feed themselves appropriately without parental control. Caregivers are therefore caught between feeding a child *too much* food, which may be treated as unhealthy or as forcing the child to eat, and *not enough* food, which may be treated as equally unhealthy or neglectful. Research by Baughcum et al. (1998) has shown how mothers caught in this dilemma may favour one option over another, believing it to be more acceptable to feed *too much* food, than to be seen as a 'bad parent' by not feeding the child enough.[2] The related concept of 'failure to thrive', due in part to perceived 'under' feeding, thus becomes an issue bound up with causes and responsible agents (e.g., Kasese-Hara et al., 2002). Equally troublesome is the issue of 'force-feeding' a child. As we shall see later in the NSPCC data, this is a particularly delicate issue in relation to potential cases of child abuse.

Negotiating food and 'appetite'

Our concern with the current literature is that while there is a focus on parental behaviour around feeding, little has been done to detail the complexity of these practices as they occur in everyday situations. Parents, health professionals and academics alike are left wondering exactly how theories about food consumption should be put into practice. This involves much more than a simple coding of 'food refusals', for example, as these gloss over the interpretation of these actions. We need to consider how a 'refusal' is produced or resisted. Our focus here is on how food is understood to be 'enough' or 'not enough'. Underlying this research is a concern not with what *is* 'normal' but with how normativity is produced and oriented to within interactions, and the discursive business to which this is attending.

The data are taken from two distinctive settings. The first are from tape-recorded interactions within family mealtimes, collected by the first author. Here, the family members themselves were responsible for recording their meals, as often as possible, according to their usual routine.[3] Our concerns here are with the ways in which quantities of food are negotiated between parents and children, and with how responsibilities and rights to claim the 'correct amount' of food are managed. This is a setting in which food management is played out in 'real time', and the consequences of such negotiations are immediate. The second source of data came from a corpus of telephone calls to an

NSPCC helpline, collected by the second author.[4] These calls are taken by child protection officers (CPO), who, amongst other activities, must decide whether the case being reported warrants further action or intervention by social services. That is, they must assess the claims being made and decide whether there is evidence of actual or potential child abuse. Our concern here is with how the reported feeding practices of caregivers might warrant such a claim, focusing in particular on the amount of food that may or may not be being fed to the child. Here, the CPOs are responsible for deciding whether or not there is a case of child abuse (or potential abuse) being reported. Callers must provide evidence or display knowledge to support their case. In both cases, this can involve the construction of feeding as a moral concern, where the 'appropriate' amount of food for a child is bound up with how parents' and children's rights and responsibilities are constructed and oriented to in interaction.

It is important to note that in analysing the NSPCC data alongside the family mealtimes, we are not suggesting that there is any significant relationship between the two, nor that 'food abuse' is something that can be evidenced by these interactions alone. As D'Cruz (2004) has noted, multidisciplinary practices are used in the evidencing of child maltreatment, and examining the ways in which specific practices are constructed does not undermine their significance. Instead, by examining these two settings in parallel, we hope to illustrate some of the different ways in which food and eating issues are discursively produced for parents and young people. We take each data set in turn.

Family mealtimes

Running through the extracts are recurring issues of *quantity* of food (and how much is enough) and *persuading* (or coercing) a child to eat, and when this might be inappropriate. The first extract is a clear illustration of how these two issues overlap. Here, the mother of the family is talking to her fourteen-year-old son, Ben, during an evening meal with the rest of the family (two other children aged ten and twelve years, and the father).[5] This fragment is taken from near the end of the meal.

Extract 1

```
1 Mum:   >do you want anything ↑else or have you had en⎯ough<
2        (0.6)
3 Ben:   m⎯m::, (.) >ahm okay.<
4        (1.0)
```

```
 5 Mum:    you: (.) >don' want< °cake then.°
 6         (1.0)
 7 Ben:    ohh (0.2) that's different (0.2) (alri' then)
 8         (1.2)
 9 Ben:    are these little cakes: °or° whate:ver
10         (0.4)
11 Mum:    well there's: (0.2) a var↑iety of °things°
12 Ben:    °can::: (.) you show them to me please°
13         (3.2)
```

'Have you had enough'

A broad gloss of this extract might code this as 'acceptance' of more food by Ben, or of 'persuasion' or 'food offer' by Mum. By considering it in closer detail, however, we can see that there are more subtle activities going on. Note first the distinction made in the opening line, between 'want' and 'had', partially used again in line 5. This is produced in speeded-up talk, indicating that this is a straightforward question, and it builds Mum's role as food provider. Since Ben responds to this as being a legitimate question (i.e., that she is in a position to ask him whether he needs or wants any more food; he doesn't challenge her question), we can start to see some of the asymmetry of the situation being produced here. However, the distinction between 'want' and 'had' suggests that Ben's fullness is not just an issue of not needing any more, but is also about his tastes or desires for food. This separation of desires versus needs subsequently allows Ben to negotiate the amount of food he takes. His elongated 'mm::,' (line 3) suggests a more lengthy consideration of the question 'have you had enough', which might display lack of certainty, and allow room for him to retract his 'okay' later on (which he does on line 7).

Mum's opening turn, 'do you want anything ↑else or have you had enough', also manages the sensitive issue of 'forcing' or coercing someone to eat. It doesn't directly tell Ben to take more, or to say how much he should take; the amounts that are being talked about here are descriptively vague: 'anything ↑else' and 'enough'. They don't specify exactly what 'else' might be required, or desired, despite the mention of cake in Mum's next turn (line 5). These terms also allow for a negotiation of exactly how much is enough. For instance, having had 'enough' suggests that there are limits to one's capacity to eat food, and that the individuals themselves would *know* what this limit is. So here Ben is treated as having greater 'access' to, or knowledge of, his own state regarding satiety or appetite.

'You don' want cake then'

What happens next is that Mum does not treat Ben's '>ahm okay.<' (line 3) as being a final response on the issue. Rather than ask 'would you like some cake?', Mum appears to be making a statement about Ben's current appetite on the basis of his brief response: 'you: (.) >don' want< °cake then.°' (line 5). The way in which this is phrased performs a number of subtle activities. First, the rather quiet and hesitant way in which this is produced displays an uncertainty on Mum's part; she cannot claim to know exactly what Ben wants (given that she has just deferred the knowledge claim to him in the first turn), but can make a guess at it. The 'then' at the end of the turn also suggests that this is a conclusion based on the prior turn. Second, it avoids *directly* offering cake, and thus treating Ben as if he doesn't know his own state of fullness. If she did offer cake directly, he might argue that he has already told her that he is 'okay'. This is important because, as we will see later, rights to issues of satiety or appetite need to be carefully managed. Third, and in relation to the last point, by metaphorically placing 'cake' on the table, Mum attends to concerns that she is providing enough without seeming to 'force' anyone to eat the food. The uptake from Ben in lines 7 to 12 thus make it appear that he has actively asked for the cake, rather than it being offered directly to him. The pressure has come from him, not his mum. Again, this deals with the sensitive issue of providing food without seeming to force-feed or coerce someone into eating, particularly when asymmetries are at play.

The notion that one might have had 'enough' of one food (say, the main course) but not of another (dessert) is also noted in the psychology of eating literature, albeit from a physiological, rather than a discursive, perspective. For instance, 'sensory-specific satiety' has been noted in the work of Barbara Rolls, amongst others (see Rolls, 1986), where individuals may be sated on one food but able to eat more food if provided with a wider selection. When we consider this notion from a discursive psychological perspective, we can examine how it is constructed, used and resisted in interaction, without needing to make any claims about its putative existence as a physiological or cognitive phenomenon. In the extract below, for example, we can see how Nick explicitly orients to being 'full', unless pudding is available. Also at issue here is the dilemma of how one can *know* another person's physiological state. There are three children in this family: Adam (twelve years old), Nick (eight years old) and Daisy (four years old). This extract is taken, again, from near the end of the family evening meal. There are dishes of food on the table and some passing and serving of the remainder of the food is going on at this time.

Extract 2

```
 1 Dad:    scuse ↓me (0.6) why hasn't anybody eat these
 2         (0.8)
 3 Mum:    they 'ave, (0.2) >look<
 4         (2.0)
 5 Mum:    >I didn't give< Daisy ↓any (0.2) >°I° thought
 6         she got enough.<
 7         (0.4)
 8 Mum:    Adam could 'ave some more=
 9 Adam:   =wha:t
10         (1.8) ((sound of scraping cutlery on plates))
11 Mum:    'stead of comin' >lookin' for< more fo:od after.
12         (0.4)
13 Mum:    ↑I'll >'ave a bit< more cabbage (.)
14         °if there is some please°
15         (1.8)
16 Dad:    >°(little bit)°<
17         (5.2) ((sound of dish being banged lightly))
18 Mum:    °'k you°
19 Dad:    °(2 syllables)°
20         (1.8)
21 Mum:    °°(might as well)°° °>finish it off<° (.) does
22         Daisy want >any more< cabbage?
23         (0.8)
24 Nick:   <I'm ↑full up un[less there's any more: pudd:ing.>
25 Mum:                    [mm?
26         (0.2)
27 Mum:    put yer knife n fork straight.
28         (3.8)
29 Mum:    might find you some if you si[t nice.
30 Daisy:                              [°wha:t°
```

'I thought she got enough'

As we noted earlier, eating is often treated as an individual activity involving physiological states that can only be 'accessed' by the speakers themselves. For the parent, then, they have to assume responsibility for another's eating behaviour, but without the privileged 'knowledge' of what that person needs or wants. In lines 5–6 above, Mum accounts for her actions ('>I didn't give< Daisy ↓any') by using a speculative claim to what Daisy had already eaten: '>°I° thought she got enough.<'. In this way, Mum can build up her entitlement to know about Daisy's physiological state without claiming it to be a fact (Potter, 1996: 868). As with extract 1, Mum also displays attention to providing food without coercing the children to eat. Note, for example, the softened use of: 'Adam could 'ave' (line 8) and 'does Daisy want' (lines 21–2). In a similar way, the quantities of food being negotiated here are also dealt with rather delicately. Again, as in extract 1, having 'enough' or 'more' is not explicated in any detail. Thus, Mum's orientations to more food treat the children as having a greater right to know, and decide, what to eat, even if the situation is not quite so simple. For instance, as we see below, the children may be held accountable if they display hunger later in the evening.

'I'm full up unless there's any more pudding'

The issue of quantities of food is combined with that of eating enough *now* so that the children don't go '>lookin' for< more fo:od after' (line 11). How much one eats (or doesn't eat) is therefore accountable later on as well. However, by stating that he is full 'unless there's any more: pudd:ing', Nick constructs the notion that one has different satiety levels for different kinds of food (in a similar way to Ben in extract 1). He can also claim to know directly how much food (and what type) he needs. By stating this claim when Mum is offering and serving more food, Nick displays an orientation to who this claim is relevant to. That is, who *needs to know* that he is 'full up unless there's any more pudding'. Note that Mum doesn't dispute his claim (compare this with Ben's more hesitant reply and his Mum's indirect 'offer', extract 1) and rather attends to behavioural requirements instead (lines 27 and 29). So in this extract we see further management of the asymmetries involved in eating practices: who has greater knowledge of/access to one's 'appetite' and who has greater responsibility for attending to the implications of this. These are issues that are collaboratively managed by the family members themselves.

The issue of being 'full' is considered again in the final mealtime extract. Chloe and Emily are the children in this family, aged thirteen and twelve years respectively. This fragment is taken from halfway through the family evening meal, when Dad asks Chloe why she doesn't want the rest of her food. This fragment provides a more explicit example of family members managing their eating patterns, in which being 'full' is itself treated as an accountable matter. But how can one hold someone accountable in this way, when speakers apparently have privileged 'access' to their appetite?

Extract 3

```
1 Dad:     >why don't you want this< Chloe?
2          (1.0)
3 Chloe:   °I'm ↑fu:ll°
```

```
4           (2.0)
5 Dad:      ↑wh*y are you always full you two.
6           (1.8)
7 Dad:      I ca:n't underst:and at your a[ge(.)
8 Emily:                                  [na-
9 Dad:      I used to be eat↓ing,
10          (0.6)
11 Emily:   haven't got very big ↑appetites=
12 Chloe:   =E-↑Emmie's no:t (.) tha::t (0.8) ↓ f:ull all the
13          time but [my-
14 Dad:              [but you keep ea:ting things in
15          be[twe:e]n ↑meals
16 Chloe:     [look-]
17 Chloe:   Mum, (0.2) can you tell him <my appetites gone.>
18          (2.4)
19 Emily:   °you've just said it°
20          (1.4)
21 Chloe:   >no but< she's been ↓here so she can ↑pro:ve it
22          (1.8)
23 Mum:     it has ↓gone (0.2) but on that basis you shouldn't
24          eat bi:scuits or a:nything between meals.
25          (5.0)
```

'Why are you always full you two'

The extract starts with a fairly typical question over why some food hasn't been eaten, and Chloe's claim that she's full (line 3). Note, however, how this claim is produced quietly and with rising intonation, as if questioning whether this is an appropriate or adequate response. What happens next is that this 'fullness' isn't challenged directly, but rather is treated as a pervasive state ('always full', line 5) and one that applies to both children ('you two.', line 5). This is a particularly interesting turn; note the rising intonation and 'squeaky voice' on the 'why', providing emphasis and displaying a sense of disbelief. Appetite and being 'full' is brought into the wider context of recurring practices and age-related expectations ('at your age(.) I used to be eat↓ing,', lines 7 and 9). Mum and Dad are then left with the situation of managing this potential problem and rather than challenge whether Chloe (or Emily) is 'really' full, they question the practices that might have resulted in this fullness (lines 23–4).

'She's been here so she can prove it'

Following a softening of the account ('E-↑Emmie's no:t (.) tha::t (0.8) ↓f:ull all the time', lines 12–13), Chloe claims an independent witness as evidence for her declining appetite. So her claim about an 'internal state' (appetite) is constructed as observable by an external source (Mum). Indeed, Mum's turn, 'it <u>has</u> ↓gone' (line 23), states this as if it were a fact, with an emphasised turn shape. The implication of this is that another person can then provide 'proof' (line 21) of someone else's physiological state by simply observing their eating habits; thus, the private becomes public. This is a particularly neat way of managing one's accountability for their appetite; if it is observable, then it can be more easily evidenced. Moreover, by focusing on her own appetite (not Emily's), Chloe resists the implication that their 'fullness' is due to collaboration or a planned, joint activity (note how Dad seems to suggest this on line 5). Losing one's appetite is hereby constructed as an individual concern, and based on physiological (and therefore less controllable) factors. It is not so much that she is 'always full', but that her appetite has 'gone' (note the temporal shift here; if it has 'gone', it must have been there before). She thus cannot be held accountable for such uncontrollable factors, and indeed the focus then shifts to what she *can* control (eating biscuits, etc.).

In this section, then, we have begun to examine the negotiation of quantities of food between parents and children in everyday settings. The sorts of issues at stake are the distinction between 'needing' and 'desiring' food, which is related to the construction of what psychologists have termed sensory-specific satiety. There is also a need to manage ownership of physiological states, and who has the rights to know one's fullness or appetite. It is not simply the case that parents have the rights and responsibilities to provide food for their children, and for children to eat this food, but that these rights are negotiated and delicately managed within interaction. So far, then, we can begin to see how psychological states and concepts relating to eating practices are played out in everyday interaction as public and accountable concerns.

NSPCC helpline interaction

We now move on to consider how issues of food quantity and coercing/persuading children to eat are raised in NSPCC helpline interaction. In this setting, the implications of poor feeding practices may be more serious, as calls may result in action being taken to protect a child from neglect or mistreatment. Unlike family mealtimes, food is not present here, so speakers are discussing retrospectively the eating habits of children and/or their parents. The concerns thus raised are whether these habits are appropriate or indicative of abuse. The way in which these are *evidenced* is thus more important; speakers must account explicitly for their concerns.

The following extract is taken from a call where the issue to be established is the mistreatment of a three-year-old girl at a day care centre. The claim from the mother in an earlier call is that the child spat food into the face of one of the staff, who then smacked the child. NSPCC requested that the father, the current caller, phone in and give more information, as he is the one who usually picks the daughter up from the centre and interacts with the staff. We are still in the initial stages of the call, and the father recounts the problem his daughter is having with eating. To some extent this issue is peripheral to the main reason for the call (whether the child was smacked at the nursery), but we have chosen it as it illustrates quite starkly some of the features of parenting and control over eating that appeared in our first data set.

Extract 4

```
 1 Caller:   Sh:e ↑has been havin problems: eatin there.=an
 2           we don't know whaddit is,
 3           (0.5)
 4 CPO:      Mh[m. ]
 5 Caller:   [>We]ll-well< when she moved there she was
 6           all right an then sort've (0.9) within a short
 7           period.
 8           (0.6)
 9 Caller:   >°or-[or-or°] a period< .hh (0.4) sh:e: was
10 CPO:           [°Mhm. °]
11 Caller:   refusing to eat >in the sense of I w'd ask
12           'er d'ye want sommink to eat< an (0.4) .hh
13           <she would> cry an say no.
14           (0.6)
15 CPO:      Mh[m.]
16 Caller:     [Er]: when I went to pick 'er up (0.2) on
17           a:- (0.7) the-the- they were .hh (0.7) saying
18           'well your daughter hhas cried but we ↑put 'er
19           food in front of 'er.=she ↑didn't <want: it:.>=
20           [an some]>times even when we took it away<
21 CPO:      [ M m :.]
22 Caller:   (0.2) she would cry.'
23           (0.4)
24 Caller:   .hh
25 CPO:      Mm.=
26 Caller:   =Er::m: (0.6) .hh td.hh (.) >an on ↑ one occasion
27           recently when I was talking to 'er about't they
28           said 'well we ↑know that she wants ↓it b'cos we
29           sometimes see 'er- whe-whe-when< .hhh >the other
```

```
30          children around 'er are eatin it< we can see her
31          face mo:vin.= s[ort've li]ke (.) .hh as if she
32 CPO:                   [ M m : .   ]
33 Caller: wants to eat it typa thing.'
34 CPO:     Mm.
35          (0.5)
```

'She was refusing to eat'

The extract begins with the caller's description of his daughter's problem with eating, and the relationship between this eating problem and his daughter's attendance at the nursery (lines 1–11). There is a lot of delicacy around the caller's implication of the nursery in the problem, for example, the timing of the onset of the problem is attended to with some interesting pauses and self-repairs. Prior to changing nurseries the child was 'all right' (line 6) then 'sort've (0.9) within a short period' of moving there, the problems with eating began. Note that the short period is qualified by 'sort've' and a fairly long delay, but is said with some emphasis. But after more delay and hesitation, the caller self-repairs to 'a period<' (line 9). This repair may be attending to the issue of whether it was the *move itself* that may have precipitated the problem, which 'a short period' might imply. Thus the problems with eating are related to the nursery rather than the parents. Note that the caller does not make this link explicitly, rather leaves it for the CPO to infer for herself. Throughout this, as is common in the 'opening narrative' sequences, the CPO provides fairly minimal continuers. So we have a puzzle – a child who has stopped eating shortly (but not too shortly) after moving to a new nursery.

'D'ye want sommink to eat'

The caller constructs his own role in his child's eating problems:

```
Caller: ..> I w'd ask 'er d'ye want sommink to eat<
         an (0.4) .hh she would> cry an say no.
```

Initially we can note two interesting features of the father's story – active voicing and script formulations. Active voicing, or the use of quotations from others or oneself to present a version of events, often occurs throughout narrative sequences, and as Wooffitt (1992) has shown, are a feature of constructing events as vividly brought to life, or as something that the teller did not expect. Here, the casualness of the caller's actively voiced utterance 'd'ye want sommink to eat' illustrates the father's role as a relaxed provider of whatever food his daughter might like.

A second feature of this utterance is what Edwards (1995) terms a 'script formulation' – an utterance that formulates events as commonplace, or 'what typically happens' – part of the script of everyday life. The use of 'would' is useful in this respect, and as well as being actively voiced, the above utterance is also scripted as an event that 'would' typically happen. So not only is the caller attending to the possible role of the nursery in his daughter's eating problem, but he is also attending to his own role in this. There is also a nice contrast between the father's casual offer of 'sommink to eat', and the daughter's (similarly scripted) response, 'sh<u>e</u> would> <u>cry</u> an say no'. The problem is not just that the daughter doesn't want to eat; it is that merely being asked about it, even in this casual way, is upsetting. Also, she is not merely upset about being asked to eat; she is also upset by her food being removed (lines 20–2). So the construction of the problem is firstly that the child is confused and upset about eating, and that this puzzling situation is something related more to the nursery than to the feeding practices of the parents. The caller moves on to describe events at the nursery.

'We know that she wants it'

The caller again employs active voicing to illustrate the perspective of the nursery staff (lines 28–33), which starts to paint a picture of a child who is confused about what she wants. The inferences about the child's state of mind are built upon through the report of a specific event at the nursery, where the caller reports that the staff know that the child wants to eat because they can see her face moving (lines 30–1). Note again how the nursery staff are actively voiced by the caller – 'they said 'well we ↑know that she <u>wants</u> ↓it', allowing a more vivid picture of events to emerge, while also providing footing for the caller, establishing this version of events as very much the nursery staff's version. The caller is careful to display the delicacy of surmising the mental states of the child on behalf of the staff: 'we can see her <u>face</u> mo:vin. = sort've like (.) .hh as if <u>she</u> wants to eat it typa thing.' Here the phrase 'she wants to eat it' is heavily qualified and softened by 'sort've', 'like' and 'typa thing' – the caller is careful not to overtly produce the staff as the kind of people who would rush into such a judgement.

This first extract has focused on establishing that something, probably the new nursery, has made the child confused and upset about eating, but that she really wants to eat. The next extract provides various justifications for then forcing her to eat. It follows on directly from the first.

Extract 5: 'You've got to eat it'

```
 1 Caller:   Er:m so what they resorted to an I mean it was
 2           with- (0.2) with my: (0.4) >let's say blessing
 3           was that well< (0.2) .hh try an be a bit firmer
 4           with her.
 5           (0.3)
 6 CPO:      Mm:.
 7           (0.8)
 8 Caller:   Because (0.2) .hhhh >we've found that sometimes we
 9           say to 'er< (0.2) y'know (0.9) 'd'you want this.'
10           (0.5)
11 CPO:      Mm.=
12 Caller:   =Er:: (0.7) she will sort've say 'no' even
13           though she might (0.4) 'n (.) ye know hh if-huh
14 CPO:      [ M m : .           ]
15 Caller:   [w(hh)e s(hh)ay] 'you've got to eat it.'
16 CPO:      .H[ tk .hh      ]
17 Caller:     [She'll eat] it.=so they [have] done
18 CPO:                               [Mhm,]
19 Caller:   >where they put 'er in a chair an they've
20           sort've< (0.5) ↑not force fed 'er but (0.5)
21           got s- puddit on the s:- s- s:poon >opened 'er
22           mouth an (then they said) 'y'ought to have it'<
23           an closed 'er- an puddit in 'er mouth.
24           (0.4)
25 CPO:      Mm.
26 Caller:   .Hh an:d (0.2) she did actually eat it.='n
27           that happened last Fri:day.=
28 CPO:      =Mm.
```

'Try an be a bit firmer with her'

The caller presents what happens next as something that was 'resorted to' (line 1), and he is careful not to sound as if he is enthusiastically giving permission for the staff to be more forceful; it is something that is qualified and hesitated over – 'an I mean it was with- (0.2) with my: (0.4) >let's say blessing<'. He also actively voices what he did say – 'well (0.2) .hh try an be a bit firmer with her', which itself contains careful qualifications – it starts as a characteristically dispreferred response, with 'well' plus hedging, and suggests that the staff 'try' to be 'a bit' firmer. The action suggested is further accounted for by the caller with an anecdote about what 'we've found':

```
Caller:  sometimes we say to 'er< (0.2) y'know
         (0.9)
```

```
              'd'you want this.'
              (0.5)
CPO:          Mm.=
Caller:       =Er:: (0.7) she will sort've say 'no' even
              though she might
```

Note the switch from 'I' to 'we' here, the responsibility for these actions now lies with the parenting team, not with the father alone. Note also the way what the child 'might' want is formulated as somehow knowable despite her ability to inform people to the contrary – 'she will sort've say "no" even though she might'. The father is here constructing and orienting to one of the normative requirements of a parent – to know what is best for your child.

'You've got to eat it'

The careful construction of compulsion to eat is continued with interpolated laughter – 'hh if-huh w(hh)e s(hh)ay you've got to eat it. She'll eat it.' (line 15). The laughter softens the impact of the command to eat, lest it be heard as an oppressive command. An interesting feature here is that '= so they have done' is latched onto this, moving seamlessly from the anecdote about the home situation back to the nursery, the moral of the prior anecdote (tell her more forcefully to eat it and she will) then serving as a go-ahead from the father to the staff to compel his daughter to eat.

So far we have noted the careful way in which the father has managed both his own responsibility and that of the nursery in the construction of his daughter's eating problem. Part of this involves attending to/carefully constructing the normative requirement that parents know when, and what, their child wants to eat. This then provides a warrant for simply commanding the child to eat, which results in 'success' – the child eats the food.

'She did actually eat it'

The final section of the extract provides the upshot to the story and is equally carefully formulated. One interesting recurring formulation is 'put 'er in a chair' (line 19) 'puddit on the spoon' (line 21) and 'puddit in 'er mouth' (line 23), 'put' being a fairly neutral description of an action of placing something somewhere, but not forcing or shoving. Indeed, the father also explicitly attends to the content of this story as being hearable as 'force feeding' and discounts this at the outset (line 20). The final 'puddit in 'er mouth' is particularly interesting as it is repaired from 'closed 'er-', which was probably going to be 'closed 'er mouth', which has more of a sense of force and coercion about it, especially coupled with 'opened 'er mouth' (lines 21–2). This course of action is then presented as successful – 'she did actually <u>eat</u> it'.

Again this shows a careful attention to the formulation of feeding practices. Evidently forcing a child to eat is not an easy thing to justify or describe, and this is marked by various qualifications, softening, hedging and false starts. As we noted earlier, this issue of feeding practices was part of a broader narrative in which the events a few days later were the main focus. Our interest in it relates to what is produced as normative in terms of the practices that accompany feeding a small child. Although forcing a child to eat is oriented to as unacceptable, being firm with a child who is confused and upset about eating is justifiable. Knowing what a child wants better than they know themselves, in this setting, seems a taken-for-granted feature of parent–child and adult–child interaction, as does possessing the rights to enforce that knowledge. We have looked in detail at how these rights and competences are produced interactionally.

Conclusions

Negotiating quantities of food for children involves a complex range of activities such as managing issues of 'appetite', and who has the rights, and responsibilities, to know or deal with these issues. This is also embedded within institutional business. In terms of the institution of the family mealtime, the business here is focused on providing appropriate food, displaying acceptable behaviour and consuming the food in appropriate quantities. Exactly what is 'appropriate' or 'acceptable' is managed on a situated level, there and then, as the activities of the mealtime unfold. In the examples we showed here, how much was enough was usually left unspecified, and children were treated as being in a position to know what this was. In all three examples, there was emphasis on having *more* rather than having *less*. The institutional business of the NSPCC helpline interaction was more focused on assessing claims about a child's consumption and whether this con-stitutes evidence of actual or potential child abuse. In the example we showed here, the concern was specifically with whether or not the child had been *forced* to eat. Again, constructions of appetite (whether the child wanted or needed to eat) and how others could 'know' this were used to provide evidence for the father's claims.

So, family eating practices are an arena in which asymmetries of competence are produced and resisted, where one party is oriented to as having a better understanding of others' needs. Yet this is troubled; the issue of eating is not simply a matter of deciding specific amounts of food and then presenting these to children. What also need to be managed are issues such as 'fullness' and 'appetite'. These are complex interactional concerns as much as individual ones; they involve negotiating rights to 'know' these things and how one can evidence this knowledge (e.g., by 'being here', extract 3, or by 'seeing her face moving', extract 4). The analysis here has enabled a small insight into how we might understand eating practices as these are embedded within childcare concerns.

There is great potential for this kind of analysis. Firstly, it provides a more thorough account of the *everyday* activities in which food and eating are central concerns, e.g., socialising with friends, reporting in at a 'slimming' group or organising a family party. This is a move away from the kind of research that tends to categorise or generalise eating practices without looking closely at the day-to-day detail of how eating is actually managed. The issues we have discussed in this chapter – such as appetite and satiety – are ones that apply not just to family situations, but to many occasions involving food. So we know more about how these issues are constructed, used and resisted, and what sorts of business they attend to. This kind of detail is useful in itself; it can inform our own eating practices and help develop research around the 'mundane' issue of meals and eating with others. Eating then is no longer just an individual or psychological concern; it requires a consideration of how seemingly 'private' physiological concepts are part of a delicate web of social and interactional concerns.

Earlier research (Hepburn, 2004, 2005, 2006) has also suggested that there can be direct practical relevance of this type of research for the NSPCC helpline. Detailed analyses of this kind can often pinpoint areas of interactional trouble that may be hard for practitioners themselves to identify. It may also be useful in showing what the day-to-day practices of the helpline are, so that good practice becomes more easily identifiable. Often CPOs find it hard to explicate exactly what they do, because it has become second nature, or because it involves subtle features of communication that are not generally focused on. The way that both callers and CPO can be heard as orienting to a set of issues (e.g., the caller's stake in making the call, the CPO's knowledge of child protection) right at the start of calls has also been focused on (Potter and Hepburn, 2003, 2004, forthcoming b).

On another level, this type of research could be used by health professionals (see Potter and Hepburn, 2005b; Stokoe and Wiggins, 2005). More specifically, our approach to the interactional features of eating may help dietitians, clinical psychologists and those working in eating disorder clinics to understand more about how food guidelines are used in practice. As noted above, it provides an insight into actual eating practices – and clearly a wider range of practices would help to develop this – and the resources used by parents and children to manage quantities of food. For example, how are claims to being 'full' understood? How can parents encourage their child to eat more (or less) without seeming to force them to eat? These are issues that are not easily resolved, and the more we understand how they work in practice, the better able we will be to pick up on occasions when they become troubled.

NOTES

1. While we are aware of the many differing kinds of caregiver relationship involved in childcare, we use the generic term 'parent' or 'parental' as a shorthand way of referring to such relationships.
2. Most research in this area has focused around maternal feeding practices (Baughcum et al., 1998; Cooper et al., 2004; Hays et al., 2001). A worrying issue here is that the importance of other caregivers is underestimated, and that it is assumed that mothers are the primary individuals responsible for (and thus also accountable for) children's eating practices.
3. For details of this data set, see Wiggins and Potter (2003).
4. For further information about the helpline, and to see prior analytic work related to this see Hepburn (2004, 2005); Hepburn and Potter (2003); Hepburn and Wiggins (2005a); Potter and Hepburn (2003, 2004).
5. We use the labels 'Mum' and 'Dad' rather than first-name pseudonyms within the data and analysis to flag up issues of parent–child interaction.

15 Discursive research: applications and implications

Sally Wiggins and Alexa Hepburn

This collection builds on an interconnected set of developments in the study of discourse. These include the powerful and rigorous approach to interaction offered by contemporary conversation analysis, the respecification of the nature of psychology in terms of practices and orientations offered by discursive psychology, and the sophisticated empiricism offered by modern ways of recording, manipulating and representing interaction. Taken together these provide the basis for a systematic, analytically based approach for studying the world as it happens. This work stands on its own intellectual merits as a contribution to the study of human life. And we should, anyway, always be cautious of the way social researchers invoke an 'ideology of application' to justify their work. Claims about application are often promissory notes that weaken as we look more closely at the connections between academic knowledge and actual practice (Potter, 1982). Nevertheless, in this final chapter we will push the discussion forward to consider how these developments can be the basis for some new ways of considering the relevance and application of social research, particularly in institutional settings.

The application of social science research has traditionally taken a variety of forms and raises a number of complex issues. For example, *what* is applied (the theory or knowledge or findings)? *Who* is application for (e.g., doctors or patients)? The style of discursive work reported in this volume offers its own possibilities in terms of the use of the findings and raises new issues about the nature of application. As this work is completely different from the factors and outcomes approach that is characteristic of much mainstream social psychology and sociology it does not lie well with input/output style evaluations.

Take research on psychotherapy, for example. There is a major tradition of largely psychology-based work that is concerned with therapeutic outcomes. The basic model here is some kind of pre-test; the therapy is delivered, and then the client is assessed again (e.g., Lambert and Ogles, 2004). Such work is appropriate for evaluation of effectiveness (although far from controversial for this). However, what it does not do is look at what goes on in the psychotherapy itself. That is, it does not consider in any way the set of embodied, situated practices that makes up any specific therapy session. The contrast with the work here is stark. It is no basis for an input/output assessment of effectiveness. And indeed, discourse researchers have been very cautious about making premature claims to application and usefulness. Yet the detailed study of therapeutic interaction might be useful in a range of different ways. It might allow therapists new ways of monitoring or understanding their own actions. It might provide insights and materials that could be drawn on in training. It might provide a more nuanced and practical account of what makes one form of therapy different from another. It might offer new ways of considering whether any particular therapist delivers the therapy effectively. And it might raise new questions about the role of therapeutic theory in particular practices. These are different models of application from the input/output assessments that factors and variable studies underpin. But they are potentially important in different ways.

To take another example, studies of medical work have suggested that there is a massive over-prescription of antibiotics to young children, often for conditions that do not respond to antibiotics. To show that there is such an over-prescription is different to showing how it happens in the specifics of any medical consultation. In a series of studies, conversation analysts Stivers, Heritage and colleagues have studied just this and highlighted not only a number of interactional features that underpin the over-prescription, but also some of the ways in which doctors can approach distressed parents of young children to avoid the unnecessary prescription (e.g., Heritage and Stivers, 1999; Stivers, 2005, forthcoming; Stivers et al., 2003).

There are nevertheless complex issues to be considered when attempting to consider the utility of discursive research. If feedback to participants is to be offered on the basis of analysis, whose knowledge and expertise are to be supported and by what criteria (Hepburn, 2006)? Who is to be helped? And to do what? The application questions are, appropriately, not easy to separate from broader social and political issues. Hepburn concluded that the 'usefulness' of the researcher becomes a complicated and contingent product of the developing relationship with those being researched. For example, in the programme of work on the NSPCC child protection helpline reported in chapter 14, the authors started with the assumption that callers and

CPOs are both competent and both working together (although sometimes in conflict, e.g., see Hepburn, 2005) to develop an understanding of the reported situation during the course of the calls. Showing how this is achieved provides practitioners with a more theorised understanding of their own practical skills and competencies. That is, it allows practitioners to turn their practical and situated know-how into a propositional form that can be communicated, considered and possibly more easily changed.

As we have seen in the chapters above, for discursive psychologists and many conversation analysts (see te Molder and Potter, 2005) 'reality' – the world that people describe and formulate – and 'subjectivity' – thoughts, feelings, beliefs and so on – are most productively seen as the *outcome* of interaction. The upshot for the application of discursive research is that rather than looking over, or into, the minds of participants to check whether they are getting things 'right', the goal is to reveal the actions performed by participants' formulations and discursive practices in different institutional environments. The contributors to this volume have developed a variety of distinctive perspectives on the way to intervene in the practices that they seek to capture and explicate.

Our aim in this concluding chapter is therefore threefold. Firstly we will draw together the contributors' developments of the 'practical relevance' of their research, and consider how the similarities and differences of approach can produce contrastive interventions. Secondly, we aim to document how similar issues can arise across different institutional settings and draw out the implications of these commonalities and differences. This will be invaluable in highlighting profound issues about the way in which institutions draw upon both context-specific and generic strategies and conversational practices, providing important resources for the development of future discursive research. Finally, we will indicate some directions for a more systematic assessment of issues of application, and the practical relevance of discursive research.

Styles of intervention

In earlier research, Hepburn (2003) developed some possible (overlapping and interlocking) ways that researchers engaged in critical and discursive research can intervene in social life. We extend and refine that discussion here with reference to the insights developed by the contributors to this volume.

Psychological actions

Part I of this collection shows the possibilities that arise from taking an action-orientated approach to what have traditionally been characterised as inner states. The early chapters deal with some of the classic items from the broad range of psychological research: dispositions (Edwards); perceptions, opinions, beliefs and attitudes (Potter and Puchta); emotions (Nikander); and descriptions of consciousness (Allistone and Wooffitt). The fifth chapter focuses on the variety of functions that apologising might have in different interactional contexts (Augoustinos, LeCouteur and Fogarty). Rather than seeing mental terms and descriptions as reflections of mental states or events, all the authors develop a focus on the interactional business performed by such terms and descriptions in their various interactional contexts. In doing so, they build challenges and possibilities for the future development of both psychology and discursive research that stays in closer touch with everyday practices. Discursive psychologists, in particular, have treated the discipline of psychology *itself* as an arena for intervention, and have developed a systematic discursive respecification of the cognitive and emotion terms previously assumed to refer to the entities and processes that make up the inner world (Edwards, Nikander).

Rather than seeing mental terms and descriptions as reflections of mental states or events, research in this tradition focuses on the actions performed by such terms, descriptions and displays in their various interactional contexts. As Potter and Puchta suggest, this style of work has developed in several ways – as a respecification of the topics of psychology, such as scripts, categories and schemata, as an investigation into the thesaurus of psychological terms such as 'anger' and 'opinion', and as an examination of various types of 'psychological display'. The book includes some powerful examples of this style of work. Cromdal et al. (Chapter 11) explore the utility of displays of emotion and reluctance for students resisting making assessments of one another. MacMartin and LeBaron (Chapter 8) examine the practical uses of 'cognitive distortions' for both therapists and clients in sex offender group therapy.

In a complex and sophisticated argument Edwards (Chapter 2) explores the construction of 'subject-side accounts', and shows how they are inextricably bound up with 'object-side accounts', in that they can work together, e.g., they can work in opposition where the subjectivity of someone's account threatens its objectivity, or they can work in unison, where I bolster my account's objectivity by presenting it as counter to my initial subjective state. Edwards suggests that discursive psychology's focus on the relationship between subject and object means that it can emphasise important features of institutional arenas such as courtrooms, police interrogations and neighbour mediation, where speakers' motivations and intentions for saying things and where doubt and dispute are commonly relevant to the interactional procedure.

One potential practical value of this style of work can be in encouraging participants to be cautious of explanations that rely on individual features such as motives or personality types, as an explanation for talk and other actions. It encourages us to see people as embedded within a complex weave of institutional relationships, constraints and possibilities. Potter and Puchta (Chapter 6) develop these ideas through a critical focus on the style of application that relies on an individualist and cognitivist notion of psychology. They argue instead for a 'dynamic and collaborative' image of psychology-in-practice.

Identification of problematic practices

In Part II of this collection we focused on studies of various therapeutic and diagnostic environments – for many the classic arena for the production and utility of professional and psychological terms and theories. Part III had a focus on the construction and treatment of young people and their 'competence'. A common feature of both sets of studies is that they both deal with professional–client interaction where both parties have different levels of knowledge and expertise. The resulting issues from both parts II and III tend to pick up on the way that these differences can be glossed over by the practitioners in the various settings. Hence many of the studies show how everyday practice does not fit well with the traditional orthodoxy in these types of environments, often due to the complexity of the tasks being performed by both practitioner and client.

For example, Fasulo and Fiore (Chapter 12) illustrated a mismatch between the stated aim of improving the social skills of autistic young people and the practices of correcting speech and controlling conversational topics that come with more educational and therapeutic goals. They show that therapists' use of 'continuous questioning' as a way of eliciting talk, and their subsequent evaluations in third position, turn what ought to be dialogues into interrogations. They recommend an appreciation of strategies that signal attention and interest, such as 'uninformed recipiency', continuers and change-of-state tokens. The issues raised in Fasulo and Fiore's chapter regarding being a 'valid person' also have resonances with other discursive and conversation analytic work in which speakers are treated as being less than competent persons. This body of work includes research by Rapley (2004) and Shakespeare (1998). Being a 'valid person', as Rapley (2004) has argued, is in part due to being able to negotiate competence in interaction, where competence is defined (according to conversation analysts) as the *accomplishment* of one's ability and/or intellectual functioning. Here, again, the focus is on practices rather than processes.

Pomerantz, Gill and Denvir (Chapter 7) highlight similar problems related to practitioners' control over the interaction, in their examination of the way that patients embed candidate explanations into initial accounts of their symptoms. Their analysis shows some of the complexity involved in this practice, such as presenting the serious condition in a sceptical way or as one of many possible explanations. Pomerantz et al. suggest that, rather than taking the explanation at face value, e.g., as evidence for the patient's views on the matter, a more contextually sensitive approach to the presentation of candidate explanations could help healthcare providers make more sense of this complex practice. They also argue that patients need more 'interactional space' to present their concerns, rather than having the interaction driven largely by the doctor's questions.

The issue of identifying problematic practices returns in Speer and Parsons' contribution (Chapter 10), although in a more complex way. The focus is on psychiatrists' clinical assessments of transsexual patients' suitability for gender reassignment surgery, and their practice of using hypothetical questions in order to assess their clients' authenticity. Speer and Parsons track through the interactional troubles that can arise with such questions, especially in the context of the institutional authority to accept or reject the case for gender reassignment surgery that the psychiatrist possesses. The analysis shows that while clients are skilled at second-guessing the function of such questions, and using their answers as a vehicle for displays of authenticity, the hypothetical question-answer sequence is nonetheless considerably troubled and marked by numerous self-repairs and hedges. Rather than recommending alternative interactional strategies however, Speer and Parsons show that it is unclear how psychiatrists could proceed without such interactional trouble, given the nature of the task in hand. This highlights again the complex relationship between analytic findings and good practice. Professionals are often working in ways that have evolved and refined over a long period of doing the job. Even if practices appear problematic or troubled to start with this does not mean that they are not successful for doing what they do, or that there is an easy alternative.

Social interventions and changes to public policy

This has been a traditional aim in much social research, with the overall goal being the development of well-supported theories through rigorous surveys and scientific testing. However, interactional research of the kind represented here cautions us against seeing the pathway to application to lie through traditional individual concepts such as opinions and beliefs (cf. Potter and Puchta). It is not that those concepts are not important or useful, but treating them simply as individual mentally encoded objects can lead to major confusions. The challenge for interaction research is to develop interventions which could feed into public information campaigns and changes to social practices such as penal policy, but which don't rely on the identification of features of individuals or pre-existing realities and social structures. In a sense, it may involve the development of a whole new vocabulary to underpin application. As yet such a vocabulary does not exist.

Our collection contains pointers toward this new way of conceiving of research utility; Fasulo and Fiore's argument about the problems emerging from therapeutic practices with autistic children is one example; MacMartin and LeBaron's discussion of sex offender therapy is another. However, we will illustrate our argument with two of the chapters, both of which, we suggest, should be interesting and provocative reading for those involved in developing educational policy. Cromdal, Tholander and Aronsson (Chapter 11) discuss the institutional dilemmas raised by the requirement for peer assessment in Swedish schools engaging in the practice of 'problem-based learning'. Their analysis shows the difficulties raised by the requirement that students evaluate one another's contributions individually, and the delicate ways that such a requirement can be managed. Cromdal et al. show the utility of emotion displays for students, such as humorous assessments and reluctance, as a way of managing such a task. They note that one of the problems for young people is in having to produce individual, rather than more general group, assessments, something which a minor change in teaching practice could address.

Buttny and Kellogg Rath (Chapter 13) also focus on school settings, this time on a high school meeting with a returning student and her family, where the student is newly a mother. Their analysis of that meeting shows how offering a 'candidate problem plus query' provides the school with a way of managing the delicacy of probing issues that are more related to family matters, rather than academic school issues. Buttny and Kellogg Rath relate their discussion to the broader home/school environment, highlighting the continuing move within North American schools towards dealing with more family-related issues. The shifting boundaries between school and family, and the difficulties that these boundaries and their fuzziness raise for the people involved in the institutional environment of the school–family meeting, are played out in the interaction. The power of this kind of analysis is that it does not merely document outcomes (a student's academic failure, another statistic of unplanned pregnancy); instead it provides a way into the weave of practices through which these things are negotiated and responded to. By opening a window on the world as it happens such studies provide a very different kind of resource for policy makers or those involved in educating counsellors or teachers.

Reworking the empirical paradigm

As Potter and Puchta (Chapter 6) note, one focus for discursive research has been the way that social research methods can constitute the objects that they claim to be studying. This style of research is starting to develop a strong critique of the traditional empirical paradigm, which relies mainly on hypothetico-deductive methods using experiments and surveys. Many of the studies in this collection highlight the limitations of this paradigm; for example, Nikander (Chapter 3) criticises psychological notions of rational information processing, which typically develop models for understanding decision making. Nikander argues that in contrast to the typical advice given to professionals to ignore background information, an understanding of the role of emotion in decision making and team-work is crucial.

However, we also need to develop a strong alternative that doesn't replicate the same problems. Allistone and Wooffitt (Chapter 4) seek to develop this style of intervention in psychology. While they illustrate the limitations of the formal experimental method for understanding what is happening in parapsychological research, they also note the finding that the success or failure of the ganzfeld experiments seems to rely quite heavily on the relationship between the experimenter and participant. They therefore suggest that the close analysis of that relationship offered by a discursive psychological/conversation analytic approach will help parapsychologists themselves to understand this phenomenon. While they may be agnostic about whether or not 'psi' phenomena exist, they do claim to offer an approach that is 'complementary' to related cognitive research (see also Wooffitt, 2005a). In this sense, the practical relevance of their work can be seen as an additional research tool for other disciplines. Allistone and Wooffitt's work may also be useful for those working in fields where claims to reality are directly questioned, such as in mental health settings or those who are treated as having a 'less than valid' account (see also the chapters in Part III).

Antaki, Barnes and Leudar (Chapter 9) also address this issue. They discuss how far a conversation analytic approach should take account of the theories that the therapist claims to be operating with in doing therapy. Their focus on therapists' formulations allows insights into the way those formulations can deliver a therapeutic message to clients, and the strategies that clients might develop for resisting those formulations. They argue that while CA does not need theories of therapy to proceed analytically, therapeutic theories and practices could be enriched by this style of analytic work.

Taking the more theoretical and linguistic tradition of speech act theory as their topic for critique, Augoustinos, LeCouteur and Fogarty (Chapter 5) argue that in order to understand how apologising is typically bound up with other actions, we need to develop a discursive approach to the topic, which can sensitise us to the many things that apologising can do (and not do) interactionally. This awareness of the complexity of apologising is lost in the standard sociological and linguistic literature, and yet, as Augoustinos et al. note, it is crucial that we understand the importance of apologising in the current Western climate of restorative justice. Their chapter also taps into the use of psychological categories to manage interpersonal transgressions. Here, the discursive act of apologising is a way of negotiating responsibilities and issues of guilt or culpability. Their example focuses on apologising at a governmental level to groups of people, and similar sorts of issues might be raised in other institutional areas. For instance, transgressions within the workplace between employers and employees, and at various levels within the organisational hierarchy, may mean that apologising becomes a real concern. An apology – at the right time, and in the right way – may ease the blow of a fairly major issue. As Augoustinos et al. note, apologies are particularly noticeable when they are absent, and it is just such absent apologies that could make the difference between a happy workforce and one that moves to dissent. The same principles could equally be used to understand individual cases: family members or neighbours involved in a dispute, a convicted individual saying 'sorry' to the victim of the crime, and so on. Whether seen as mundane or not, understanding how apologies are produced can be key to understanding part of the complexity of everyday interaction.

Turning institutional practices into strategies

Application has traditionally been characterised in terms of the authority of social scientists' definitions, where the researcher possesses the expertise – for example, insights into participants' thought processes, or insights into social realities – and judges the adequacy of participants' knowledge against that expertise. By contrast, many of the studies reported here have focused on both explicating the knowledge and skills of practitioners themselves, and appreciating the varied ways in which they coordinate social interaction, manage various difficulties, and achieve certain outcomes. We noted earlier some of the interactional problems that can arise through the complexity of the tasks being performed by both practitioners and clients. The aim with this style of intervention is to develop training materials aimed at highlighting features of good practice, and documenting the complexities of how the job is done. This notion of intervention has been discussed by Potter and Puchta (Chapter 6) and was also topicalised by Hepburn (2006).

Taking the NSPCC project discussed in our chapter as an example of this approach, in the longer term the aim is to provide child protection officers (CPOs) with a more analytically informed set of resources, in which different interactional practices will be made more explicit, so that they can be used strategically. This will comprise a digitised archive of examples of calls and elements of calls that can be used to illustrate particular problems and ways of dealing with them. The aim will be to produce a small number of CDs which allow both trainees and experienced practitioners to work though a simple menu of topics (problem closings, say, or styles of soothing upset children) each generating an on-screen presentation which takes them through problems and solutions using instances from calls. As well as providing examples of calls that the NSPCC themselves find difficult to deal with, we will also supply analytic insights that identify common features and interactional functions. Silverman (1998) has argued that practical input into training of this kind is important for the application of interaction research.

This raises further issues of the relation of training materials to practice – in the NSPCC training materials work with normative reconstructions of everyday practice, which is probably why CPOs have found records of their own interaction so useful. What they show (and what we aim to clarify for future training materials) is the way in which CPOs' practices can be doing several things simultaneously. This can give them the sense that they are doing a bad job – they don't measure up to the idealised versions of helpline interaction that they get in training. When CPOs reflect on their own practices they can easily appear messy or haphazard in comparison. Puchta and Potter's (2004) study of focus group moderation found something similar, in that the claims in training manuals were often at odds with the practices of skilled moderators. They suggest in this volume (Chapter 6) that training manuals available for focus group moderators do not capture the complexity of everyday practice, and suggest that for applied work to be more effective, it may need to take examples of good practice and explicate its operation. Thus one use of interaction analysis is to clarify the complex organisation of talk that might appear chaotic, and to show some of the art of doing the job. The aim of these kinds of practical interventions is not to tell practitioners how to do their job better, but to provide resources that they can draw on in their training and practice.

Epilogue

One of the features of interaction research of this kind is that it has encouraged a major reappraisal of what kind of thing an institution is, of what kind of thing psychology is, and, most fundamentally, of the nature of interaction. Although we have indicated some different ways in which utility and social relevance can flow from this work we are also cautious that our models of utility are too shaped by previous forms of social research. One of the challenges here will be to develop new concepts of application. This is likely to be stimulated by the reflexive study of application practices. Rather than stipulate on the appropriateness of particular applications we suggest that interaction researchers should take social research applications as a topic of study. This might, for example, focus on training, on the implementation of systems or the use of claims and findings in warranting practices. It is a challenging research field, partly because the topic can seem so ephemeral. However, that is part of what makes it interesting and important.

Appendix: transcription notation

The following conventions were developed by Gail Jefferson.

[ ]	Square brackets mark the start and end of overlapping speech, and are aligned where the overlap occurs.
↑↓	Vertical arrows precede marked pitch movement, over and above normal rhythms of speech. They are for marked, hearably significant shifts – and even then, the other symbols (full stops, commas, question marks) mop up most of that. As with all these symbols, the aim is to capture interactionally significant features, hearable as such to an ordinary listener – especially deviations from a commonsense notion of 'neutral', which admittedly has not been well defined.
→	Side arrows are not transcription features, but draw analytic attention to particular lines of text. Usually positioned to the left of the line.
Underlining	Underlining signals vocal emphasis; the extent of underlining within individual words locates emphasis, but also indicates how heavy it is.
CAPITALS	Capitals mark speech that is obviously louder than surrounding speech (often occurs when speakers are hearably competing for the floor by raising volume rather than doing contrastive emphasis).
°I know it°	'Degree' signs enclose obviously quieter speech (i.e., hearably produced as quieter, not just someone distant).
that's r*ight.	Asterisks precede a 'squeaky' vocal delivery.
(0.4)	Numbers in round brackets measure pauses in seconds (in this case, four-tenths of a second). Placed on new line if not assigned to a speaker.
(.)	A micropause, hearable but too short to measure.
((text))	Additional comments from the transcriber, e.g., context or intonation.
she wa::nted	Colons show degrees of elongation of the prior sound; the more colons, the more elongation.
hhh	Aspiration (out-breaths); proportionally as for colons.
.hhh	Inspiration (in-breaths); proportionally as for colons.

292

Yeh,	'Continuation' marker – speaker has not finished; marked by fall-rise or weak rising intonation, as when enunciating lists.
y'know?	Question marks signal stronger, 'questioning', intonation, irrespective of grammar.
Yeh.	Periods (full stops) mark falling, stopping intonation ('final contour'), irrespective of grammar, and not necessarily followed by a pause.
bu-u-	Hyphens mark a cut-off of the preceding sound.
>he said<	'Greater than' and 'less than' signs enclose speeded-up talk. Sometimes used the other way round for slower talk.
solid. ==We had	'Equals' signs mark the immediate 'latching' of successive talk, whether of one or more speakers, with no interval. Also used where an unbroken turn has been split between two lines to accommodate another speaker on the transcript page.
heh heh	Voiced laughter. Can have other symbols added, such as underlinings, pitch movement, extra aspiration, etc.
sto(h)p i(h)t	Laughter within speech is signalled by an h in round brackets.
Several£	The pound sterling sign signifies a 'smiley' voice

For further details see Jefferson (2004).

References

Abel, G. G., Becker, J. V. and Cunningham-Rathner, J. (1984). Complications, consent, and cognitions in sex between children and adults. *International Journal of Law and Psychiatry*, 7, 89–103.

Abel, G. G., Gore, D. K., Holland, C. L., Camp, N., Becker, J. V. and Rathner, J. (1989). The measurement of cognitive distortions of child molesters. *Annals of Sex Research*, 2, 135–52.

Abu-Lughod, L. and Lutz, C. A. (1990). Introduction: emotion, discourse and the politics of everyday life. In C. A. Lutz and L. Abu-Lughod (eds.), pp. 1–23.

Antaki, C. (1999). Assessing quality of life of persons with a learning disability: how setting lower standards may inflate well-being scores. *Qualitative Health Research*, 9, 437–54.

(2001). 'D'you like a drink then do you?': dissembling language and the construction of an impoverished life. *Journal of Language and Social Psychology*, 20, 196–213.

(2006). Producing a cognition, *Discourse Studies*, 8 (1), 9–15.

Antaki, C., Leudar, I. and Barnes, R., (2004). Trouble in agreeing on a client's problem in a cognitive-behavioural therapy session. *Rivista di Psicolinguistica Applicata*, 4, 127–38.

Antaki, C. and Rapley, M. (1996). 'Quality of life' talk: the liberal paradox of psychological testing. *Discourse and Society*, 7, 293–316.

Antaki, C. and Widdicombe, S. (eds.) (1998). *Identities in talk*. London: Sage.

Aronsson, K. and Cederborg, A.-C. (1996). Perspective setting in multiparty problem formulations. *Discourse Processes*, 21 (2), 191–212.

Aronsson, K. and Evaldsson, A.-C. (1993). Pedagogic discourse and interaction orders: sharing time and control. In N. Coupland and J. Nussbaum (eds.), *Discourse and Lifespan Identity*, Language and Language Behaviours series, vol. IV (pp. 103–31). London: Sage.

Astington, J. W. and Gopnik, A. (1991). Theoretical explanations of children's understanding of the mind. *British Journal of Developmental Psychology*, Special Issue on Children's Theories of Mind, 9, 7–31.

Atkinson, J. M. (1984). Public speaking and audience responses: Some techniques for inviting applause. In J. M. Atkinson and J. Heritage (eds.), *Structures of social action: studies in conversation analysis* (pp. 370–409). Cambridge: Cambridge University Press.

(1992). Displaying neutrality: formal aspects of informal court proceedings. In P. Drew and J. Heritage (eds.), pp. 199–211.

Atkinson, J. M. and Drew, P. (1979). *Order in court: the organization of verbal interaction in judicial settings*. London: Macmillan.

Atkinson, J. M. and Heritage, J. C. (eds.) (1984). *Structures of social action: studies in conversation analysis*. Cambridge: Cambridge University Press.

Atkinson, P. (1999). Medical discourse, evidentiality and the construction of professional responsibility. In S. Sarangi and R. Roberts (eds.), *Talk, work and institutional order: discourse in medical, mediation and management setting* (pp. 75–108). Berlin: Mouton de Gruyter.

Auburn, T. (2005). Narrative reflexivity as a repair device for discounting 'cognitive distortions' in sex offender treatment. *Discourse and Society*, 16, 697–718.

Auburn, T. and Lea, S. (2003). Doing cognitive distortions: a discursive psychology analysis of sex offender treatment talk. *British Journal of Social Psychology*, 42, 281–98.

Augoustinos, M., LeCouteur, A. and Soyland, J. (2002). Self-sufficient arguments in political rhetoric: constructing reconciliation and apologising to the Stolen Generations. *Discourse and Society*, 13, 105–42.

Austin, J. L. (1961). A plea for excuses. In J. O. Urmson and G. J. Warnock (eds.), *Philosophical papers* (pp. 175–205). Oxford: Oxford University Press.
  (1962). *How to do things with words*. Oxford: Clarendon Press.

Barkan, E. (2000). *The guilt of nations: restitution and negotiating historical injustices*. New York: W. W. Norton and Company.

Baron-Cohen, S., Tager-Flasberg, H. and Cohen, D. (eds.) (1993). *Understanding other minds: perspectives from autism*. Oxford: Oxford University Press.

Baruch, G. (1981). Moral tales: parents' stories of encounters with the health professions. *Sociology of Health and Illness*, 3 (3), 275–95.

Baughcum, A. E., Burklow, K. A., Deeks, C. M., Powers, S. W. and Whitaker, R. C. (1998). Maternal feeding practices and childhood obesity. *Archives of Pediatrics and Adolescent Medicine*, 152 (10), 1010–14.

Beach, W. (1993). Transitional regularities for 'casual' 'Okay' usages. *Journal of Pragmatics*, 19, 325–52.

Beach, W. A. and Metzger, T. R. (1997). Claiming insufficient knowledge. *Human Communication Research* 23 (4), 562–88.

Beattie, G. (2004). *Visible thought: the new psychology of body language*. London: Routledge.

Bem, D. and Honorton, C. (1994). Does psi exist? Replicable evidence for an anomalous process of information transfer. *Psychological Bulletin*, 115, 4–18.

Bem, D. J., Palmer, J. and Broughton, R. S. (2001). Updating the Ganzfeld database: a victim of its own success? *Journal of Parapsychology*, 65, 207–18.

Bendelow, G. and Williams, S. J. (eds.) (1998). *Emotions in social life: critical themes and contemporary issues*. London: Routledge.

Bergmann, J. R. (1992). Veiled morality: notes on discretion in psychiatry. In P. Drew and J. Heritage (eds.), pp. 137–62.

Bierman, D. J. (1995). The Amsterdam Ganzfeld Series III and IV: target clip emotionality, effect sizes and openness. In N. L. Zingrone (ed.), *Proceedings of presented papers*, 38th Annual Parapsychological Association Convention (pp. 27–37). Fairhaven, MA: Parapsychological Association.

Billig, M. (1992). *Talking of the Royal family*. London: Routledge.

(1996). *Arguing and thinking: a rhetorical approach to social psychology* (2nd edn). Cambridge: Cambridge University Press.

(1999). *Freudian repression: conversation creating the unconscious*. Cambridge: Cambridge University Press.

(2005). *Laughter and ridicule: toward a social critique of humour*. London: Sage.

Billig, M., Condor, S. Edwards, D., Gane, M. Middleton, D. and Radley, A. (1988). *Ideological Dilemmas*. London: Sage.

Birch, L. L. (1990). The control of food intake by young children: the role of learning. In E. D. Capaldi and T. L. Powley (eds.), *Taste, experience and feeding* (pp. 116–35). Washington, DC: American Psychological Association.

Boden, D. (1990). The world as it happens: ethnomethodology and conversation analysis. In G. Ritzer (ed.), *Frontiers of social theory: the new synthesis* (pp. 185–213). New York: Columbia University Press.

Boden, D. (1994). *The business of talk: organizations in action*. Cambridge: Polity.

Boden, D. (1995). Agendas and arrangements: everyday negotiations in meetings. In A. Firth (ed.), *The discourse of negotiation: studies of language in the workplace* (pp. 83–99). Oxford: Pergamon.

Boden, D. and Zimmerman, D. (eds.) (1991). *Talk and social structure: studies in ethnomethodology and conversation analysis*. Cambridge: Polity.

Boersma, P. and Weenink, D. (2004). *Praat: doing phonetics by computer*. Software version 2.4.19, Department of Phonetics, University of Amsterdam. Available at http://www.fon.hum.uva.nl/praat/.

Bonaiuto, M. and Fasulo, A. (1997). Rhetorical intentionality attribution: its ontogenesis in ordinary conversation. *British Journal of Social Psychology*, 36, 511–37.

Boud, D. and Feletti, G. (eds.) (1991). *The challenge of problem based learning*. London: Kogan Page.

Broughton, R. S. and Alexander, C. (1995). Autoganzfeld II: the first 100 sessions. In N. L. Zingrone (ed.), *Proceedings of presented papers*, 38th Annual Parapsychological Association Convention (pp. 53–61). Fairhaven, MA: Parapsychological Association.

Brown, M. and Rounsley, C. (2003). *True selves: Understanding transsexualism for families, friends, co-workers and helping professionals*. San Francisco: Jossey-Bass.

Bruner, J. (1983). *Child's talk: learning to use language*. New York: Norton.

Bryan, J. (2004). School counselors' perceptions of their involvement in school-family-community partnerships. *Professional School Counseling*, 7, 162–71.

Burns, C. (2004a). Something rotten in the state of the profession. http://www.pfc.org.uk/pfclists/news-arc/2004q4/msg00069.htm.

Burns, C. (2004b). UK: Echoes of a bygone age. http://www.pfc.org.uk/pfclists/news-arc/2004q4/msg00073.htm.

Burns, C. (2005). Health Trust to examine comments by psychiatrist. http://www.pfc.org.uk/pfclists/news-arc/2005q1/msg00061.htm.

Bushwick, N. L. (2001). Social learning and the etiology of autism. *New Ideas in Psychology*, 19, 49–75.

Buttny, R. (1993). *Social accountability in communication*. London: Sage.
  (1999). Discursive construction of racial boundaries and self-segregation on campus. *Journal of Language and Social Psychology*, 18 (3), 247–68.
  (2004). *Talking problems: studies on discursive construction*. Albany: State University of New York Press.
Buttny, R. and Jensen, A. D. (1995). Telling problems in an initial family therapy session: The hierarchical organization of problem-talk. In G. H. Morris and R. J. Chenial (eds.), *The talk of the clinic: explorations in the analysis of medical and therapeutic discourse* (pp. 19–47). Hillsdale, NJ: Erlbaum Publications.
Carper, J. L., Fisher, J. O. and Birch, L. L. (2000). Young girls' emerging dietary restraint and disinhibition are related to parental control in child feeding. *Appetite*, 35, 121–9.
Clayman, S. and Heritage, J. (2002). *The news interview: journalists and public figures on the air*. Cambridge: Cambridge University Press.
Cooper, P. J., Whelan, E., Woolgar, M., Morrell, J. and Murray, L. (2004). Association between childhood feeding problems and maternal eating disorder: role of the family environment. *British Journal of Psychiatry*, 184, 210–15.
Corsaro, W. (1979). 'We're friends right?': children's use of access rituals in a nursery school. *Language in Society*, 8, 315–36.
Coulter, J. (1979). *The social construction of mind*. London: Macmillan.
  (1990). *Mind in action*. Oxford: Polity.
  (1999). Discourse and mind, *Human Studies*, 22, 163–81.
Couper-Kuhlen, E. and Ford, C. (eds.) (2004). *Sound patterns in interaction*. Amsterdam: John Benjamins.
Couper-Kuhlen, E. and Selting, M. (eds.) (1996). *Prosody in conversation: interactional studies*. Cambridge: Cambridge University Press.
Cowie, R. and Cornelius, R. (2003). Describing the emotional states that are expressed in speech. *Speech Communication*, 40, 5–32.
Craig, M. E. (1990). Coercive sexuality in dating relationships: a situational model. *Clinical Psychology Review*, 10, 395–423.
Cromdal, J. (2006). Socialization. I. In *Encyclopedia of language and linguistics*, vol. XI (2nd edn), (pp. 462–6). North-Holland: Elsevier.
Cruttenden, A. (1997). *Intonation* (2nd edn) Cambridge: Cambridge University Press.
Cullen, K. W., Baranowski, T., Rittenberry, L., Cosart, C., Hebert, D. and De Moor, C. (2001). Child-reported family and peer influences on fruit, juices and vegetable consumption: reliability and validity of measures. *Health Education Research*, 16 (2), 187–200.
Danby, S., and Baker, C. (1998). How to be masculine in the block area. *Childhood*, 5 (2), 151–75.
Da Silva, F. E., Pilato, S. and Hiraoka, R. (2003). Ganzfeld vs. no ganzfeld: an exploratory study of the effects of ganzfeld conditions on ESP. In *Proceedings of presented papers*, 46th Annual Parapsychological Association Convention (pp. 31–48). New York: Parapsychological Association.

Davies, B. and Harré, R. (1999). Positioning and personhood. In R. Harré and L. van Langenhove (eds.), *Positioning theory* (pp. 32–52). Oxford: Blackwell.

Davis, K. (1986). The process of problem (re)formulation in psychotherapy. *Sociology of Health and Illness*, 8 (1), 44–74.

D'Cruz, H. (2004). The social construction of child maltreatment: the role of medical practitioners. *Journal of Social Work*, 4 (1), 99–123.

Denzin, N. K. (1984). *On understanding emotion*. San Francisco: Jossey-Bass.

Douglas, J. (ed.) (1971). *Understanding everyday life: toward the reconstruction of sociological knowledge*. London: Routledge and Kegan Paul.

Drew, P. (1987). Po-faced receipts of teases. *Linguistics*, 25, 219–53.

(1991). Asymmetries of knowledge in conversational interactions. In I. Markova and K. Foppa (eds.), *Asymmetries in dialogue* (pp. 21–48). Hemel Hempstead: Harvester Wheatsheaf.

(1992). Contested evidence in courtroom cross-examination: the case of a trial for rape. In P. Drew and J. Heritage (eds.), pp. 470–520.

(1998). Complaints about transgressions and misconduct. *Research on Language and Social Interaction*, 31, 295–325.

(2003). Comparative analysis of talk-in-interaction in different institutional settings: a sketch. In P. J. Glenn, C. D. LeBaron and J. Mandelbaum (eds.), *Studies in language and social interaction: in honor of Robert Hopper* (pp. 293–308). Mahwah, NJ: Erlbaum.

(2005). Is *confusion* a state of mind? In H. te Molder and J. Potter, (eds.), (pp. 161–83).

Drew, P. and Heritage, J. C. (eds.) (1992a). *Talk at work: interaction in institutional settings*. Cambridge: Cambridge University Press.

Drew, P. and Heritage, J. C. (1992b). Analyzing talk at work: an introduction. In P. Drew and J. Heritage (eds.), pp. 3–65.

Drew, P. and Holt, E. (1998). Figures of speech: figurative expressions and the management of topic transition in conversation. *Language in Society*, 27, 495–522.

Drucker, R. R., Hammer, L. D., Agras, W. S. and Bryson, S. (1999). Can mothers influence their child's eating behavior? *Developmental and Behavioral Pediatrics*, 20 (2), 88–92.

DSM-IV (1994). *Diagnostic and statistical manual of mental disorders* (4th edn). Washington, DC: American Psychiatric Association.

Duranti, A. and Goodwin, C. (eds.) (1992). *Rethinking context: language as an interactive phenomenon*. Cambridge: Cambridge University Press.

Edge, H. L., Morris, R. L., Palmer, J. and Rush, J. H. (1986). *Foundations of parapsychology: exploring the boundaries of human capability*. Boston: Routledge and Kegan Paul.

Edley, N. (2001). Analysing masculinity: interpretative repertoires, ideological dilemmas and subject positions. In M. Wetherell, S. Taylor and S. J. Yates (eds.), *Discourse as data: a guide for analysis* (pp. 189–228). London: Sage.

Edwards, D. (1994). Script formulations: an analysis of event descriptions in conversation. *Journal of Language and Social Psychology*, 13, 211–47.

(1995). Two to tango: script formulations, dispositions, and rhetorical symmetry in relationship troubles talk. *Research on Language and Social Interaction*, 28, 319–50.

(1997). *Discourse and cognition*. London: Sage.

(1999). Emotion discourse. *Culture and Psychology*, 5 (3), 271–91.

(2000). Extreme case formulations: softeners, investment, and doing nonliteral. *Research on Language and Social Interaction*, 33, 347–73.

(2003). Analyzing racial discourse: the discursive psychology of mind–world relationships. In H. van den Berg, M. Wetherell and H. Houtkoop-Steenstra (eds.), *Analyzing race talk: multidisciplinary approaches to the interview* (pp. 31–48). Cambridge: Cambridge University Press.

(2004). Discursive psychology. In K. Fitch and R. Sanders (eds.), *Handbook of language and social interaction*. (pp. 257–73). Mahwah, NJ: Erlbaum.

(2005). Moaning, whinging and laughing: the subjective side of complaints. *Discourse Studies*, 7, 5–29.

(2006a). Facts, norms and dispositions: practical uses of the modal *would* in police interrogations. *Discourse Studies*, 8 (4), 475–501.

(2006b). Discourse, cognition and social practices: the rich surface of language and social interaction. *Discourse Studies*, 8, 41–9.

Edwards, D. and Fasulo, A. (2006). 'To be honest': sequential uses of honesty phrases in talk-in-interaction. *Research on Language and Social Interaction*, 39 (4), 343–76.

Edwards, D. and Middleton, D. (1986). Joint remembering: constructing an account of shared experience through conversational discourse. *Discourse Processes*, 9, 423–59.

Edwards, D., Middleton, D. and Potter, J. (1992). Toward a discursive psychology of remembering. *The Psychologist*, 5, 56–60.

Edwards, D. and Potter, J. (1992). *Discursive psychology*. London: Sage.

(2001). Discursive psychology. In A. McHoul and M. Rapley (eds.), *How to analyse talk in institutional settings: a casebook of methods* (pp. 12–24). London and New York: Continuum International.

(2005). Discursive psychology, mental states and descriptions. In H. te Molder and J. Potter (eds.), pp. 241–59.

Fairclough, N. (1995). *Critical discourse analysis*. Harlow: Longman.

Fairclough, N. and Wodak, R. (1997). Critical discourse analysis. In T. A. van Dijk (ed.), *Discourse as social interaction: a multidisciplinary introduction*, Discourse studies 2 (pp. 258–84). London: Sage.

Faith, M. S., Scanlon, K. S., Birch, L. L., Francis, L. A. and Sherry, B. (2004). Parent–child feeding strategies and thier relationships to child eating and weight status. *Obesity Research*, 12, 1711–22.

Fasulo, A. (1997). Other voices, other minds: the use of reported speech in group therapy talk. In L. Resnick, R. Säljö, C. Pontecorvo and B. Burge (eds.), *Discourse, tools and reasoning: essays on situated cognition* (pp. 203–23). New York: Springer.

Fasulo, A. and Girardet, H. (2002). Il dialogo nella situazione scolastica [Dialogue in the school situation]. In C. Bazzanella (ed.), *Sul dialogo* [On dialogue] (pp. 59–72). Milan: Guerini.

Fatigante, M., Fasulo, A. and Pontecorvo C. (1998). Life with the alien: role casting and face–saving techniques in family conversation with young children. *Issues in Applied Linguistics*, 9 (2), 97–121.

Fineman, S. (ed.) (2000). *Emotion in organizations* (2nd edn). London: Sage.

Fiore, F. (2003). Autismo e comunicazione [Autism and communication]. Graduation thesis. Rome: University of Rome 'la Sapienza'.

Fiske, S. T. (1989). Examining the role of intent: toward understanding its role in stereotyping and prejudice. In J. S. Uleman and J. A. Bargh (eds.), *Unintended thought: the limits of awareness, intention and control* (pp. 253–83). New York: Guilford.

Fiske, S. T. and Taylor, S. E. (1984). *Social cognition.* New York: McGraw-Hill. (1991). *Social cognition* (2nd edn). New York: McGraw-Hill.

Forman, E., Minick, N. and Stone, A. (1993). *Contexts for learning: sociocultural dynamics in children's development.* Oxford: Oxford University Press.

Forsberg, H. (1999). Speaking of emotions in child protection practices. In J. Jokinen and Pösö (eds.), *Constructing social work practices* (pp. 116–32). Aldershot: Ashgate.

Freese, J. and Maynard, D. W. (1998). Prosodic features of bad news and good news in conversation. *Language in Society*, 27 (2), 195–219.

Frith, U. (1989). *Autism: explaining the enigma.* Oxford: Blackwell.

Gable, S. and Lutz, S. (2001). Nutrition socialization experiences of children in the Head Start program. *Journal of the American Dietetic Association*, 101 (5), 572–7.

Gale, J. E. (1991). *Conversation analysis of therapeutic discourse.* Norwood, NJ: Ablex.

Gardner, R. (1997). The conversational object *Mm*: a weak and variable acknowledging token. *Research on Language and Social Interaction*, 30, 131–56.

Garfinkel, H. (1963). A conception of, and experiments with, 'trust' as a condition of stable concerted actions. In O. J. Harvey (ed.), *Motivation and social interaction* (pp. 187–238). New York: The Ronald Press Company. (1967). *Studies in ethnomethodology.* Englewood Cliffs, NJ: Prentice-Hall.

Garfinkel, H. and Sacks, H. (1970). On formal structures of practical actions. In J. C. McKinney and E. A. Tiryakian (eds.), *Theoretical sociology* (pp. 337–66). New York: Appleton-Century-Crofts.

Gergen, K. (1982). *Toward transformation of social knowledge.* New York: Springer Verlag. (1994). *Realities and relationships: soundings in social construction.* Cambridge, MA: Harvard University Press.

Gergen, K. J. and Semin, G. (eds.) (1990). *Everyday understanding: social and scientific implications.* London: Sage.

Gibson, J. J. (1979). *The ecological approach to visual perception.* Boston, MA: Houghton Mifflin.

Giesler, P. V. (1986). Sociolinguistics and the psi conducive context of laboratory and field setting: a speculative commentary. In D. H. Weiner and R. D. Radin (eds.), *Research in parapsychology 1985* (pp. 111–15). Metuchen, NJ and London: Scarecrow Press.

Gilbert, N. and Mulkay, M. (1984). *Opening Pandora's box: a sociological analysis of scientists' discourse.* Cambridge: Cambridge University Press.

Gill, V. T. (1995). The organization of patients' explanations and doctors' responses in clinical interaction. Unpublished Ph.D. dissertation. University of Wisconsin, Madison.

Gill, V. T. (1998). Doing attributions in medical interaction: patients' explanations for illness and doctors' responses. *Social Psychology Quarterly*, 61, 342–60.

Gill, V. T. and Maynard, D. (2006). Explaining illness: patients' proposals and physicians' responses. In J. Heritage and D. Maynard (eds.), *Communication in medical care: interaction between primary care physicians and patients* (pp. 115–50). Cambridge: Cambridge University Press.

Gill, V. T., Pomerantz, A. and Denvir, P. (2004). On patients' ruling out explanations for illness: a case building strategy. Pacific Sociological Association annual meeting, San Francisco, April 2004.

Glenn, P. J. (1995). Laughing *at* and laughing *with*: negotiations of participant alignments through conversational laughter. In P. ten Have and G. Psathas (eds.), *Situated order: studies in the social organization of talk and embodied activities* (pp. 43–56). Washington, DC: University Press of America.

(2003). *Laughter in interaction.* Cambridge: Cambridge University Press.

Goffman, E. (1967). Embarrassment and social organization. In E. Goffman, *Interaction ritual* (pp. 97–112). New York: Pantheon Books.

(1971). Remedial interchanges. In E. Goffman, *Relations in public: microstudies of the public order* (pp. 95–197). New York: Basic Books.

(1981). *Forms of talk.* Oxford: Basil Blackwell.

(1983). The Interaction Order, *American Sociological Review*, 48, 1–17.

Goodwin, C. (1981). *Conversational organization. interaction between speakers and hearers.* New York: Academic Press.

(1984). Notes on story participation and the organization of participation. In J. M. Atkinson and J. Heritage (eds.), *Structures of social action* (pp. 225–46). Cambridge: Cambridge University Press.

(1986). Gesture as a resource for the organization of mutual orientation. *Semiotica*, 62, 29–49.

(ed.) (2003). *Conversation and brain damage.* New York: Oxford University Press.

Goodwin, M. H. (1980). He said/she said: formal cultural procedures for the construction of a gossip dispute activity. *American Ethnologist*, 7, 674–94.

Goodwin, M. H. and Goodwin, C. (2000). Motion within situated activity. In A. Duranti (ed.), *Linguistic anthropology: a reader* (pp. 239–57). Malden, MA, and Oxford: Blackwell.

Greatbatch, D. and Dingwall, R. (1999). Professional neutralism in family mediation. In S. Sarangi and R. Roberts (eds.), *Talk, work and institutional order: discourse in medical, mediation and management setting* (pp. 271–92). Berlin: Mouton de Gruyter.

Green, R. (1974). *Sexual identity conflict in children and adults.* New York: Basic Books.

(1987). *The 'Sissy boy syndrome' and the development of homosexuality.* New Haven: Yale University Press.

(2000). Gender identity disorder in adults. In M. Gelder, J. Lopez-Ibor and N. Andreasen (eds.), *The new Oxford textbook of psychiatry.* Oxford: Oxford University Press.

(2004). Gender development and reassignment. *Psychiatry,* 26–9.

Gumperz, J. J. (1982). *Discourse strategies.* Cambridge: Cambridge University Press.

Haakana, M. (1999). *Laughing matters: a conversation analytical study of laughter in doctor–patient interaction.* Department of Finnish Language 303. Helsinki: University of Helsinki.

Hak, T. and de Boer, F. (1996). Formulations in first encounters. *Journal of Pragmatics,* 25, 83–99.

Halkowski, T. (2006). Realizing the illness: patients' reports of symptom discovery in primary care visits. In J. Heritage and D. Maynard (eds.), *Communication in medical care: interaction between primary care physicians and patients* (pp. 86–114). Cambridge: Cambridge University Press.

Hall, R. (1998). *Black armband days: truth from the dark side of Australia's past.* Milsons Point, NSW: Random House.

Hammersley, M. (1997). On the foundations of Critical Discourse Analysis, *Language and communication,* 17, 237–48.

Hammersley, M. and Woods, P. (eds.) (1976). *The process of schooling: a sociological reader.* London: Routledge and Kegan Paul.

Harré, R. (ed.) (1988). *The social construction of emotions.* Oxford: Blackwell.

Harré, R. and Gillet, G. (1994). *The discursive mind.* Thousand Oaks, CA: Sage.

Harré, R. and Parrott, G. W. (eds.) (1996). *The emotions: social, cultural and biological dimensions.* London: Sage.

Harry Benjamin International Gender Dysphoria Association (2001). *Standards of care for gender identity disorders,* sixth version. http://www.tc.umn.edu/~colem001/hbigda/hstndrd.htm.

Harvey-Berino, J. and Rourke, J. (2003). Obesity prevention in preschool Native American children: a pilot study using home visiting. *Obesity Research,* 11 (5), 606–11.

Hays, J., Power, T. G. and Olvera, N. (2001). Effects of maternal socialisation strategies on children's nutrition knowledge and behaviour. *Applied Developmental Psychology,* 22, 421–37.

Heath, C. (1986). *Body movement and speech in medical interaction.* Cambridge: Cambridge University Press.

(1988). Embarrassment and interactional organization. In P. Drew and A. Wootton (eds.), *Erving Goffman: exploring the interaction order* (pp. 136–60). Boston: Northeastern University Press.

(1992). The delivery and reception of diagnosis in the general-practice consultation. In P. Drew and J. Heritage (eds.), pp. 235–67.

Heelas, P. (1988). Emotion talk across cultures. In R. Harré (ed.), pp. 234–66.

Heider, F. (1958). *The psychology of interpersonal relations.* New York: Wiley.

Hellermann, J. (2003). The interactive work of prosody in the IRF exchange: teacher repetition in feedback moves. *Language in Society,* 32, 79–104.

Henderson, N. (1991). The art of moderating: a blend of basic skills and qualities. *Quirk's Marketing Research Review*, 18, 19–39.

Hepburn, A. (2000). Power lines: Derrida, discursive psychology and the management of accusations of school bullying. *British Journal of Social Psychology*, 39, 605–28.

(2003). *An introduction to critical social psychology*. London: Sage.

(2004). Crying: notes on description, transcription, and interaction. *Research on Language and Social Interaction*, 37, 251–90.

(2005). 'You're not takin me seriously': ethics and asymmetry in calls to a child protection helpline. *Journal of Constructivist Psychology*, Special Issue on Constructivist Ethics, 18, 255–76.

(2006). Getting closer at a distance: theory and the contingencies of practice. *Theory and Psychology*, Special Issue on Theory in Action, 16 (3), 325–52.

Hepburn, A. and Potter, J. (2003). Discourse analytic practice. In C. Seale, D. Silverman, J. Gubrium and G. Gobo (eds.), *Qualitative research practice* (pp. 180–196). London: Sage.

Hepburn, A. and Wiggins, S. (2005a). Size matters: constructing accountable bodies in NSPCC helpline interaction. *Discourse and Society*, 16, 625–46.

(2005b). Discursive psychology, Special Issue of *Discourse and Society*, 16 (5), 595–602.

Heritage, J. (1984). A change-of-state token and aspects of its sequential placement. In J. M. Atkinson and J. Heritage (eds.), *Structures of social action: studies in conversation analysis*. (pp. 299–346). Cambridge: Cambridge University Press.

(1985). Analyzing news interviews: aspects of the production of talk for an overhearing audience. In T. A. Van Dijk (ed.), *Handbook of discourse analysis*, vol. III. London: Academic Press.

(1998). Oh-prefaced responses to inquiry. *Language in Society*, 27, 291–334.

Heritage J. and Raymond G. (2005). The terms of agreement: indexing epistemic authority and subordination in talk-in-interaction. *Social Psychology Quarterly*, 68, 15–38.

Heritage, J. and Sefi, S. (1992). Dilemmas of advice: aspects of delivery and reception of advice in interactions between health visitors and first-time mothers. In P. Drew and J. Heritage (eds.), pp. 359–417.

Heritage, J. and Stivers, T. (1999). Online commentary in acute medical visits: a method of shaping patient expectations. *Social Science and Medicine*, 49 (11), 1501–17.

Heritage, J. and Watson, R. (1979). Formulations as conversational objects. In G. Psathas (ed.), pp. 123–62.

Hester, S. and Eglin, P. (eds.) (1997). *Culture in action: studies in membership categorization analysis*. Washington, DC: International Institute for Ethnomethodology and Conversation Analysis and University Press of America.

Hewstone, M. (1989). *Causal attribution: from cognitive processes to collective beliefs*. Oxford: Basil Blackwell.

Hochschild, A. R. (1983). *The managed heart: commercialization of human feeling*. Berkeley and Los Angeles: University of California Press.

Hollway, W. and Jefferson, T. (2000). *Doing qualitative research differently: free association, narrative and the interview method*. London: Sage.

Holstein, J. A. (1983). Grading practices: the construction and use of background knowledge in evaluative decision-making. *Human Studies*, 6, 377–92.

Holt, E. (1993). The structure of death announcements: looking on the bright side of death. *Text*, 13, 189–212.

(1996). Reporting on talk: the use of direct reported speech in conversation, *Research on Language and Social Interaction*, 29, 219–45.

Honorton, C. (1985). Meta-analysis of psi ganzfeld research: a response to Hyman. *Journal of Parapsychology*, 49, 51–91.

Honorton, C., Ramsey, M. and Cabibbo, C. (1975). Experimenter effects in extrasensory perception. *Journal of the American Society for Psychical Research*, 69, 135–9.

Housley, W. (2003). *Interaction in multidisciplinary teams*. Cardiff Papers in Qualitative Research. Aldershot: Ashgate.

Houtkoop-Steenstra, H. (2000). *Interaction and the standardized survey interview: the living questionnaire*. Cambridge: Cambridge University Press.

Huisman, M. (2001). Decision-making in meetings as talk-in-interaction. *International Studies of Management and Organization*, 31 (3), 69–90.

Human Rights and Equal Opportunities Commission (HREOC) (1997). *Bringing them home: report of the National Inquiry into the Separation of Aboriginal and Torres Strait Islander Children from Their Families* (Chair: Sir Ronald Wilson). Canberra: Australian Government Printing Service.

Hutchby, I. (1996a). *Confrontation talk: arguments, asymmetries, and power on talk radio*. Mahwah, NJ: Lawrence Erlbaum.

(1996b). Power in discourse: the case of arguments on a British talk radio show. *Discourse and Society*, 7 (4), 481–97.

(2002). Resisting the incitement to talk in child counselling: aspects of the utterance 'I don't know'. *Discourse Studies*, 4 (2), 147–68.

Hutchby, I. and Ellis, J. M. (eds.) (1998). *Children and social competence: arenas of action*. London: Palmer.

Hutchby, I. and Wooffitt, R. (1998). *Conversation analysis*. Cambridge: Polity Press.

Irwin, H. J. (1999). *An introduction to parapsychology* (3rd edn). Jefferson, NC: McFarland.

Jackson, S. (1993). Even sociologists fall in love: an exploration in the sociology of emotions. *Sociology*, 27 (2), 201–20.

Jaggar, A. M. and Bordo, S. (eds.) (1989). *Gender/body/knowledge: feminist reconstructions of being and knowing*. New Brunswick, NJ: Rutgers University Press.

James, A. and Prout, A. (eds.) (1990). *Constructing and reconstructing childhood: contemporary issues in the sociological study of childhood*. London: Falmer Press.

Jefferson, G. (1983). On exposed and embedded correction in conversation. *Studium Linguistik*, 14, 58–68.

(1984a). *On the organization of laughter in talk about troubles*. In J. M. Atkinson and J. Heritage (eds.), pp. 346–69.

(1984b) 'On stepwise transition from talk about a trouble to inappropriately next-positioned matters'. In J. M. Atkinson and J. Heritage (eds.), *Structures of social action: studies in conversation analysis* (pp. 191–222). Cambrdige: Cambridge University Press.

(1985). An exercise in the transcription and analysis of laughter. In T. A. Van Dijk (ed.), *A handbook of discourse analysis*, vol. III: *Discourse and dialogue* (pp. 25–34). London: Academic Press.

(1987). On exposed and embedded correction in conversation. In G. Button and J. R. E. Lee (eds.), *Talk and social organization* (pp. 86–100). Philadelphia: Multilingual Matters.

(1990). List construction as a task and resource. In G. Psathas (ed.), *Interaction competence* (pp. 63–92). Lanham, MD: University Press of America.

(2004 [1984]). 'At first I thought': a normalizing device for extraordinary events. In G. H. Lerner (ed.), *Conversation analysis: studies from the first generation* (pp. 131–67). Amsterdam and Philadelphia: John Benjamins.

(2004). Glossary of transcript symbols with an introduction. In G. H. Lerner (ed.), *Conversation analysis: studies from the first generation* (pp. 13–31). Amsterdam and Philadelphia: John Benjamins.

Jefferson, G., Sacks, H. and Schegloff, E. A. (1987). Notes on laughter in pursuit of intimacy. In G. Button and J. R. E. Lee (eds.), *Talk and social organization* (pp. 152–205). Clevedon: Multilingual Matters.

Jenks, C. (1997). *Childhood: key ideas*. London: Routledge.

Johnston, L. and Ward, T. (1996). Social cognition and sexual offending: a theoretical framework. *Sexual Abuse: A Journal of Research and Treatment*, 8, 55–80.

Kasese-Hara, M., Wright, C. and Drewett, R. (2002). Energy compensation in young children who fail to thrive. *Journal of Child Psychology and Psychiatry*, 43 (4), 449–56.

Kelly, J. and Local, J. (1989). On the use of general phonetic techniques in handling conversational material. In D. Roger and P. Bull (eds.), *Conversation: an interdisciplinary perspective* (pp. 197–212). Clevedon: Multilingual Matters.

Kitzinger, C. (2005). Heteronormativity in action: reproducing normative heterosexuality in 'after hours' calls to the doctor, *Social Problems*, 52, 477–98.

(2006). After cognitivism, *Discourse Studies*, 8 (1), 67–84.

Klesges, R. J., Coates, T. J., Brown, G., Sturgeon-Tillish, J., Modenhauer-Klesges, L. M., Holzer, B., Woolfrey, J. and Vollmer, J. (1983). Parental influences on children's eating behavior and relative weight. *Journal of Applied Behavioral Analysis*, 16, 371–8.

Koivisto, U.-K., Fellenius, J. and Sjoden, P.-O. (1994). Relations between parental mealtime practices and children's food intake. *Appetite*, 22, 245–58.

Koole, T. (2003). Affiliation and detachment in interviewer answer receipts. In H. van den Berg, M. Wetherell and H. Houtkoop-Steenstra (eds.),

Analyzing race talk: multidisciplinary approaches to the interview (pp. 178–99). Cambridge: Cambridge University Press.

Kotani, M. (2002). Expressing gratitude and indebtedness: Japanese speakers' use of 'I'm sorry' in English conversation. *Research on Language and Social Interaction*, 35 (1), 39–72.

Kremer-Sadlik, T. (2004). How children with autism and Asperger Syndrome respond to questions: a 'naturalistic' theory of mind task. *Discourse Studies*, 6, 185–206.

Kremers, S. P. J., Brug, J., De Vries, H. and Engels, R. C. M. E. (2003). Parenting style and adolescent fruit consumption. *Appetite*, 41, 43–50.

Labov, W. (1972). *Language in the inner city*. Oxford: Basil Blackwell.

Labov, W. and Waletzky, J. (1967). Narrative analysis: oral versions of personal experience. In J. Helm (ed.), *Essays on the verbal and visual arts* (pp. 12–44). Seattle: University of Washington Press.

Lambert, M. J. and Ogles, B. M. (2004). The efficacy and effectiveness of psychotherapy. In A. E. Bergin, S. L. Garfield and M. J. Lambert (eds.), *Handbook of psychotherapy and behaviour change* (pp. 139–93). London: John Wiley.

Lang, F., Floyd, M. R. and Beine, K. L. (2000). Clues to patients' explanations and concerns about their illnesses. *Archive of Family Medicine*, 9, 222–7.

Lawes, R. (1999). Marriage: an analysis of discourse. *British Journal of Social Psychology*, 38 (1), 1–20.

Lea, S. and Auburn, T. (2001). The social construction of rape in the talk of a convicted rapist. *Feminism and Psychology*, 11 (3), 11–33.

LeCouteur, A. and Augoustinos, M. (2001). Apologising to the stolen generations: argument, rhetoric, and identity in public reasoning. *Australian Psychologist*, 36 (1), 51–61.

LeCouteur, A., Rapley, M. and Augoustinos, M. (2001). This very difficult debate about Wik: stake, voice and the management of category memberships in race politics. *British Journal of Social Psychology*, 40, 35–57.

Lee, Y.-J. and Roth, W.-M. (2004). Making a scientist: Discursive 'doing' of identity and self-presentation during research interviews. *Forum: Qualitative Social Research* [Online Journal], 5 (1), Art. 12. Available at: http://www.qualitative-research.net/fqs-texte/1–04/1–04leeroth-e.htm.

Leiter, K. (1976). Teacher's use of background knowledge to interpret test scores. *Sociology of Education*, 49, 59–65.

Lerner, G. H. (1991). On the syntax of sentence in progress. *Language in Society*, 20, 441–58.

Leslie, A. L. (1987). Pretense and representation: the origins of 'theory of mind'. *Psychological Review*, 94, 412–26.

Li, S. and Arber, A. (2006). The construction of troubled and credible patients: a study of emotion talk in palliative settings. *Qualitative Health Research*, 16 (1), 27–46.

Lieberman, A. (2004). Confusion regarding school counselor functions: school leadership impacts role clarity. *Education*, 124, 552–8.

Liefooghe, A. P. D. (2003). Employee accounts of bullying at work. *International Journal of Management and Decision Making*, 4 (1), 24–34.

Linell, P. (1990). The power of dialogue dynamics. In I. Markova and K. Foppa (eds.), *The dynamics of dialogue*. Hemel Hempstead: Harvester Wheatsheaf.

Local, J. and Walker, G. (forthcoming). Explicit lexical formulations of speaker states and some of their uses in everyday conversation. *Journal of Pragmatics*.

Local, J. and Wootton, A. (1993). Interactional and phonetic aspects of immediate echolalia in autism: a case study. *Clinical Linguistics and Phonetics*, 9 (2), 155–84.

Locke, A. and Edwards, D. (2003). Bill and Monica: memory, emotion and normativity in Clinton's grand jury testimony. *British Journal of Social Psychology*, 42, 239–56.

Loseke, D. R. (1993). Constructing conditions, people, morality, and emotions: expanding the agenda of constructionism. In J. Miller and J. Holstein (eds.), *Constructionist controversies: issues in social problems theory*. New York: Aldine de Gruyter.

Luhmann, N. (1968). *Vertrauen*. Stuttgart: Lucius and Lucius.

Lumbelli, L. (1992). Glossa, parafrasi e risposta riflesso' [Gloss, paraphrase and mirror-response]. In L. Brasca and M. L. Zimbelli (eds.), *Grammatica del parlare e dell'ascoltare a scuola* [Grammar of talking and listening in school] (pp. 137–56). Florence: La Nuova Italia.

Lumme-Sandt, K., Jylhä, M. and Hervonen, A. (2000). Interpretative repertoires of medication among the oldest-old. *Social Science and Medicine*, 50, 1843–50.

Lupton, D. (1998). *The emotional self: a sociocultural exploration*. London: Sage.

Lutz, C. A. (1988a). Morality, domination and understanding of 'justifiable anger' among the Ifaluk. In G. Semin and K. Gergen (eds.), *Everyday understanding: social and scientific implications* (pp. 204–26). London: Sage.

(1988b). *Unnatural emotions: everyday sentiments on a Micronesian atoll and their challenge to Western theory*. Chicago: University of Chicago Press.

(1990). Engendered emotion: gender, power, and the rhetoric of emotional control in American discourse. In C. A. Latz and L. Abu-Lughod (eds.), pp. 69–91.

Lutz, C. A. and Abu-Lughod, L. (eds.) (1990). *Language and the politics of emotion*, Studies in Emotion and Social Interaction series. Cambridge: Cambridge University Press, and Pars: Editions de la Maison des Sciences de l'Homme.

Lynch, M. and Bogen, D. (2005). 'My memory has been shredded': a non-cognitivist investigation of 'mental' phenomena. In H. te Molder and J. Potter (eds.), pp. 226–40.

Mackay, R. (1974). Conceptions of children and models of socialization. In Turner (ed.), pp. 180–93.

MacMartin, C., and LeBaron, C. D. (2006). Multiple involvements within group interaction: a video-based study of sex offender therapy. *Research on Language and Social Interaction*, 39, 41–80.

MacMillan, K. and Edwards, D. (1999). Who killed the Princess? Description and blame in the British press. *Discourse Studies*, 1 (2), 151–74.

Madill, A., Widdicombe, S. and Barkham, M. (2001). The potential of conversation analysis for psychotherapy research. *Counseling Psychologist*, 29, 413–34.

Manne, R. (2000). In denial: the Stolen Generations and the right. *The Australian Quarterly Essay*, 1, 1–113.

Marshall, W. L. (1999). Current status of North American assessment and treatment programs for sexual offenders. *Journal of Interpersonal Violence*, 14, 221–39.

Marshall, W. L., Serran, G., Fernandez, Y. M., Mulloy, R., Mann, R. and Thornton, D. (2003). Therapist characteristics in the treatment of sexual offenders: tentative data on their relationship with indices of behaviour change. *Journal of Sexual Aggression*, 9, 25–30.

Marshall, W. L., Serran, G., Moulden, H., Mulloy, R., Fernandez, Y. M., Mann, R., et al. (2002). Therapist features in sexual offender treatment: their reliable identification and influence on behaviour change. *Clinical Psychology and Psychotherapy*, 9, 395–405.

Maynard, D. W. (2003) *Bad news, good news: conversational order in everyday talk and clinical settings*. Chicago: University of Chicago Press.

Maynard, D. W., Houtkoop-Steenstra, H., Schaeffer, N. C. and van der Zouwen, J. (eds.) (2002). *Standardization and tacit knowledge: interaction and practice in the survey interview*. New York: Wiley.

Maynard, D. W. and Marlaire, C. L. (1992). Good reasons for bad testing performance: the interactional substrate of educational exams. *Qualitative Sociology*, 15, 177–202.

Mehan, H. (1984). Institutional decision-making. In B. Rogoff and J. Lave (eds.), *Everyday cognition: its development in social context* (pp. 41–66). Cambridge: Cambridge University Press.

Meier, A. J. (1998). Apologies: what do we know? *International Journal of Applied Linguistics*, 8 (2), 215–31.

Mercer, N. (1995). *The guided construction of knowledge: talk amongst teachers and learners*. Clevedon: Multilingual Matters.

Mey, J. (ed.) (2006). *Encyclopedia of language and linguistics*, vol. X: *Pragmatics* (2nd edn). North-Holland: Elsevier.

Milton, J. (1999). Should ganzfeld research continue to be crucial in the search for a replicable psi effect? Part I: discussion paper and an introduction to an electronic mail discussion. *Journal of Parapsychology*, 63 (4), 309–33.

Milton, J. and Wiseman, R. (1997). Ganzfeld at the crossroads: a meta-analysis of the new generation of studies. In *Proceedings of presented papers*, 46th Annual Parapsychological Association Convention (pp. 277–92). New York: Parapsychological Association.

Morris, G. H. and Chenail, R. (eds.) (1995). *The talk of the clinic: explorations in the analysis of medical and therapeutic discourse*. Hillsdale, NJ: Lawrence Erlbaum.

Morris, R. L., Dalton, K., Delanoy, D. and Watt, C. (1995). Comparison of the sender/no sender condition in the ganzfeld. In N. L. Zingrone (ed.), *Proceedings of presented papers*, 38th Annual Parapsychological Association Convention (pp. 244–59). Fairhaven, MA: Parapsychological Association.

Moscovici, S. (1984). The phenomenon of social representations. In R. M. Farr and S. Moscovici (eds.), *Social representations*. Cambridge: Cambridge University Press.

Murphy, W. D. and Smith, T. A. (1996). Sex offenders against children: empirical and clinical issues. In J. Briere, L. Berliner, J. A. Bulkley, C. Jenny and T. Reid (eds.), *The APSAC handbook on child maltreatment* (pp. 175–91). Thousand Oaks, CA: Sage.

Myers, G. (1998). Displaying opinions: topics and disagreement in focus groups. *Language in Society*, 27 (1), 85–111.

(2004). *Matters of opinion: talking about public ideas*. Cambridge: Cambridge University Press.

Myers, G. and Macnaghten, P. (1999). Can focus groups be analysed as talk? In R. S. Barbour and J. Kitzinger (eds.), *Developing focus group research* (pp. 173–85). London: Sage.

Newman, L. K. (2000). Transgender issues. In J. Ussher (ed.), *Women's health: contemporary international perspectives*. Leicester: BPS Books.

Nikander, P. (2000). 'Old' versus 'little girl': a discursive approach to age categorisation and morality. *Journal of Aging Studies*, 14 (4), 335–58.

(2001). Kenneth Gergen: Konstruktionistinen ja postmoderni sosiaalipsykologia [Kenneth Gergen: constructionist and postmodern social psychology]. In V. Hänninen and J. Ylijoki Oili-Helena ja Partanen (eds.), *Sosiaalipsykologian suunnannäyttäjiä* [Beacons of social psychology] (pp. 275–98). Tampere, Vastapaino.

(2002). *Age in action: membership work and stage of life categories in talk*. Helsinki: Finnish Academy of Science and Letters.

(2003). The absent client: case description and decision-making in interprofessional meetings. In J. Hall, N. Parton and T. Pösö (eds.), *Constructing clienthood in social work and human services: identities, interactions and practices* (pp. 112–28). London: Jessica Kingsley.

(forthcoming). Interprofessional decision making in elderly care: morality, criteria, and help allocation. In I. Paoletti (ed.), *Family caregiving*. New York: Nova Science.

Norrick, N. R. (1978). Expressive illocutionary acts. *Journal of Pragmatics*, 2, 277–91.

Ochs, E. (1983). Conversational competence in children. In E. Ochs and B. Schieffelin (eds.), *Acquiring conversational competence* (pp. 3–25). London: Routledge and Kegan Paul.

Ochs, E., Kremer-Sadlik, T., Solomon, O. and Gainer-Sirota, K. (2001). Inclusion as social practice: views from children with autism. *Social Development*, 10 (3), 399–419.

Ochs, E. and Solomon, O. (2004). Practical logic and autism. In R. B. Edgerton and C. Casey (eds.), *A companion to psychological anthropology: modernity and psychocultural change* (pp. 140–67). Oxford: Blackwell.

Ogden, R. (2001). Turn transition, creak and glottal stop in Finnish talk-in-interaction. *Journal of the International Phonetic Association*, 31, 139–52.

Orsolini, M. and Pontecorvo, C. (1992). Children's talk in classroom discussion. *Cognition and Instruction*, 9 (2), 113–36.

Osvaldsson, K. (2004). On laughter and disagreement in multiparty assessment talk. *Text*, 24 (4), 517–45.

Park, R. J., Lee, A., Woolley, H., Murray, L. and Stein, A. (2003). Children's representation of family mealtime in the context of maternal eating disorders. *Child: care, health and development*, 29 (2), 111–19.

Parker, A. (2000). A review of the ganzfeld work at Gothenburg University. *Journal of the Society for Psychical Research*, 64, 11–15.

Parker, A., Grams, D. and Pettersson, C. (1998). Further variables relating to psi in the ganzfeld. *Journal of Parapsychology*, 62, 319–37.

Parker, I. (2002). *Critical discursive psychology*. London: Palgrave.

Parker, I. and Burman, E. (1993). Against discursive imperialism, empiricism, and constructionism: thirty-two problems with discourse analysis. In E. Burman and I. Parker (eds.), *Discourse analytic research: repertoires and readings of texts in action* (pp. 155–72). London: Routledge.

Parrott, G. W. (ed.) (2001). *Emotions in social psychology: essential readings*. Philadelphia, PA: Psychology Press, Taylor and Francis Group.

Peeters, T. (1998). *Autism: from theoretical understanding to educational intervention*. New York: Wiley.

Peräklyä, A. (1993). Invoking a hostile world: discussing the patient's future in AIDS counselling. *Text*, 13 (2), 291–316.

  (1995). *AIDS counselling: institutional interaction and clinical practice*. Cambridge: Cambridge University Press.

Peräkylä, A. and Silverman, D. (1991). Owning experience: describing the experience of other persons. *Text*, 11 (3), 441–80.

Peräkylä, A. and Vehviläinen, S. (2003). Conversation analysis and the professional stocks of interactional knowledge. *Discourse and Society*, 14, 727–50.

Peyrot, M. (1987). Circumspection in psychotherapy: Structures and strategies of counsellor–client interaction. *Semiotica*, 65 (3/4), 249–68.

Phillips, B. (1999). Reformulating dispute narratives through active listening. *Mediation Quarterly*, 17, 161–80.

Phillips, L. and Jørgensen, M. W. (2002). *Discourse analysis as theory and method*. London: Sage.

Pomerantz, A. (1984a). Agreeing and disagreeing with assessments: some features of preferred/dispreferred turn shapes. In J. M. Atkinson and J. Heritage (eds.), pp. 57–101.

  (1984b). Giving a source or basis: the practice in conversation of telling 'how I know'. *Journal of Pragmatics*, 8, 607–25.

  (1986). Extreme case formulations: a way of legitimizing claims. *Human Studies*, 9, 219–29.

  (1987). Descriptions in legal settings. In G. Button and J. R. E. Lee (eds.), *Talk and social organisation* (pp. 226–43). Clevedon and Philadelphia: Multilingual Matters.

  (2005). Using participants' video stimulated comments to complement analyses of interactional practices. In H. te Molder and J. Potter (eds.), pp. 93–113.

Potter, J. (1982). Nothing so practical as a good theory: the problematic application of social psychology. In P. Stringer (ed.) *Confronting social issues: applications of social psychology* (pp. 23–49). London: Academic Press.

(1996). *Representing reality: discourse, rhetoric, and social construction.* London and Thousand Oaks, CA: Sage.

(1998a). Cognition as context (whose cognition?), *Research on Language and Social Interaction,* 31, 29–44.

(1998b). Discursive social psychology: from attitudes to evaluative practices. In W. Stroebe and M. Hewstone (eds.), *European Review of Social Psychology,* vol. IX (pp. 233–66). Chichester: Wiley.

(2003). Discourse analysis and discursive psychology. In P. M. Camic, J. E. Rhodes and L. Yardley (eds.), *Qualitative research in psychology: expanding perspectives in methodology and design* (pp. 73–94). Washington, DC: American Psychological Association.

(2004). Discourse analysis as a way of analysing naturally occurring talk. In D. Silverman (ed.), *Qualitative Research: Theory, Method and Practice* (2nd edn) (pp. 200–21). London: Sage.

(2005). A discursive psychology of institutions, *Social Psychology Review,* 7, 25–35.

Potter, J. and Edwards, D. (2001a). Discursive social psychology. In W. P. Robinson and H. Giles (eds.), *The new handbook of language and social psychology* (pp. 103–18). Chichester: Wiley.

(2001b). Sociolinguistics, cognitivism and discursive psychology. In N. Coupland, S. Sarangi and C. Candlin (eds.), *Sociolinguistics and social theory* (pp. 88–103). London: Longman.

(2003a). Sociolinguistics, cognitivism, and discursive psychology. *International Journal of English Studies,* 3, 93–109.

(2003b). Rethinking cognition: on Coulter, discourse and mind, *Human Studies,* 26, 165–81.

Potter, J. and Hepburn, A. (2003). 'I'm a bit concerned': early actions and psychological constructions in a child protection helpline. *Research on Language and Social Interaction,* 36 (3), 197–240.

(2004). Analysis of NSPCC call openings. In S. Becker and A. Bryman (eds.), *Understanding research methods for social policy and practice* (pp. 311–13). London: The Policy Press.

(2005a). Qualitative interviews in psychology: problems and possibilities. *Qualitative Research in Psychology,* 2, 38–55.

(2005b). Discursive psychology as a qualitative approach for analysing interaction in medical settings. *Medical Education,* 39, 338–44.

(forthcoming a). Chairing democracy: psychology, time and negotiating the institution. In J. McDaniel and K. Tracy (eds.), *Rhetoric, discourse and ordinary democracy.* Tuscaloosa, AL: University of Alabama Press.

(forthcoming b). Somewhere between evil and normal: traces of morality in a child protection helpline. In J. Cromdal and M. Tholander (eds.), *Children, morality and interaction.* New York: Nova Science.

Potter, J. and Wetherell, M. (1987). *Discourse and social psychology: beyond attitudes and behaviour.* London: Sage.

Psathas, G. (ed.) (1979). *Everyday language: studies in ethnomethodology.* New York: Irvington.

Puchta, C. and Potter, J. (1999). Asking elaborate questions: focus groups and the management of spontaneity, *Journal of Sociolinguistics*, 3, 314–35.

(2002). Manufacturing individual opinions: market research focus groups and the discursive psychology of attitudes. *British Journal of Social Psychology*, 41, 345–63.

(2004). *Focus group practice.* London: Sage.

Puchta, C., Potter, J. and Wolff, F. (2004). Repeat receipts: a device for generating visible data in market research focus groups, *Qualitative Research*, 4, 285–309.

Radin, D. (1997). *The conscious universe: the scientific truth of psychic phenomena.* San Francisco: Harper Edge.

Raevaara, L. (1998). Patients' etiological explanations in Finnish doctor–patient consultation. Presented at the Netherlands Institute for Primary Health Care conference, 'Communication in Health Care', June 1998. The Netherlands: The Free University.

Raevaara, L. (2000). Patients' candidate diagnoses in the medical consultation: a conversation analytical study of patient's institutional tasks. Unpublished Ph.D. dissertation. University of Helsinki, Finland.

Rapley, M. (2004). *The social construction of intellectual disability.* Cambridge: Cambridge University Press.

Rapley, T. (2001). The art(fullness) of open-ended interviewing: some considerations on analysing interviews. *Qualitative Research*, 1 (3), 303–23.

Rayburn, C. (2004). Assessing students for morality education: a new role for school counselors. *Professional School Counseling*, 7, 356–62.

Raymond, J. (1979). *The transsexual empire: the making of the she-male.* New York: Teachers College Press.

(1994). Introduction to the 1994 edition. In *The transsexual empire: the making of the she-male.* New York: Teachers College Press.

Reid, R. (1998). NHS v private treatment for transsexuals. GENDYS Conference. http://www.gender.org.uk/conf/1998/reid.htm.

Robinson, J.D. (1998). Getting down to business: talk, gaze, and body orientation during openings of doctor–patient consultations. *Human Communication Research*, 25, 98–124.

(2004). The sequential organization of 'explicit' apologies in naturally occurring English. *Research on Language and Social Interaction*, 37 (3), 291–330.

(2006). Soliciting patients' presenting concerns. In J. Heritage and D. Maynard (eds.), *Communication in medical care: interaction between primary care physicians and patients* (pp. 22–47). Cambridge: Cambridge University Press.

Robinson, S. (2000). Children's perceptions of who controls their food. *Journal of Human Nutrition and Dietetics*, 13, 163–71.

Rolls, B. (1986). Sensory-specific satiety. *Nutrition Reviews*, 44, 93–101.

Ruusuvuori, J. (2005). Empathy and sympathy in action: attending to patients' troubles in Finnish homeopathic and GP consultations. *Social Psychology Quarterly*, 68 (3), 204–22.

Sacks, H. (1979). Hotrodder: a revolutionary category. In Psathas (ed.), pp. 7–14.

    (1984). On doing 'being ordinary'. In J. M. Atkinson and J. Heritage (eds.), pp. 413–29.

    (1992). *Lectures on conversation* ed. Gail Jefferson. Oxford: Blackwell.

Sacks, H., Schegloff, E. and Jefferson, G. (1974). A simplest systematics for the organization of turn taking for conversation. *Language*, 50, 696–735.

Säljö, R. (2000). *Lärande i praktiken* [Learning in practice]. Stockholm: Prisma.

Sarangi, S. (1998). Interprofessional case construction in social work: the evidential status of information and its reportability. *Text*, 18 (2), 241–70.

Sarbin, T. R. (1988). Emotion and act: roles and rhetoric. In R. Harré (ed.), pp. 83–97.

Schaeffer, N. C. and Maynard, D. W. (2005). From paradigm to prototype and back again: interactive aspects of cognitive processing in standardized survey interviews. In H. te Molder and J. Potter (eds.), pp. 114–33.

Schegloff, E. (1979). The relevance of repair for a syntax-for-conversation. In T. Givòn (ed.), *Syntax and semantics*, vol. XI: *Discourse and syntax* (pp. 261–88). New York: Academic Press.

    (1988). Discourse as an interactional achievement II: An exercise in conversation analysis. In D. Tannen (ed.), *Linguistics in context: connecting observation and understanding* (pp. 135–58). Norwood, NJ: Ablex.

    (1992). On talk and its institutional occasions. In P. Drew and J. Heritage (eds.), pp. 101–34.

    (1997). Whose text? Whose context? *Discourse and Society*, 8, 165–87.

    (1999). Discourse, pragmatics, conversation, analysis, *Discourse Studies*, 1, 405–36.

    (2000). On granularity. *Annual Review of Sociology*, 26, 715–20.

    (2006). On possibles. *Discourse Studies*, 8, 141–57.

Schegloff, E. A. and Lerner, G. (2004). Beginning to respond. Paper presented at the Annual Meeting of the National Communication Association, Chicago, IL, November.

Schegloff, E. A. and Sacks, H. (1973). Opening up Closings. *Semiotica* 8 (4), 289–327.

Schiffrin, D. (1987). *Discourse markers*. Cambridge: Cambridge University Press.

Schlitz, M. J. and Honorton, C. (1992). Ganzfeld psi performance within an artistically gifted population. *Journal of the American Society for Psychical Research*, 86, 83–98.

Schmiedler, G. R. and Edge, H. (1999). Should ganzfeld research continue to be crucial in the search for a relicable psi effect? Part II: edited ganzfeld debate. *Journal of Parapsychology*, 63 (4), 335–88.

Schneider, R., Binder, M. and Walach, H. (2000). Examining the role of neutral versus personal experimenter–participant interactions: An EDA-DMILS experiment. *Journal of Parapsychology*, 64, 181–94.

Schuler, A. (2003). Beyond echoplaylia. promoting language in children with autism. *Autism*, 7 (4), 455–69.

Searle, J. (1969). *Speech acts: an essay in the philosophy of language*. Cambridge: Cambridge University Press.

(1976). A classification of illocutionary acts. *Language in Society*, 5, 1–23.

Selting, M. (1994). Emphatic speech style – with special focus on the prosodic signalling of heightened emotive involvement in conversation. *Journal of Pragmatics*, 22, 375–408.

Serran, G., Fernandez, Y., Marshall, W. L. and Mann, R. E. (2003). Process issues in treatment: application to sexual offender programs. *Professional Psychology: Research and Practice*, 34, 368–74.

Shakespeare, P. (1998). *Aspects of confused speech: a study of verbal interaction between confused and normal speakers*. London: Lawrence Erlbaum Associates.

Sharrock, W. (1974). On owning knowledge. In R. Turner (ed.), pp. 45–53.

Showers, C. and Cantor, N. (1985). Social cognition: a look at motivated strategies. *Annual Review of Psychology*, 36, 275–305.

Shweder, R. A. and Haidt, J. (2000). The cultural psychology of the emotions: ancient and new. In M. Lewis and J. M. Haviland-Jones (eds.), *Handbook of emotions* (2nd edn) (pp. 397–414). New York: Guilford Press.

Siegfried, J. (ed.) (1995). *Therapeutic and everyday discourse as behavior change: towards a micro-analysis in psychotherapy process research*. Norwood, NJ: Ablex.

Sigman, M. and Capps, L. (1997). *Autism: a developmental perspective*. Cambridge, MA: Harvard University Press.

Silverman, D. (1997). *The discourse of counselling: HIV counselling as social interaction*. London: Sage.

Silverman, D. (1998). *Harvey Sacks: social science and conversation analysis*. Oxford: Policy Press.

Silverman, D., Baker, C. and Keogh, J. (1998). The case of the silent child: advice-giving and advice reception in parent–teacher interviews. In I. Hutchby and J. M. Ellis (eds.), pp. 220–40.

Silverman, D. and Bor, R. (1991). Delicacy of describing sexual partners in HIV-test counseling: implications for practice. *Counselling Psychology Quarterly*, 4, 177–90.

Sinclair, J. and Coulthard, M. (1975). *Towards an analysis of discourse: the English used by teachers and pupils*. London: Oxford University Press.

Smith, D. (1990). *Texts, facts and femininity: exploring the relations of ruling*. London: Routledge.

Smith, M. D. (2003). The role of the experimenter in parapsychological research. *Journal of Consciousness Studies*, Special Edition: Psi Wars, 10 (6–7), 69–84.

Sneijder, P. and te Molder, H. F. M (2005). Moral logic and logical morality: attributions of responsibility and blame in online discourse on veganism, *Discourse and Society*, 16, 675–96.

Speer, S. (2002). 'Natural' and 'contrived' data: a sustainable distinction. *Discourse Studies*, 4, 511–25.

(forthcoming a). The form and function of hypothetical questions in the gender identity clinic. Alice F. Freed and Susan Ehrlich (eds.), *'Why do you ask?' The function of questions in institutional discourse.* Oxford: Oxford University Press.

(forthcoming b) Hypothetical questions.

Speer, S. A. and Green, R. (forthcoming). Transsexual identities. Constructions of gender in an NHS gender identity clinic. ESRC award no. RES-148-0029.

Speer, S. A. and Parsons, C. (2006). Gatekeeping Gender: some features of the use of hypothetical questions in the psychiatric assessment of transsexual patients. *Discourse and Society* 17 (6), 785–812.

Speier, M. (1971). The everyday world of the child. In J. Douglas (ed.), pp. 188–217.

(1976). The child as conversationalist: some culture contact features of conversational interactions between adults and children. In M. Hammersley and P. Woods (eds.), pp. 98–103.

Spruijt-Metz, D., Lindquist, C. H., Birch, L. L., Fisher, J. O. and Goran, M. I. (2002). Relation between mothers' child-feeding practices and children's adiposity, *American Journal of Clinical Nutrition*, 75 (3), 581–6

Stivers, T. (2002). Presenting the problem in pediatric encounters: 'Symptoms only' and 'Candidate diagnoses'. *Health Communication*, 14 (3), 299–338.

(2005). Parent resistance to physicians' treatment recommendations: one resource for initiating a negotiation of the treatment decision. *Health Communication*, 181 (1), 41–74.

(forthcoming). The interactional process of reaching a treatment decision in acute medical encounters. In J. Heritage and D. Maynard (eds.), *Communication in medical care: interactions between primary care physicians and patients.* Cambridge: Cambridge University Press.

Stivers, T. and Heritage, J. (2001). Breaking the sequential mold: answering 'more than the question' during comprehensive history taking. *Text*, 21, 151–85.

Stivers, T., Mangione-Smith, R., Elliott, M., McDonald, L. and Heritage, J. (2003). Why do physicians think parents expect antibiotics? What parents report vs what physicians believe. *Journal of Family Practice*, 52 (2), 140–8.

Stokoe, E. H. and Hepburn, A. (2005). 'You can hear a lot through the walls': noise formulations in neighbour complaints. *Discourse and Society*, 16, 647–73.

Stokoe, E. H. and Wiggins, S. (2005). Discursive approaches. In J. Miles and P. Gilbert (eds.), *A handbook of research methods for clinical and health psychology* (pp. 161–174). Oxford: Oxford University Press.

Stone, S. (1993). The 'empire' strikes back: a Posttranssexual manifesto. http://sandystone.com/empire-strikes-back.

Storm, L. (2000). Research note: replicable evidence of psi: a revision of Milton's 1999 meta-analysis of the ganzfeld databases. *Journal of Parapsychology*, 64 (4), 411–16.

Storm, L. and Ertel, S. (2002). The ganzfeld debate continued: a response to Milton and Wiseman. *Journal of Parapsychology*, 66, 673–82.

Suchman L. and Jordan, B. (1990). Interactional troubles in face-to-face survey interviews. *Journal of the American Statistical Association*, 85, 232–41.

Sudnow, D. (1965). Normal crimes: sociological features of the penal code in a public defender's office. *Social Problems*, 24, 255–76.

Swanson, D., Case, S. and Vleuten, C. van der (1991). Strategies for student assessment. In Boud and Feletti (eds.), pp. 260–73.

Tavuchis, N. (1991). *Mea culpa: a sociology of apology and reconciliation.* Stanford: Stanford University Press.

te Molder, H. and Potter, J. (eds.) (2005). *Conversation and cognition.* Cambridge: Cambridge University Press.

Tholander, M. and Aronsson, K. (2002). Teasing as serious business: collaborative staging and response work. *Text*, 22, 559–95.

Tiggemann, M. and Lowes, J. (2002). Predictors of maternal control over children's eating behaviour. *Appetite*, 39, 1–7.

Todorov, Tzvetan (1995) *Les Abus de la mémoire.* Paris: Arléa.

Tracy, K. (1997). *Colloquium: dilemmas of academic discourse.* Norwood, NJ: Ablex.

Turner, R. (ed.) (1974). *Ethnomethodology: selected readings.* Harmondsworth: Penguin.

Utts, J. M. (1995). An assessment of the evidence for psychic functioning. *Journal of Parapsychology*, 59, 289–320.

van den Berg, H., Wetherell, M. and Houtkoop-Steenstra, H. (eds.) (2003). *Analyzing race talk: multidisciplinary approaches to the interview.* Cambridge: Cambridge University Press.

Vehviläinen, S. (2001). Evaluative advice in educational counseling: the use of disagreement in the 'stepwise entry' to advice. *Research on Language and Social Interaction*, 34, 371–98.

Verkuyten, M. (2000). School marks and teachers' accountability to colleagues. *Discourse Studies*, 2 (4), 452–72.

(2003). Preparing and delivering interpretations in psychoanalytic interaction, *Text*, 23, 573–606.

Ward, T., Hudson, S. M., Johnston, L. and Marshall, W. L. (1997). Cognitive distortions in sex offenders: an integrative review. *Clinical Psychology Review*, 17, 479–507.

Watson, D. R. (1983). The presentation of victim and motive in discourse: the case of police interrogations and interviews. *Victimology*, 8, 31–52.

Watson, G. and Seiler, R. M. (1992). *Text in context: contributions to ethnomethodology.* Newbury Park, CA: Sage.

Watt, C. (2002). Experimenter effects with a remote facilitation of attention focusing task: a study with multiple believer and disbeliever experimenters. In *Proceedings of presented papers*, 45th Annual Parapsychological Association Convention (pp. 306–18). Fairhaven, MA.: Parapsychological Association.

West, D. J. (1954). *Psychical research today.* London: Penguin.

West O. (2004). Report into the medical and related needs of transgender people in Brighton and Hove: the case for a local integrated service. www. pfc.org.uk/medical/spectrum.pdf.

Wetherell, M. (1996). Romantic discourse and feminist analysis: Interrogating investment, power and desire. In S. Wilkinson and C. Kitzinger (eds.), *Feminism and discourse: psychological perspectives* (pp. 128–44). London: Sage.

(1998). Positioning and interpretative repertoires: conversation analysis and post-structuralism in dialogue. *Discourse and Society*, 9 (3), 387–412.

Wetherell, M. and Potter, J. (1992). *Mapping the language of racism: discourse and the legitimation of exploitation.* Hemel Hempstead: Harvester Wheatsheaf.

Whalen, J. and Zimmerman D. H. (1998). Observations on the display and management of emotion in naturally occurring activities: the case of 'hysteria' in calls to 9–1–1. *Social Psychology Quarterly*, 61 (4), 141–59.

White, G. M. (1990). Moral discourse and the rhetoric of emotions. In Lutz and Abu-Lughod (eds.), pp. 46–68.

White, S. (2002). Accomplishing 'the case' in paediatrics and child health: medicine and morality in inter-professional talk. *Sociology of Health and Illness*, 24 (4), 409–35.

Widdicombe, S. and Wooffitt, R. (1995). *The language of youth subcultures: social identity in action.* Hemel Hempstead: Harvester Wheatsheaf.

Wieder, L. (1974). *Language and social reality: the case of telling the convict code.* The Hague: Mouton.

Wiggins, S. (2001). Construction and action in food evaluation: conversational data. *Journal of Language and Social Psychology*, 20 (4), 445–63.

(2002). Talking with your mouth full: gustatory 'mmms' and the embodiment of pleasure, *Research on Language and Social Interaction*, 35, 311–36.

Wiggins, S. and Potter, J. (2003). Attitudes and evaluative practices: category vs. item and subjective vs. objective constructions in everyday food assessments. *British Journal of Social Psychology*, 42, 513–31.

Wilkinson, S. and Kitzinger, C. (2006). Surprise as an interactional achievement: reaction tokens in conversation. *Social Psychology Quarterly*, 69 (2), 150–82.

Winn, M. E. (1996). The strategic and systemic management of denial in the cognitive/behavioral treatment of sexual offenders. *Sexual Abuse: A Journal of Research and Treatment*, 8, 25–36.

Wiseman, R., and Schlitz, M. (1997). Experimenter effects and the remote detection of staring. *Journal of Parapsychology*, 61, 197–207.

Wittgenstein, L. (1958). *Philosophical investigations*, trans. G. E. M. Ascombe, 2nd edn. Oxford: Blackwell.

Woods, D. (1994). *Problem-based learning: how to gain the most from PBL.* Hamilton: Griffin Printing.

Wooffitt, R. (1991). 'I was just doing X ... when Y': some inferential properties of a device in accounts of paranormal experiences. *Text*, 11, 267–88.

(1992). *Telling tales of the unexpected: the organization of factual discourse.* London: Harvester/Wheatsheaf.

(2005a). From process to practice: language, interaction and 'flashbulb memory'. In H. te Molder and J. Potter (eds.), pp. 203–25.

(2005b). *Conversation analysis and discourse analysis: a comparative and critical introduction.* London: Sage.

Wooffitt, R. and Widdicombe, S. (2006). Interaction in interviews. In P. Drew, G. Raymond and D. Weinberg (eds.), *Talk and interaction in social research methods* (pp. 28–49). London: Sage.

Wootton, Anthony (1999). An investigation of delayed echoing in a child with autism. *First Language*, 19, 359–81.

Index